The End(s) of Religion

Also Available from Bloomsbury:

Death Anxiety and Religious Belief,
Jonathan Jong and Jamin Halberstadt

The Demise of Religion,
Edited by Michael Stausberg,
Stuart A. Wright, and Carole M. Cusack

Understanding Sport as a Religious Phenomenon,
Eric Bain-Selbo and D. Gregory Sapp

The End(s) of Religion

A History of How the Study of Religion Makes Religion Irrelevant

Eric Bain-Selbo

BLOOMSBURY ACADEMIC
LONDON • NEW YORK • OXFORD • NEW DELHI • SYDNEY

BLOOMSBURY ACADEMIC
Bloomsbury Publishing Plc
50 Bedford Square, London, WC1B 3DP, UK
1385 Broadway, New York, NY 10018, USA
29 Earlsfort Terrace, Dublin 2, Ireland

BLOOMSBURY, BLOOMSBURY ACADEMIC and the Diana logo
are trademarks of Bloomsbury Publishing Plc

First published in Great Britain 2022
This paperback edition published 2023

Copyright © Eric Bain-Selbo, 2022, 2023

Eric Bain-Selbo has asserted his right under the Copyright, Designs and
Patents Act, 1988, to be identified as Author of this work.

For legal purposes the Preface on pp. viii–ix constitutes an extension
of this copyright page.

Cover design by Toby Way
Cover image © Getty Images

All rights reserved. No part of this publication may be reproduced or
transmitted in any form or by any means, electronic or mechanical,
including photocopying, recording, or any information storage or retrieval
system, without prior permission in writing from the publishers.

Bloomsbury Publishing Plc does not have any control over, or responsibility for,
any third-party websites referred to or in this book. All internet addresses given
in this book were correct at the time of going to press. The author and publisher
regret any inconvenience caused if addresses have changed or sites have
ceased to exist, but can accept no responsibility for any such changes.

A catalogue record for this book is available from the British Library.

Library of Congress Control Number: 2021949407

ISBN:	HB:	978-1-3500-4525-5
	PB:	978-1-3502-8776-1
	ePDF:	978-1-3500-4526-2
	eBook:	978-1-3500-4527-9

Typeset by Integra Software Services Pvt. Ltd.

To find out more about our authors and books visit www.bloomsbury.com
and sign up for our newsletters.

This book is dedicated to my amazing spouse, Laura, and my awesome children, Zach and Hannah. Throughout my professional career, their very existence has continually reminded me of what I consider to be my greatest accomplishments—being a decent (I hope) husband and father.

This book also is offered in memory of two dear friends who died in the years in which I was writing it. To Gregory Sapp, a wonderful colleague who became an even better friend. I cherish the work we did together, but far more the camaraderie we shared. And to Richard Haberman, my University of Chicago and Democratic Socialists of America comrade. He had a great mind, heart, and delightful (sometimes obnoxious) sense of humor. I expected to grow old (well, older) with each of them. I miss them both terribly.

Contents

Preface		viii
Introduction: Very Brief Comments to Get Us Started		1
1	The Ethical/Philosophical Function of Religion: Kant, Hegel, and So Forth	5
2	The Sociological Function of Religion: Durkheim and Weber	27
3	The Psychological Function of Religion: Freud, Jung, and Beyond	47
4	The Existential Function of Religion: Eliade and Tillich	81
	Interlude	105
5	The Religion of Culture	113
6	What Happens Next? Some Concluding Remarks	157
Postscript: A Cautionary Tale		203
Notes		224
Bibliography		264
Index		275

Preface

First of all, I want to make clear that this book is not written for specialists—though I would hope they would find it of interest. It is written for the educated reader who wants to learn something about the study of religion, our present situation (particularly in the Western world), and how religion may factor (or not) in our future. It also is written for undergraduate students (maybe graduate students) in a variety of religious studies or even philosophy courses. I think this book might serve as a wonderful supplement in a number of such courses or even as the primary text in courses about the history of the study of religion, atheism, religion and culture, secularization, or other related topics.

Second, I am much too young (only mid- to late-fifties) to be writing one of those career-culminating books. And there are far more accomplished and wiser scholars than I who should be writing such books. Still, this book does seem like the end of something (the title of the book, therefore, is personally ironic). It seems to be the result of many years of thinking and working along a specific line of inquiry. I feel like I am at the end of that line.

The line of inquiry is roughly the study of the religious elements or dimensions of culture (specifically popular culture)—what I will call the "religion of culture" in this text. It started with the late, great Stan Lusby at the University of Tennessee. As an undergraduate, he introduced me (and really every one of his students) to the work of Mircea Eliade (one of the most prominent scholars of religion in the history of the field, and one of the scholars featured here). That introduction included thinking about culture more broadly, and how *homo religiosus* expresses itself in all kinds of phenomena that we otherwise would deem secular or profane.

In the many years that followed, my scholarly work went in a lot of different directions, but I often came back to the religion of culture. I was especially interested in sport and having grown up in the South the sport was college football. I floated the idea of a book about college football to Joe Price (a leading and truly groundbreaking figure in the study of religion and sport) and he liked it. Joe was editor of the Mercer University Press series in this area, and our conversation led to my book *Game Day and God: Football, Faith, and Politics in the American South*. While much of my work afterward focused on sport,

I dabbled in other areas of culture (film, consumerism, etc.) and eventually ended up here. This book has given me the opportunity to think deeply about formative theorists in my past as well as the current state of the study of religion. It also has allowed me to think a lot about the future—something I really like to do. And, it has permitted me the opportunity to bring many of my social and cultural concerns to bear on these really interesting areas in religious studies.

So, this book really does bring a lot of ideas to closure for me. But I stress that it is "for me." There is so much more to be thought and said and written in these areas—about the religion of culture, about the academic study of religion, and about historical trajectories that we can trace in our past and project into the future. I offer this book as just one scholar's (and a minor one at that) perspective on some very interesting and pretty profound questions.

Naturally, I have a lot of people to thank for helping me finish this book. I asked a few people to read portions of the text, and they all provided wonderful feedback. Simply in alphabetical order, they are Hannah Bain-Selbo, Laura Bain-Selbo, Zachary Bain-Selbo, Stephen Baker, Chris Conner, Joshua Mugg, and Terry Shoemaker. As I mention in endnotes in the text, there are portions of some chapters that are reworked from previous journal articles or book chapters. In those endnotes, I thank several other people who helped with those publications and thus, indirectly, with some of this one. The two anonymous peer reviewers also provided critical and extremely helpful feedback on the penultimate draft of this manuscript.

All the folks at Bloomsbury are awesome. This is my second opportunity to publish with them. I want to thank Lalle Pursglove for helping me get started on this book (she worked with Greg Sapp and me on the previous book too) and Lily McMahon for helping to make sure I finished. During the research and writing, a career move necessitated a couple of deadline extensions. I very much appreciate the generosity and support shown to me in this regard, as well as the gentle nudging to get the book done.

Finally, let me return to the beginning (intellectually, at least) and thank Stan Lusby. Not only did he get me started on this line of inquiry, he got me into graduate school (long story) and got me on my way. He really exemplified what a teacher and mentor is all about. He also was just a wonderful person. He passed away several years ago, and I am sorry he cannot read my humble work. But I really wanted to remember him here.

Introduction

Very Brief Comments to Get Us Started

In part, this book is a story. It is a story about some of the central figures in the study of religion in the last several centuries—particularly in the last century. It also is a story that I think informs our present moment in the Western world. I think it helps us understand our culture and much of our cultural behavior. Finally, it is a story that I think provides us some insight into the future, including the future of institutional religion (the world's major religions like Buddhism, Christianity, etc.) and how human beings detached from that kind of religion will meet some of their basic human needs in different ways.

By no means is this a comprehensive history of the study of religion. There are much more substantive and worthwhile texts in that regard. For example, I would recommend Eric J. Sharpe's *Comparative Religion: A History*[1] or Walter H. Capps's *Religious Studies: The Making of a Discipline*.[2] In regard to the individual thinkers I examine, of course, there is a thorough and extensive literature on each (I have cited some of the secondary literature in the following chapters). For a single text in this regard, I recommend Daniel L. Pals's *Eight Theories of Religion* (second edition), which includes (among others) chapters on Sigmund Freud, Emile Durkheim, Max Weber, and Mircea Eliade (figures that I cover, though not nearly as thoroughly).[3] Thus, my aim is not to provide a comprehensive history of religious studies or even each particular historical figure. My aim is to use the thinkers as touchpoints to highlight particular aspects or truths of the story of religious studies—aspects or truths that have led us in certain theoretical directions and will continue to do so in the future. I fully understand that other scholars could take the same figures, movements, and ideas and construct a different story. And I definitely know that other scholars could draw different conclusions. But I hope readers find my narrative compelling and my conclusions reasonable given the story I am telling.

In short, here is the story I am telling. Over the last few centuries, a lot of smart people have thought about religion—what it is, how it works, what it does for us, and where it is headed. This thinking was pretty novel. People for millennia have thought and believed religiously, but only relatively recently have so many smart people spent so much time thinking about religion itself. In Chapters 1 through 4, I focus on many of those smart people. My choice of figures should not be taken as an endorsement of their ideas or conclusions—though I think each of them certainly got some things right. My choices rather are guided by the fact that these figures have had a significant impact on the study of religion in the Western world and likely will continue to do so. Because of the racism and sexism throughout the centuries covered, very few people of color or women ever had a platform to share their insights and perspectives and even fewer had any impact on the field of the study of religion. Thus, the figures examined in Chapters 1 through 4 are all white men. Today, of course, the field is much more diverse, and we are so much better for it. But, as Christopher M. Driscoll and Monica R. Miller might say, the scholars featured in the first four chapters are the "ghosts" that continue to haunt our work in religious studies.[4]

The first chapter focuses on philosophy and the work of Immanuel Kant and G.W.F. Hegel (eighteenth to nineteenth century) in particular. The second chapter turns to the discipline of sociology and the work of Emile Durkheim and Max Weber (nineteenth to twentieth century), while Chapter 3 is on psychology and the work of Sigmund Freud and Carl Jung (twentieth century). The fourth chapter focuses on two key twentieth-century figures in the study of religion, historian of religion Mircea Eliade and theologian Paul Tillich—both incredibly influential from the middle of the century onward. In all four of these chapters, I dabble with some more contemporary questions and theorists, but the main point of these chapters is to present a historical narrative. Thus, I extensively quote from these figures so that (so to speak) they tell the story in their own words.[5] Given their historical context and their cultural and academic norms, some of their writing will strike the reader as culturally insensitive (even racist) and/or sexist. The use of terms like primitive, savage, and the like is unacceptable in academic writing today (as they should be). In addition, nobody uses "man" any more to refer to human beings in general. In quoting these authors, I assumed we all knew that some of their language is inappropriate, so I chose not to pepper the text with the convention [sic] to show such disapproval.

The main conclusion of the first four chapters is that the academic study of religion has advanced a fundamentally functionalist understanding of religion— even at times in ways contrary to what one or more of these theorists intended.

By "functionalist understanding," I mean that religion is seen as a cultural phenomenon that does something for human beings. What religion does for human beings is to achieve certain ends—certain goods that human beings want and need (these ends might be psychological, social, or both). Thus, the title of this book: the ends of religion. My hope is that these four chapters will provide a useful introduction to some of the history of religious studies for those (from students to the general public) who know little or nothing about it. Scholars who are familiar with these thinkers may want to skip ahead if they really are more interested in what I think all this history means for us now.

The first four chapters are followed by an interlude that begins to work out what this history of the study of religion has to tell us about its object of study and how that history impacted and continues to impact the work of religious studies scholars. Part of what that history tells us is that religious expression and practice are not limited to stereotypical or institutional religion—that religious expression and practice can be found in a wide range of cultural phenomena because those phenomena can and often do *function* religiously. Thus, the subtitle of the book: how the study of religion makes religion irrelevant. Admittedly, there may be some hyperbole in the subtitle. Irrelevant is a strong word. But the point here is that stereotypical or institutional religion is increasingly irrelevant to many religious studies scholars because they are busy studying religious expression and practice in so many other cultural phenomena (art, economy, sport, and so much more). In this regard, I draw inspiration from and position my approach relative to the groundbreaking work of Mark C. Taylor.

The fifth chapter looks at the explosion of work that looks at how seemingly non-religious cultural phenomena function religiously—work that I eventually put under the umbrella of the *religion of culture*. My claim is that those engaged in the study of the religion of culture are the necessary consequence of the history detailed in Chapters 1 through 4. Religious studies scholars did not simply stumble upon the study of the religion of culture; they were led there by the theorists who were foundational to the very establishment of religious studies as a "discipline." I put this last word in scare quotes because religious studies is not really a discipline (sorry, Eliade), it really is more of an area studies. It does not have its own methodology, for example, but draws upon other disciplines like psychology, anthropology, sociology, and many others to investigate incredibly varied and complex cultural phenomena. In recent decades, religious studies scholars have used all the tools (again, borrowed from more standard academic disciplines) at their disposal to study stereotypical religious institutions, communities, beliefs, and practices, but they increasingly have turned their attention to so many other cultural phenomena—using those same tools to arrive at new understandings of those phenomena and new insights about the human beings who engage those phenomena.

In the final chapter, I draw conclusions from all this history and these contemporary efforts. Here I engage with a number of scholars concerned with secularism, secularization, and the secular age. These conclusions include my educated guesses about the future of the study of religion. But the main conclusions are about the subject of religion and the future of humanity (particularly the near future and in the Western world). In the end, I conclude (spoiler alert!) that stereotypical or institutional religion will continue to decline in the Western world (no surprise there). Thus, the twist on the title of the book: the end of religion. I also conclude that human beings will increasingly have their religious needs (the ends of religion) met through other cultural phenomena, and I provide a humanistic and pragmatic account of how that could be. I then add a Postscript that raises lingering concerns about my conclusions—especially about how economic forces pose a potential danger to many cultural phenomena. But there is reason to be optimistic if we can recognize the pernicious effects of the market and consumerism and protect the internal goods of so many of our cultural phenomena.

Let us begin.

1

The Ethical/Philosophical Function of Religion: Kant, Hegel, and So Forth

For millennia, religion has been intertwined with ethical rules and moral behavior. The relationship has not been an uncomplicated one. As far back (at least) as Plato's *Euthyphro*, philosophers, theologians, and others have grappled with the nature of this relationship. Does morality arise from religion? Or is it a mere addendum to religion? Can we have morality without religion or vice versa?

For most of Western history, the relationship of religion and morality was so close that one hardly could separate them. Living a moral life was part of what it meant to be religious. Living a moral life was pleasing to God, and one's eternal life might depend on how morally good one was in this life (a belief held at the popular level, even if not always theologically or doctrinally). Something changed, however, in the eighteenth century during the Enlightenment. Instead of seeing morality as founded or grounded on religion, many philosophers and theologians (often these were one and the same, since the sharp divide between philosophy and theology was a later development) sought to discover and explicate the rational basis for morality. By doing so, however, they also had to account for the historical relationship of morality to religion and explain why religion still was relevant to morality. In other words, if morality was based on rationality, and all human beings have a rational capacity, then do we really need religion to enable us to be morally good creatures?

In this chapter we examine one line of development related to these issues. We begin with Immanuel Kant (1724–1804), *the* Enlightenment philosopher, and then shift our focus to subsequent critical figures in German philosophy. Through such an examination we will find that the effort to justify the moral relevance of religion failed, and that in fact the work of these philosophers implicitly or explicitly made religion *less* relevant in the Western world. These philosophers, then, are the first characters in the story I want to tell.

Kant and Rational Religion

In "An Answer to the Question: What Is Enlightenment?", published in 1784, Kant defines his particular historical moment. But his essay also expresses sentiments and motivations that would form the basis of philosophical, cultural, religious, and political movements for centuries to come. He begins that famous essay by immediately answering the question: "*Enlightenment is the human being's emancipation from its self-incurred immaturity. Immaturity* is the inability to make use of one's intellect without the direction of another."[1] There are at least four important aspects or implications to this statement. First, there is the emphasis on the use of one's intellect or our ability to think. Second, there is the claim that we ought to use our intellect (and, we are all capable of doing so) free from the direction or manipulation of others. Third, the use of the idea of immaturity signals some kind of temporal development or growth. In short, to be Enlightened is to be able to freely use one's intellect—it is to be a mature rational creature as opposed to a child. Simply put, to be Enlightened is to *think for yourself*. By analogy, then, the Enlightenment period is one of liberation and maturity for the Western world. The Western world *was* immature but was becoming mature during the Enlightenment period.[2] Fourth, rational maturity is inevitable. Just as an individual develops from a child to a more rational adult, so society will develop from a childish state and become more rational as well.

Immediately we see the potential conflict with institutional religion. Certainly in the eighteenth century but even today in many religions, the veracity of the authority figure or leadership or at least the authority of a text or set of texts is accepted without question. For example, think about certain pronouncements from the Vatican or a powerful Imam. Such pronouncements are deemed to be true by virtue of the authority that expresses them, not as a consequence of rational assessment of the pronouncement. The latter at least is subordinate to the former and often seems like a *post hoc* justification. Such is the case as well with sacred scripture, which many religious adherents accept as true with little rational scrutiny. For example, think about beliefs in the existence of God or the Christian idea of the Trinity (the idea that God has three aspects or beings—Father, Son, and Holy Spirit—in one ultimate being). There are a lot of theological arguments or justifications for these beliefs, but most people still accept them (and often are asked to accept them) on faith alone.

So, if religion often asks us to accept certain truths with little or no reflection on our part, what are we to do with Kant's insistence that we be more mature and enlightened? Should religion simply be rejected? Kant answers this question negatively. He wants to defend and preserve religion and does so via his moral theory. Kant's moral theory represents one of the three major approaches to ethics (the other two being utilitarianism and virtue theory). While his moral argument can rationally stand on its own, separate from any religious assumptions or claims, Kant nevertheless finds room for religion in his overall theory.

Kant begins the first chapter of his *Groundwork of the Metaphysic of Morals*, a canonical text in college ethics courses, with the famous claim: "It is impossible to conceive anything at all in the world, or even out of it, which can be taken as good without qualification, except a *good will*."[3] By "good without qualification," Kant means that the good will is "good in itself," and that its "usefulness or fruitlessness can neither add to, nor subtract from, this value."[4] For example, imagine someone (we will call this person Bob) is about to be trampled by a rhinoceros. I have a gun, however, that can kill the rhinoceros and save Bob's life. But, when I try to shoot the rhinoceros, I accidentally shoot and kill Bob instead (actually, a pretty likely scenario, since I do not own a gun nor have I shot one very often). My desire to save Bob is an expression of my good will, and my will (that which leads to the action) remains good even though the consequences of the action were quite bad. Indeed, Kant's moral theory is radically non-consequentialist, which separates it from utilitarianism (generally, an action is good or better to the extent that it creates happiness) and virtue theory (generally, an action is good or better to the extent that it contributes to the goal of human flourishing, of which being a virtuous person is the central part). For Kant, an action is judged to be good or bad *not* by the outcome of the action but by the intention or motivation of the agent. Using the same example, imagine that I really want to kill Bob and I take aim at him. But, I accidentally shoot and kill a rhinoceros that suddenly has appeared and was just about to trample Bob to death. In this case, the consequence of my action is good but my intention or motivation was bad. Nobody would say that I somehow had a good will in this scenario.

So, if what really matters is intention or motivation, are there ways to determine whether someone is acting from a good will or not? For Kant, we can never really know the true intentions or motivations of our own actions, let alone others. But reason can provide us with criteria for figuring out what moral acts look like. Reason is what separates us from animals. Reason allows us to transcend our instincts—for example, "I want that doughnut because I'm hungry" or "I want to kill Bob because he made me angry." Reason is not about producing happiness or the achievement of any particular goal. So many other instincts or human capacities are better in that regard (e.g., sexual intercourse, which generally can be accomplished without our rational capacity, can make us happy or at least bring us pleasure). But if the only good without qualification is the good will, then perhaps that is what reason is for. Indeed, Kant asserts that reason's "true function must be to produce a *will* which is *good*, not as a *means* to some further end [such as pleasure or happiness], but *in itself*."[5] So how does reason accomplish this function?

Reason performs this function in part by providing us with the ability to act freely. Of course, for Kant reason allows us to be free, to be autonomous, in part because it allows us to question authority and to think for ourselves. But it also liberates us psychologically, by helping us to overcome our desires and inclinations. When we act out of our desires or inclinations, we act in ways that animals act. Like an animal, I act to eat food when I am hungry. If I acted only from that desire or inclination, however, I likely would act in very non-human ways. For example, I might just wander into a restaurant and start eating off of other people's plates (much like our cat, Rocky, does on a regular basis at home). As a rational creature, though, I know I should not act in such a way. I know that the moral law requires me to respect the property or belongings (in this case, their dinner!) of others. But I am not following the moral law because society tells me to do so or because I will be arrested for not doing so; I follow the moral law because it is *my law*—it springs from my reason. I am not bound or compelled to follow the moral law. I do so freely as a consequence of the fact that it is rational and thus a product of my reason (which, of course, I share with all other human beings). Thus, for Kant, I am *autonomous* when following the moral law, but I am in a *heteronomous* condition when I am driven by desire or inclination or simply follow some sort of external authority.[6] He concludes that autonomy "is the property the will has of being a law to itself."[7] As a rational creature, I produce the law that I freely follow.

But what is the moral law? Kant's term for the moral law is *categorical imperative*. The categorical imperative is contrasted with the *hypothetical imperative*.[8] The latter are calls or reasons for action (an imperative) that generally follow an if/then pattern. For example, if I am hungry then I should eat dinner. In other words, the action is chosen in order to achieve a particular end or goal. A more morally relevant example might be: If it makes me feel happy to help others, then I should provide funding to organizations that feed the hungry. Providing such funding is a morally good thing to do, but in this particular example Kant would claim that I am not acting ethically. I am not acting unethically either. My action simply is not moral or immoral because the intention or motivation is not moral or immoral. So, it is not the act that is a problem (again, the focus is not on consequences), but the reason (intention or motivation) for the act. Kant certainly could see two people providing funding to organizations that feed the hungry—with one of them not acting morally or immorally at all and the other acting morally. The former is acting out of inclination (the desire to be happy) while the latter would be acting out of duty.[9] The former is acting out of passion (I want to be happy) while the latter would be acting through reason alone. The former is an act of prudence (doing something to achieve a particular individual good) while the latter would be acting morally. The latter, in fact, would be acting in accordance with the categorical imperative.

Kant famously provided three formulations of the categorical imperative, the first two generally being more prominent than the third. These are not three different moral laws, but just three different ways of expressing the single moral law. The first formulation is "*Act only on that maxim through which you can at the same time will that it should become a universal law.*"[10] Take lying as an example. Imagine I am at a restaurant and discover that the restaurant gives patrons a free dessert on their birthdays. Though it is not my wife's birthday, I tell the waiter that it is her birthday so that she can get the free dessert (which, I am hoping, she will share with me). In this case, the consequence is great (free dessert, pleasure, etc.). But could we will that the maxim of my action (the reason for it, the justification) could be a universal law? The maxim in this case is that I should lie when it serves my interests. But if everyone did that (if that maxim was followed universally) then we never could trust anyone. The world would be a chaotic mess. But it is not that mess as a consequence that is the crux of the issue for Kant. What is the crux of the issue is that I cannot universalize this maxim because it contradicts the very notion of speaking truthfully—it destroys the rational purpose of speech (to communicate clearly, to share legitimate and truthful information, etc.). That contradiction makes lying contrary to reason and thus immoral.

The second formulation goes "*Act in such a way that you always treat humanity, whether in your own person or in the person of any other, never simply as a means, but always at the same time as an end.*"[11] Take the example of lying again. In the case above, I use the waiter as a mere means to the achievement of my goal or end (free dessert, happiness, etc.). But I should respect the waiter enough as a rational creature to *not* use him merely as a means to my ends. Again, this is the flip side of the universalization formulation. If we universalized lying to achieve one's ends, then we would do nothing but treat others as mere means. Such universalization would lead to terrible consequences, and few of us would want to live in such a world. But beyond the consequences, such universalization violates the fundamental dignity of human beings—a dignity that they have by virtue of their rationality, which separates them from all other creatures.[12]

While this brief description of Kant's moral theory hardly does it justice, the key point to note here is that there is no need for religious concepts. No God is needed to understand our moral obligations. Human beings, using their reason, can determine what is morally correct. Indeed, Kant does not view the moral law as something that he creates and then shares with the world through his account of the categorical imperative. His account is simply a philosophical description of how our mind naturally works morally. But Kant was a philosopher in Christian Europe during a time when religion was a very large part of cultural life. While religious concepts do not seem to be needed in his moral theory, he nevertheless seems compelled to work them in. So, he brings God and immortality back into the moral equation. For Kant, religious concepts are necessary to complete his moral theory.

Kant claims that we cannot know God nor be certain that there is an afterlife (where our worldly actions that are pleasing to God lead to eternal happiness), but morality leads us to postulate their existence. As stated earlier, morality for Kant has nothing to do with our happiness. The latter is merely an end or goal that may result from our moral action, but it cannot be the basis for our action. If happiness is the basis for our action, then we are acting according to a hypothetical imperative (e.g., "If I want to be happy, then I should help my spouse with the dishes so he won't be angry with me") that may not be immoral, but certainly has no moral worth (it may be non-moral). Only an action that is in accord with the categorical imperative, in which happiness may or may not be a consequence (happiness being merely a non-relevant consequence), can be an action with moral worth.

While Kant rejects happiness as a basis for moral action, we also know through experience that moral goodness does not seem to lead to happiness—at least not consistently. We know that some very morally worthy people end up suffering great tragedies and even living lives of great sorrow, while truly immoral people (we may even call them evil) seem to end up being excessively happy. Though Kant rejects happiness as a basis for moral action (it can be the basis of non-moral or prudential action), he recognizes that the way things are seems unreasonable and unjust—the good are unhappy, the evil are happy. Certainly, it must be the case that moral goodness will receive its just reward. In fact, he calls the combination of moral goodness and happiness (something that is not guaranteed on this earth, and in fact often does not happen) the *highest good*. Thus, reason demands that we postulate that there is a God who ensures that goodness is rewarded with happiness. And we must postulate the immortality of the soul so that such reward can be attained by the individual.[13] As Kant concludes, "morals is not really the doctrine of how to make ourselves happy but of how we are to be *worthy* of happiness. Only if religion is added to it can the hope arise of someday participating in happiness in proportion as we endeavored not to be unworthy of it."[14]

If religion (at least the concepts of God and immortality) seems like an unnecessary appendage to Kantian moral theory, his *Religion within the Limits of Reason Alone* demonstrates a more substantive albeit counter-productive attempt to preserve the relevance if not importance of religion for humanity. In the "Preface" to the text, Kant makes the bold claim (particularly for his time period), "So far as morality is based upon the conception of man as a free agent who, just because he is free, binds himself through his reason to unconditioned laws, it stands in need neither of the idea of another Being over him, for him to apprehend his duty, nor of an incentive other than the law itself, for him to do his duty."[15] Even more starkly, he adds that "morality does not need religion at all."[16] Our reason is sufficient to provide us with the moral law. Even the moral example of Jesus Christ as a role model for humanity, in this sense, is unnecessary. Kant insists that we need "no empirical example to make the idea of a person morally well-pleasing to God our archetype; this idea as an archetype is already present in our reason."[17] The idea of Jesus, of a perfectly holy or moral being, would exist in our reason even if no human being (Jesus) had existed.

In a certain sense, it almost is as if religion needs morality rather than the other way around. Indeed, for Kant, a religion is worthwhile to the extent that it embodies, supports, and promotes moral duty. Kant argues that all religions "can be divided into those which are *endeavors to win favor* (mere worship) and *moral religions, i.e.,* religions of *good life-conduct*."[18] The former are associated with superstition and cult activity, whereas the latter are associated with reason and moral conduct. The latter are far superior. Indeed, only the latter really matter. Kant concludes, "*Whatever, over and above good life-conduct, man fancies that he can do to become well-pleasing to God is mere religious illusion and pseudo-service of God*."[19] He even lists various activities, various external forms of religion as opposed to internal moral disposition, that all seem of equal (lower) value to him—for example, pilgrimages to holy sites, attending church, and prayers. He warns his readers to avoid believing these "pious playthings" are central to religion, when the only thing that really matters is moral conduct.[20] By focusing on moral conduct, we can hope to achieve the kind of "ethical commonwealth" that is the proper aim of human beings. The ethical commonwealth "can be thought of only as a people under divine commands, *i.e., as a people of God*, and indeed *under laws of virtue*."[21]

But if morality is a function of our reason, then why do we need religion at all? For Kant, religion helps to spark our reason or support our reason in the discovery of the moral law. Religion (or, as he says, the church) is critical in that process of discovery. He even states that the establishment of a church is something that is "required" of human beings as part of their effort to achieve moral conduct.[22] Indeed, the way that Kant interprets or explains the meaning of certain religious practices, artifacts, or ideas drives home the point that religion serves morality, not the other way around.

For example, Kant interprets the life and teachings of Jesus through a moral prism. Jesus came to spread the message of a "moral religion," and because of its "closest relation with reason" this religion (i.e., Christianity) was able "to be spread at all times and among all peoples."[23] This focus on morality is also the primary purpose of scripture. "For the final purpose even of reading these holy scriptures, or of investigating their content, is to make men better," Kant writes, adding "and since … the moral improvement of men, constitutes the real end of all religion of reason, it will comprise the highest principle of all Scriptural exegesis."[24]

In contrast to moral religion is "statutory religion," the religion of cult-like rules and practices—the kind of rules and practices that have no rational and thus moral basis. Again, statutory religions may be a helpful means toward the teaching of moral religion (morality being the true core of any religion). Kant concludes that "pure *moral* legislation, through which the will of God is primordially engraved in our hearts [by virtue, one might add, of our being rational creatures], is not only the ineluctable condition of all true religion whatsoever but is also that which really constitutes such religion; statutory religion can merely comprise the means to its furtherance and spread."[25] For Kant, the danger is that we take this statutory religion for the genuine (moral) religion.[26] In fact, Kant believes that his historical moment is one in which statutory religion increasingly is not needed as support for or justification of genuine religion. He asserts that "the true religion … from now on is able to maintain itself on rational grounds."[27]

Kant recognizes that in statutory religion there are certain rules and practices that are non-rational at best and perhaps irrational (either way, they have no direct moral content, though they might help lead one to moral religion). These rules and practices easily can become a form of *fetishism* (in this case, worship of that which has no moral content) and *clericalism* (when a church is organized around fetish-worship).[28] Kant describes *fetish-faith* as "the persuasion that what can produce no effect at all according either to natural laws or to moral laws of reason, will yet, of itself, bring about what is wished for, if only we firmly believe that it will do so, and if we accompany this belief with certain formalities [such as praying, making sacrificial offerings, etc.]."[29] This kind of faith reminds us of the hypothetical imperative. Ritual behavior (the means) is driven by a desire to achieve a specific end or goal (a good harvest, victory in war, our eternal happiness, etc.) rather than being a manifestation of the moral law. The core of genuine religion, however, must be moral and rational. Thus, genuine religion, real religion, moral religion, is really rational religion. And any specific religion that runs counter to reason reveals itself as illusory religion. Kant concludes that the "fanatical religious illusion … is the moral death of reason; for without reason, after all, no religion is possible."[30]

The emphasis that Kant puts on reason also runs counter to the strategy of locating religion in emotions or feelings. Kant rejects such a strategy, since feelings are merely subjective and particular to the individual, whereas reason is objective and universal (shared in common by everyone).[31] In addition, feelings cannot be the basis of knowledge, whereas reason (of course) is the most fundamental basis of knowledge (at least according to Kant).[32]

As an effort to demonstrate some ways in which religion can be interpreted in light of a strong commitment to a rationalistic moral theory (a moral theory based on the claim of a universal human capacity to reason), Kant's *Religion within the Limits of Reason Alone* is a significant achievement. But, I argue, in the end it fails to "save" religion. Kant claims in the "Preface" to the text that "a religion which rashly declares war on reason will not be able to hold out in the long run against it."[33] In so tying the essence or core of religion to reason, however, he ends up making the distinctive beliefs and practices of religion mere ornaments to the rational morality that gives to religion its value. Religion becomes a mere means to the end of morality. As Burkhard Tuschling states, religion in this view "comes to be treated as a mere means of preparing humankind for its destination to be able to use its own reason and to be free to determine itself."[34] This destination, of course, is the very aim of the Enlightenment.

If it is true, then, that religion is a mere means, then once the end is achieved (rational society, moral clarity, etc.) we will not need religion any more. Kant sees this as a real possibility even in his day. He raises the question of "whether an historical (ecclesiastical) faith [characterized at times by fetishism, clericalism, etc.] must always be present as an essential element of saving faith, over and above pure religious faith [the religion of reason and morality], or whether it is only a vehicle which finally—however distant this future event may be—can pass over into pure religious faith."[35] While Kant argues forcefully against the prioritization of fetishism and clericalism and defends "true" or "pure" religion, might it be that here we have the beginning of the end of a need for any religion at all? In a conclusion that sounds distinctly secular, Kant writes that "in the end religion will gradually be freed from all empirical determining grounds and from all statutes which rest on history and which through the agency of ecclesiastical faith provisionally unite men for the requirements of the good; and thus at last the pure religion of reason will rule over all."[36]

For Kant, the end or goal of religion is reason and morality, but the full flourishing of reason and morality likely means the end of religion. Indeed, Charles Taylor notes, "In spite of the continuing place of God and immortality in his scheme, he is a crucial figure also in the development of exclusive humanism [that dispenses with religion], just because he articulates so strongly the power of inner sources of morality."[37]

In the Aftermath of Kant

After Kant, German thought about religion went in many interesting directions. But the pre-occupation, if not obsession, with figuring out the relationships among religious ideas, rationality, and morality remained front and center.

The most significant figure after Kant (in fact, overlapping historically with him) was Georg Wilhelm Friedrich Hegel (1770–1831). His approach to thinking about morality differed greatly from Kant. But, like Kant, his philosophy ended up subordinating (by, in fact, subsuming) religion to both morality and reason.

Hegel associates God with Spirit, and it is the latter term that takes priority. Spirit is not a static, unchanging, and eternal being, but a reality that unfolds and comes to know itself through human history and culture. As he insists, Spirit is "never at rest but always engaged in moving forward."[38] The primary way in which Spirit accomplishes its unfolding and self-knowledge is through rationality, because it is pure rationality. Hegel claims that "God is essentially rational, rationality, which as Spirit is in and for itself."[39]

But how does Spirit come to know itself? And what do history and culture have to do with it? In short, in order for Spirit to know itself it must become an object to itself. It does this through the human mind, as the human mind (through history) produces various artifacts of culture (literature, philosophy, art, and more) that reflect rationality (which, of course, is Spirit itself).[40] It is through history and culture—through human activity—that Spirit expresses itself and comes to know itself.

Religion is a key element of culture, and it too is one of the ways in which Spirit unfolds and comes to self-knowledge. Religion, in fact, comes from the Spirit—just as all cultural phenomena do. "Religion is a product of the Divine Spirit," Hegel insists, "it is not a discovery of man, but a work of divine operation and creation in him."[41]

Hegel recognizes different "shapes" in the variety of religions, different characteristics that are representative of the Spirit and its movements.[42] But these different "shapes" do not change the fact that the phenomenon of religion is universal.[43] Religion crosses all cultures because the Spirit itself is universal. For Hegel, "religion is the Divine Spirit's knowledge of itself through the mediation of finite spirit."[44] While the "Divine Spirit" is infinite, it manifests itself in the world in particular religions ("finite spirit"). And by manifesting itself in the world, Spirit is able to make an object of itself and thus can know itself. Spirit works through human beings to create particular religions (e.g., Christianity) that as objects (externalized, finite spirits) allow human beings to know Spirit. But because human reflection is itself a manifestation of Spirit, our participation in religion is really a matter of Spirit reflecting on itself, of Spirit gaining self-knowledge.

Hegel's framework for thinking about religion as a cultural phenomenon obviously shapes how he views its various stereotypical elements. Worship, for example, becomes a practice symbolic of "the movement of God toward man, and of man toward God"[45]—this movement being the integral part of the unfolding and self-knowledge of Spirit. Worship, however, is not restricted to institutional religion. Art and philosophy join with religion, for Hegel, as three central cultural forms in which worship occurs.[46] Art is a cultural phenomenon that very early was a way in which Spirit was revealed. Art engages the mind through the senses—through touch, sight, and hearing. "The law and content of art is Truth as it appears in mind or Spirit," Hegel writes, "and is therefore spiritual truth, but spiritual truth in such a form that it is at the same time *sensuous* truth, existing for perception in its simple form."[47] Art and religion often are intertwined, as one sees in the history of art across the planet. Philosophy also engages the mind, of course, but not through the senses. Instead, it engages the mind simply through ideas. Hegel insists that "Philosophy is itself, in fact, worship; it is religion, for in the same way it renounces subjective notions and opinions in order to occupy itself with God."[48]

It seems then we need to distinguish two senses or uses of religion in Hegel. On the one hand, there is stereotypical institutional religion. While institutional religion is one cultural element among many, Hegel sees a special role for it in the history of Spirit and its task of unfolding and coming to self-knowledge. In thinking about it along with science, art, law, and morals, Hegel insists that religion "occupies the highest position."[49] On the other hand, Hegel uses religion as an umbrella concept for various cultural phenomena like art and philosophy that function in the same essential way as institutional religion (i.e., as part of the unfolding and coming to self-consciousness of Spirit). But while Hegel may have privileged institutional religion (in one sense), we need not follow his lead to be properly Hegelian. The key point here is that Spirit unfolds itself and comes to self-knowledge through *many* elements of culture, and we need not privilege one over another. Religion has been a particularly important element in this regard, but it is not clearly the only element needed and Hegel prepares the ground for imagining other elements that can fulfill a similar function to religion.

Perhaps the most effective way to view Hegel's perspective is to use *culture* as the large umbrella term.[50] Within that umbrella we find art, philosophy, religion, and many other phenomena that may be part of the unfolding and coming to self-knowledge of Spirit. Remember, the individual person *is* Spirit to the extent that he or she shares in the fundamental rationality of what Spirit is. Culture is the way that human beings both individually and collectively project Spirit out of themselves, making themselves and Spirit objects of themselves, in order to not only express themselves but to know themselves. Thus, this process is the mechanism by which Spirit comes to know itself. When Hegel writes that "the measure of its [humanity's] culture is the measure of its actuality and power,"[51] he means that the quality or worth of culture derives from the foundational character and force of Spirit working through human beings. Hegel concludes:

> It is by reason of his being Spirit, that man is man; and from man as Spirit proceed all the many developments of the sciences and arts, the interests of political life, and all those conditions which have reference to man's freedom and will. But all these manifold forms of human relations, activities, and pleasures, and all the ways in which these are intertwined; all that has worth and dignity for man, all wherein he seeks his happiness, his glory, and his pride, finds its ultimate centre in religion, in the thought, the consciousness, and the feeling of God. Thus God is the beginning of all things, and the end of all things.[52]

Again, Hegel is using "religion" in this sense as an umbrella term, but clearly a variety of cultural phenomena are working in concert to achieve a similar goal.

For Hegel, cultural phenomena connect significantly with the moral life of a people. But this is not the narrow morality of Kant—the kind of morality that focuses on the analysis of actions and how to determine their moral worth. Morality for Hegel is more associated with the *ethos* of a community—their moral norms, customs, presuppositions, core resources, etc. He insists that "Spirit is the *ethical life* of a nation" and that the "*living ethical* world is Spirit in its *truth*."[53] This truth of Spirit "speaks its *universal language* in the customs and laws of its nation."[54] These customs and laws may differ (sometimes quite dramatically), but they all promote (some to a greater, others to a lesser, extent) reason in our relationships with others, a care for others, and a sense of being part of an ethical whole or community.

The German term for this more expansive understanding of morality is *Sittlichkeit*. Charles Taylor notes that while Kant's theory focuses on specific acts and motivation, focuses in the end on the individual, with *Sittlichkeit* "morality reaches its completion in a community."[55] Indeed, the "norms of a society's public life are the content of *Sittlichkeit*."[56]

In the modern world, it is the State that represents the Spirit of the people. For Hegel, "the State is the actually existing, realized moral life."[57] And the Law of the State "is the objectivity of Spirit."[58] The State is the expression of the Spirit through the people. "The State is the true form of reality," Hegel concludes, "In it the true moral will comes into the sphere of reality, and Spirit lives in its true nature."[59] Thus, while religion may contribute to the expression and promotion of moral truth, it is not the only or even the final means to achieve this function. Other cultural phenomena can do it. And, in fact, the State takes a special priority in the historical development of morality.

In sum, the Spirit of a people, the Spirit working through the reason and artifacts of the people, is the culture of the State or Nation. The Spirit of a people "exists and persists in a particular religious form of worship, customs, constitution, and political laws—in the whole complex of its institutions—in the events and transactions that make up its history. That is its work—that is what this particular Nation *is*."[60] Another way of putting this is to simply say that the Spirit of a people is expressed in its culture—including everything from political institutions and laws to literary texts and music.[61] The development of culture through history then is the movement of the Spirit. Hegel insists that the "history of the divine content" is "essentially the history of mankind as well—the movement of God toward man, and of man toward God. Man knows himself to be essentially included in this history, woven into it."[62] He sums this up quite succinctly: History is "Spirit emptied out into

Time."[63] And because Spirit is reason or rationality, Hegel can conclude that history is a "rational process."[64]

But to what goal is all this history, this unfolding and coming to knowledge of Spirit, directed? There are at least three answers to this question.

Spirit coming to full knowledge of itself. The unfolding of Spirit begins in various human activities, with religion being the most prominent. But its full realization awaited our modern historical period, when Science came to fruition. Hegel claims that "the content of religion proclaims earlier in time than does Science, what *Spirit is*, but only Science is its true knowledge of itself."[65] Indeed, it is through Science that the final goal, "Absolute Knowing," is achieved.[66]

Absolute freedom. Spirit is the embodiment of freedom. Hegel claims that "the essence of Spirit is Freedom."[67] And Spirit's working through human beings allows them to be free too. Because Spirit is reason, this freedom is very much like the freedom we see in Kant—the freedom from material constraints in order to act rationally.

Morality achieving its ultimate good. Unlike Kant, for whom the ultimate good is achieved only for individuals in an afterlife, for Hegel the ultimate good is achieved in this life, in this world. Burkhard Tuschling summarizes this key difference between the two thinkers:

> The realization of virtue or morality in a commonwealth and ethico-religious unification with God is not postponed, as in Kant, until the end of history, or transferred to a domain separate from actual life. Rather [for Hegel] it is actual, present in this life by the individual's becoming a member and active participant in the spiritual and material life of the people, by the individual's life becoming the means of the realization of the spirit of the whole, a subjective-objective unity, or, in short, by becoming objective spirit.[68]

While with Kant we saw that religious ideas seemed to be a superfluous appendage to his moral theory, here we see really a secular vision of the moral relationship of the individual and community—a vision couched in religious verbiage but that easily can stand without it. Indeed, we will see that much of future German philosophy would extend and develop Hegel's work while dispensing with the religious language.

Kant and Hegel are giants in the history of philosophy, and their work has had far-ranging implications even beyond philosophy. In some cases, those implications were extensions of their thought into new times or new problems. In other cases, those implications were a consequence of critiques of their work.

In either case, however, subsequent thought continued a trajectory in which religion would become more and more irrelevant. Let us look at three thinkers, in particular, to trace some of this trajectory.

Schleiermacher, Feuerbach, and Marx

One very common objection to the kind of rationalization of religion that is found in Kant and Hegel is to claim that religion is beyond reason or rationality—that religion is fundamentally about or grounded in feelings or emotions. This is exactly the kind of claim made by Friedrich Schleiermacher (1768–1864).

Perhaps Schleiermacher's most famous work is *On Religion: Speeches to Its Cultured Despisers* (1799). Published just a few years after Kant's *Religion within the Limits of Reason Alone*, it represents one of the earliest and still most important responses to the Enlightenment critique and appropriation of religion. In this regard, Schleiermacher provides us with a compelling contrast to Kant and Hegel.

Whereas Kant and Hegel try to account for religion within a larger rational framework, Schleiermacher insists that religion is completely separate (though not necessarily opposed) from reason and morality. "It springs necessarily and by itself from the interior of every better soul," he writes, "it has its own province in the mind in which it reigns sovereign, and it is worthy of moving the noblest and the most excellent by means of its innermost power and by having its innermost essence known by them."[69] In what can be read as a direct critique of Kant and Hegel, he insists that "metaphysics and morals have therefore invaded religion on many occasions, and much that belongs to religion has concealed itself in metaphysics or morals under an unseemly form."[70] In other words, the attempt to account for or even meld religion into a rational or moral framework inevitably distorts it—twists it into something contrary to its essence.

What is truly essential about religion is the experience of the individual with the divine, the finite with the infinite. This experience is not about reason, but about feeling or sense or intuition. For Hegel as for Kant, feeling is too subjective, too uncertain, to be a guide for our thoughts and behavior. Only reason can provide a secure foundation for us.[71] But for Schleiermacher, feeling (also referred to as sense or intuition) is the very basis of religion. And while Kant and Hegel would find such a basis to be a critical flaw in regard to religion (thus, they sought to "save" religion through their rationalist accounts), for Schleiermacher this basis is the very mark of distinction and uniqueness for religion.

Schleiermacher's emphasis on psychological experience as central to religion can be seen clearly in his concluding statement to his second speech: "To be one with the infinite in the midst of the finite and to be eternal in a moment, that is the immortality of religion."[72] While Schleiermacher was a committed Christian, he nevertheless thinks of this experience as something that is shared or held in common across religions. He concludes that "the basic intuition of a religion can be nothing other than some intuition of the infinite in the finite, some universal element of religion that may also occur in all other religions."[73] While Kant and Hegel use universal rationality as that which binds the religions of all people together, Schleiermacher uses a universal sense or feeling. "A person is born with the religious capacity as with every other," he writes, "and if only his sense is not forcibly suppressed, if only that communion between a person and the universe—these are admittedly the two poles of religion—is not blocked and barricaded, then religion would have to develop unerringly in each person according to his own individual manner."[74]

In the fifth and final speech, Schleiermacher asks the cultural despisers of religion to reject the "enlightened religions" of thinkers like Kant and Hegel. Such religions, heavy on rationalist justifications and moral theory, miss the deep and powerful experiential core of what religion is. In addition, their universalizing leads us away from the particulars of concrete religions. One central passage is worth quoting at length:

> Thus if you are serious about considering religion in its determinate forms, turn back from these enlightened religions to the despised positive religions where everything real, powerful, and determinate appears, where every particular intuition has its specific content and its own relationship to the rest. Turn to the religions where every feeling has its own circle and its special connection; where you encounter every modification of religiousness somewhere and every state of mind into which only religion can transpose a person; where you find each part of religion formed somewhere and each of its effects completed somewhere; where all communal institutions and all individual expressions prove the high worth that is put on religion to the point of forgetting all the rest; where the holy zeal with which it is contemplated, communicated, and enjoyed and the childlike longing with which one looks forward to new revelations of heavenly powers guarantee for you that none of its elements that could already be perceived from this point has been overlooked and that none of its moments has disappeared without leaving a monument.[75]

Schleiermacher's turn to experience (in the passage above, note terms like "intuition," "feeling," "holy zeal," and "longing"), to the psychology of religion, would become an important approach to the study of religion in the many decades to come. I will elaborate on that approach and its history in Chapter 3. For now, I merely note how the effort by figures like Kant and Hegel to defend religion against rationalist critiques and to even "save" religion by integrating it into a rationalist framework failed in the eyes of many people. Those like Schleiermacher who testified to that failure simply rejected the project of trying to preserve religion through rationalist means, claiming instead that religion essentially was about experience, about a psychological state or intuition or feeling that has nothing (or very little) to do with reason. As we will see in Chapter 3, this psychological approach also has its limitations.

Ludwig Feuerbach (1804–1872) also dabbled in psychological speculation, but his work leads us more in the direction of the sociology of religion. Indeed, it often is difficult to separate causes and effects that are psychological from those that are sociological. What distinguishes someone like Feuerbach, as well as Karl Marx (1818–83), whom I discuss below, is the attention they pay to the social origins of religious beliefs and behaviors as well as the social consequences of them. Both Feuerbach and Marx are considered Hegelians, but they took Hegel's philosophical approach in a very different direction.

Feuerbach's most influential work is *The Essence of Christianity*, one that would greatly influence Marx's theory of religion. One of the most obvious and critical departures for Feuerbach from Hegel is the former's materialism. Where Hegel begins or at least focuses on Spirit, Feuerbach begins with human beings, concrete existence, and matter. His approach "generates thought from the *opposite* of thought, from Matter, from existence, from the senses."[76] Where Hegel can be viewed as engaging in theological inquiry, Feuerbach insists that he is doing anthropology. In short, for Feuerbach, the ground or basis of religion is not some transcendent God, but human beings—in particular the human mind. He concludes, "Religion is the dream of the human mind."[77] In this conclusion, however, Feuerbach does not see a denigration of religion, but the exaltation of the human. He insists that while he is "reducing theology to anthropology" he also "exalt[s] anthropology into theology, very much as Christianity, while lowering God into man [the incarnation of God in Jesus Christ], made man into God."[78]

Long before the concept of "projection" became common in the world of psychology and then even part of everyday discourse in the Western world, Feuerbach was making an argument about religion that centered on this idea. For Feuerbach, religious ideas are projections of human characteristics onto a transcendent being. "Religion being identical with the distinctive characteristics of man," he writes, "is then identical with self-consciousness—with the consciousness which man has of his nature."[79] The three distinct characteristics for Feuerbach are the ability to think, to will, and to love.[80] While human beings embody these characteristics in a finite manner, God is the being who has these characteristics in a perfect form, in an infinite manner. It is by projecting these characteristics on to God that human beings come to know themselves.[81] Whereas Hegel imagines Spirit (the transcendent) expressing itself through human rationality and culture (the immanent) in order to come to know itself, Feuerbach reverses the relationship. It is human beings (immanent) who project their characteristics out onto a transcendent object (God) in order to know themselves. That is why Feuerbach concludes that "religion is man's earliest and also indirect form of self-knowledge."[82]

Given Feuerbach's argument, we see then that the religious adherent's experience of God is really just her experience of her own nature—in particular, those characteristics that human beings find of greatest value. "Consciousness of God is self-consciousness, knowledge of God is self-knowledge," Feuerbach writes. "By his God thou knowest the man, and by the man his God; the two are identical. Whatever is God to a man, that is his heart and soul; and conversely, God is the manifested inward nature, the expressed self of a man—religion the solemn unveiling of a man's hidden treasures, the revelation of his intimate thoughts, the open confession of his love-secrets."[83]

As with Kant and Hegel, thinking (rationality) is critical to Feuerbach's theory. Like them, Feuerbach views reason as a marker, an attribute that distinguishes human beings from creatures governed by instinct. Reason is what provides human beings with freedom, and (of course) God is that infinite being who has unlimited freedom. "To think is to be God," Feuerbach concludes. "The act of thought, as such, is the freedom of the immortal gods from all external limitations and necessities of life."[84] He also affirms that "God as God—as a purely thinkable being, an object of the intellect—is thus nothing else than the reason in its utmost intensification become objective to itself."[85] But whereas God as reason has its source in a transcendent being (or, in Hegel's terms, the Spirit), for Feuerbach the true source is humanity itself. Again, his is a work of anthropology first and theology second (or, we might say, it is anthropology as theology).

Feuerbach's anthropology changes the way in which we view a whole range of religious ideas or concept. Take, for example, the incarnation (God becoming human through Jesus) in Christianity. "The mystery of the incarnation is the mystery of the love of God to man," Feuerbach writes, "and the mystery of the love of God to man is the love of man to himself."[86] The incarnation then is symbolic of humanity coming to love itself.

Morality, central to the philosophy of religion of both Kant and Hegel, also looks very different.[87] "God as a morally perfect being is nothing else than the realised idea, the fulfilled law of morality, the moral nature of man posited as the absolute being," Feuerbach argues, "man's own nature, for the moral God requires man to be as he himself is."[88] God, in this theory, is the ideal of moral perfection—not (as in the case of Kant) the being who guarantees the reward for human moral excellence. As the ideal of moral perfection, God shows us our limitations. God is an infinite concept, while we only are finite. Feuerbach notes that "while it [God, the morally perfect being] proclaims to me what I ought to be, it also tells me to my face, without any flattery, what I am not."[89] The moral God may reflect my moral nature, but it also shows me my human limitation (as, for example, a "sinner"). Religion, he continues, "sets man's own nature before him as a separate nature, and moreover as a personal being, who hates and curses sinners, and excludes them from his grace, the source of all salvation and happiness."[90] The incarnation, subsequently, brings that ideal of moral perfection back into human beings (Jesus, in other words) and his sacrifice is able to redeem all of humanity.[91] While the moral God reveals our foibles, the incarnation insists that we must accept and love ourselves—a worldly form of salvation, but a salvation nonetheless.

Feuerbach is very aware that many people would view his theory of religion as atheistic. Such a criticism, of course, makes sense given that he reduces theology to anthropology. But he expresses no concern about such a charge. "If therefore my work is negative, irreligious, atheistic, let it be remembered that atheism—at least in the sense of this work—is the secret of religion itself," he responds, "that religion itself, not indeed on the surface, but fundamentally, not in intention or according to its own supposition, but in its heart, in its essence, believes in nothing else than the truth and divinity of human nature."[92] Besides this embrace of the idea of atheism, Feuerbach's approach further diminishes religion when he argues that there is nothing peculiar to religion that cannot be found in other areas of human life and culture. In this sense, he is echoing the same point that we identified in Hegel. "Religion has thus no dispositions and emotions which are peculiar to itself," he states, "what it claims as belonging exclusively to its object, are simply the same dispositions and emotions that man experiences either in relation to himself (as, for example, to his conscience), or to his fellow-man, or to Nature."[93] As with Hegel, religion then for Feuerbach is just one particular cultural phenomenon among many. It is not unique.

The atheism of Feuerbach is powerfully extended by Karl Marx, though the latter's focus is more on the social (political, economic, etc.) implications of the kind of projection theory advanced by Feuerbach. In short, Marx very much adopts that projection theory. He accepts the anthropological claim that the objects of religion do not exist "out there"—that those objects and the religions around them are wholly (holy?) human creations. In a critique of Hegel's *Philosophy of Right*, Marx reverses his forerunner's theological position by insisting that "*man makes religion; religion does not make man.*"[94] He describes religion as an "inverted world consciousness."[95] Whereas the real world (immanent) is one of suffering and injustice, religion poses a transcendent world (the heavenly realm) where there is only happiness and justice. The fixation of human beings on the heavenly realm prevents them from working diligently to ease the suffering and fight the injustices in this world. In particular, it is the poor, the lower class, those who suffer the most and experience the greatest injustices, who are most encouraged (generally by the rich, the upper class, those who inflict suffering and injustice) to focus their attention on the world beyond instead of on this world. In this way, the unjust status quo is never challenged. Marx concludes that religion "is the sigh of the oppressed creature, the sentiment of a heartless world, and the soul of soulless conditions. It is the *opium* of the people."[96] It is opium, a drug, because it dulls our senses to the world around us. It makes us believe in an illusion (the heavenly realm) while we suffer here in this world.[97] Therefore, Marx calls us to action. "The abolition of religion as the *illusory* happiness of men," he argues, "is a demand for their *real* happiness."[98]

In the end, Marx takes the fundamental theory of Feuerbach and politicizes it. In doing so, he simply extends it to its natural conclusion in the social arena. For him, religion is not just irrelevant (or, it should be irrelevant), it is a powerful obstacle to human progress.

Conclusion

This trek through eighteenth- and nineteenth-century German thought (a small portion, of course) was necessarily brief, but I hope the following conclusions (not just about German thought, but about Western philosophy more generally) have become clear.

- The Enlightenment period, with its championing of reason and turn to science, brought with it a powerful critique of religion. Certain Enlightenment thinkers like Kant attempted to "rescue" or "save" religion by finding a necessary role for it in moral philosophy. Hegel did this too, but went even further in weaving religious ideas into a grand philosophical/theological theory of human history and culture. Both attempts, however, failed vis-à-vis religion—at least religion in its stereotypical and institutional form. One may adopt a Kantian perspective or a Hegelian outlook without necessarily buying into their religious or theological claims.

- In response to overly rationalistic accounts of religion as we see in Kant and Hegel, some thinkers sought to separate religion from reason. Such was the attempt of Schleiermacher. We will see in Chapter 3 that such an attempt has its own limitations, though such attempts continue to be made even today.
- The work of figures like Feuerbach and Marx are understandable extensions of the line of thought begun by their Enlightenment predecessors. Their atheism was not a radically new way of thinking in opposition (in this case) to Hegel, but a mere working out of Hegel without the theological baggage.
- All of these thinkers work across the divide between transcendence (other worldly) and immanence (this worldly) in ways that prioritize the latter over the former. For Kant, the transcendent is but a practical supposition that must be accepted as a consequence of our very immanent moral reasoning. For Hegel, the immanent (history and culture) is not the opposite of the transcendent, but that through which the transcendent unfolds. While Schleiermacher resists Enlightenment rationalism, he grounds religion in human feeling or intuition (immanent) more than in some transcendent reality—setting the stage for a psychologizing of religion in the centuries to come. And both Feuerbach and Marx dispense with the transcendent (for them, it might truly be irrelevant or even an obstacle) and insist on the sole reality of the immanent instead.

In the end, the point is that some philosophical efforts to preserve religion contained within them the seeds of lines of thought that would come to denigrate, diminish, deny, and/or dismiss religion. While this conclusion is seen clearly in the German thought covered in this chapter, it nevertheless could be traced in French thought, in the English-speaking world, and elsewhere. And while most Westerners know very little, if anything, about Kant, Hegel, or any of the other philosophers mentioned in this chapter, they necessarily are inheritors of debates and perspectives that have leaked out of the philosophical realm and seeped into the general culture.

2

The Sociological Function of Religion: Durkheim and Weber

In one sense, the divide between sociology and psychology is artificial. Individual psychology and society are inextricably linked. They really are two sides of the same coin—the coin being, more generally, the human condition. But psychologists do focus more on the individual, while sociologists do focus more on the greater society. In this chapter, we will look at two key figures in the development and promotion of the sociology of religion, before turning in the next chapter to two key figures in the development and promotion of the psychology of religion. What all these figures share is a commitment to the idea that rational inquiry can reveal new insights into the phenomenon known as religion and that the phenomenon of religion serves human beings in particular ways. In short, religion functions in certain ways for human beings. As we will see, this way of seeing religion (functionally) will be critical to advancing the argument of this book.

Introduction

In his *Alternative Sociologies of Religion: Through Non-Western Eyes*, James V. Spickard challenges the "default view" of the sociology of religion by imagining how the area of study might have developed in other (non-Western) cultures. While those thought experiments are a little too far afield for our purposes, his description of the "default view" is a great place for us to start our inquiry.

According to Spickard, the "default view" in sociology holds "that religions are primarily about beliefs and are embodied in religious organizations."[1] Such a view that focuses on beliefs and organizations will necessarily miss a lot of religious behavior and phenomena. As Spickard concludes:

> Like all views, the default view focuses on some aspects of religions and fails to focus on others. It does a good job of understanding formal religious organizations. It does a poorer job of understanding religion that takes other forms. It does a good job of tracking people's religious beliefs. It does a poorer job of understanding people's religious practices. It recognizes the importance of religious symbols. It too often fails to recognize the importance of religious experiences. It typically treats religion as a separate institutional sphere, which prevents it from easily seeing religions' connections with other spheres: race, ethnicity, inequality, war, peace, and so on.[2]

Spickard argues that the "default view" is one that arises out of a specific Western and Christian context. Thus, that view reflects some specific Western and Christian assumptions about religion—for example, the binding of the concept of religion to that of church.[3] He argues that a more expansive and helpful alternative view can be developed by thinking sociologically through other non-Western cultural lenses—in particular, Chinese, Muslim, and Native American.

While Spickard is critical of both Durkheim and Weber for succumbing to some of the shortcomings of the "default view," we will see that their work also avoids many of those shortcomings and provides the conceptual tools for a very progressive and even radical view of religion. And in the same way that non-Western cultural lenses can expand our sociology of religion, so (I will argue) can the study of cultural phenomena—especially popular culture—expand our very understanding of religion.

Durkheim and the Foundations of Moral Community

Emile Durkheim (1858–1917) was a French scholar and one of the founding figures of the discipline of sociology.[4] His work covered a range of institutions and issues in society, from the division of labor to the social causes of suicide. He also wrote on religion, and much that he wrote on that subject continues to carry weight today.

Durkheim divides religious phenomena into two categories: beliefs and rites (rituals or practices).[5] These two categories are dependent on one another, though Durkheim certainly emphasizes the role of collective action (rituals or practices) as preeminent. As Robert N. Bellah concludes in regard to Durkheim's position, beliefs "arise from and express the homogeneous physical movements that constitute the ritual, not the other way around."⁶ In other words, religion is more about what we *do* than what we *think*. "He thus defined religion by what it accomplishes," Spickard notes, "the separation of the sacred from the profane and the unification of the moral community for which it does so."⁷

All religious beliefs and rites, Durkheim notes, presuppose the dichotomy between the sacred and the profane. He argues that the sacred and profane are radical opposites, and that a central aspect of the religious life is the continual separation of the sacred from the profane. This process and maintenance of separation are not something done simply by individuals. Beliefs are held and rites performed by individuals who are part of a group that holds the beliefs and performs the rites in common. Indeed, it is the holding of beliefs and the performance of rites in common that help to form the group itself.

> Religious beliefs proper are always shared by a definite group that professes them and that practices the corresponding rites. Not only are they individually accepted by all members of that group, but they also belong to the group and unify it. The individuals who comprise the group feel joined to one another by the fact of common faith.⁸

Durkheim calls such a group a "Church" (though predominantly a Christian term, by "Church" he simply means any religious community). Thus, he arrives at the following definition of religion: "*A religion is a unified system of beliefs and practices relative to sacred things, that is to say, things set apart and forbidden—beliefs and practices which unite into one single moral community called a Church, all those who adhere to them.*"⁹

While Durkheim believes that his definition of religion holds universally, his particular interest in *The Elementary Forms of Religious Life* is totemic religion in aboriginal Australia. In a sustained argument, Durkheim makes the case that the totem (e.g., a particular animal, let us say a kangaroo) of a tribe or clan is what is most sacred. It also is what represents the tribe or clan. For Durkheim, these are one and the same. Take a hypothetical example of a tribe with a kangaroo as its totem. What is most sacred (*set apart, forbidden*) may be the kangaroo, but the kangaroo simply represents the tribe. Thus, it is the tribe or clan that is most sacred and is the object of religious devotion—only not directly but via the totem. Chris Shilling describes Durkheim's point this way:

> Totemism is a mode of ritual religious practice which has at its center the symbolic equation of a clan or tribe with an animal, plant or other object most frequently found in its place of ceremonial meeting. Totemism unites individuals around a

system of symbols (which organize thought) and an associated system of norms and prohibitions (which organize ritual action) and ultimately is explicable ... as a result of the social group's worship of itself.[10]

The totemic principle is that which comes to organize all people, animals, and things. It helps to designate the relative importance of everything by virtue of any particular thing's affinity or relatedness to the totem. For example, a particular field where kangaroos tend to congregate would be especially sacred, as would be the water in the stream that runs through the field. Stones from the field might be used in certain rituals, as will (of course) the kangaroos themselves (particularly in sacrifices). The result is a coherent system of beliefs (organized around the totem) about the world around the tribe or clan as well as a set of rituals that generate, affirm, and sustain those beliefs.

Of particular interest to Durkheim is how the totemic principle comes to organize human beings and other human-like beings such as great ancestors, gods, and goddesses. Gods and goddesses (culminating in the idea, eventually, of one god) developed from the idea of ancestors. The idea of ancestors living on after the death of the body was inferred by the empirical evidence of the survival of the tribe or clan even as individuals pass away. Individuals have temporal limitations, but the tribe or clan is eternal (at least it can seem that way). The idea of ancestors also can be understood as a consequence of our sense that we have something eternal and objective in us—separate from our bodies and idiosyncratic thoughts. This eternal and objective thing is the soul.

The soul is what is sacred about human beings, as opposed to the body that is profane. The soul is the spark or fragment of the totem (in later epochs, this might be considered a spark or fragment of the divine) that connects human beings to ancestors, gods, and goddesses. It is our moral conscience, that which guides our thoughts and actions and somehow seems other than ourselves. This is why Durkheim writes of our "double nature." Any person is both an individual and something else—this something else is denoted by the idea of the soul. But this something else is not unique to the individual, it is what is shared in common with everyone else (or at least everyone else in the tribe or clan). Our soul then is really a spark or fragment of the collective soul (as represented in the totem). Durkheim writes that "there truly is a parcel of divinity in us, because there is in us a parcel of the grand ideals that are the soul of collectivity."[11] In short, we are both individual and social beings, and the soul simply is the idea of the social side of us. Thus, Durkheim concludes that "man is double. In him are two beings: an individual being that has its basis in the body and whose sphere of action is strictly limited by this fact, and a social being that represents within us the highest reality in the intellectual and moral realm that is knowable through observation: I mean society."[12]

The soul then represents what is transcendent. It is immortal—greater than any individual life. Durkheim observes:

> In sum, belief in the immortality of souls is the only way man is able to comprehend a fact that cannot fail to attract his attention: the perpetuity of the group's life. The individuals die, but the clan survives, so the forces that constitute his life must have the same perpetuity. These forces are the souls that animate the individual bodies, because it is in and by them that the group realizes itself. For that reason, they must endure. Indeed, while enduring, they also must remain the same. Since the clan always keeps its characteristic form, the spiritual substance of which it is made must be conceived of as qualitatively invariable.[13]

The soul is identical to that which makes the ancestors, gods, and goddesses sacred, and it is what connects us to them. But the soul is nothing more nor less than society itself. The soul is our social nature, experienced by us as something other and greater than ourselves. Ultimately our soul is identified with God (the ultimate, most powerful totem), and God is society. In this move, Durkheim takes what are transcendent (spirit, gods, etc.) and makes them immanent (society). It is a move that other theorists (some of whom we met in Chapter 1) make, and it is central to the larger argument of this book.

The idea of transcendence, represented by the concept of the soul as the psychological experience of the power of the collectivity (tribe or clan) within us, helps us to understand what rituals achieve. Rituals entail our participation in something greater than ourselves—that something greater being society itself. This understanding of ritual is true for Muslims who gather for prayer, for Christians joining for communion, but also for people engaged in a wide variety of ritual activities.

Sporting events are great illustrations of how Durkheim's work is applicable beyond what we view as stereotypically religious—and foreshadows developments in religious studies that we take up in Chapter 5. Anyone who has been to a sporting event (particularly in major team sports) may be struck by how well Durkheim's account fits with what fans often do to themselves as part of their participation in the event. Whether it is wearing the totem (team mascot) on apparel or painting it on their faces or chests, fans seem to engage in the same kind of totemic representation that Durkheim found among totemic tribes and clans. Anthropologist Victor Turner also writes about the following characteristics of the rites or rituals that he observed or studied: "singing, dancing, feasting, wearing of bizarre dress, body painting, use of alcohol or hallucinogens."[14] All of these, for good or ill, also are characteristic of the sporting experience for millions of fans across the globe.

Durkheim divides rituals into the "negative cult" and the "positive cult." The negative cult has to do with that which is prohibited—often those things that are associated with the totem. What is prohibited is considered taboo. Certain things associated with the totem, certain powerfully sacred things, are too great to be handled at will. They are taboo for most people. That is, most people are prohibited from touching them. Priests or others who conduct rituals may be allowed to handle taboo elements, but even they may have to go through rites of purification to do so. There are few elements of the sporting experience that are taboo in this sense, that people are prohibited from touching. There are, however, elements that *some* people at least are excluded from touching. For example, fans generally are excluded from touching or handling the balls and equipment necessary for the play of a sport that they are watching. They also are prohibited from being on the fields or courts. In other words, the fields or courts are open to athletes and officials, but taboo for spectators.

The positive cult is not about avoiding the sometimes dangerous power of sacred elements, but bringing the participants of the ritual into communion with the sacred. Thus, it is a system of ritual practices that "regulate and organize" our bilateral relationship with the sacred.[15] So it is through the collective enactment of ritual that people are brought into contact with the sacred—the sacred ultimately being that very collective enactment itself (when properly performed and engaging the appropriate emotions).

A great example of the positive cult is the sacrificial feast. Here the power of the totem is released and incorporated by the tribe or clan through, as one example, the killing (sacrifice) and eating of a representative totemic animal. Remember, however, that the totem is a symbol for the society itself, and in this instance any particular totemic animal is like an individual. Just as a particular totemic animal may be sacrificed (and through its being consumed, its power is distributed throughout the members of the tribe or clan), so any individual in a society must be prepared to sacrifice himself or herself for the good of the whole.

The sacrificial feast is not simply about consumption, however; it also entails renunciation—a giving up of some of the totemic animal and/or other goods to the gods. Sacrifice "always presupposes that the worshipper relinquishes to the gods some part of his substance or his goods."[16] But what is even more important as an offering in the sacrificial feast is the thought of the participants.[17] The ritual is performed to strengthen the society as a whole (albeit through the strengthening of individual members) through an act of communion. And while it is believed that this strength comes from oblation to the gods and/or the ingesting of the totemic animal, it really comes from the active participation of the community's members in the ritual—it comes from the care and concern that they demonstrate toward the whole as demonstrated by and as a consequence of their participation. So, while it is believed that the ritual strengthens members of the tribe or clan, and through the offering strengthens the totem and/or the gods, according to Durkheim's analysis it is society itself that is preserved and revived by the ritual. Robert Alun Jones explains Durkheim's approach this way:

> Metaphorically, therefore, the gods (i.e. society) depend upon men (i.e. individuals) for their existence, just as men (individuals) depend upon the gods (society) for the best attributes of themselves; and once this is recognized, Durkheim concluded, the task of the science of religions becomes clear—i.e. to explain the nature and origin of the forces upon which our social actions rely.[18]

What happens to the participants in the sacrificial feast or other rituals of the positive cult is what Durkheim describes as "collective effervescence." He notes that the "state of effervescence in which the assembled faithful find themselves is translated outwardly by exuberant emotions that are not easily subordinated to ends that are defined too strictly."[19] In other words, the effervescence is not about achieving some other practical end. It is an end in itself. It is an end because it represents the social and psychological unity of the community itself—and the community is the highest good (and thus, is not a means to some other good).[20] It is central to our collective lives.[21] As Spickard concludes, the "collective feeling that comes from group ritual is experienced as something special, something set apart. It does not just change people's beliefs; it changes their lives."[22] This collective feeling is one of the "ends of religion" that is central to my argument in this book.

While collective effervescence is an end-in-itself, it does have practical and quite important effects in building and sustaining the community and its moral order. This end or goal of religion—the formation and sustaining of community—is *the* central function of religion for Durkheim. Shilling notes that, for Durkheim, "there can be no society without a sense of the sacred: the sacred energizes the symbolic order of society and motivates people to act [through rituals that lead to collective effervescence] in relation to the moral norms of that order."[23] Rituals give rise to collective effervescence that then is the psychological energy and capacity for the moral order (rules, roles, authority, etc.) that defines society.

It also is worth noting that the relationship between the sacred and collective effervescence is circular rather than linear. It is not simply that the experience of the sacred through rituals and contact with particular objects leads to collective effervescence, but that collective effervescence also helps to make those rituals and objects sacred. As Elisa Heinamaki concludes, "the intense, contagious affect of effervescent gatherings is projected onto things, which are thus deemed sacred."[24] Our communion with those sacred things then also leads to collective effervescence.

What Durkheim refers to as collective effervescence is similar to what Turner describes as *communitas*. Communitas refers to the direct relationship of concrete, particular individuals with one another. This relationship is not between, for example, a teacher and a student or a clerk and a customer; it is between two human beings stripped of their roles and statuses in society.[25] Such a relationship between human beings, though the most fortuitous and beneficial of encounters, cannot be maintained indefinitely. All human societies need (or, at least, seem to need) some kind of division of labor, clearly understood power relations and duties/obligations for their citizens, and orderly and effective social institutions with accompanying hierarchies. All of this is what Turner calls *structure*. Structure is "a more or less distinctive arrangement of mutually dependent institutions and the institutional organization of social position and/or actors which they imply."[26] Structure allows societies to function effectively. The "spontaneity and immediacy" of communitas inevitably gives way to structure.[27] But it is communitas that provides the powerful emotional bond to one another that human beings need as social creatures. It is through communitas that "*anomie* [the psychological distress caused by chaos in the social order; a term popularized by Durkheim] is prevented or avoided and a milieu is created in which a society's members cannot see any fundamental conflict between themselves as individuals and society. There is set up, in their minds, a symbiotic interpenetration of individual and society."[28] What we have then is a continual tension, a dialectic, between communitas (also called anti-structure) and structure. Both are necessary for human life, and our objective should be finding the appropriate balance between the two. Turner concludes:

> Spontaneous communitas is richly charged with affects, mainly pleasurable ones. Life in "structure" is filled with objective difficulties: decisions have to be made, inclinations sacrificed to the wishes and needs of the group, and physical and social obstacles overcome at some personal cost. Spontaneous communitas has something "magical" about it. Subjectively there is in it the feeling of endless power. But this power untransformed cannot readily be applied to the

organizational details of social existence. It is no substitute for lucid thought and sustained will. On the other hand, structural action swiftly becomes arid and mechanical if those involved in it are not periodically immersed in the regenerative abyss of communitas. Wisdom is always to find the appropriate relationship between structure and communitas under the *given* circumstances of time and place, to accept each modality when it is paramount without rejecting the other, and not to cling to one when its present impetus is spent.[29]

Today, the rituals of various sporting events, musical concerts, and other cultural phenomena, like religious rituals, contribute to the establishment of communitas and collective effervescence. Durkheim notes, for example, that games originated in a religious context, and that recreation "is one form of the moral remaking [society itself] that is the primary object of the positive cult."[30] Games or recreation helps to create communitas, for the players encounter one another directly—not mediated by the structures of the social order. In the end, there are numerous rituals—religious and apparently non-religious—that allow communitas to occur.

What Durkheim's work clearly indicates is the great need we have for all collective rituals. "There can be no society," he writes, "that does not experience the need at regular intervals to maintain and strengthen the collective feelings and ideas that provide its coherence and its distinct individuality."[31] There can be no society that does not engage in rituals to achieve collective effervescence or communitas. Religion has served an important role in human history in functioning to provide these moments of collective effervescence or communitas. But, as Edward A. Tiryakian notes, at the end of *The Elementary Forms of Religious Life*, we are left with the following question: "[C]an the moments of 'collective effervescence' regenerative of societal solidarity occur in the modern world, and under what circumstances?"[32]

My answer to this question and, indeed, the answer of this book, is "yes." While religion is one example of an institution or set of practices that fulfills this function, it by no means is the only one. As noted above, sport may fulfill this function at times, but so too might beliefs and practices revolving around the nation (e.g., the bald eagle may serve as a totem for the United States, Independence Day as a critical ritual, Thanksgiving as a communal feast) or simply the emotionally charged and powerful sights and sounds of a popular music concert.

Durkheim's work is an excellent representation of a functional interpretation of religion. He explains religion by describing and analyzing what functions it fulfills. But once we understand these functions, we find that they may be fulfilled by other means. In short, then, religion loses its uniqueness and becomes but one important social institution among others. In this sense, stereotypical religion may not be irrelevant, but it certainly is much less relevant.

Weber and the Social and Economic Power of Ideas

A contemporary of Durkheim, Max Weber (1864–1920) takes a different approach to the study of religion—though still firmly within the field of the sociology of religion. As with Durkheim, we will see that Weber also views religion as playing a particular and important role in society—guiding individuals and groups in their behavior with one another.

In his summary of Weber's sociology, Lawrence A. Scaff identifies five key theses: *capitalism thesis, rationalization thesis, disenchantment thesis, thesis of subjectivist culture,* and *democratization thesis*.[33] Each thesis reveals something important about Weber's view of society (Western society in particular), but the most important ones for our purposes are the first three. And the three are all very much related.

Weber recognizes that, as Scaff notes, "capitalism transformed the material conditions of modern life in such a way as to affect dramatically the nature of cultural forms and cultural production."[34] We will see this impact in regard to religion—in particular, Christianity in the West. Capitalism brings with it a kind of rationalization of economic activity that comes to define other areas of human life. Of course, rationalization also leads to a certain kind of development of economic activity. In short, capitalism and rationalization can be seen as two sides of the same coin. For Weber, this rationalization "must be understood in terms of means-ends categories, purposive or goal-oriented actions, and 'instrumental' standards."[35] The process of rationalization then leads to disenchantment, "a loss of the sacred sense of wholeness and reconciliation between self and world provided by myth, magic, tradition, religion, or immanent nature."[36]

These theses about the modern world are the parameters in which to consider Weber's approach to the study of religion. While the religious impulse may have originated in non-rational responses of wonder or awe in relation to the natural world or the universe, religions (for Weber) are very much products of rational processes. A primary example of such development can be found in "doctrine." "We may assume that the outstanding marks of doctrine," Weber writes, "are the development of a rational system of religious concepts and ... the development of a systematic and distinctively religious ethic based upon a consistent and stable doctrine which purports to be a 'revelation.'"[37] Both the "rational system" and the "religious ethic" are results of rationalization. This rationalization entails also the development of a group of people who serve as authorities of the tradition and ethical guides. As Weber notes, "The full development of both a metaphysical rationalization and a religious ethic requires an independent and professional trained priesthood, permanently occupied with the cult and with the practical problems involved in the cure of souls."[38] These authority figures then are the bearers of the institutions that *are* our religious traditions (Judaism, Islam, etc.).

While Weber recognizes the broad reach of rationalization in religion, his primary focus is in the area of religious ethics—and he is particularly renowned in regard to the relationship between religious ethics and economic beliefs and behaviors. Indeed, for Weber, religion and the economic sphere are intricately connected. He insists that "religious or magical behavior or thinking must not be set apart from the range of everyday purposive conduct, particularly since even the ends of the religious and magical actions are predominantly economic."[39] The "ends" of "religious and magical actions" tend to be about the acquisition of goods—an abundant harvest, protection from natural catastrophes that destroy the necessities (food, shelter, etc.) of life, attaining an eternal afterlife where all our needs are met, and much more. All of these "ends" are economic in the broadest sense. And, in the West in particular, Weber identifies an "affinity between economic rationalism and certain types of rigoristic ethical religion."[40]

The most famous treatment of religion and economics by Weber (or perhaps by anyone) is his *The Protestant Ethic and the "Spirit" of Capitalism*. The book weaves an amazing narrative of the relationship between early Protestant theological ethics and the rise and then triumph of capitalism in the Western world. Weber notes that one of the goals of the text is to "perhaps play a modest part in illustrating the manner in which 'ideas' become effective in history."[41] His approach is not some form of idealism, however, as we see with Hegel. But it is a counter-methodology to the powerful and prevalent (in his day) materialism of Marxism. Instead, Weber is trying to find a middle ground. Thus, he notes that he is not arguing that certain Protestant ideas *caused* the rise of capitalism. What he seeks to do is "to establish whether and to what extent religious influences *have in fact* been *partially* responsible for the qualitative shaping and the quantitative expansion of that 'spirit' [of capitalism] across the world, and what concrete aspects of capitalist culture originate from them."[42] He concludes that "it cannot, of course, be our purpose to replace a one-sided 'materialist' causal interpretation of culture and history with an equally one-sided spiritual one.

Both are equally possible, but neither will serve historical truth if they claim to be the *conclusion* of the investigation rather than merely the *preliminary work for it*."[43]

So what exactly is the relationship between Protestantism and capitalism? Here we need to tell the tale of two historical plot lines that come together in interesting ways. The first involves industrialization and the rise of capitalism. The second involves the different economic attitudes and behavior that began to emerge between Protestants and Catholics.

What is critical for Weber is not the mechanics of capitalism, but the moral outlook that accompanies that economic system. In this regard, it is important to note that capitalism is not simply greed. Greed has been around for millennia—long before capitalism ever developed. What distinguishes capitalism is not greed for money, but the pursuit of money as an end-in-itself. "The aim of a man's life is indeed moneymaking," Weber writes, "but this is no longer merely the means to the end of satisfying the material needs of life."[44] He goes on to talk about "the *irrational* element of this way of conducting one's life, whereby a man exists for his business, not vice versa."[45] By "irrational," Weber means that a focus on business and moneymaking for its own sake, and even in spite of our general happiness, appears contrary to our self-interest.[46] We can think here of the business person working tirelessly to accumulate vast amounts of money, but who never seems satisfied with life. In general, we identify people who act contrary to their self-interest to be acting irrationally.

The reason why the capitalist might be committed to a moral outlook and economic behavior that seems counter to his self-interest is that he considers his work, his business, to be a "calling." This is a religious term that we flesh out below, but for now we can say that a calling in economic terms is the idea that one has a duty or obligation to work hard and make money in their particular vocation. It is here that we find the "spirit of capitalism," which Weber defines as "that attitude which, *in the pursuit of a calling*, strives systematically for profit for its own sake."[47]

Weber argues that the idea of a calling played out differently among Catholics and Protestants. Weber claims that in his time "business leaders and owners of capital, as well as the skilled higher strata of the labor force, and especially the higher technical or commercially trained staff of modern enterprises tend to be predominantly *Protestant*."[48] These leaders of industry and commerce contrast with their Catholic counterparts, who tend to fill the ranks of everyday laborers and crafts people. Thus, Weber concludes (for example) that "among journeymen the Catholics show the greater inclination to *remain* in craft work and thus more often tend to become *master* craftsmen, while the Protestants to a greater degree tend to flock to the factories where they form the upper echelons of skilled workers and management."[49] The idea that Catholics tend to "remain" at a previous historical stage of economic activity leads Weber to speak of their "traditionalism." Early in his text Weber gives the example of workers who are paid a piecework rate.[50] What he finds is that, among the "traditionalists," the higher the rate the less work they do. For example, imagine a worker getting paid $2 for each widget he makes. And imagine that $10 per day fulfills all his basic needs, so he works to make five widgets. Weber claims that if the price for a widget is raised to $2.50, then the traditionalist worker will only make four widgets instead of five. The reason is that he is only interested in fulfilling his basic needs, and if he can do that by working less then that is what he will do. He would rather spend time at home with his family or join his friends at the local beer hall than waste the day making more widgets. On the other hand, the non-traditionalist (Protestant) seems compelled to not only make the fifth widget (thus earning $12.50 that day) but to make as many widgets as possible to earn as much money as possible. In short, the non-traditionalist, Protestant worker is infused with the spirit of capitalism.

But what explains the difference in economic outlook and behavior between Catholics and Protestants? Here is where their distinctive theological positions come to the fore. For example, Weber surmises that "one might be tempted to express the contrast by saying that the greater '*unworldliness*' of Catholicism and the ascetic features which express its highest ideals must necessarily induce in its followers a greater indifference toward worldly goods."[51] But Weber focuses much more on the elements of Protestantism that would come to differentiate it from its Catholic predecessor.

We begin then with Martin Luther and the Reformation (sixteenth century), which leads us back to the idea of a calling. In the medieval Catholic world, the population was divided between the general population and the officials of the Church. The latter were governed by a rigorous asceticism that required celibacy and other austerities—exemplified best by the members of monastic orders. The sins of the general population were condemned though expected, and the Church provided the means by which individuals could free themselves from the punishment that necessarily applied to those sins. For example, an individual could go to the Church to confess his sins and receive prescribed practices to cleanse him of them. The goal was to minimize the harm of sins enough to guarantee an eternal life in heaven for the individual. To that extent, life in this world was mainly an obstacle to that final goal. It certainly was not a good to celebrate. Only the ascetic (a priest, but especially a monk or nun) achieves God's will in some way in this world. In contrast, Protestantism (arising in the sixteenth century out of the Reformation) "recognizes, as the *only* means of living a life pleasing to God, not the surpassing of innerworldly [*innerweltlich*] morality through the pursuit of monastic asceticism, but exclusively the fulfillment of innerworldly duties which arise from the individual's station in life. This then becomes one's 'calling.'"[52] In other words, fulfilling one's calling *in this world* is a way of achieving God's will—and that calling can be a vocation other than simply a priest or monastic.

To understand the importance of this notion of the calling, we need to understand a critical theological divide between Catholics and Protestants, between the idea of salvation by works and the idea of salvation by faith alone. While Christianity always has included both ideas and any particular Christian may embrace both to some degree, they do represent some important tendencies in Catholicism and Protestantism. The idea of salvation by works is straightforward. It is the idea that one can do good deeds and earn their way to eternal salvation. Alternatively, by confessing one's sins and engaging in acts of penance, one at least can mitigate the spiritual damage of the bad deeds that one may have done (thus avoiding eternal damnation). Depending on the balance of one's deeds or "works," one might end up in hell or heaven or purgatory (between heaven and hell, where one's sins may be purified through suffering, allowing one to then move on to heaven).

During the Renaissance, this Catholic view of salvation came under attack, most prominently by Luther. For example, he and other leaders of the Protestant Reformation railed against the selling of indulgences—basically a payment to the church that allows one to lessen the punishment that rightfully should result from one's sins (or, they even can be purchased on behalf of the dead, who might be languishing in purgatory). Luther and others challenged the corruption and superficiality of the practice and the hubris of imagining that a person can earn (or buy) one's way into heaven. As Luther writes in his "Ninety-Five Theses," the famous document he nailed to the Castle church door in Wittenberg in 1517, which generally is seen as marking the beginning of the Protestant Reformation: "All those who believe themselves certain of their own salvation by means of letters of indulgence, will be eternally damned, together with their teachers. We should be most carefully on our guard against those who say that the papal indulgences are an inestimable divine gift, and that a man is reconciled to God by them."[53] Instead of salvation by works (or by purchase), Luther insists on salvation through faith alone.

Luther and others who led the Protestant Reformation focused on the "original sin" of humanity. We are unworthy of eternal salvation, and we certainly cannot achieve it on our own. The only way to achieve it is through faith in Jesus Christ as the Son of God who died for our sins. Even then, we can never be sure that our faith is pure or even meritorious. To believe that one knows that they will attain eternal salvation is to claim to know God's mind—an act of hubris certainly equivalent to the belief that one can earn their way into heaven. In truth, we really have little control over our salvation, and we cannot even know if we will achieve it. We only can hope that God will show mercy upon us.

Many of these Reformation ideas are worked out to their logical conclusions in Calvinism—a particularly important Reformation denomination. While few if any key ideas in Calvinism were held exclusively by its adherents, the particular combination of ideas and fanaticism associated with them really led Calvinists to stand out from their other Christian brethren. And, of great interest to Weber is the fact that Calvinism was a major cultural influence in "the countries in which capitalism was most highly developed (the Netherlands, England, and sixteenth- and seventeenth-century France)."[54]

In Calvinist theology, one's salvation or damnation is predetermined. This belief is reflected in the doctrine of predestination. God's knowledge is perfect—past, present, and future. In God's mind, if I am on the path to hell, then there is nothing I can do to change that fact. The very idea that I could change that fact suggests that God's knowledge is *not* perfect. But God's knowledge is not simply a matter of knowing everything about a creation that already exists. God created everything. So my salvation or damnation is determined by God at the beginning of creation. My salvation or damnation then is not a consequence of anything I do. As Weber summarizes the position, "To assume that human merit or fault had any influence on one's fate would be to regard God's absolutely free decisions, which had stood for all eternity, as capable of being changed by human influence—an impossible idea."[55] And because I cannot know God's will (at least not in the sort of particularity that I need), I can never know if I am one of the elect (saved) or not. I only will know when I finally die and go to heaven or hell. And, of course, I cannot know the ultimate destination of any member of my family or my friends. Thus, Weber argues that the doctrine had "one principal consequence for the mood of a generation which yielded to its magnificent logic: it engendered, *for each individual*, a feeling of tremendous inner *loneliness*."[56]

This spiritual loneliness springs from the lack of knowledge about my ultimate destination. Such doubt about such an ultimate question is unbearable.

And even if I come to believe that I *am* one of the elect, what evidence is there to support such a belief? As Weber frames them, the questions are: "Am I one of the elect? And how can I be certain of my election?"[57]

While there is nothing I can do to ever earn my way into heaven, Calvinists concluded, my activity in the world might give me some indication of whether or not I am one of the elect. Such an indication or sign can go a long way toward easing the burden of spiritual uncertainty—the loneliness of which Weber speaks. Contrary to a stereotypical rejection of the world in Catholicism, Calvinists believed God cared about the world, that the world represented his will, and that "the world" obviously includes the social, political, and economic spheres. One's "calling" then was to fulfill one's role in these different spheres—to play one's part. Take work in the economic sphere as an example. Fulfilling one's "calling" in work (whether you are a laborer, merchant, or industrial tycoon) means working hard and being successful. Properly fitting in to the divine order then is a sign of one's grace, a sign that you are among the elect. As Weber notes, "*tireless labor in a calling* was urged as the best possible means of *attaining* this self-assurance. This and this alone would drive away religious doubt and give assurance of one's state of grace."[58] Or, put differently, "work is *the* end and purpose of life commanded by God. ... Unwillingness to work is a symptom of the absence of the state of grace."[59] My behavior cannot cause my salvation, but my already determined salvation might be reflected in my behavior.

Here is where Christian asceticism returns to play a critical role—not as a way of earning one's place in heaven (reminiscent of salvation by works) but merely as a sign of one's election (salvation by grace alone). Whereas withdrawal from the world and subjection to ascetic practices were once the way to prepare oneself or even become worthy of eternal salvation (Catholicism), a disciplined and dispassionate commitment to one's vocation or work in the world along with the tangible fruits of success in the world became a sign of one's predestined salvation (Protestantism, especially Calvinism). The difference between these two purposes, however, should not detract us from what is held in common. Weber summarizes that commonality well:

> The *goal* of asceticism was, in contrast to many widely held notions, to be able to lead a watchful, aware, alert life. The most urgent *task* was the eradication of *uninhibited* indulgence in instinctive pleasure. The most important *means* employed by asceticism was to bring *order* into the conduct of life of those who practiced it. All of these vital points are found equally clearly both in the rules of Catholic monasticism and in the principles of conduct of the Calvinists.[60]

One of the consequences, then, of the Protestant Reformation was that "the spiritual aristocracy of the monks, who stood outside and above the world, was replaced by the spiritual aristocracy of the saints *in* the world, predestined by God from all eternity."[61] Nobody could know for sure who was part of this latter aristocracy, but we could make a pretty good educated guess—they were those whose discipline and hard work in their "calling" led to worldly success. Thus, the "consequence for the individual was the drive to *keep a methodical check on his state of grace as shown in how he conducted his life and thus to ensure that his life was imbued with asceticism*."[62] This asceticism was less religious but more rationalistic. Thus, Weber describes such a person as a "worldly ascetic." "The person who lives as a worldly ascetic is a rationalist," Weber writes, "not only in the sense that he rationally systematizes his own conduct, but also in his rejection of everything that is ethically irrational, esthetic, or dependent upon his own emotional reactions to the world and its institutions. The distinctive goal always remains the alert, methodical control of one's own pattern of life and behavior."[63]

While medieval asceticism would persist even into the present age, it was the "this-worldly" ethic of Protestantism that would come to dominate Western civilization. "The dogmatic roots of ascetic morality died (admittedly only after terrible struggles)," Weber concludes. "But the original attachment to those dogmas left clear traces in later 'undogmatic' ethics."[64] This "undogmatic ethics" was the Protestant ethic, which Weber found so critical historically in the development of the "spirit" of capitalism.[65] "Above all," he declares, "Protestantism interpreted success in business as the fruit of a rational mode of life"[66]—and, consequently, as a sign of one's election.[67] Such a conclusion seems counter to the very idea of asceticism, however, with its stereotypically prescribed and celebrated poverty. But this is the great transformation that Weber traces. "Riches are only dangerous when they tempt us to idleness and sinful indulgences; and striving for riches is only dangerous when it is done with the aim of later leading a carefree life of pleasure," he notes. "As an exercise of the duty of the calling, however, it is not only morally permissible but actually commanded."[68] The result of a disciplined pursuit of wealth without enjoying it results in the steady accumulation of it. The accumulation of wealth, or capital, is then the prerequisite for the rapid expansion of the capitalist order.[69] Weber is worth quoting at length here:

> If we may sum up what has been said so far, then, innerworldly Protestant asceticism works with all its force against the uninhibited *enjoyment* of possessions: it discourages *consumption*, especially the consumption of luxuries.

> Conversely, it has the effect of liberating the *acquisition of wealth* from the inhibitions of traditionalist ethics; it breaks the fetters on the striving for gain by not only legalizing it, but (in the sense described) seeing it as directly willed by God.[70]

In short, we see in Weber's work the argument for how certain theological beliefs and religious behaviors in one sphere of life can influence the beliefs and behaviors of people in another (economic) sphere of life. We are the inheritors of this influence even if completely unaware that our economic beliefs and behaviors are shaped by theological beliefs and religious behaviors that long since have diminished or even vanished in public consciousness. Weber summarizes this point:

> The Puritans *wanted* to be men of the calling—we, on the other hand, *must be*. For when asceticism moved out of the monastic cells and into working life, and began to dominate innerworldly morality, it helped to build that mighty cosmos of the modern economic order (which is bound to the technical and economic conditions of mechanical and machine production). Today this mighty cosmos determines, with overwhelming coercion, the style of life *not only* of those directly involved in business but of every individual who is born into this mechanism, and may well continue to do so until the day that the last ton of fossil fuel has been consumed.[71]

This idea of modern humanity being imprisoned in this mechanism is described by Weber as "a shell as hard as steel"[72] or famously the "iron cage" of the modern world.

Part of what Weber identifies and traces is the historical and cultural transformation that orients us less to the transcendent realm (heaven) and more to the immanent realm (this world). This transformation has significant consequences for thinking about religion and the modern world. The latter is characterized by an increasing rationalization of economic life and other spheres, interspersed with diversions and amusements that make such rationalization bearable (one thinks here of Guy Debord's *Society of the Spectacle*[73] as a powerful, contemporary analysis of what Weber envisions).[74]

If this all sounds a bit depressing and an imprisoning of true freedom (an "iron cage"), that is because it is depressing and imprisoning. Modern human beings cannot but succumb to the rationalization of so many areas of their lives. And while they have an array of amusements from which to choose (popular entertainment, sports, various forms of consumption, etc.), they cannot *not* choose. The "freedom" of modern humanity is an illusion. We will return to this predicament in Chapter 6, but even more so in the Postscript.

So, what can we make of religion in the modern period? It is easy to see how rationalization can lead to disenchantment—to viewing the world in less magical or spiritual ways. The combination of rationalization and disenchantment then can be part of a story of secularization, of a decline in the power of religion in the world and of adherents to religion. "With every advance of scientific rationalism," Fritz Ringer notes, "religion is pushed further out of the realm of the rational and thus at last becomes *the* purely irrational or antirational power."[75] And who, in the modern age, wants to be associated with the "irrational or antirational"? We will return as well to questions of secularization in Chapter 6.

The stereotypical narrative of rationalization/disenchantment/secularization has some value, but is often too simplistic. Weber shows us that the story is much more complex. The "traces" or theological residue of Calvinism that he finds in modern capitalist beliefs and behavior make it clear that religion is *not* simply an institution that either will exist or not exist. It certainly can be found in specific institutions (the Vatican, for example), but it is a collection of beliefs and behaviors that very much can persist—in some fashion—long after any particular institution may fade away. Indeed, these beliefs and behaviors may persist even in disguised forms that are difficult to discern. But once discerned, they can reveal insights not only into our past but into our present and perhaps the future. Such traces of religious beliefs and practices are central to the argument of this book—and are the objects of study of many scholars featured in Chapter 5.

Conclusion

So, what are the lessons we learn from Durkheim and Weber and, more generally, the sociological approach to the study of religion? There are many, but let me highlight just three.

First, we learn that religion functions in particular ways for societies—helping them to form cohesive units (or, one might say, religion is that very process of forming a society) and both expressing and affecting the core beliefs and behaviors of society. What we will see later in Chapter 5 is that this functional approach to religion is the beginning of separating out certain functions from religion itself. Once separated, we then can find other cultural phenomena (phenomena seemingly secular or even anti-religious) that fulfill the same functions.

Second, we learn that religious beliefs and behaviors can persist in ways that are not recognizably religious or even seem downright irreligious (e.g., think of Weber's worldly asceticism). Maybe, then, some or all of these beliefs and behaviors are not necessarily religious but simply part of the human condition. We can find these beliefs and behaviors in religion, but we also may find them in a wide variety of human activities, projects, and institutions.

Third, we see that Western history reflects a gradual shift from the transcendent to the immanent—from the other-worldly to the this-worldly. This shift will have an incredible impact on religion and culture more generally. The Interlude and final two chapters will investigate this shift in various ways.

While in the previous chapter we saw how philosophers blurred the line between the religious and the secular, in this chapter we have seen how sociology has done something analogous. And, in the next chapter, we will see that a similar phenomenon occurs in the historical roots of the psychology of religion as we turn to the work of Sigmund Freud and Carl Jung.

3

The Psychological Function of Religion: Freud, Jung, and Beyond

In opening the previous chapter, I suggested that sociology and psychology are two sides of the same coin. Neither approach to the study of the human condition can isolate itself from the other. The sociologist or psychologist who sought to isolate his or her approach from the other necessarily would diminish prospects for genuine insights. Of course, sociologists and psychologists alike will champion the priority or even superiority of their discipline against all others. Some might even try to subordinate one to the other. The famed psychologist Sigmund Freud, for example, insists that sociology "cannot be anything but applied psychology."[1] Obviously, both are critical to the understanding of the human condition. In regard to religion, what both disciplines have in common is a functionalist approach to the cultural phenomenon.

I realize that many scholars in the psychological sciences might not claim Freud or Carl Jung as one of their own. Both may be identified as psychoanalysts or psychiatrists rather than psychologists. But many if not most lay people would include them under the broad psychology umbrella, and both are central to the area of inquiry that is called the psychology of religion. We will examine each in turn, and then review some more contemporary efforts in the psychological study of religion.

Sigmund Freud and the Psychological Purposes of Religion

Perhaps nobody in the broad field of psychology is better known by people across the planet than Sigmund Freud (1856–1939). His fame is not unwarranted. Not only did he play a central role in the development of psychology (especially psychoanalysis and psychiatry) as an academic discipline and therapeutic practice, but many of his ideas or terminology became part of everyday language (e.g., the Freudian slip, Oedipus complex, the id/ego/superego, and penis envy). Covering the full breadth of his work is impossible here. Instead, I will focus on key theories or arguments about religion: (1) an origin story that speaks to the development of taboo, ritual, and gods; (2) a theory about the civilizing of human creatures and the role that religion plays; and (3) an argument for why religion will fade into history in light of the rise of science and reason.

Origin Story

Freud's origin story appears in both *Totem and Taboo* and *Moses and Monotheism*. Like Durkheim, Freud focuses on totemism, how it began, and how we continue to live with its consequences. Freud probably did not believe that there was a historical event that occurred in exactly the way that he describes, but he clearly imagined that particular historical interactions (particularly conflicts) among our distant ancestors set in motion certain psychological complexes and social practices that continue to this day.

The story begins with a "primal horde" of early human beings who are ruled by a domineering father. The father's sexual desire was strong (for Freud, this is generally true of all men), and he kept all the women to himself. As Robert A. Paul describes the horde:

> The primal horde probably never existed; but it does ideally embody the *fantasy* of what any male in a sexually reproducing species like ours might *aspire* to in his narcissistic and reproductive self-interest: to father offspring by as many women as possible, and to eliminate all rival males from competition by depriving them—one way or another—of reproductive potential, that is, by "castrating" them.[2]

As Paul notes, the castration of the young men need not be literally so—though certainly physical castration was an option. But in effect and symbolically the young men were castrated by being cut off from sexual relations with the women.[3] Either way, the young men (his sons) became sexually frustrated in the absence of such sexual relations. Thus, they banded together and killed their father. They then ate him (Freud assumed our ancestors were cannibals).[4] According to Freud, the cannibalistic act was the origin of the totem meal in what he called primitive or savage religions:

> Cannibal savages as they were, it goes without saying that they devoured their victim as well as killing him. The violent primal father had doubtless been the feared and envied model of each one of the company of brothers: and in the act

of devouring him they accomplished their identification with him, and each one of them acquired a portion of his strength. The totem meal, which is perhaps mankind's earliest festival, would thus be a repetition and a commemoration of this memorable and criminal deed, which was the beginning of so many things—of social organization, of moral restrictions and of religion.[5]

While killing the father allowed for a broader distribution of the women,[6] the act had powerful and negative psychological consequences. The brothers experienced significant feelings of guilt. Freud notes that "we need only suppose that the tumultuous mob of brothers were filled with the same contradictory feelings which we can see at work in the ambivalent father-complexes of our children and of our neurotic patients."[7] As compensation for and in an effort to overcome their guilt, the brothers (and their descendants) valorized their father and even began treating the idea of their father as a real thing (a spirit, for example). This process is what led to the development of totemic religion and the accompanying creation of the idea of gods. "Totemic religion arose from the filial sense of guilt, in an attempt to allay that feeling and to appease the father by deferred obedience to him," Freud writes. "All later religions are seen to be attempts at solving the same problem [of ambivalent feelings toward the father]."[8] In other words, the father becomes—via the totemic stage, in which he is symbolized as (most typically) an animal—a god because the sons felt so guilty about killing him. Freud insists that "while the totem may be the *first* form of father-surrogate, the god will be a later one, in which the father has regained his human shape."[9] Particular beliefs and rituals then developed around this father/god figure—most specifically the totem sacrifice and meal. For Freud, the totem sacrifice serves two functions. "The importance which is everywhere, without exception, ascribed to sacrifice lies in the fact that it offers satisfaction to the father for the outrage inflicted on him [the sacrificed animal is a gift]," he writes, "in the same act in which that deed is commemorated [the totem is a symbol for the father; so the killing of the totem is a reenactment of the killing of the father]."[10] Freud elaborates:

> Totemic religion not only comprised expressions of remorse and attempts at atonement, it also served as a remembrance of the triumph over the father. Satisfaction over that triumph led to the institution of the memorial festival of the totem meal, in which the restrictions of deferred obedience no longer held. Thus it became a duty to repeat the crime of parricide again and again in the sacrifice of the totem animal [which represents the father], whenever, as a result of the changing conditions of life, the cherished fruit of the crime—appropriation of the paternal attributes—threatened to disappear.[11]

While the connection of the totem to the historical father slowly disappeared, the sacrifice remained as "an act of renunciation in favour of the god [the natural symbolic development of the totem]."[12] Even Jesus Christ is a mere development of the origin narrative. As Freud concludes, Christ "sacrificed his own life and so redeemed the company of brothers from original sin."[13] Even today, Christians symbolically eat their god—flesh and blood—in the communion ritual.

The original crime or set of crimes did not just lead to religion, but to many aspects of society—including morality and law. Freud claims that "Society was now based on complicity in the common crime; religion was based on the sense of guilt and the remorse attaching to it, while morality was based partly on the exigencies of this society and partly on the penance demanded by the sense of guilt."[14] In short, the primordial psycho-sexual drama gave rise to myriad cultural norms and phenomena—all ultimately tied to fundamental psychological needs or instincts.[15]

The Civilizing Process

A second though related theory of religion involves its role in the civilizing process of humanity. To fully understand this theory, we must begin with Freud's view of the tripartite psyche. This view is so famous and ubiquitous that most people have at least a rudimentary understanding of its constitutive parts—the id, ego, and superego.

The id is generally seen as the repository of our most basic desires and instincts—often associated with our more animalistic side, but they also can be distinctively human. The id is "linked to the pleasure principle" and "knows no judgements of value: no good and evil, no morality."[16] Freud claims that it "is the dark, inaccessible part of our personality."[17] If the id is one side of our psychic spectrum, the superego is at the other. It is associated with order, morality, and conscience. The superego is the counterbalance to the id.

Both the id and the superego are necessary psychical elements, but both have drawbacks. If people act from their uncontrolled id, they necessarily will end up in conflict—sometimes bloody or even deadly. On the other hand, dominance by the superego can lead to a repressive existence that has negative psychic consequences and can manifest in destructive behavior. It is the ego that mediates these two psychic elements—and a strong and effective ego can lead to a fruitful life.

The control of desires or instincts not only benefits the individual, but it is critical for the development of civilization. Of particular concern are those desires or instincts that are aggressive, since "they make human communal life difficult and threaten its survival. Restriction of the individual's aggressiveness is the first and perhaps the severest sacrifice which society requires of him."[18]

Freud recognizes that the satisfaction of our desires and instincts is a determining factor in achieving happiness. But, as already noted, the uncontrolled pursuit of fulfilling our desires and instincts would lead to incredible conflicts. Civilization, the ordered and organized collection of human beings living peacefully together, is the result of a process through which individuals curb or control desires and instincts. Certainly, the immediate satisfaction of our desires makes us happy, but existence outside of or free from civilization is a dangerous one. We very likely will be the victim of someone else's pursuit of pleasure. In short, life outside civilization is a war of all versus all in the pursuit of fulfilling desires and instincts. Civilization limits the satisfaction that leads to happiness, but it provides a stable structure and order in which individuals can live much longer and within which they still can satisfy desires and instincts (even if less frequently). Freud concludes:

> If civilization imposes such great sacrifices not only on man's sexuality but on his aggressivity, we can understand better why it is hard for him to be happy in that civilization. In fact, primitive man was better off in knowing no restrictions of instinct. To counterbalance this, his prospects of enjoying this happiness for any length of time were very slender. Civilized man has exchanged a portion of his possibilities of happiness for a portion of security.[19]

Clearly there is a political dimension to the civilizational process, and Freud's approach fits nicely with the kind of social contract theory that we find in classical political philosophy. Social contract theory (John Locke and Thomas Hobbes are paradigmatic examples) sees the creation of political units as an effort by the majority to advance the interests of individuals through mutual cooperation[20] and to protect the majority from the whims (often violent) of any particular individual. Freud writes:

> Human life in common is only made possible when a majority comes together which is stronger than any separate individual and which remains united against all separate individuals. The power of this community is then set up as 'right' in opposition to the power of the individual, which is condemned as 'brute force'. This replacement of the power of the individual by the power of a community constitutes the decisive step of civilization.[21]

Whereas social contract theorists like Locke and Hobbes focused mainly on political association, Freud really expands upon what we might see as the rudimentary psychology that underlies their theories.[22] As noted above, entering into a social order entails some renunciation of desires and instincts. Freud insists that "every civilization must be built up on coercion and renunciation of instinct"[23] because "every individual is virtually an enemy of civilization."[24] This process of renunciation that leads to civilization has important benefits, and not just the advancing of individual interests through collective action and the mutual protection of individuals. Freud notes that the "sublimation of instinct" also "makes it possible for higher psychical activities, scientific, artistic or ideological, to play such an important role in civilized life."[25] At the same time, it is impossible to deny and we have to recognize that this process of renunciation can be very painful psychologically and can have social implications. For Freud, the "non-satisfaction (by suppression, repression or some other means?) of powerful instincts" leads to "'cultural frustration' [that] dominates the large field of social relationships between human beings."[26]

Perhaps the greatest renunciation, and one that ties in with our origin narrative, is the human willingness to curb the uncontrolled pursuit of sexual satisfaction and to establish instead an order of sexual relations. In a passage that clearly predates the sexual revolution in Western civilization, Freud writes:

> Present-day civilization makes it plain that it will only permit sexual relationships on the basis of a solitary, indissoluble bond between one man and one woman, and that it does not like sexuality as a source of pleasure in its own right and is only prepared to tolerate it because there is so far no substitute for it as a means of propagating the human race.[27]

Most societies in the Western world probably do not hold such a negative view toward sex as we find in this passage, but nevertheless Freud's larger point still holds. We do not live in societies where we are encouraged to satisfy our sexual desires or instincts at will. Rape and sexual assault are crimes. Marriage or at least monogamous relationships are standard if not ideal. Strict norms and laws prohibit sexual relations among family members. In short, there still is a sexual order that involves some level of renunciation in order to preserve the basic structure of civilization. But there also is a price to this renunciation. Carl E. Schorske summarizes his reading of *Civilization and Its Discontents* as follows:

> The progress of our technical mastery over nature and the perfection of our ethical self-control are achieved at the cost of instinctual repression in the "civilized" man—a cost so high as not only to make neurotics of individuals, but of whole civilizations. An excess of civilization [too much superego] can produce its own undoing at the hands of instinct avenging itself against the culture that has curbed it too well.[28]

The renunciation that accompanies the rise of civilization, however, is not something that occurs just once and for all. "In consequence of this primary mutual hostility of human beings," Freud notes, "civilized society is perpetually threatened with disintegration."[29] To prevent such disintegration, societies need structures that can enforce or (even better) encourage renunciation. Psychologically, this means strengthening the superego in order to control the id. "Such a strengthening of the super-ego is a most precious cultural asset in the psychological field," Freud concludes. "Those in whom it has taken place are turned from being opponents of civilization into being its vehicles."[30] What Freud is describing is the development of conscience.[31] Conscience then is this "internalization" of renunciation that otherwise would have to be imposed by external force. Because the renunciation is internalized, there is even greater stability in the society.[32]

Perhaps the first and most important institution for this process of internalization is religion. Freud argues that gods have a threefold task: "they must exorcize the terrors of nature, they must reconcile men to the cruelty of Fate, particularly as it is shown in death, and they must compensate them for the sufferings and privations which a civilized life in common has imposed on them."[33] Long after many peoples came no longer to imagine that there is a religiously magical way of controlling nature, religion has continued to provide many people with hope of conquering death through the promise of an eternal afterlife. At the same time, this belief in an afterlife—in particular, an afterlife in a heaven where all our desires are satisfied—makes the earthly renunciation of these desires more bearable. In other words, "religious ideas have arisen from the same need as have all the other achievements of civilization: from the necessity of defending oneself against the crushingly superior force of nature. To this a second motive was added—the urge to rectify the shortcomings of civilization which made themselves painfully felt."[34]

The fact that religion promises an afterlife of desire fulfillment in compensation for renunciation in this life is what makes religious beliefs illusory. For Freud, "we call a belief an illusion when a wish-fulfillment is a prominent factor in its motivation, and in doing so we disregard its relations to reality, just as the illusion itself sets no store by verification."[35] Indeed, for Freud, religious beliefs and doctrines "are illusions and insusceptible to proof."[36] But religion has been an effective illusion, because it has contributed to the internalization of renunciation (strengthening of the superego, development of conscience) and the rise of civilization (stable and ordered societies).

The Future of Religion

Though religion may have been central to the development of civilization, Freud argues that the rise of reason and science will lead to the decline and eventual disappearance of religious belief. Central to this argument is the analogy between the development of civilization and the development of the individual. In short, primitive societies were like children and modern (predominantly) Western societies are more like adults. Religion is part of our past or at least eventually will be part of our past. It is part of the childhood of civilization. As Freud claims, the "origin of the religious attitude can be traced back in clear outlines as far as the feeling of infantile helplessness."[37]

But religion is not simply a benign leftover from civilization's childhood. Rather, it is equivalent to an individual's neurosis. Freud perhaps states the argument best in *The Future of an Illusion*:

> We know that a human child cannot successfully complete its development to the civilized stage without passing through a phase of neurosis sometimes of greater and sometimes of less distinctness. This is because so many instinctual demands which will later be unserviceable cannot be suppressed by the rational operation of the child's intellect but have to be tamed by acts of repression, behind which, as a rule, lies the motive of anxiety. Most of these infantile neuroses are overcome spontaneously in the course of growing up, and this is especially true of the obsessional neuroses of childhood. The remainder can be cleared up later still by psycho-analytic treatment. In just the same way, one might assume, humanity as a whole, in its development through the ages, fell into states analogous to the neuroses, and for the same reasons—namely because in the times of its ignorance and intellectual weakness the instinctual renunciations indispensable for man's communal existence had only been achieved by it by means of purely affective forces.[38]

To get human beings to renounce their most basic instincts and desires, civilizations had to manipulate them psychologically through fear (punishment by the gods, who serve as parental figures) and rewards (eternal bliss in the afterlife). While successful at establishing and preserving social order, this psychological manipulation nevertheless took a toll on individuals and (collectively) societies.[39]

Freud argues for a three-stage development of civilization that mirrors the development of the individual. The three stages are the animistic, religious, and the scientific or rational. He explains:

> At the animistic stage men ascribe omnipotence to *themselves* [e.g., they believe they have the power to manipulate natural laws through magic or sorcery]. At

the religious stage they transfer it to the gods but do not seriously abandon it themselves, for they reserve the power of influencing the gods in a variety of ways according to their wishes. The scientific view of the universe no longer affords any room for human omnipotence; men have acknowledged their smallness and submitted resignedly to death and to the other necessities of nature. None the less some of the primitive belief in omnipotence still survives in men's faith in the power of the human mind, taking account, as it does, of the laws of reality.[40]

These stages in the development of civilization correspond to the stages in the psychological development of the individual.

The animistic phase would correspond to narcissism [e.g., unreasonable assessment of one's own powers] both chronologically and in its content; the religious phase would correspond to the stage of object-choice of which the characteristic is a child's attachment to his parents [who are, of course, analogous to the gods]; while the scientific phase would have an exact counterpart in the stage at which an individual has reached maturity, has renounced the pleasure principle, adjusted himself to reality and turned to the external world for the object of his desires.[41]

Just as the individual must move to the stage of maturity in order to be a psychologically healthy adult, so do civilizations have to move to the scientific stage in order to be psychologically healthy.

Freud is no blind or naïve believer in reason. He does not believe that it will usher in a new utopian age for humankind. Psychologically, the human condition is difficult. It necessarily will include various trials and tribulations. A child always will struggle at times (in some cases, a lot of the time) in the family unit, as she negotiates relationships with parents and (perhaps) siblings while simultaneously developing sexually, emotionally, and intellectually. The entire family unit and childhood trajectory are fraught with peril. And adulthood can be equally trying, with efforts to secure sexual and life partners and working through parent-child relationships—only this time from the parent side of the equation. There is no amount of reason that magically will make these challenges go away. At the same time, however, Freud does insist that there "is no appeal to a court above that of reason."[42] Whatever our difficulties might be, only reason and science (a particular expression of reason) are viable and healthy ways of confronting them.

As civilizations have matured and reached the stage of reason and science, adherence to animistic and religious beliefs has faded. Freud notes that "the greater the number of men to whom the treasures of knowledge become accessible, the more widespread is the falling-away from religious belief."[43] His account of the fading away of religion is not simply descriptive; however, it is also normative. Freud believes religion is dangerous. Just as we do not want human beings to be stuck psychologically at the adolescent stage of development, so do we not want societies to be stuck at the religious stage of development. For Freud, human beings "cannot remain children for ever; they must in the end go out into 'hostile life'. We may call this '*education to reality*.'"[44]

Freud believes that such "education to reality," an education relying heavily on reason and science, will not only allow human beings to mature, it will make life better. Or, to put it another way, it will allow human beings to be more successful at improving their lives. "By withdrawing their expectations from the other world [the focus of religion] and concentrating all their liberated energies into their life on earth," Freud surmises, in a passage reminiscent of Marx, "they will probably succeed in achieving a state of things in which life will become tolerable for everyone and civilizations no longer oppressive to anyone."[45] Civilization still will continue to require us to repress our instincts and desires, but at least we will have a clear understanding as to why that is the case. No longer will we forgo the pleasures of our instincts and desires for the mere affirmation of God or the gods, but we will forgo them because we know it is the rational thing to do and only by such individual sacrifice can the other goods of civilization (e.g., order, stability, advances in science and technology) be achieved.[46]

John Deigh notes that Freud's views of the future of human civilization varied—including between *The Future of an Illusion* (1927) and *Civilization and Its Discontents* (1930), two of the books central to my account of Freud's treatment of religion. Deigh concludes that the former text ends on an optimistic note. "Just as healthy individuals overcome their childish ways as they mature, as reason comes to play a greater role in the governance of their lives," he writes, "so too healthy societies should overcome their primitive practices [many of them religious] as they mature, as science comes to play a greater role in the governance of their lives."[47] But *Civilization and Its Discontents*, published only a few years later, has a darker tone. "He ended the work on a somber note," Deigh concludes. "No one, Freud observed, in this age of great technological advances can be confident that the struggle between life-giving and life-destroying forces that shapes civilization will not have a ruinous outcome."[48]

While Freud certainly expresses some ambivalence about the development of civilization, there is no doubt that he sees a steady maturation in civilization just as we see a steady maturation in the individual. His ambivalence makes sense based on the analogy. Everyone who makes it through adolescence and certainly those who parent children through that stage know well the emotional challenges faced by teenagers. But everyone also recognizes it as a necessary stage of development. Moving from childhood to adulthood is difficult, and childish things must be given up in order to fully embrace adulthood. In terms of civilization, religion is one of those childish things that must be given up. It served humanity well for quite a long time. Indeed, it helped to usher in civilization and allowed human beings to make incredible advances. But we can move beyond it now. We can turn to reason and science to guide us, and they are far superior guides given our intellectual and psychological development. As Freud concludes with the last sentences of *The Future of an Illusion*: "No, our science is no illusion. But an illusion it would be to suppose that what science cannot give us we can get elsewhere."[49]

In the end, Freud complements the sociologists we examined in the previous chapter. He recognizes positive functions of religion for individual psychology and the development of societies (though, in both cases, religion is limited and ultimately problematic). He also is part of a movement (including thinkers in psychology, sociology, philosophy, etc.) that advocates that human beings are shifting and should be shifting from a focus on the transcendent (gods, heavens, etc.) to a focus on the immanent (this world). Freud describes such a shift as a historical necessity, in the same way that a child necessarily becomes an adult. In this way, his work also leads us to the discussion of secularization in Chapter 6.

Carl Jung and the Collective (Religious) Unconscious

Whereas Freud has a decidedly negative view of religion, Carl Jung (1875–1961) embraces religion in a way very different from his one-time teacher/mentor. Whereas Freud views religion as a relic that holds us back psychologically, Jung views it as an important aid in psychologically healthy individuals. "Freud has unfortunately overlooked the fact that man has never yet been able single-handed to hold his own against the powers of darkness—that is, of the unconscious," Jung writes. "Man has always stood in need of the spiritual help which each individual's own religion held out to him."[50] Whereas Freud views the symbols of religion as indicators of neuroses that linger in modern humanity, Jung sees them as the very means to help modern humanity escape its spiritual crisis. As Philip Rieff notes, "Jung's aim was to reach a new compromise between the patient and his sufferings, which are individuated representations of a permanent and superior spiritual order. In the very symbols from which Freud had wanted to free mankind, Jung saw the principle of salvation."[51]

Like Freud, Jung begins with the unconscious. He divides the unconscious into the personal unconscious and the collective unconscious.[52] The former is the residue of individual experience that can impact us at various times, but upon which we often do not reflect or to which we may not even have much access. For example, a frightening experience with a dog as a young child might make an adult dislike movies about dogs. Perhaps the adult could reflect about his or her dislike of movies about dogs and realize that it was connected to the experience as a child. But it also could be the case that the childhood experience was so long ago or even so early in life that the adult does not have much of a conscious memory about it. However, the experience still has an impact on his or her life (in this case, whether he or she likes movies about dogs).

The collective unconscious similarly can have unexpected consequences but is very different. Whereas the personal unconscious is dependent on an individual's experience, the collective unconscious is not. Jung writes:

> The collective unconscious is a part of the psyche which can be negatively distinguished from a personal unconscious by the fact that it does not, like the latter, owe its existence to personal experience and consequently is not a personal acquisition. ... the contents of the collective unconscious have never been in consciousness, and therefore have never been individually acquired, but owe their existence exclusively to heredity.[53]

Jung has a number of ways of describing the existence of the collective unconscious. For example, he notes that "just as there is a society outside the individual, so there is a collective psyche outside the personal psyche, namely the collective unconscious."[54] Elsewhere, he surmises that "[i]f it were permissible to personify the unconscious, we might call it a collective human being combining the characteristics of both sexes, transcending youth and age, birth and death, and, from having at his command a human experience of one or two million years, almost immortal."[55] In short, the collective unconscious is a universal inheritance received by every human being.

Though the collective unconscious is found in the individual mind, it is hardly subjective. It, in fact, is found in every mind, and thus is the opposite of subjective. As Jung concludes, "the collective unconscious is anything but an incapsulated personal system; it is sheer objectivity, as wide as the world and open to all the world."[56] Thus, one of the ways in which a human being can transcend the self is by virtue of tapping into the collective unconscious. "There I am utterly one with the world [in the collective unconscious]," Jung writes, "so much a part of it that I forget all too easily who I really am [my personal identity]."[57]

So how should we imagine the relationship of consciousness to the collective unconscious? "We shall probably get nearest to the truth if we think of the conscious and personal psyche as resting upon the broad basis of an inherited and universal psychic disposition which is as such unconscious," Jung advises, "and that our personal psyche bears the same relation to the collective psyche as the individual to society."[58] This complicated relationship can function better or worse. "Normally the unconscious collaborates with the conscious without friction or disturbance, so that one is not even aware of its existence," Jung notes. "But when an individual or a social group deviates too far from their instinctual foundations, they then experience the full impact of unconscious forces."[59] This experience can be exhilarating or benign, but it also can be overwhelming and even dangerous.

It is very important that individuals recognize the difference between their personal consciousness and the collective unconscious. As Jung warns, "if the collective psyche is taken to be the personal possession of the individual, it will result in a distortion or an overloading of the personality which is very difficult to deal with. Hence it is imperative to make a clear distinction between personal contents and those of the collective psyche."[60] Indeed, he concludes, "If the unconscious simply rides roughshod over the conscious mind, a psychotic condition develops."[61] The problem is that the failure to clearly distinguish between the content of the personal psyche and the collective unconscious can lead to uncertainty about one's identity. As Jung explains it, "under certain conditions the unconscious is capable of taking over the role of the ego. The consequence of this exchange is insanity and confusion, because the unconscious is not a second personality with organized and centralized functions but in all probability a decentralized congeries of psychic processes."[62]

The collective unconscious contains this vast wealth of evolutionary inheritance built up by humanity. More specifically, Jung describes the distinct contents of the collective unconscious as archetypes. The concept of the archetype "indicates the existence of definite forms in the psyche which seem to be present always and everywhere."[63] These forms take a wide range of shapes. For example, a short list of archetypes would include mother, father, child, trickster, hero, and spirit. These archetypes are infused with meaning. For example, the mother archetype represents qualities such as "maternal solicitude and sympathy; the magic authority of the female; the wisdom and spiritual exaltation that transcend reason; any helpful instinct or impulse; all that is benign, all that cherishes and sustains, that fosters growth and fertility."[64] Yet, at the same time, the mother archetype "may connote anything secret, hidden, dark; the abyss, the world of the dead, anything that devours, seduces, and poisons, that is terrifying and inescapable like fate."[65] Therefore, the mother archetype can appear in the fertile and nurturing form of Mother Earth, but also in various goddess forms that are highly sexualized and dangerous.

The archetypes are the "inherited possibilities of human imagination as it was from time immemorial."[66] And they did not just magically appear. They are the consequence of "typical situations in life" and "[e]ndless repetition has engraved these experiences into our psychic constitution."[67] It is through the archetypes that we connect with the depths of the collective unconscious. For Jung, the archetype "represents or personifies certain instinctive data of the dark, primitive psyche, the real but invisible roots of consciousness."[68] By bringing the archetypes to consciousness, by engaging with them, we tap into our deepest history. As Jung concludes, "they bring into our ephemeral consciousness an unknown psychic life belonging to a remote past. It is the mind of our unknown ancestors, their way of thinking and feeling, their way of experiencing life and the world, gods and men."[69]

There are many places where we find the archetypes. One of the most immediate and personal proofs of their existence is our dreams, "which have the advantage of being involuntary, spontaneous products of the unconscious psyche and are therefore pure products of nature not falsified by any conscious purpose."[70] The archetypes do not appear, however, only when we are unconscious. They permeate our everyday existence and reveal themselves prominently in cultural creations. For example, they are prominent in myths and fairytales.[71] Jung describes myths as "original revelations of the preconscious psyche, involuntary statements about unconscious psychic happenings."[72] For example, the hero archetype is dominant in a lot of mythology, where it "always refers to a powerful man or god-man who vanquishes evil in the form of dragons, serpents, monsters, demons, and so on, and who liberates his people from destruction and death."[73]

The archetypes also are manifest in much more recent literature, including contemporary literature and really all forms of art. Jung writes:

> Great poetry draws its strength from the life of mankind, and we completely miss its meaning if we try to derive it from personal factors. Whenever the collective unconscious becomes a living experience and is brought to bear upon the conscious outlook of an age, this event is a creative act which is of importance to everyone living in that age. A work of art is produced that contains what may truthfully be called a message to generations of men.[74]

Not only are the archetypes and the collective unconscious a resource for the artist, but there is a sense in which the artist is a mere vehicle for these psychic realities.

> The artist is not a person endowed with free will who seeks his own ends, but one who allows art to realize its purposes through him. As a human being he may have moods and a will and personal aims, but as an artist he is "man" in a higher sense—he is "collective man"—one who carries and shapes the unconscious, psychic life of mankind. … Whenever the creative force predominates, human life is ruled and moulded by the unconscious as against the active will, and the conscious ego is swept along on a subterranean current, being nothing more than a helpless observer of events.[75]

Here we see an important move by Jung. While religion is a very typical institution through which archetypes and the collective unconscious can be expressed (through, for example, myth), other cultural phenomena like art also are vehicles for such expression.

As mentioned before, failure to distinguish between the contents of the collective unconscious and personal consciousness can lead to disastrous psychological consequences. "Possession by an archetype turns a man into a flat collective figure," Jung states as an example, "a mask behind which he can no longer develop as a human being, but becomes increasing stunted."[76] Freeing oneself from the unbeknownst effects of the collective unconscious is part of the process of individuation—which Jung defines as "coming to selfhood" and "self-realization."[77] This process establishes firm psychological ground for the individual to "divest the self of the false wrappings of the persona on the one hand [that which is imposed by one's specific social context], and of the suggestive power of primordial images on the other [the collective unconscious]."[78] It is the latter part of the process that concerns us here, the part that seeks "to integrate the unconscious into consciousness."[79] Ann Belford Ulanov acknowledges the positive benefits of individuation,[80] while noting the following implications of failing to go through the process well:

> If we fail to engage in that process, our ego can easily be taken over by archetypal contents, as we see to our horror in any kind of religious or political fanaticism. Under such pressures, we rush out against others, compelled by the force of the archetypal. Convinced we alone possess the truth, we know no bounds in dealing with others who may disagree with, or even defy, us; segregating, maligning, oppressing, imprisoning, murdering others are crimes we can commit in the name of our twisted version of truth and salvation.[81]

Jung believes that modern humanity is hampered in its ability to work through the process of individuation, including an inability to come to terms psychologically with the archetypal content of the collective unconscious. Part of the problem is that human beings today (especially, perhaps, in the Western world) believe that they are fully autonomous and rational creatures. They believe that they are freed from the superstition and restriction of the past—particularly elements associated with our mythical and/or religious past. "The values and strivings of those past worlds no longer interest him save from the historical standpoint. Thus he has become 'unhistorical' in the deepest sense and has estranged himself from the mass of men who live entirely within the bounds of tradition," Jung writes. "Indeed, he is completely modern only when he has come to the very edge of the world, leaving behind him all that has been discarded and outgrown, and acknowledging that he stands before a void out of which all things may grow."[82] But despite what the modern person may think, there is no final or permanent escaping from the power of the collective unconscious. It always will have an impact on the consciousness of the individual, no matter how modern (rational, scientific, etc.) that person might be. As Jung observes, explicitly connecting the archetypes and collective unconscious to religion:

> A man may be convinced in all good faith that he has no religious ideas, but no one can fall so far away from humanity that he no longer has any dominating *representation collective* [collective representations or archetypes]. His very materialism, atheism, communism, socialism, liberalism, intellectualism, existentialism, or what not, testifies against his innocence. Somewhere or other, overtly or covertly, he is possessed by a supraordinate idea.[83]

The question is not whether or not the collective unconscious will manifest itself in modern humanity, but how that will look and what modern humanity can do to mediate it.

The fact that modern humanity has turned its back on the past is part of what has led to what Jung identifies as a spiritual crisis. "Our intellect has achieved the most tremendous things," Jung insists, "but in the meantime our spiritual dwelling has fallen into disrepair."[84] Jung does not think we can have a simple return to that "old time religion," but we also cannot ignore the powerful and meaningful archetypes of the collective unconscious. "[Modern man] has freed himself from 'superstition' (or so he believes), but in the process he has lost his spiritual values to a positively dangerous degree," Jung observes. "His moral and spiritual tradition has disintegrated, and he is now paying the price for this break-up in world-wide disorientation and dissociation."[85] The loss of connection to the contents of the collective unconscious (often expressed through the myths and rituals of our religious traditions) results in certain "loneliness" that is the basis of the "disorientation and dissociation."[86]

What Jung identifies as a problem is, in one sense, the problem of secularism. Modern humanity has abandoned religion, which provided access to the archetypal content of the collective unconscious as well as institutional and ritual structures to mediate that content. Without access to that content, the world is empty and devoid of meaning (at least the wealth of meaning that it previously had). At the same time, we have a compulsion or even instinct to engage that content. As Jung insists, "every civilized human being, whatever his conscious development, is still an archaic man at the deeper levels of his psyche."[87]

The archetypal content of the collective unconscious finally cannot be suppressed. It is bound to impact us—even if not in the traditional contexts of religious traditions. As mentioned before, the content will find expression in other cultural artifacts—literature, music, art, sport, and so much more. Jung shares this viewpoint in the powerful final paragraph of *Modern Man in Search of a Soul*:

> The living spirit grows and even outgrows its earlier forms of expression; it freely chooses the men in whom it lives and who proclaim it. This living spirit is eternally renewed and pursues its goal in manifold and inconceivable ways throughout the history of mankind. Measured against it, the names and forms which men have given it mean little enough; they are only the changing leaves and blossoms on the stem of the eternal tree.[88]

In this imagery, the eternal tree is the collective unconscious and its archetypes. The various leaves and blossoms are the cultural artifacts in which it is expressed. Even in an otherwise "secular" society, then, the collective unconscious and its archetypal contents will still impact our lives. The danger is when we deny these impacts, guard against them, or even fail to recognize their influence.

Whereas Freud generally views the unconscious as a repository of trauma and self-centered and often violent desire, Jung has a much more positive assessment. Certainly, the unconscious can wreak havoc on the conscious life and may pose an obstacle to the process of individuation, but it also is an ancient source of wisdom and meaning. As Philip Rieff notes, "The general solution for neuroses in a culture that has exhausted its particular symbolic capital is an infusion of new capital from the unconscious or, perhaps, even the appropriation of capital from the collective unconscious of another culture."[89]

For both Freud and Jung, though, it is important to note that religion serves a particular psychological function. For Freud, religion can help individuals face an often confusing and frightening world. It also played an important role in the history of civilization. But it is a form of neurosis that must be overcome. He believes reason can help us survive without religion. Jung thinks reason is much more limited in its ability.[90] As Daniel L. Pals notes, for Jung religion (as with "mythology, folklore, philosophy, and literature") "draws on the resources of this 'collective unconscious' not as a form of neurosis but as the healthy expression of true and deep humanity."[91] Thus, Jung views religion as but one important cultural phenomenon for the human psyche, and suggests that other cultural artifacts, other cultural symbols, may be able to fulfill the same kind of psychological needs that religion fulfills.[92] Today, for example, we might think of the hero archetype. In Judaism, we see it in key figures like King David and Moses. But is there much distance between those ancient models of the hero and the ones we now have through the Marvel franchise (Spider-Man, Captain America, etc.)? From Moses to Marvel there certainly is a gap of thousands of years, but the hero archetype is fundamentally one and the same. But do these other cultural artifacts, these cultural symbols, function just like religion or only somewhat like religion? This is a critical question that will be addressed in subsequent chapters. But it also is a question central to a relatively new approach to the psychology of religion—affect theory. In the remainder of this chapter, we will examine this recent development, for it too provides important insights about how to think about religion and the academic study of it.

Affect Theory: A Contemporary Approach to the Psychology of Religion[93]

Introduction to Affect Theory

Affect theory is one of the newer approaches to the psychology of religion, differing in many ways from Freudian and Jungian psychology. But we will see that it shares certain continuities with those psychologies—including a functionalist orientation.

Affect theorists often describe their object of study in negative terms—what affects are *not* or what they are *not* connected to. For example, two primary characteristics of affects are, first, that they are pre-discursive or *not* directly related to or dependent upon language; and, second and relatedly, that affects are *not* to be understood as necessarily inferior to reason.

Donovan O. Schaefer, a leading scholar in this area, describes affects as "the flow of forces through bodies outside of, prior to, or underneath language."[94] In other words, "affect or affects can be understood as the propulsive elements of experience, thought, sensation, feeling, and action that are not necessarily captured or capturable by language or self-sovereign 'consciousness.'"[95] Take the example of joy. John Corrigan writes: "So, affect theorists see in the smile a sign of an affective *fact*, the affect of joy. That joy, displayed on the face, is not something that persons have to talk themselves into. It is a physically embodied emotion, but not one that requires the discourse of culture—however those are defined and displayed—in order to take place."[96]

The idea that emotions or affects must be dependent on language is part of what Schaefer calls the "linguistic fallacy." He explains:

> The linguistic fallacy affirms that depth can't exist without language—that we can't want things without being told that we want them, without deciding that we want them, or without learning to want them. This is the presupposition of classical psychological behaviorism as much as textualism. But affect theory suggests that our animal intimacy with the world precedes constitution inside a linguistic frame—that there are "Proustian nooks" that pull us into the world without the application of language. The relationship between the affect and power moves bodies transversally through and across the grids of language, consciousness, or cognition. The compulsions of affect are better understood as addictions, as thick passions for bodies, objects, and relationships.[97]

Not only are affects independent of language, but they often are more powerful. "Affects are not passive receptors of inconsequential feeling that serve as window dressing on the linguistic architecture of power," Schaefer concludes, "power moves bodies through the pulsing of mobile, uneven affective systems. The linguistic *I* is a figurehead monarch in this field of recalcitrant attachments."[98] Language may be king, but it often or even frequently is powerless. The real power is with affects.

Because language and reason are so bound together, it is not surprising that affects are seen as being in a complicated if not contentious relationship to reason. "To study affects is to explore nonsovereign bodies, animal bodies," Schaefer argues, "bodies that are propelled skittering forward by a lattice of forces rather than directed by a rational homunculus."[99]

But it is not the case that we now have a dichotomy with elements or aspects (affects and reason) that never interact and remain solely in their domains. In other words, there is not feeling and thinking separately. There are feelings to thinking, feelings to knowledge production as well as the holding of knowledge. "Within the framework of affect theory, affect animates every aspect of embodied life, including the ostensibly affect-neutral domain of knowledge-production," Schaefer insists. "Affect theory prompts us to ask not just what we know, not just how we know, but *how knowledge feels*."[100]

By elevating the role of affects vis-à-vis reason and knowledge, affect theorists deconstruct a powerful and persistent view of the hierarchical structure of the human being—a hierarchical structure that Freud certainly accepted, but one that was challenged or problematized by Jung. This hierarchy certainly dates back millennia and posits our rational nature as superior and controlling and our affectual or emotional nature as inferior and in need of control. "Separating reason and emotion denigrates the embodied nature of cognition, resorts to an ancient dualism of mind and body, and erects a hierarchy of thought, feeling, and body that skews the explanation of human behavior as properly rational," David Morgan observes. "The resulting dualism is strongly disposed to regard emotion as suspect for its inherent tendency to move one independent of reason."[101]

Liberated from language and rationality, affects can be seen as "ends in themselves."[102] What Schaefer means by this is that affects cannot be reduced to other phenomena. For example, they are not merely the epiphenomena of language or culture or rationality. In this sense, we might see an analogy between the way that affect theorists treat affects as *sui generis* and the way that Mircea Eliade (featured in the next chapter), perhaps the twentieth century's most prominent scholar of comparative religion, treats the sacred as *sui generis*.[103] There are then two related questions: Are affects *sui generis*? Or, are *religious* affects *sui generis* (though other affects may not be)? Answering affirmatively to the second question in particular might provide the theoretical basis for a "protective strategy" for religious phenomena that isolates or protects certain claims about religious affects from rational inquiry.

The independence of affects from language and reason is critical when studying religion. Affect theory draws us to these powerful elements in human beings—elements that are not simply activated by or determined by language and rationality but exist independently and prior to or outside of all language and reason. Schaefer insists that "affects are not simply to be understood as passive channels activated by the play of language hovering over them. Rather, affects surge through bodies, producing semistable structures that become the tough, raw materials of religion."[104]

Part of the problem with the past study of religion has been its focus on language—the "linguistic fallacy." "The linguistic fallacy misunderstands religion as merely a byproduct of language," Schaefer writes, "and misses the economies of affect—economies of pleasure, economies of rage and wonder, economies of sensation, of shame and dignity, of joy and sorrow, of community and hatred—that are the animal substance of religion and other forms of power."[105] Looking behind or before language leads scholars then to a new and very different approach to the study of human beings and culture in general and religion in particular. For Schaefer, such an approach even closes the gap between human beings and other animals. He insists that "at the emotional and preemotional levels, affects are the flexible architecture of our animal lifeways, the experiential shapes that herd together and carry religion on their backs. Affect theory makes available a set of approaches to religion that work through animality by probing the thick forms moving outside of the narrow lighted circle of language."[106] Affects are like the foundation of a house upon which reason, desires, and human action build cultural phenomena—for example, religion.

For Schaefer, affects are both the prelinguistic foundation of religion and a consequence of religious activity. "Religion as a composite of compulsions is made possible by existing, intransigent bodily technologies," he writes, "but it also motivates, activates, and drives those technologies."[107] Rather than arguing for a simplistic cause-and-effect position (religion causes affects or affects cause religion), Schaefer is defending a more circular understanding of the relationship.[108]

In situating affect theory in the broader history of the study of religion, it is reasonable to wonder if it is a new version of the phenomenological approaches of figures like Rudolf Otto or Mircea Eliade. In one sense, affect theory can embrace that phenomenological history. Like Otto's "idea of the holy" or Eliade's experience of the sacred, affects have a *sui generis* character. In other words, affects appear to be universal and fundamental elements of the human condition and cannot be reduced to any other elements or functions. On the other hand, someone like Schaefer is hesitant to embrace the "ahistorical metaphysical essentialism of Eliade"[109]—insisting on the cultural context and historical grounding of affects. The question is: Are there *religious* affects or simply affects that tend to occur as a consequence of religious practices or in religious settings? If the latter, then we certainly have something very different than the phenomenological approach of Otto or Eliade. But if it is the former, affect theory would seem to come particularly close to the kind of *sui generis* arguments of scholars like Otto and Eliade. Before answering the question, however, it will be helpful to look at the work of Wayne Proudfoot, the philosopher of religion who offers a powerful critique of the phenomenological approach—one that might serve as a warning to affect theorists.

Wayne Proudfoot on Religious Experience and Protective Strategies

Affect theory is far from the first attempt to draw our attention away from language and reason and focus on emotion or feeling instead. In the nineteenth century, theologians and scholars of religion started to identify feeling or emotion as that which was most characteristic of religion. Wayne Proudfoot argues that this primarily occurred for two reasons. First, it was deemed that feelings or emotions are more grounded in the lived experience of adherents than is doctrine. Feelings or emotions are more powerful than dogma. Second, the move to feelings or emotions helped to avoid a rationalist critique of religion. At least since the Enlightenment, religious doctrine had been subject to powerful philosophical criticism. Indeed, in the nineteenth century, through the twentieth century, and continuing into the twenty-first century, many intellectuals (Freud, for example) predicted and still predict the demise of religion as individuals and whole societies become more rational. But reason often reaches a certain limitation (so it is thought) when confronted with feelings or emotions. At the very least, feelings or emotions do not seem subject to the same level of rational critique as does doctrine.[110] One might be able to offer a compelling rational critique against the Christian doctrine of the Trinity or the Hindu and Buddhist doctrine of reincarnation, but what would a critique of the feelings or emotions of the infinite or ecstatic spiritual experiences even look like? Our feelings or emotions are natural or intrinsic elements of the human condition (irreducible to propositions of reason) in the same way that today some theorists speak of affects.

Christian theologians like Friedrich Schleiermacher (Chapter 1) and Rudolf Otto, whose interests included the more general study of religion as well, were instrumental in moving the study of religion in this theoretical direction. The former emphasizes the role of non-cognitive feelings or intuitions as foundational to religion, while the latter describes feelings of awe, energy, and mystery (among others) that are constitutive of religious experience. William James, the early twentieth-century philosopher and psychologist, also emphasizes the subjective experience of religious phenomena as central to the study of religion. His *Varieties of Religious Experience* is a seminal work in the typology of religious experience. He describes religion not in terms of doctrines or institutions, but as "*the feelings, acts, and experiences of individual men in their solitude, so far as they apprehend themselves to stand in relation to whatever they may consider the divine.*"[111] We will see in the next chapter that Eliade also focuses on subjective experience. In his phenomenology of religion, Eliade argues for the qualitatively greater experience associated with the sacred as opposed to what is associated with the profane.

Wayne Proudfoot offers a compelling critique of this historical and theoretical development in the study of religion. He finds that many of the approaches to understanding religious experience simply protect that experience against rational investigation and criticism. One cannot rationally dismiss, for example, that which precedes or is beyond reason (a popular argumentative strategy, of course, for those who defend claims about the existence of God or gods). But these "protective strategies" fail philosophically. Take, for example, Proudfoot's critique of Schleiermacher—one that can be (and is) extended to other theorists as well.

Schleiermacher describes religious experience as an immediate apprehension of the divine or religious object or being. By making the religious experience immediate, Schleiermacher preserves it against the argument that it is the "idea" or "thought" of the divine that causes the experience and, extending this, that the divine is *merely* an "idea" or "thought" and thus has no external reality (or, at least, following Kant, that we cannot have epistemological certainty about that reality). Religious consciousness, according to Proudfoot's reading of Schleiermacher, "is both intentional, in that it is directed toward the infinite as its object, and immediate. It is not dependent on concepts or beliefs, yet it can be specified only by reference to the concept of the whole or the infinite."[112] Taken together, however, these claims are contradictory. "If the feeling is intentional," Proudfoot writes, "it cannot be specified apart from reference to its object and thus it cannot be independent of thought."[113] In other words, Schleiermacher "defends the incoherent thesis that the religious consciousness is both independent of thought and can only be identified by reference to concepts and beliefs."[114] He cannot have it both ways. Either religious experience is truly immediate (i.e., not mediated by thought), in which case it becomes hard to identify it vis-à-vis an intentional object (Thus, why even call it "religious"?), or it is mediated by thought, in which case it is not immediate and thus open to rational inquiry and criticism.

There are at least two key points that come out of Proudfoot's critique of Schleiermacher—again, points that can be extended to subsequent theorists who attempt (either explicitly or implicitly) to protect religious experience from critical inquiry. First, Proudfoot makes the point that religious language is both expressive and formative of experience. Religious language may describe an experience but the words and ideas that we associate with religious language also cause or at least shape the experience itself. Thus, Proudfoot argues that religious language "is not only the expressive, receptive medium Schleiermacher takes it to be. It also plays a very active and formative role in religious experience."[115] The second (related) point is that it is illegitimate to separate religious feeling or emotion (in short, religious experience) from thought. Proudfoot admits that Schleiermacher "is correct to view primary religious language as the expression of a deeply entrenched moment of consciousness," but he is "incorrect to portray that moment as independent of thought and belief. Schleiermacher has mistaken a felt sense of immediacy for a guarantee that piety is not formed or shaped by thought or inference."[116] Do affect theorists make a similar mistake?

The question of the cognitive status of feelings or emotions is critical and deserves more of our attention here. Take the example of anger. Anger may be an innate affect in that we all are born with the ability to be angry. But it is not an immediate emotional experience, unmediated by thought. How do we know when someone is angry? It certainly is not because we empathically feel what they are feeling. We ascribe anger to them based on the public evidence, based on how they are reacting. This ascription will include our interpretation of their actions relative to our understanding of the entire context in which they are acting. Frank seems agitated, and I interpret that as anger because I know he has just been told by his boss that he will not be receiving a raise in his salary this year (the boss, of course, being an uncaring, miserly character). In short, my ascription of anger to someone is a consequence of my reflection about all sorts of pieces of evidence provided to me. What is even more interesting is that our self-ascription of anger is very similar. As Proudfoot argues, "I don't appeal to private inner states in ascribing emotions to myself any more than I do in ascribing them to others. I often come to know what I am feeling by interpreting physiological changes or my behavior in exactly the same way in which another might interpret them if the data were available to him."[117] Coming out of a meeting with my boss (yes, the same miserable boss who screwed over Frank), I may notice that my heart is racing and my teeth are clenched. These physiological changes alone are not enough for me to determine that I am angry. Certainly they can contribute to such a determination, but I will come to ascribe anger to myself by interpreting the situation, realizing that my boss is a jerk, and that I have been treated poorly or unfairly by her. Indeed, I may not even realize that I am angry based just on increased heart rate and clenched teeth. I may not even notice these physiological changes. To that extent, the physiological changes alone do not constitute anger. Only when interpreted and understood within a context of perceived sleight, injury, etc., can we connect these physiological changes to the feeling or emotion of anger. The word "anger" is not merely a description of our experience, but is an interpretation of it. Proudfoot concludes that emotion words "are employed, not as simple descriptions of bodily changes, behavior, or dispositions to behave, but as interpretations and explanations of those phenomena."[118] Even more, the interpretation is constitutive of the very experience.

Proudfoot turns to the psychological research of Stanley Schachter to further his argument. Schachter's experiments confirm that physiological changes alone are not clear indicators of particular emotions or feelings. In other words, the same physiological changes may be interpreted in different ways depending on the person who is experiencing them and the context in which they occur. But what is the relevance of Schachter's work for Proudfoot's interest in religious experience and for our concerns here? "Given the results of Schachter's experiments," Proudfoot concludes, "it seems quite plausible that at least some religious experiences are due to physiological changes for which the subject adopts a religious explanation."[119] Thus, if understood in the same way that we should understand other emotions or feelings, the physiological changes (the felt experience) of the religious experience are in fact religious to the extent that they are interpreted religiously—they are not intrinsically religious.

This understanding of what constitutes an experience is critical to Proudfoot's distinction between descriptive and explanatory reduction in the study of religious experience. Descriptive reduction is "the failure to identify an emotion, practice, or experience under the description by which the subject identifies it. This is indeed unacceptable."[120] Proudfoot uses the example of a hiker seeing a bear in the woods, the sighting leading to an experience of fear in the hiker. As it turns out, it really was not a bear but a tree stump instead. It would be a case of descriptive reduction to claim that the hiker was in fear of a tree stump. The tree stump indeed was the object he saw, but he perceived it was a bear. To say that he was afraid of a tree stump would be to fail to make sense of the story. Still, it would not be wrong to say that the cause of his fear was a tree stump that looked to him (perhaps at a distance, through some fog or mist, etc.) like a bear. We also must take account of the hiker's understanding of the danger of bears or even his past experience with bears (maybe he was mauled as a child?). Including this information in our account of the incident would be leading us toward explanatory reduction, "offering an explanation of an experience in terms that are not those of the subject and that might not meet with his approval. This is perfectly justifiable and is, in fact, normal procedure."[121] It might be the hiker refuses to believe that there was no bear; that what he really saw was a tree stump. I certainly am not obligated simply to accept his account of the experience, especially if I have strong evidence supporting the claim that what he saw really was a tree stump. In other words, I must take him seriously when he says that he saw a bear and that this is what made him afraid, but I need not accept that as the final explanation of the event. I clearly have solid evidence of the tree stump, and I might even be able to make the case that the hiker suffers from paranoia vis-à-vis bears (thus leading to the mistaken identification of the tree stump as a bear). Proudfoot concludes:

> Where it is the subject's experience which is the object of study, that experience must be identified under a description that can plausibly be attributed to him. … The explanation the analyst offers of that same experience is another matter altogether. It need not be couched in terms familiar or acceptable to the subject. It must be an explanation of the experience as identified under the subject's description, but the subject's approval of the explanation is not required.[122]

All of this can be applied to religious experience in the following way. If a religious adherent claims to have had a religious experience of God's love, a uniquely *religious* love unlike any other experience of love, then any investigation of this experience must begin with the adherent's description. But a full explanation of the experience may entail an account of the full context in which the experience occurred in order to more accurately identify the factors or causes that gave rise to the experience. For example, perhaps it was an emotionally taxing period in the adherent's life. Maybe she was part of a prayer group that emphasized the experience of God's love during its communal activity. Maybe she was even on medication or ecstasy (the illegal drug with the curiously religious name) that fostered such loving emotions. In short, many factors may have led to her experience of God's love—and we need not accept the *sui generis* character of that experience any more than we need accept the reality of God. Naturally, she might reject our explanations. But while we must begin with her description, we need not end up there. As Proudfoot argues, "To require that any explanation of a religious experience be one that would be endorsed by the subject is to block inquiry into the character of that experience."[123] In other words, if all I can do is to accept her description of the experience, then there is no room for any other explanation nor even for an investigation of her experience in the first place. I may as well simply record her account and be done with it—no further study is necessary.

Proudfoot concludes that the "distinguishing mark of a religious experience is not the subject matter but the kind of explanation the subject believes is appropriate."[124] Another way of putting this is that it is not the content (increased heart rate, feelings of elation, forms of ecstasy, etc.) of the experience that defines it, but the explanation we give to that content. For example, think of experiences that are seemingly *not* religious. In the case of experiences surrounding the participation (either as an athlete or spectator) in sporting events, it very well could be that the participants have similar physiological and psychological experiences that religious practitioners have—but the former are not having "religious" or "spiritual" experiences because they simply do not label them that way as do the latter. If, for example, the participants in the sporting event had a different understanding of what religion is or what a spiritual experience is, perhaps they more likely would apply these terms to describe their experiences and, thus, those experiences legitimately could be considered religious or spiritual.

The approach Proudfoot represents certainly opens up cultural phenomena to a deeper and more thorough investigation. There are other theorists whose work supports or is supported by such an approach. Mihaly Csikszentmihalyi champions the psychological concept of "flow." Flow involves the immersion of the individual psyche in an activity that is productive, creative, and personally valuable. Flow is "the state in which people are so involved in an activity that nothing else seems to matter; the experience itself is so enjoyable that people will do it even at great cost, for the sheer sake of doing it."[125] Flow experiences can occur in all sorts of activities, ranging from sports to sculpture, from dancing to making a cabinet. They can occur in religious settings. "Play, art, pageantry, ritual, and sports are some examples [of flow]," Csikszentmihalyi writes. "Because of the way they are constructed, they help participants and spectators achieve an ordered state of mind that is highly enjoyable."[126] The flow experience is common or universal whether it occurs in the art studio, the church, or the stadium—it is just that the contexts will shape how we label the flow experience.

If the content of the experience is similar (ecstasy, "flow," etc.) but we simply label it differently, then it should not surprise us when people decide that it is appropriate and perhaps necessary to use religious language to more accurately describe experiences that on the surface seem non-religious. They have come to believe that the content of the experience is similar to if not identical with those experiences described by religious practitioners (e.g., mystics). In regard to sport, for example, Howard Slusher insists: "Something of faith, something of peace, a touch of power, a feeling of right, a sense of the precarious—all of these and more is what *real spirit* of sport *is*."[127] He acknowledges the mystical dimension of sport and religion, concluding that both "open man towards the acceptance and actualization of being."[128]

It is important to remember, however, that Proudfoot makes a convincing case that our labels of experiences do not merely describe them but help to constitute them. There still might be something different about the religious experience—because it in part is constituted by religious concepts and ideas—that separates it from the often equally powerful experiences of other cultural phenomena. But here we are pushed to our reflective limits, and the recognition that we now are probing psychological and existential areas where we cannot have anything close to definitive answers.[129] Is there a difference between the ecstasy in the pews and the ecstasy at the Grateful Dead concert (the latter, probably not the former, aided, perhaps, by hallucinogenics)? Given the complexities and subtleties of psychological states, we probably can never know. But we should not begin our investigations with theories that are "protective strategies," that separate out some experiences as *sui generis*, that close off avenues of inquiry about the similarities or even identical natures of human experiences.

Critique of Affect Theory

So, what of affect theory? Does Proudfoot's critique of the phenomenological approach pose a threat to affect theory as an approach to the study of religion? As with a lot of questions, it depends. It depends most significantly on whether we think there are fundamental affects as part of the human condition or that there are specific affects that are irreducibly religious.

If the claim by affect theorists is that there are affects that are exclusively religious affects, then we return to something like the *sui generis* argument of Otto, Eliade, and others—the kind of argument that Proudfoot identifies as a "protective strategy." On the other hand, if we are talking about a set of general affects, some of which encourage and/or are activated by religious thought and actions, then we recognize the possibility that that subset of affects may also encourage and/or be activated by thought and actions that may be stereotypically secular in character.

I do not think that Schaefer is always clear on this issue. Generally, he writes about affects as universals that can be connected to a wide variety of practices, institutions, and structures. At other times, however, he suggests the existence of specifically *religious* affects. Indeed, even the frequent reference to *religious* affects (including in the title of his book, *Religious Affect: Animality, Evolution, and Power*) suggests that there are actual affects that are religious in nature. Beyond just the use of the adjective "religious," however, there are passages that seem to claim the existence of specific religious affects. For example, Schaefer states that affects "surge through bodies and compose themselves in religious forms."[130] What are these "religious forms"? And what can it mean that they "compose themselves"? The phrase leads one to believe that affects change somehow into forms that are specifically religious. But how? Is simple joy different than religious joy? In another passage, Schaefer goes further, making it sound like there are permanent or eternal religious affects. In *Religious Affects*, he writes of "the multitude of subterranean ways that religion flows through our bodies."[131] Is religion a "thing" that flows through bodies? We would hardly think so. Does Schaefer mean then that religious affects flow through bodies? In short, both passages suggest a return to the sort of *sui generis* arguments of the older phenomenological approach of Otto, Eliade, and others.

Schaefer, in fact, tries to separate himself from this phenomenological approach. He imagines a line that goes roughly from Eliade and Otto to J.Z. Smith to affect theory. He considers Smith to be an important advance beyond the phenomenological tradition represented by Eliade and Otto, and sees affect theory as an important advance beyond Smith.

What would Proudfoot say about the affect theory we find in Schaefer? Clearly, the claim that there are pre-linguistic affects that are "religious" (whatever that means) leads us right into the same problems that Proudfoot critiques in the phenomenological tradition. If they are pre-linguistic, then why call them "religious." In this sense, *religious* affects are akin to Eliade's experience of the sacred or Otto's *mysterium tremendum*. But if affects are viewed as merely emotional experiences or states that can be elicited or activated in a number of different settings—some stereotypically religious and others seemingly secular—then we open up a much richer and defensible approach to the study of culture and cultural institutions and the human experience of them. In this regard, I agree with Abby Kluchin who warns, "Affect theory cannot afford to be so enchanted with itself—with its own bewitching linguistic formulations to capture the nonlinguistic—that it unwittingly re-enchants our thoroughly disenchanted world."[132] We cannot consider ourselves critical and enlightened twenty-first-century scholars and then naïvely insist on the existence of mystical or magical religious affects that flow miraculously through our bodies.

In his essay on religion, sport, and nationalism, David Morgan attempts to "thread the needle" on the problems raised above. "My contention will *not* be that sport or national piety is the new religion of modern society," he writes, "but rather that there is no need for the social or cultural analyst to erect a strong distinction among the three. They are not fully discrete any more than they are merely interchangeable."[133] In other words, the affects associated with these three areas of cultural life are neither unique and irreducible nor exactly the same and interchangeable. There may not be a discrete set of religious affects wholly different from all other affects, but we still can talk about affects that either arise in a religious context or have a religious "flavor" to them.

Morgan relies upon the notion of "sacralization." "*Sacralization* is a procedure at work in any number of cultural activities, including but not limited to religion," he notes. "Thus, when fans say *soccer is my religion*, they may be understood to say something like *soccer is how my people and I feel our common identity*. They might say the very same of their nation and their religion."[134] Morgan then rejects the notion that any of these categories needs to be "reduced" to the other—that sport is *really* religion or that religion is *really* nationalism or even that nationalism is *really* sport (which, by the way, would be a really fruitful line of inquiry). He insists that "sacralization is not synonymous with religion nor is it essentially religious, but is rather the pervasive social mechanism for making something, someone, or someplace special. It happens in sports, art, politics, commerce, the family, and religions."[135] In a sense, the point is that the noun (sport, art, "the sacred," etc.) is less important than the verb (sacralize)—than the process by which something is made special. Morgan concludes that rather than reducing other cultural phenomena to the phenomenon of religion or vice versa, "we get further by describing such modern experiences as sport, nationalism, and religion as ritual practices that generate powerful cultures of thought and feeling that enable moderns to imagine the bonds of affection that tell them who their group is and what matters to them."[136]

Morgan cites Ann Taves as a kindred spirit in this regard, and certainly her work makes a substantial contribution. She argues against the *sui generis* approach typical of phenomenologists like Eliade—the idea that sacredness or holiness is some irreducible reality in the world. She argues that the "basic problem with the sui generis model is that it obscures something that scholars of religion should be studying: that is, the process whereby people constitute things as religious or not."[137] In order to get away from problematic terms like sacred and holy, Taves instead writes of "specialness." Objects, people, places, actions, or times that are special can vary greatly—but specialness is not some irreducible reality in the world or beyond. Many things that are special are stereotypically religious (e.g., a temple, a priest, a ritual, etc.), but what is special also can appear in contexts that are secular. In other words, the process of making something special is the big umbrella under which religion is but one institution—along with music, sport, nationalism, and much more. Special things, for Taves, are the "building blocks" of religion but also of many other cultural phenomena.[138] There is an analogy here to Hegel. Just as he posits an umbrella (Spirit) under which religion, art, and philosophy are covered, so does Taves posit a different umbrella (specialness) under which religion, sport, the arts, and other cultural phenomena are covered. The key difference, however, is that whereas Spirit for Hegel is both a reality and a process, specialness for Taves has no external reality (there is no substance called specialness in the world). It is all process—a purely human process.

Both Taves and Morgan, then, suggest a world of experiences or affects that are more universal in character and fluid between cultural phenomena. They represent a very different position than those who might posit the existence of uniquely *religious* experiences or affects.

In the end, it might help for us to imagine a spectrum of positions to take on the status of religious affects. At one extreme is the claim that there are affects that *are* religious—not reducible to other affects, unique, *sui generis*, etc. We might imagine Eliade and Otto occupying this position (for the former, we will see why in the next chapter), and Schaefer sometimes seems to drift in this direction (though, as stated, his position is not always clear). Thus, one might argue that there is a distinct religious experience of transcendence, of feeling part of something larger than oneself, and that this experience is unlike any similar sorts of experiences in different contexts.

At the other extreme is the claim that "affects *are* affects"—that affects are basic building blocks (to borrow Taves' term) of the human condition that can be found in religious contexts but in many other contexts as well. In this sense, *religious* affects are not unique affects. Rather, the word "religious" simply designates where the affects arise or are manifested or how they are interpreted rather than any irreducible or *sui generis* character that they have. Thus, one would argue that the experience of transcendence, of feeling part of something larger than oneself, is an experience that can happen in a religious context, but it also may happen at a political rally or in a sports stadium. The affect is the same, though the context might change. This position is supported by the work of Proudfoot, and Taves certainly can be read in this direction.

Between these two extremes, of course, are a myriad of other positions—Morgan being but one example. But it is hard to occupy a middle position on this issue, because the two extremes require an either/or choice. Either religious affects are *sui generis* or they are not. Proudfoot opens the door to such middle positions by noting how language and/or context might shape experience rather than serve as mere interpretation. But, as I noted earlier, we then are "in over our heads" in terms of really figuring out and disentangling cause and effect here. We are beyond being able to come up with definitive answers. That said, and while I cannot fully defend the claim here (the claim may even be indefensible or at least unproveable), I believe Morgan's position ends up being a theoretically untenable compromise.

In the end, I support Proudfoot's side of the spectrum. There certainly is a danger that affect theory turns us back to the problematic kind of protective strategy that Proudfoot powerfully identifies in the phenomenological tradition. I argue that the study of the full range of human affects in culture is only possible by avoiding that protective strategy and that the study of the full range of human affects in culture also helps us to avoid that protective strategy. Seeing the experiences of joy, "flow," and transcendence in a sporting event "disenchants" those experiences—frees them from the limitations of specifically religious contexts. If there is such a thing as *religious* joy, for example, that can mean one of two things. First, that there is an intrinsically religious character in a particular kind of joy that makes it different from any other joy-like affect. Here we are in the neighborhood of Eliade and other classical phenomenologists. In that neighborhood, our questioning or inquiry into that joy is limited, for we first must accept the intrinsically religious character and that character, at least, cannot be questioned. Second, one might say that *religious* joy is the joy that occurs in a religious context. But then the very phrasing "religious joy" is misleading, for what we really mean is that one might experience joy as part of a religious ritual or being in a religious building, but one also could experience that same joy in the symphony hall or theatre. Thus, instead of calling it *religious* joy, we simply should talk about joy as it may occur in a religious context. Now we are in the neighborhood of Proudfoot—the neighborhood that I prefer. And in this neighborhood we can query more fully the nature of this joy and how it arises and how its appearance in a variety of contexts (religious or secular, in the temple or the stadium) can lead to powerful insights about it.

The study of culture by religious studies scholars is most fruitful when we avoid protective strategies (either ones we inherit or new ones of our own creation) and that same study implicitly makes the case against those protective strategies. Affect theory can be a powerful tool for religious studies scholars studying culture, but only if it avoids becoming a new protective strategy.

Conclusion

The conclusion of our review of affect theory leads us back to a psychologically functionalist approach. Though the details of what affect theorists are doing in regard to affects and "specialness" (to borrow Taves' term) are different from key concepts and arguments in Freud and Jung, the fundamental approach is the same. Religion is a set of ideas and actions that function psychologically in particular ways for people—tapping into or eliciting affects, compensating us psychologically for the burdens of civilization, mediating our relationship with the archetypes of the collective unconscious, and much more. But other cultural phenomena also may function in these ways. Discovering the ways in which cultural phenomena (including religion) psychologically function for human beings ends up making religion less special. It is no longer the *sui generis* reality of an Eliade or the *numinous* of Otto. Instead, it is merely one cultural phenomenon among many. Once that truth is realized, we are well on the way to recognizing the irrelevance of religions. They may remain models of where and how religious experiences occur. But they are not the only models and today, in our more secular age, they may not even be our best models.

That said, human beings for millennia have claimed that religious experiences are unique—in terms of both their felt experience and their meaning. Have we taken that claim seriously enough? To make sure we do, the next chapter presents the work of two monumental figures of the twentieth century, both responding to the kind of functionalist arguments of the preceding chapters. They are the historian of religion Mircea Eliade and theologian Paul Tillich.

4

The Existential Function of Religion: Eliade and Tillich

As the study of religion progressed through the twentieth century, many religious studies scholars and theologians were concerned about what they perceived as "reductionist" tendencies in scholarship about religion. Can religion be reduced to a set of rational principles (as Kant does in regard to the moral law) that represent its essence? Or can religion be reduced to a particular function (as Durkheim does in regard to religious practices being critical to building community) that then minimizes or excludes its other elements? Or can religion be reduced to a set of beliefs and practices that merely allow human beings to cope psychologically (as Freud and Jung argue)? Is such reductionism a threat to the essential nature of religion—leading to both its demystification, marginalization, and ultimately irrelevance and decline?

In this chapter, we will examine two different, yet complementary responses to the threat of reductionism. Both represent phenomenological (focus on the specific phenomena of religion, without imposing external theoretical apparatuses) and existentialist (focus on the lived experience and meaning of phenomena for human beings) approaches to religion. Both insist on an immutable core to religion. At the same time, it is a core that has a place (necessarily so) in what on the surface are very non-religious or secular phenomena. What we see in the end, then, is that the very effort to preserve religion against reductionism simply pushed two prominent figures into another kind of reductionism—more psychological than sociological or philosophical, but a reductionism nevertheless.

Mircea Eliade, the Sacred, and *Homo Religiosus*

Mircea Eliade, the renowned twentieth-century scholar of comparative religion, was central in popularizing the comparative study of religion, legitimating the study of religion in higher education, and consequently in establishing departments of religion or religious studies across the United States and even across the globe.

Eliade (1907–86) claims that the "ultimate aim of the historian of religions is to understand, and to make understandable to others, religious man's behavior and mental universe."[1] But this aim is far from merely of historical interest. He argues that the study of religion is not only of interest in and of itself, but that the comparative study of religion is an existential imperative—particularly for the Western world. "One day the West will have to know and to understand the existential situations and the cultural universes of the non-Western peoples," he writes, "moreover, the West will come to value them as integral with the history of the human spirit and will no longer regard them as immature episodes or as aberrations."[2] By understanding these other "existential situations" and "cultural universes," those of us in the West will better understand the human condition and improve our lives.

Eliade typically uses the term "historian of religions" to describe the scholar of religion. While certainly the scholar may be engaged in some historical inquiry, the term really is broader than that. It refers to scholars of religion engaged in comparative work—investigating the religious dimensions of humanity across religious traditions, across time periods, and across geographical locations. In order to properly conduct such investigations, Eliade advances the phenomenological approach.

The phenomenological approach has three distinct characteristics. First, the scholar must attempt to view the object of study (a particular religious community or tradition) from the *inside* and to see the world from that perspective. As Eliade insists, "there is no other way of understanding a foreign mental universe than to place oneself *inside* it, at is very center, in order to progress from there to all the values that it possesses."[3] It is not enough to gather evidence or data about a religious community or tradition, one must then make "an effort to understand them *on their own plane of reference*."[4] In this way, the scholar avoids what Wayne Proudfoot describes as "descriptive reduction" (see Chapter 3).

The key to the phenomenological approach, and its second characteristic, is *epoche*. This idea is borrowed from the phenomenological tradition in philosophy (which, still, is quite different from what we are discussing here). It refers to the "bracketing" of one's ideas and beliefs so that they do not interfere in the effort to understand the other. It also refers to the "bracketing" of the question of truth or reality of the entities, forces, or beings that are part of the other world. "Rather than assuming either the existence or non-existence of religious realities," Jason N. Blum writes, "the phenomenologist of religion suspends or brackets this question in order to disclose meanings as constructed and experienced from the perspective of religious consciousness."[5] The result of such bracketing is the ability to immerse oneself in a different cultural reality. As Eliade concludes, the "historian of religions is forced by his hermeneutical endeavor [his methods of understanding] to 'relive' a multitude of existential situations."[6] While such immersion is necessary, according to Eliade, it also can be dangerous—as the scholar might lose her "self" and even is subject to some kind of transformation. Eliade writes:

> The historian and phenomenologist of religions does not confront these myths and rituals as external objects, like an inscription to be deciphered, an institution to be analyzed. In order to understand that world from within, he must live it. He is like an actor assuming his roles, embodying them. Sometimes the gulf between the archaic world and our everyday world is so great that one's very personality can be at stake.[7]

The phenomenological approach also is existentialist, in the sense that it focuses on the lived experience of religion and the meaning derived from it. "Like it or not, the scholar has not finished his work when he has reconstructed the history of a religious form or brought out its sociological, economic, or political contexts," Eliade insists. "In addition, he must understand its meaning—that is, identify and elucidate the situations and positions that have induced or made possible its appearance or its triumph at a particular historical moment."[8]

In the end, the phenomenological approach serves as a shield against reductionism. Eliade insists that religion is *sui generis*, that it is irreducible to a single function or disciplinary way of understanding it. Certainly religious beliefs and practices have various aspects—from sociological to economic, psychological to political. But Eliade insists that the "confusion starts when *only one* aspect of religious life is accepted as primary and meaningful, and the other aspects or functions are regarded as secondary or even illusory."[9] So, for example, Eliade recognizes the contributions of socioeconomics to the study of religion. But such an approach only provides one view of religion, and certainly is not the most important view. Eliade argues:

> The socioeconomic explanations of historical phenomena [like religion] sometimes seem to me exasperatingly simplistic. It's because of these platitudes that original, creative minds are no longer interested in history. Reducing historical phenomena to lower "conditioning" is to empty them of all exemplary meaning; thus, everything that is still valid and significant in human history disappears.[10]

While recognizing the contributions of figures like Sigmund Freud and Carl Jung,[11] Eliade has a similar critique for psychology. "It is when the psychologist 'explains' a mythological Figure or Event by reducing it to a process of the unconscious," he insists, "that the historian of religions—and perhaps not he alone—hesitates to follow him."[12]

Even history is limited in its utility. The task of the phenomenologist or historian of religion is not simply to understand one religious expression or one religious tradition, but to understand the universal nature of religious humanity—*homo religiosus*. As he insists, "the very dialectic of the sacred tends indefinitely to repeat a series of archetypes, so that a hierophany [manifestation of the sacred] realized at a certain 'historical moment' is structurally equivalent to a hierophany a thousand years earlier or later."[13] Regardless of the particularities of a specific community or country or even time, there are certain essential elements to religious life that transcend those particularities and thus cannot be understood adequately by academic disciplines that study society, human psychology, economics, or history. Understanding the deeper, universal structures and meanings of hierophanies (these can be parts of nature, like the sun, moon, mountains, etc., or human, such as mythological heroes) across space and time is a morphological task—the third characteristic of the phenomenological approach. In this way we get to the essential and irreducible nature of religion—its *sui generis* core. "At the very heart of the discourse on sui generis religion," Russell McCutcheon, who is critical of such an approach, writes, "lies the assumption that certain aspects of human experience can be, and are, divorced from the interactions and negotiations of people embedded within historical, social situations characterized by power imbalances—in a word, the world of politics."[14]

Religion, then, for Eliade is a unique object for study—not simply one human phenomenon that can be studied exhaustively by standard academic disciplines. He insists that religion is "an experience of existence in its totality, which reveals to a man his own mode of being in the World."[15] There are no other experiences that are like this experience—neither political nor social, economic nor aesthetic. And only the unique approach and sensibilities of the historian of religion can reveal its meaning.

At the heart of religion is the experience of the sacred. "Religion 'begins' when and where there is a total revelation of reality," Eliade concludes, "a revelation which is at once that of the sacred—of that which supremely *is*, of what is neither illusory nor evanescent—and of man's relationship to the sacred, a relationship which is multiple, changing, sometimes ambivalent, but which always places man at the very heart of the real."[16] Eliade equates the sacred with the real. He writes:

> The sacred is pre-eminently the *real*, at once power, efficacity, the source of life and fecundity. Religious man's desire to live *in the sacred* is in fact equivalent to his desire to take up his abode in objective reality, not to let himself be paralyzed by the never-ceasing relativity of purely subjective experiences, to live in a real and effective world, and not in an illusion.[17]

The insistence on the reality of the sacred as opposed to the idea of it as illusory is a clear rejection of Freudian or other psychologizing approaches to religion. As the real, the sacred is that which is significant rather than insignificant, meaningful rather than meaningless. It is that which infuses our life with purpose and value. Participation in a specific ritual, for example, adds a depth or quality to life that is not there outside the ritual (i.e., in profane existence). "Man becomes aware of the sacred because it manifests itself, shows itself," Eliade writes, "as something wholly different from the profane."[18] Consequently, the sacred makes profane existence bearable. It is something greater than us (not "purely subjective"). This is what it means to identify the sacred with the transcendent—that which is beyond any single individual. Transcendence is a quality or characteristic of the sacred.

The experience of the sacred then is more than any profane experience of the world. It is qualitatively different and greater. For Eliade, the sacred and profane "are two modes of being in the world, two existential situations assumed by man in the course of his history."[19] The human propensity and even necessity of experiencing the sacred are what make us *homo religiosus*. The experience does not just happen, however, and it is not simply an individual or cultural desire—like wanting to experience great art or delicious ice cream. And it is not simply imposed by some greater force. It is a result of deep existential needs shared by all human beings as human beings. "Religious man thirsts for *being*," Eliade argues. "His terror of the chaos that surrounds his inhabited world corresponds to his terror of nothingness."[20] The profane world is finite, contingent, and fragile, the sacred world is infinite, necessary, and eternal. Thus, *homo religiosus* "wishes to be *other* than he is on the plane of his profane experience."[21]

Cultural Elements of the Sacred

Religions are collections of myths and legends, symbols, and rituals (among other elements) that help to create connections between human beings and the sacred. Through religious practices human beings experience certain spaces, objects, and times as qualitatively greater than other spaces, objects, and times. In short, these become manifestations of the sacred.

To the extent that anything has religious value, it has it through its relation with the transcendent or sacred. "Objects or acts," Eliade writes, "acquire a value, and in so doing become real, because they participate, after one fashion or another, in a reality that transcends them."[22] What the transcendent is called varies historically and culturally. It can be Brahman, God, nirvana, or Allah—but all these terms point to the same sacred reality.

Myths and legends can mean many things. Often there is a pejorative connotation, in that myths and legends are deemed to be false or imaginary (as in "That's *just* a myth" or "That's *just* a legend"). More positively, myths and legends can be stories or narratives about great heroes, heroines, gods, or goddesses that tell us something important about human existence—how it ought to be lived, what its purpose is, etc. Of course, most myths and legends are about people who lived a long time ago, or, in the case of gods or goddesses, about things they did a long time ago. But through the process of mythicization, more recent or even contemporary figures can take on qualities typically associated with great heroes, heroines, gods, or goddesses.

The "metamorphosis of a historical figure into a mythical hero" may involve the assimilation of the historical personage to a pre-existing mythical model.[23] When a historical figure demonstrates certain human excellences (as determined by the community in which he or she lives), accomplishes great tasks, or demonstrates a superior way to live (thus revealing something about the very meaning or purpose of human life), stories about that person are circulated and often embellished. That does not mean that the stories lack any historical validity. It simply means that what they did and how they did it are so valued by the community that stories about them are told and retold as a way for community members to affirm their own identity and the values of the community.

Symbols and signs both point us in the direction of something else. But whereas signs are *merely* pointers to something else, symbols somehow embody what they point toward.

For Eliade, symbols of the sacred are hierophanies—manifestations or appearances or expressions of gods and goddesses or, more generally, the sacred.[24] A symbol or hierophany "effects a permanent solidarity between man and the sacred."[25] Symbols or hierophanies bring us into contact with the sacred. While there are certain things that may be more predisposed to be hierophanies or that have served humans symbolically more frequently (e.g., the sun and the moon have been popular hierophanies in the history of humankind), hierophanies really can be anywhere and anything. It is unlikely that any Jew or Roman before the life and death of Jesus would have imagined that a simple wooden cross used to punish criminals would become a sacred symbol or hierophany. Therefore:

> We must get used to the idea of recognizing hierophanies absolutely everywhere, in every area of psychological, economic, spiritual and social life. Indeed, we cannot be sure that there is *anything*—object, movement, psychological function, being or even game—that has not at some time in human history been somewhere transformed into a hierophany.[26]

In this case, we see that the sacred object, the hierophany, "transforms the place where it occurs: hitherto profane, it is thenceforward a sacred area."[27] As Eliade notes, the sacred object disrupts the profane homogeneity of space and creates something sacred instead.[28] It is better, more meaningful, to be in some places rather than others.

One important consequence of all rituals is to demarcate sacred time from profane time. Just as objects and spaces can be charged with meaning and value and thus made different (greater) than other objects and spaces, so it is with periods of time as well. Some time is simply more meaningful and valuable than other time, and such sacred time is initiated and sustained by rituals. For example, the sacrality of a church (sacred space) service may begin when the minister calls the congregants to prayer or when the choir leads them in the opening hymn—rituals that mark the beginning of a sacred time.

Eliade recognizes that human beings seek periods of heightened states of experience—they desire sacred time. Indeed, profane time—that time spent struggling for survival and performing all the mundane yet necessary tasks that we must do as human beings—only is bearable because human beings break it up with periods of sacred time. Sacred time makes life worth living.[29]

The desire for sacred time has not abated simply because many people no longer find traditional religions attractive or compelling. As Eliade notes, we "find in man at every level, the same longing to destroy profane time and live in sacred time."[30] Living in sacred time is not the creation of some new time, but is achieved through the repetition of rituals (like archetypes or models) that have proven capable of giving rise to sacred time. Indeed, part of what we think of when we think about rituals is repetition—something done over and over again. This common sense understanding is fundamentally correct. Rituals (established, for example, by custom or scripture) are repetitive, and each time we engage in them we repeat the actions of those (sometimes divine beings, sometimes heroes or ancestors) who established those rituals as effective means of bringing us into contact with the sacred, of initiating sacred time.[31] For example, in Judaism the lighting of the menorah during the Hanukkah celebration is a repetition of the rededication of the temple in Jerusalem in the second century BCE. Or, in Christianity the communion ritual is a repetition of the actions of Jesus at the Last Supper. Both rituals are examples of the establishing of sacred time that can be and has been repeated for millennia. Thus, it is more appropriate to speak here not of the creation of a new time but of a regeneration of sacred time.[32] Practitioners, in some sense, are transporting themselves back to a sacred time that breaks up the mundane profane time of their everyday existence.

The Pervasiveness and Permanence of the Sacred

This fundamental urge for human beings to be in contact with the sacred is an indispensable element of human life. Even among the most secular individuals and in the seemingly most unreligious societies, our relationship to the sacred, to that which separates the meaningful and valuable from the insignificant and profane, persists. For Eliade, "even the most desacralized existence still preserves traces of a religious valorization of the world."[33] He insists that "[s]omething of the religious conception of the world still persists in the behavior of profane man, although he is not always conscious of this immemorial heritage."[34]

As these quotations suggest, there is a kind of inevitability and inescapability to the religious life. No matter how much an individual or society rejects religion, it is a necessary part of the human condition—surviving in the contemporary, largely secular world despite the proclamations of many people that religion is dead (or, at least, dying). Thus, Eliade claims that "profane man cannot help preserving some vestiges of the behavior of religious man, though they are emptied of religious meaning. Do what he will, he is an inheritor."[35] As an inheritor, he behaves religiously whether or not he wants to do so. "The majority of the 'irreligious' still behave religiously," Eliade argues, "even though they are not aware of the fact."[36] For Eliade, unearthing this hidden religiosity in the contemporary world is a task that he finds incredibly important. As he notes, "I wanted to show that even beneath its radically desacralized forms, Western culture camouflages magico-religious meanings that our contemporaries, with the exception of a few poets and artists, do not suspect."[37]

While he rejects the mere reduction of religion to psychological "facts" about human beings, Eliade nevertheless identifies the human unconscious as the place where we can find our religious inheritance. In this regard, he comes very close to the kind of psychological perspective of Jung.

For Eliade, "profane man is the descendant of *homo religiosus* and he cannot wipe out his own history—that is, the behavior of his religious ancestors which has made him what he is today. This is all the more true because a great part of his existence is fed by impulses that come to him from the depths of his being, from the zone that has been called the 'unconscious.'"[38] The contents of the unconscious are the result of humanity's lived experience—the result of its existential situation. "[T]he contents and structures of the unconscious are the result of immemorial existential situations, especially of critical situations, and this is why the unconscious has a religious aura," Eliade observes. "For every existential crisis once again puts in question both the reality of the world and man's presence in the world."[39]

For Eliade, to understand what is sacred is to understand something critical about the way human beings *are* at the most fundamental level. Human beings have some fundamental characteristics. While individuals and cultures do differ, the differences remain within certain limits. Nobody and no culture is absolutely different from all others. Human beings and cultures all have a need for and relation to the sacred, and thus exhibit characteristically religious behavior. The sacred may change and look very different from one epoch to another, from one culture to another. People may even fail to be fully conscious of the sacred or fail to recognize their religious behavior, but they remain inextricably drawn to what is sacred in the sense described—a desire to identify and associate with that which is "really real," an orientation toward the transcendent, and a need for deeper, more meaningful experiences—and thus they are undeniably religious.

As a consequence of being *homo religiosus*, Eliade is able to identify a plethora of examples in contemporary society that *seem* profane but nevertheless have a religious element or dimension.

- National flags: Flags function like other symbols from "archaic societies"—they elicit powerful "affective experiences" related to our participation in a social order. In this sense, Eliade argues that there is "no break in the continuity between the archaic world and the modern world."[40]
- Festivals: Ancient new year rituals and festivals marked the end of a cosmic cycle and the beginning of a new one. They signaled the regeneration of time. For example, "the seasonal feasts which close one cycle of time and

open another set out to achieve a *complete regeneration of time.*"⁴¹ This regenerated time allows for renewal of the cosmos, the society, and the individual. It reorders the world and provides renewed opportunities. While the contemporary New Year's Eve celebrations may be devoid of explicit religious content (though they generally resemble Durkheim's account of "collective effervescence"), they nevertheless function in a similar way.⁴² The revelry of the evening gives way to the return to order on New Year's Day. Thus, there is significant continuity with the past, for "the meaning of the carnivalesque orgy at the end of the year is confirmed by the fact that the chaos is always followed by a new [ordered and orderly] creation of the cosmos."⁴³ To return to Victor Turner's distinction, New Year's Eve in even the most secular cultures is an opportunity for *communitas*, followed the next day by a return to profane structure.

- Heroes: Our heroes today may not be equated with gods, but they nevertheless serve as "archetypes" or role models of exemplary behavior—just as ancient heroes/gods served our distant ancestors. Thus, Eliade observes that "real and imaginary" heroes "play an important part in the formation of European adolescents: the characters in tales of adventure, heroes of war, screen favourites, etc."⁴⁴
- Place: While the archaic world was characterized by a clear understanding of the sacred and profane, our contemporary world nonetheless bears some resemblance. Take the way we distinguish—even individually—some places from others. "There are, for example, privileged places, qualitatively different from all others—a man's birthplace, or the scenes of his first love, or certain places in the first foreign city he visited in youth," Eliade notes. "Even for the most frankly non religious man, all these places still retain an exceptional, a unique quality; they are the 'holy places' of his private universe, as if it were in such spots that he had received the revelation of a reality *other* than that in which he participates through his ordinary [profane] daily life."⁴⁵
- Construction: The specialness or sacrality of certain places is a consequence of the human creations in those locations. Regardless of how religious we consider ourselves, "*every construction or fabrication has the cosmogony as paradigmatic model*," Eliade argues. "The creation of the world becomes the archetype [model] of every creative human gesture, whatever its plane of reference may be."⁴⁶ The creation of our habitat is not simply of practical benefit, but an act of extracting something sacred and meaningful out of the profane and mundane. "Every new town, every new house that is built, imitates afresh, and in a sense repeats, the creation of the world," Eliade

concludes. "Indeed, every town, every dwelling stands at the 'centre of the world', so that its construction was only possible by means of abolishing profane space and time and establishing sacred space and time."[47]

- Literature: Our literature today is not explicitly religious like the Quran or even more ancient texts, but it still serves a similar function. It still provides heroes and narratives that open up worlds of meaning, that allow us to see reality in a qualitatively different way. Thus, Eliade insists that "the literary imagination is the continuation of mythological creativity and oneiric [related to dreams or dreaming] experiences."[48]
- Communism: Even an avowedly atheistic economic and political movement like communism still bears the traces of our religious past and expresses our intrinsically religious nature. Eliade writes of the "mythological structure of communism" and, in particular, its "eschatological content."[49] That content includes a deterministic view of history that culminates in the great victory of the good and the just (the proletariat) over the evil and exploitative (the capitalists). For Eliade, this victory ushers in a "Golden Age" that is very much like a religious vision—indeed, it builds upon classic visions in the Abrahamic traditions of what Christians call the "Kingdom of God."

Eliade's work is replete with such accounts of seemingly secular phenomena whose meanings are forged through the dialectic of the sacred and profane.

The kind of expansion of our thinking about the sacred and religion that Eliade initiates can be seen in the work of more contemporary scholars who expand it further into interpretations of cultural artifacts and practices. David Chidester—especially in *Authentic Fakes: Religion and American Popular Culture*—is a good example. Chidester writes:

> Religious ways of being human engage the transcendent—that which rises above and beyond the ordinary. They engage the sacred—that which is set apart from the ordinary. And they engage the ultimate—that which defines the final, unavoidable limit of all our ordinary concerns.[50]

This approach to religion does not focus on the existence or character of the transcendent or sacred or ultimate (all very much synonymous), but the ways that these phenomena are "engaged" by human beings and how such engagement responds to and shapes our existential circumstances. Again, the approach here is phenomenological and existential.

Chidester describes the engagement of the human and the sacred as a kind of "work." He writes that "something is doing religious work if it is engaged in negotiating what it is to be human."[51] In other words, something is doing religious work if it helps to tell us who we are, what we should seek, how we should conduct ourselves, and so on. That said, we can see that many ideas, activities, objects, or institutions might contribute to "negotiating what it is to be human." Certainly there are stereotypically religious ideas, activities, objects, and institutions that help us negotiate what it is to be human. But many things may do this, including elements of popular culture. This is what Chidester tries to show throughout *Authentic Fakes*. He concludes:

> Traces of religion, as transcendence, as the sacred, as the ultimate, can be discerned in the play of popular culture. As a result, we can conclude that popular culture is doing a kind of religious work, even if we cannot predict how that ongoing religious work of American popular culture, now diffused all over the globe, will actually work for the United States of America.[52]

Seeing popular culture not only as a place where religions express themselves, but as religious itself, is one of the more compelling theoretical moves in religious studies in recent years—one that we explore in some depth in Chapter 5. And it complicates our understanding of Eliade's critique of the contemporary Western world.

The Critique of the Contemporary World

After learning about Eliade's argument that *homo religiosus* remains religious even in the seemingly secular world, his critique of and grave concern for the contemporary Western world may seem contradictory.

The basic critique is clear: Contemporary humanity is drifting ever further into the profane, secular world. The sacred breaks through at times, as we noted above, but it is less powerful and coherent as compared to the more pervasive and structural religious lives of the past. As a consequence, contemporary humanity is threatened by the potential chaos of the world and finds it ever more difficult to find and experience that world as meaningful. Eliade writes that "the modern world is in the situation of a man swallowed by a monster, struggling in the darkness of its belly; or of one lost in the wilderness, or wandering in a labyrinth which itself is a symbol of the Infernal—and so he is in anguish, thinks he is already dead or upon the point of dying, and can see no way out except into darkness, Death or Nothingness."[53] Such experiences occur in archaic or religious societies as well. In fact, such experiences may even be prompted by religious rituals. Such existential crises certainly appear in sacred literature.

But religious cultures also have ways (spiritual practices, rituals, and other collective actions) that provide meaning to such experiences and then raise individuals out of the depths of despair and into contact with the sacred. People in the contemporary world simply have no ability to grapple with such situations nearly as effectively. They have a crisis of meaning. As Eliade concludes, the "crises of modern man are to a large extent *religious* ones, insofar as they are an awakening of his awareness to an absence of meaning."[54]

For religious people, religious beliefs and actions are able to turn the profane into something more than the profane; they sacralize the ordinary in order to give it more depth and meaning. Take the simple act of eating, which all human beings must do to nourish the body. But certain dietary practices, rituals, and blessings can turn an ordinary meal into a sacred activity—into an experience that is greater than it appears. For "nonreligious man, all vital experience—whether sex or eating, work or play—have been desacralized. This means that all these physiological acts are deprived of spiritual significance, hence deprived of their truly human dimension."[55] The stark contrast between the religious and the secular is made clear in this final passage of Eliade's *Patterns in Comparative Religion*:

> The cosmic myths and the whole world of ritual thus appear as existential experiences to primitive man: he does not lose himself, he does not forget his own existence when he fulfils a myth or takes part in a ritual; quite the reverse; he finds himself and comes to understand himself, because those myths and rituals express cosmic realities which ultimately he is aware of as realities in his own being. To primitive man, every level of reality is so completely open to him that the emotion he felt at merely *seeing* anything as magnificent as the starry sky would have been as strong as the most 'intimist' personal experience felt by a modern. For, thanks chiefly to his symbols, the *real existence* of primitive man was not the broken and alienated existence lived by civilized man to-day.[56]

It might be best to imagine a spectrum, with a fully infused sacred life on the one end and a purely profane life on the other end. Even in the most religious cultures, the fully infused sacred life is not achieved. There are always parts or aspects of life that remain profane. But certainly the lives of the religious are on that side of the spectrum. The purely profane life also is not a reality—at least not now, and not even in the most secular societies. But we may be moving ever further in that direction. "For nonreligious man, birth, marriage, death are events that concern only the individual and his family; or occasionally—in the case of heads of governments or political leaders—events that have political repercussions," Eliade argues. "In a nonreligious view of life, all these 'passages' have lost their ritual character ... However, we must repeat that a drastically nonreligious experience of the whole of life is seldom found in the pure state, even in the most secularized societies. Possibly such a completely nonreligious experience will become commoner in a more or less distant future; for the present, it is still rare."[57]

Eliade identifies contemporary humanity's relationship with history as particularly problematic—existentially problematic. Religious people have the ability to escape history. Through rituals, spiritual exercises, and other individual and collective practices, they transcend profane time, history, by bringing themselves into contact with the sacred and by returning to the mythological, sacred time of the origin of the world, the moment of the creation of order. Increasingly, however, contemporary humanity does not have access to such sacred time. "Modern nonreligious man assumes a new existential situation," Eliade notes, "he regards himself solely as the subject and the agent of history, and he refuses all appeal to transcendence."[58]

The reason that contemporary humanity's approach to history is so problematic is that it leaves people subject to the chaos, death, and nothingness of history—manifested in widespread anomie, two world wars and a myriad of violent conflicts, and other social and psychological ailments. Nothing has any ultimate or sacred meaning. It all is meaningless. Such a realization is summed up in Eliade's phrase "the terror of history." Eliade recognizes that modern movements like Marxism may offer some protection against "the terror of history."[59] The belief that all of history leads inevitably to an ideal social order (the communist utopia) provides all of history with meaning. But such safety from "the terror of history" generally is lacking among people living in contemporary secular societies. While such societies champion the freedom of their citizens, that freedom "is powerless to justify history; and this, for every man who is sincere with himself, is equivalent to the terror of history."[60] Given the limitations of secular social and political movements and the general spiritual vacuity of contemporary freedoms, Eliade argues that a recognition of our religious nature and a return to a more explicit expression and practice of religion can save us.[61] Short of a return to institutional religion, however, Eliade also advocates for a sort of cultural and existential revitalization of our spiritual selves. He insists that "the best defense against the terror of history, next to religious experience, is spirituality, creation, culture."[62] The term he uses to describe this cultural and existential revitalization is the "New Humanism."

Eliade asserts that to "know the situations assumed by religious man, to understand his spiritual universe, is, in sum, to advance our general knowledge of man."⁶³ It is the history of religions, with its phenomenological and existential approach, that is best situated to advance our knowledge in this way. "The history of religions is not merely a historical discipline," Eliade notes. "It is equally a *total hermeneutic*, being called to decipher and explicate every kind of encounter of man with the sacred, from prehistory to our day."⁶⁴ Such a hermeneutic or way of understanding is not just about advancing knowledge, though; it is about transforming humanity. In this sense, it is creative. "In the end, the creative hermeneutics *changes* man; it is more than instruction, it is also a spiritual technique susceptible of modifying the quality of existence itself."⁶⁵

Eliade argues that "by attempting to understand the existential situations expressed by the documents he is studying, the historian of religions will inevitably attain to a deeper knowledge of man. It is on the basis of such a knowledge that a new humanism, on a world-wide scale, could develop."⁶⁶ This "New Humanism" is like secular humanism in that it advances the projects of human beings and improves their existential situation. It is unlike secular humanism, however, in that it depends on tapping into the spiritual or religious nature of human beings.

It is the history of religions, the study of comparative religion from this particular phenomenological and existential approach, that will lead to the "New Humanism." Eliade insists that "the history of religions envisages, in the end, cultural *creation* and the *modification* of man."⁶⁷ In an equally bold statement, he adds that the "history of religions can play an essential role in the effort toward a *planetisation* of culture; it can contribute to the elaboration of a universal type of culture."⁶⁸ As he notes in one of his journal entries, Eliade is in search of a "new, wider humanism" and he "dreamed of rediscovering the model of a 'universal man.'"⁶⁹

In the end, then, Eliade's work moves beyond the simple understanding of religious phenomena. For Eliade, the understanding of these phenomena potentially can change (in a positive way) the person who comes to that understanding and even has the possibility of revitalizing and saving Western culture. In short, for Eliade the history of religions promises a kind of personal and cultural conversion—transforming our individual and collective existential situation.⁷⁰ As Charles H. Long notes, Eliade is proposing what might be called "a therapy that will prepare our culture for a new beginning."⁷¹

But there is a paradox at the heart of Eliade's approach—or at least an uncomfortable contradiction. On the one hand, he claims that we need to engage again our religious traditions in order to experience the sacred and save our cultures. But, on the other hand, he claims that the sacred is unavoidable—that we are *homo religiosus* whether or not we explicitly engage in religious practices. Why do we need to engage again with our religious traditions if we can experience the sacred in the seemingly secular world? Eliade has an answer for this question, which is that these remnants of the sacred in the secular world are not enough to fend off the "terror of history" and the existential crisis of contemporary humanity. Eliade believes that the chaos and destruction of the twentieth century (including two world wars) confirm his assessment of contemporary humanity. But one could argue that the Western world is less chaotic and destructive than ever before, certainly less violent.[72] Perhaps secularism is good for Western culture. And maybe our experience of the sacred (broadly conceived) in our otherwise secular culture is more than enough to sustain us existentially. That proposition will be examined in more depth in Chapters 5 and 6.

Paul Tillich and Ultimate Concern

If Eliade can be seen as the preeminent scholar of the twentieth century in the comparative study of religion, Paul Tillich (1886–1965) likewise can be seen as the preeminent theologian—certainly, at least, one of the most influential. Like Eliade (who was Romanian), the German-born Tillich immigrated to the United States where he completed his astounding career. Like Eliade, Tillich was shaped greatly by the turmoil in his native Europe, and believed that Western culture was in the midst of a serious spiritual and existential crisis—a crisis that only could be resolved through a spiritual or religious revival. And, like Eliade, Tillich's work would have a great impact on the study of religion and how religion would be understood in the late twentieth century. As Jonathan Z. Smith states, although Tillich was a theologian, he was instrumental in the academic as well as popular "shift in understanding religion from a theological to an anthropological perspective." He writes:

> What Tillich appeared to provide was both a rationale for and a translation language to enable and express this shift. This was especially so in three areas: (i) a translation that reflected an anthropological definition of religion (one that was taken up in college textbooks and, later, by the Supreme Court); (ii) a focus on symbols and their interpretation (an issue that would later contribute to the centrality of Paul Ricoeur's work in the discourse of the academy); (iii) a privileged relation between religion and culture which seemed particularly appropriate to the new setting of the study of religion within public institutions

(recall the revival of interest, within the academy, in the category "civil religion" beginning in the late 1960s). It is activity in these three areas, among others, with the AAR [American Academy of Religion] and the academic study of religion in North America that undergirds the proposition that Tillich was "the unacknowledged theoretician of our entire enterprise."[73]

In sum, Tillich joins Eliade as a foundational figure not only in the study of religion in academic circles, but in how religion is conceived at a popular level.

Tillich's complete theological project is complex, extensive, and comprehensive. A full account of it cannot be taken up here, nor would it be necessary for our purposes. Our focus will be on Tillich's theology of culture. This more limited project parallels Eliade's work in that it is an effort to avoid the kind of reductionism that was increasingly prevalent in the academy. For example, even though Tillich engages psychology quite substantively and recognizes its important contributions to understanding the human condition, he nonetheless notes that it "is a reductionist profanation of self-transcendence to attempt to derive religion, especially in its ecstatic side, from psychological dynamics."[74] Religion, in other words, is as *sui generis* for Tillich as it is for Eliade.

The key to Tillich's theology of culture is the relation between ultimate reality (the sacred, the transcendent, God, etc.) and the world, the universe that we inhabit. As he writes, "if we say that the universe is an expression of ultimate reality we say that the universe and everything in it, both reveals and hides ultimate reality."[75] Let us look at some key concepts and arguments at the core of this theology of culture.

Tillich's *Theology of Culture* very succinctly explicates his argument about the nature and importance of religion. For Tillich, religion is not one human institution among others. Nor is it simply the best or most important of our human institutions. "Religion is not a special function of man's spiritual life," Tillich writes, "but it is the dimension of depth in all of its functions."[76] Religion is about our orientation to the world, the way we find meaning and spiritual sustenance. "It is at home everywhere, namely, in the depth of all functions of man's spiritual life," Tillich concludes. "Religion is the dimension of depth in all of them. Religion is the aspect of depth in the totality of the human spirit."[77]

But what is this depth? For Tillich, it is more than simply a feeling that might accompany our beliefs and practices.[78] Depth "means that the religious aspect points to that which is ultimate, infinite, unconditional in man's spiritual life. Religion, in the largest and most basic sense of the word, is ultimate concern. And ultimate concern is manifest in all creative functions of the human spirit."[79]

"Ultimate concern" is a key theological concept for Tillich. He sees it manifested in three spheres or functions. He affirms that it "is manifest in the moral sphere as the unconditional seriousness of the moral demand"; "is manifest in the realm of knowledge as the passionate longing for ultimate reality"; and "is manifest in the aesthetic function of the human spirit as the infinite desire to express ultimate meaning."[80] Because religion or "ultimate concern" permeates all these functions of human beings, one cannot deny religion without denying our very humanity. Indeed, if you seriously deny religion, you in fact are expressing the kind of "ultimate concern" for reality that is at the very heart of religion. "You cannot reject religion with ultimate seriousness, because ultimate seriousness, or the state of being ultimately concerned, is itself religion," Tillich insists. "Religion is the substance, the ground, and the depth of man's spiritual life. This is the religious aspect of the human spirit."[81]

Tillich notes that this approach to religion is "an existential, not a theoretical, understanding of religion."[82] The existential situation of human beings, particularly in the twentieth century, is one of "estrangement"—"the situation of the estrangement of man from his true being. One could rightly say that the existence of religion as a special realm is the most conspicuous proof of man's fallen state."[83] Religion should not be something that one does only on a specific day in a specific place (e.g., Friday at the mosque), but it should permeate our whole life. Like Eliade, Tillich views the horrors and alienation of the twentieth century as a particularly spiritual crisis—the inevitable consequence of our "estrangement."

Faith for Tillich is "the state of being grasped by an ultimate concern."[84] This ultimate concern is meaning producing, and thus fights against the kind of estrangement and alienation that typify our contemporary predicament. As a consequence of this formal definition, Tillich insists that nobody can be without faith. "Nobody can escape the essential relation of the conditional spirit to something unconditional in the direction of which it is self-transcendent in unity with all life," he writes. "However unworthy the ultimate concern's concrete content may be, no one can stifle such concern completely."[85] The difference between the stereotypically religious person and the more secular person is the content itself. Some content is truly unconditional (religious) and other content is not (profane), but all content can be the object of ultimate concern. Tillich concludes that the "continuing struggle through all history is waged between a faith directed to ultimate reality and a faith directed toward preliminary realities claiming ultimacy."[86] For example, I can have ultimate concern directed toward the divine (unconditional, infinite, etc.) or something less than divine (such as socialism or sensual pleasure or any other conditional and finite good).

Though insisting on the difference between the religious and the secular, the sacred and the profane, Tillich nonetheless understands that these ideas of ultimate concern and faith close the gap between the two ends of these dichotomies. As he notes, a "consequence of the existential concept of religion is the disappearance of the gap between the sacred and secular realm. If religion is the state of being grasped by an ultimate concern, this state cannot be restricted to a special realm."[87]

The closing of the gap between the sacred and the secular is reflected in the distinction that Tillich makes between the manifest Church and the latent Church. "The Church," Tillich notes, "has the function of answering the question implied in man's very existence, the question of the meaning of this existence."[88] The manifest Church is the stereotypical church—most likely with a building, a congregation of some sort, perhaps some sort of leadership structure, etc. The latent Church is "a Church in which the ultimate concern which drives the manifest Church is hidden under cultural forms and deformations."[89] Even a political and economic movement as atheistic as communism is connected to the latent Church. "Not even communism could live if it were devoid of all elements of the Spiritual Community," Tillich observes. "Even world communism is teleologically related to the Spiritual Community."[90]

This idea of the manifest and the latent Church is one of many examples of the ways in which Tillich sees religion as intimately intertwined with culture. Most generally, "churches silently give Spiritual substance to the society in which they live, and the churches silently receive Spiritual forms from the same society."[91] Churches provide an indispensable spiritual and meaning-producing element to society, but the specific forms of Churches (particular rituals, symbols, architecture, organization, etc.) also are drawn from the society itself. "For its [the Church] forms are created by culture," Tillich concludes, "as its religious substance makes culture possible. The Church and culture are within, not alongside, each other."[92]

The way Tillich views the relationship between religion and culture is reflected as well in his approach to religious symbols. Religious symbols, Tillich notes, are like all symbols, "they open up a level of reality, which otherwise is not opened at all, which is hidden."[93] All symbols work in this way, but religious symbols get at particular existential or spiritual content—at least in a more direct and explicit way. However, other cultural symbols (in the visual arts, literature, etc.) may still function in this particularly religious way. These symbols may even reveal existential or spiritual content—though perhaps not as effectively or deeply.

What I have explained about Tillich's work so far makes the compelling case that religion and culture are intrinsically intertwined. You cannot have one without the other. Religion provides the existential or spiritual substance to culture (across all its forms) and culture provides the forms and resources for the expression of religion. Because this relationship is so critical to the story I am telling, let us delve a bit more into it.

In the Foreword to *Theology of Culture*, Tillich notes that "the present volume attempts to show the religious dimension in many special spheres of man's cultural activity. This dimension ... is never absent in cultural creations even if they show no relation to religion in the narrower sense of the word."[94] He insists later that "in every cultural creation—a picture, a system, a law, a political movement (however secular it may appear)—an ultimate concern is expressed, and that it is possible to recognize the unconscious theological character of it."[95]

The theological reality that Tillich sees working through all cultural phenomena (religious or not) is Spirit. Here we see the influence of Hegel's philosophical and theological work. In his *Systematic Theology*, Tillich states that Spirit "as a dimension of life unites the power of being with the meaning of being. Spirit can be defined as the actualization of power and meaning in unity."[96] While stopping short of an identity of Spirit with culture, an identity of the sacred and the profane, Tillich nevertheless insists on the "principle of the consecration of the secular"—meaning "that it is open to the impact of the Spirit even without the mediation of a church."[97] The Spirit is like the thread that weaves together religion and culture, the sacred and the profane.

But Tillich goes much further in his *Theology of Culture* in blurring the line between the sacred and the profane—stating positions that seem even more Hegelian. "Religion as ultimate concern is the meaning-giving substance of culture, and culture is the totality of forms in which the basic concern of religion expresses itself," he writes. "In abbreviation: religion is the substance of culture, culture is the form of religion."[98] He adds that "there is no cultural creation without an ultimate concern expressed in it."[99]

Given that religion and culture, the sacred and profane, the transcendent and immanent, are so intertwined, it makes sense that Tillich would see Spirit or ultimate concern or religion (in some way, these are interchangeable) throughout various cultural elements or creations. In fact, only the religious dimension of the human condition truly can reveal the import or depth of cultural creations.

> The great works of the visual arts, of music, of poetry, of literature, of architecture, of dance, of philosophy, show in their style both the encounter with non-being, and the strength which can stand this encounter and shape it creatively. Without

this key, contemporary culture is a closed door. With this key, it can be understood as the revelation of man's predicament, both in the present world and in the world universally.[100]

After a description of myths and symbols, Tillich writes that philosophy and art "take from their depth and abundance. Their validity is the power with which they express the relation of man and his world to the ultimately real. Out of a particular relation of this kind they are born. With the end of this relation they die."[101] As a theologian, it is not surprising that Tillich engages with various philosophical figures and movements. But neither is it surprising that he would engage with art. As a cultural form, it is Spirit or ultimate concern or religion that is its real depth. "A work of art is authentic," Tillich argues, "if it expresses the encounter of mind and world in which an otherwise hidden quality of a piece of the universe (and implicitly of the universe itself) is united with an otherwise hidden receptive power of the mind (and implicitly of the person as a whole)."[102] In this encounter, meaning is generated and a deeper understanding of the human condition is achieved. This encounter is at the heart of what Tillich means by ultimate concern. In short, this encounter is religious even if the work of art is superficially secular or profane.[103] Even in considering the development of particular artistic styles, Tillich sees the hidden power of Spirit or ultimate concern or religion. "A new style appears in the course of the self-creation of life under the dimension of spirit," he insists. "A style is created by the autonomous act of the individual artist and, at the same time, by historical destiny. But religion can influence historical destiny and autonomous creativity indirectly."[104] Again, this is true regardless of whether or not the artist or artists consider themselves religious in any stereotypical sense. "Whatever the subject matter which an artist chooses, however strong or weak his artistic form, he cannot help but betray by his style his own ultimate concern, as well as that of his group, and his period," Tillich concludes. "He cannot escape religion even if he rejects religion, for religion is the state of being ultimately concerned."[105]

What is true for the visual arts is also true for literature. Tillich argues that in "all literature and every use of language, the Spiritual Presence can grasp him who speaks and elevates his words to the state of bearers of the Spirit."[106] While every literature and language is particular to a place, a culture, and a history, it nevertheless has the ability to express something that is universal. It is a vehicle for ultimate concern, and thus the Spirit can be manifest in it. "Every language is particular because it expresses a particular encounter with reality," Tillich concludes, "but the language which is a bearer of the Spirit is at the same time universal because it transcends the particular encounter which it expresses in the direction of that which is universal, the Logos, the criterion of every particular logos."[107]

Moral life is of particular interest to Tillich. It is the sphere where doubt and uncertainty create particularly powerful existential *angst*, and where the spiritual crisis of the twentieth century affects our relationships with one another. It also is central to him theologically. "The act in which man actualizes his essential centeredness is the moral act," Tillich notes. "Morality is the function of life by which the realm of the spirit comes into being. Morality is the constitutive function of spirit."[108] In thinking about the moral imperative, which is demanded of us by the presence of the other, Tillich claims that "the moral imperative is valid because it represents our essential being over against our state of existential estrangement."[109]

For Tillich, a central element of morality is transcendence—specifically, the ability of human beings to transcend the self in the moral act. "There is no self-transcendence under the dimension of the spirit without the constitution of the moral self by the unconditional imperative," Tillich writes, "and this self-transcendence cannot take form except within the universe of meaning created in the cultural act."[110] Again, we see the central role that culture plays in Tillich's theology.

> Culture provides the contents of morality—the concrete ideals of personality and community and the changing laws of ethical wisdom. Religion gives to morality the unconditional character of the moral imperative, the ultimate moral aim, the reunion of the separated in *agape* [unselfish or unconditional love] and the motivating power of grace. Culture, or the creation of a universe of meaning in *theoria* and *praxis*, is essentially related to morality and religion.[111]

An important point to make here is that while Tillich draws theological conclusions from morality, he seems to indicate that morality is not dependent on theology. We know that human beings can perform moral acts without being explicitly religious. So do we even need religion? Tillich seems to anticipate this line of critique. "The many forms of ethics without Spiritual Presence are judged by the fact that they cannot show the power of motivation, the principle of choice in the concrete situation, the unconditional validity of the moral imperative," he argues. "Love can do it, but love is not a matter of man's will. It is a creation of the Spiritual Presence. It is grace."[112] He seems to be arguing that even the secular moral act is still religious or spiritual at its depth. Only grace or love can motivate truly moral behavior, *whether we know it or not*. While this may be a compelling argument for the religious believer, however, it makes no claim on the secular individual. He or she can say that there is no religious or spiritual depth to the moral act. There is just the moral act, informed by the customs and norms of the culture. There is nothing more nor less to it.

What Tillich argues in relation to morality holds more generally for what he deems to be a certain limitation to culture—secular culture more specifically. "Morality and culture in existential separation from religion become what is usually called 'secular,'" Tillich notes. "Their greatness is contradicted by their profanity."[113] Morality and culture can work on a mere horizontal plane, but only religion can connect them vertically with the ultimate, the divine, that is the real source of their depth and meaning anyway. As Tillich insists, "Meaning cannot live without the inexhaustible source of meaning to which religion points."[114] In this regard, ultimate reality serves Tillich's theology in the same way that the sacred serves Eliade's project.

Tillich views the finite (morality, culture, religious institutions, etc.) and the infinite (ultimate reality, God, Spirit, etc.) in a constant relationship and even tension. The finite, in fact, prevents life from becoming "swallowed by the infinite."[115] He writes:

> In this sense the secular is the necessary corrective of the holy. Yet, it itself drives toward the holy. It cannot resist indefinitely the function of self-transcendence, which is present in every life, however secularized, for the resistance against it produces the emptiness and meaninglessness which characterizes the finite when cut off from the infinite.[116]

So, while Tillich certainly sees religion, Spirit, ultimate reality, working throughout culture (however secular it may appear), he still insists that religion holds a special place in human life—an indispensable place. In fact, in the wake of the terrible wars and genocide of the twentieth century and the general malaise or *anomie* in Western culture, religion for Tillich may be more important than ever.

Conclusion

So, what are the lessons we learn from Eliade and Tillich? While both acknowledge the existence of a transcendent reality (the sacred, God, Spirit, ultimate reality, etc.), they nevertheless focus their attention on the immanent. Such a focus is inherent in any scholarly approach that is phenomenological or existential—any approach that focuses on the human condition and lived experience. This focus on the immanent rather than (or, at least, more so than) the transcendent is an important thread in the history of the study of religion. It is a thread that we already have seen in other theorists in previous chapters and one that will be further developed later in this work.

Both Eliade and Tillich also identify existential (and thus universal) problems or questions to which they then claim only religion can best respond. For Tillich, of course, it is Christianity that best responds—though he recognizes how all religions can do so. For Eliade, on the other hand, religion generally responds to those existential problems and questions, and he is much more pluralist in his approach (with the exception of a nod to Christianity at the end of *Myth of the Eternal Return*). Now, however, we must push further.

The existential problems or questions that Tillich and Eliade identify may not be universal or even the right problems or questions. Or they may have been the right problems or questions earlier in our history, but not now. And even if they are the right problems or questions, why is institutional religion the only way or the best way to respond to them? Both Tillich and Eliade acknowledge that a wide range of cultural phenomena can function religiously or, more, intrinsically have a religious dimension. In short, they prioritize or privilege stereotypical or institutional religion, but there is not a convincing argument to do so. Their defense of stereotypical or institutional religion seems to be more of a residual, cultural bias than a convincing and necessary conclusion of their work. *Homo theologicum* leaves us in a similar position as *homo religiosus*. Tillich and Eliade can claim that we are inherently theological or religious, but there are no conclusive reasons for accepting those propositions. And, prescriptively, we confront the added paradox or contradiction of advocating for something (ultimate meaning, experience of the sacred, etc.) that is supposed to already permeate our lives.

In critiquing the elitism of Tillich's theology of culture (his preference, for example, for great literary works, high art, etc.), Kelton Cobb concludes: "The range of sources for theology of culture should be opened up to include any vortex of valuation that functions to attract and repel and otherwise activate or alter the way people value reality. A case could be made that popular culture discloses more of this than high culture."[117] I agree with Cobb's valuation of popular culture but add that we not even bother with the "theology" part of theology of culture. The fact of the matter is that culture functions in some important ways for human beings. You can use religious terms or secular terms to describe it, but the terms do not really matter. In this sense, we have the beginning of the argument that religion does not really matter—at least not stereotypical or institutional religion. Ironically, then, we have the beginning of an argument that does not begin simply with secular or even atheist writers, but with scholars like Tillich and Eliade who saw themselves as defenders of religion.

Interlude

We now are at an important transition point in our historical narrative and in the argument of this book. So far we have looked at a wide range of theorists and disciplinary approaches to the study of religion. They emphasize different elements of religion (as they understood it). They have different views about the future of religion, and they have different assessments of the merits of religion and potential changes in the future. But what they all have in common is some version of a functional understanding of religion. In other words, they all think that religion does something for human beings. It has value or is good because it does that thing or those things for us.

We may believe that the supposed object of religion—whether it be God or the gods or spiritual powers—is good in itself. In other words, God is good not because God does something for us (though believers certainly believe God does), but God is good in itself. And while some people might feel that religion is good in itself, as an institution it only exists because of the way it functions. That function might be psychological, sociological, existential, ethical, or something else. But it does function for us. However, multiple phenomena can have similar functions. A horse can get us from point A to point B, but so can a bicycle or an automobile. Watching a Greek tragedy in ancient Athens can entertain us and provide us meaningful ways to look at the world, but so can reading Dostoyevsky's novels or watching the television program *Game of Thrones*. By analogy, we can say that religion functions for us in certain ways but there may be other cultural phenomena that can function in similar ways.

Check out Table 1:

Table 1

Historical figure	Functional type	Description of religion	Displacement or substitution	Assessment of historical change or secularization
Immanuel Kant	Philosophical Moral	Religion as a means by which to communicate the Categorical Imperative; religion is a supposition of practical reason	Practical reason can delineate Categorical Imperative without the need of religion	UNCERTAIN Kant claims role for religion, but it is not rationally necessary
G.W.F. Hegel	Philosophical Theological	Spirit unfolds and comes to self-consciousness through human history and culture	Religion plays special role but not a unique role in the work of the Spirit	UNCERTAIN Hegel claims special role for religion, but it could be viewed as just one among many important historical and cultural institutions
Emile Durkheim	Sociological	Religion as a means of forming and energizing community; a way for a community to express and understand itself	Other rituals may perform the same function as religion	UNCERTAIN or POSITIVE Durkheim suggests that the future may require different forms of "collective effervescence," yet functioning in a similar way as religion
Max Weber	Sociological	Religion as a means of providing meaning, including to otherwise secular activities (e.g., economic behavior)	In a "disenchanted world," it is unclear whether or not the residues of religion are sufficient to continue to provide meaning to otherwise secular activities	UNCERTAIN Weber does not offer a clear or unambiguous assessment of the "disenchanted world"

Sigmund Freud	Psychological	Religion is an illusion that allows people to cope psychologically with the difficulties of nature and society	Reason and science will supplant religion	POSITIVE Religion will disappear in a mature society just as fantasies and illusions disappear when children become mature adults
Carl Jung	Psychological	Religion is one means by which the collective unconscious and its archetypes are expressed in human culture	The archetypes of the collective unconscious will still impact human lives through various cultural phenomena	UNCERTAIN Religious practices and institutions allow for a healthy interaction with the archetypes of the collective unconscious; it is unclear whether or not other cultural practices and institutions can fill this same role
Mircea Eliade	Phenomenological Existential	Religion is one means by which human beings experience the sacred	As *homo religiosus*, humans will continue to express their innate religiosity through various cultural phenomena	NEGATIVE Though humans are innately religious, only explicit and self-conscious religious practice can prevent existential angst and despair
Paul Tillich	Theological Existential	Religion is the primary (but not only) means by which Spirit is expressed	The Spirit always will be expressed through various cultural practices	NEGATIVE Only explicit and self-conscious religious practice (Christianity in particular) can prevent existential angst and despair

Here we have a summary of each theory, the functional argument they make, to what extent that function may be taken up by other cultural phenomena, and how each figure might assess changes to religion or even the supplanting of religion.

The table summarizes the story I have been trying to tell. This story overlaps at points with the work of Mark C. Taylor. Though his work is more theological than my orientation, his approach parallels what I am trying to do in this work. He argues that much of the theological and philosophical development of the Western world is grounded in its religious history—particularly the Protestant Reformation in the sixteenth century. But the effects of that historical moment are not restricted to just theology and philosophy. Indeed, Taylor makes a comprehensive and compelling argument that the effects can be seen more broadly throughout Western culture—from art to economy, from architecture to politics.

As I also have argued in the preceding chapters, Taylor insists that religion permeates culture. "Religion is not a separate domain," he states, "but pervades all culture and has an important impact on every aspect of society."[1] Given his position, one that we have seen in so many of the theorists examined here, it is not surprising that he rejects the simple opposition between the religious and the secular.

> Religion is not limited to what occurs in churches, synagogues, mosques, and temples; rather, there is a religious dimension to all culture. Religion, moreover, is often most influential where it is least obvious. Supporters as well as critics fail to discern the pervasive influence of religion because their understanding of it is too limited. When the invisible as well as the visible aspects of religion are recognized, the simplistic opposition between secularity and religion collapses and the terms of analysis are effectively recast.[2]

To get to the point of collapsing the religious and the secular, however, Taylor takes us back to Martin Luther. Luther's impact on Western culture is sweeping, but one significant contribution that he made was in regard to the very understanding of human subjectivity. Prior to the Reformation that Luther ignited, the relationship of the individual to God was mediated by the Catholic Church. In short, one's relationship to God was only through the Church. But Luther championed the idea that our relationship to God was a *private* affair— that our relationship was between our interior, subjective nature and the divine. There is no need for a separate mediating institution. This idea would have powerful repercussions. As Taylor notes, "this inward turn eventually leads to the self-legislating autonomous subject [for example, the one we find in Kant and in moral and political philosophy ever since] without which the political revolutions of the modern era would have been impossible."³

Of course, Luther was not the only Reformer. John Calvin also played an instrumental role in the historical trajectory that Taylor traces. The key here is the relationship between God and the world. In particular, the issue is how transcendent or immanent God is. Taylor elaborates:

> God can disappear in two ways: on the one hand, God can become so transcendent that he is functionally irrelevant, and on the other, the divine can become so immanent that God and world are one. By pushing God's transcendence to the limit, Calvin unwittingly affirms divine immanence. If God is everything and I am nothing, then my deeds are never merely my own but are always also the expression of divine providence operating through me. ... In other words, when I act, Christ acts through me. The affirmation of human impotence and divine omnipotence leads to the unexpected identification of God with self and by extension world. At this point, the logic of opposition reverses itself in a logic of identity and creates the implosion of the sacred and the profane.⁴

In other words, Taylor is finding here the theological roots of the same blurring of sacred and profane, the transcendent and immanent, that I have argued for through the development of the study of religion (at least in the key figures I have highlighted in previous chapters).

The play between the transcendent and immanent is at the center of Taylor's account of the Western understanding of religion. Even more, it is at the center of many philosophical, cultural, political, and economic developments in the Western world. For example, take the political philosophy of Jean-Jacques Rousseau from the eighteenth century. "Rousseau's translation of the sovereign will of the transcendent God into the sovereign will of the people repeats the dialectical reversal, which we have discovered at the heart of Calvin's theology," Taylor argues. "When the Creator God is so powerful that everything is a representation of his free will, divine and human action become indistinguishable."⁵

Hegel, of course, is the preeminent theorist in this regard. Taylor argues that Hegel's God "is not a transcendent center of creative self-consciousness but the immanent structural ground of the cosmohistorical process, which gradually becomes self-conscious in the course of its own development."⁶ It is most completely through Hegel that we find the full mediation of the transcendent and immanent, the sacred and profane.⁷ As I explained in Chapter 1, with Hegel the divine and the world become one, and history the unfolding and coming to consciousness of Spirit. As we learned there, "world history is marked by the steady march of freedom"[8]—not ultimately human freedom, but spiritual freedom (rather, these are one and the same). This "march of freedom," coming to consciousness of Spirit, or unfolding of the divine, or revelation of Truth (again, these ultimately are the same process) "first appears sensually in artistic images and religious representation and then is articulated in philosophical concepts."[9]

For Taylor, Hegel is the philosophical bridge between the theological developments of the Reformation and the rest of Western historical and cultural development. Philosophically, Hegel's worldview is carried forward by key figures like Marx, Freud, and Nietzsche (among others). They ultimately do not overcome the transcendent/immanent divide, though (like Hegel) they move us further in that direction.[10] The historical trajectory that Taylor traces culminates in the twentieth century in the "Death of God theology" and what we have described as the blurring of the sacred and profane, the transcendent and immanent. In fact, though, we end up with the complete dissolution of the sacred/profane or transcendent/immanent divide. Thomas Altizer is the great prophet of "Death of God theology." Taylor writes of his work that "the death of the otherworldly God issues in a worldly faith that deems the secular sacred and the sacred secular."[11] At this point, we have the culmination of the Hegelian revolution. As Taylor summarizes it:

> The good news of the Hegelian system is that the Kingdom is not still to come but is present here and now. In preaching this gospel, Hegel declares art to be a thing of the past, and God, in the words of Luther's memorable hymn, to be dead. When philosophy arrives, art and religion pass away. From Hegel's dialectical perspective, the end of art and the death of God are necessary negations through which art and religion are fully realized. When the world truly becomes a work of art, everyone becomes an artist and art as such disappears. In a similar manner, the death of God is not merely the negation of the divine but the disappearance of transcendence in an immanent process that finally reconciles the secular and the sacred.[12]

As artists, theologians, and philosophers increasingly merged the sacred and profane, the transcendent and immanent, we were left only with world—the sacred profane or should we say the profane sacred (the terminology, ultimately, does not matter).

Given the history that he covers and the reading he makes of it, Taylor concludes that secularism is not the opposite of religion but in fact a religious phenomenon. Secularism did not develop independently as a negation of religion but emerged naturally out of it. More specifically, as Taylor insists, "secularity is a *religious* phenomenon, which grows directly out of the Judeo-Christian tradition as it develops in Protestantism."[13] As a consequence, "the gods or their functional equivalents do not simply disappear but go underground, where they continue to support human life."[14] As opposed to scholars who cite the rise of religious fundamentalism as a sign of the "return" of religion, Taylor claims that such a conclusion is mistaken—but not for the reason that many might think. "Religion does not return," he writes, "because it never goes away; to the contrary, religion haunts society, self, and culture even—perhaps especially—when it seems to be absent."[15]

Given where Taylor ends up, the study of religion cannot possibly restrict itself to the study of institutional religions (Buddhism, Christianity, etc.) and their adherents. The study of religion embraces all of culture as potentially worthy of investigation. "Religion, it seems, is often most effective when it is least obvious," Taylor argues. "Sociocultural processes that appear to be thoroughly secular harbor tacit traces of religion, which continue to influence cultural production and reproduction in ways that usually go undetected."[16] The role of the scholar of religion, one who is open to all of culture, is to be a detective—to find the "traces of religion" (behaviors, beliefs, and values) where we least expect them and where they potentially are the most impactful.

As I said, the story I am telling overlaps with the story Taylor tells. I am less concerned with the theological roots that he identifies. Those roots indeed may be as formative as he argues, though I am not prepared to offer an evaluation here. What I have done in the preceding chapters is to identify more current roots. These roots may not go as deep historically, but I believe their influence on our contemporary understanding of religion and the study of religion (especially in the last several decades) is easier to see. And those roots lead us to a similar understanding of our current situation—one where transcendence is superseded by immanence and the sacred/profane dichotomy is obviated.

While the earlier chapters focused on the historical roots of our current moment, the next two chapters will investigate the impact of those historical developments. Chapter 5 reviews some of the developments in the last several decades in the study of religion and culture—especially popular culture. The chapter will provide some reflection on contemporary theoretical approaches to the study of religion and culture (more specifically, the religion *of* culture)—an area of study that is a consequence of the history of religious studies as detailed in the preceding chapters. Chapter 6 explores more deeply the idea of secularization. It then draws conclusions about the future of religion (and, by definition, the future of secularism) and the future of the study of religion. It is necessarily speculative in nature, but I believe many of the conclusions will make sense to the reader who has worked through the full argument presented in this book.

5

The Religion of Culture

Recent decades have seen an explosion in the study of religious elements in or religious dimensions of culture—of phenomena that one would not immediately consider religion. This new area of study is the result of the broader history of the study of religion—a history that I have described through the work of some of its central figures. We will see in this chapter that their theories, ideas, and approaches are peppered explicitly or implicitly throughout this new area of research. At the same time, we will see in the next chapter that this new area of scholarship has emerged during a larger historical trajectory—one typically referred to as the process of secularization. I am not making an argument that religious studies caused secularization, since such an argument would be too simplistic, too difficult to make, and impossible to prove. But there undoubtedly is some historical correlation here between developments in religious studies and larger social transformations.

I propose then that we imagine two historical processes in the Western world that have been in circular relation—both reciprocally reacting and reinforcing one another. One is the modern history of the study of religion. This history dates back in my narrative to the eighteenth century and the Enlightenment. The other is the process of secularization that some scholars date back to the Protestant Reformation, but that really took root in the same Enlightenment period. Both processes are causes and effects. In other words, how scholars thought about religion had a causal impact on the process of secularization while the process of secularization had a causal impact on how scholars thought about religion.

In this chapter, I bring my narrative of the history of the study of religion to a penultimate conclusion by examining the relatively recent study of the *religion of culture*.[1] It is "penultimate" because the next chapter will take the narrative one step further—connecting it with the broader and more sweeping process of secularization and speculating where the story goes in the future.

The Emerging of the Study of the Religion of Culture

While scholars have been interested in the intersection of religion *with* culture for hundreds of years, only very recently has the study of the religion *of* culture more generally become prevalent. For example, since 1991 approximately forty articles in the *Journal of the American Academy of Religion* (one of the most prestigious journals in religious studies) have focused on the study of culture *as* religious.[2] The last decade of the twentieth century featured articles on art, fetishism (from Coca-Cola to baseballs), Rock and Roll music (Elvis in particular), conceptions of cyborgs in literature, television, and film, and "the market" (macroeconomically speaking). The first decade of the twenty-first century featured articles on country music, dance, aquatic nature religion, and industrialism. And in the last decade we have seen articles on Star Wars fans, Bollywood, gaming, and *goop* (the Gwyneth Paltrow brand/website/lifestyle). And across multiple decades, there were articles on topics like film, Disney (both media and theme parks), and civil religion. This plethora of research in *JAAR* is powerful evidence of the growth of the area of study, combined with the emergence of a number of specialty journals like the *Journal of Religion and Popular Culture*, the *Journal of Religion and Film*, the *International Journal of Religion and Sport* (defunct now, but surviving in part through an existing monograph series), special issues of journals focusing on culture (specifically popular culture), and much more.

In addition to journals and other publication series, a number of books have been published in this emerging area. One of the most influential works by a single author is David Chidester's *Authentic Fakes: Religion and American Popular Culture*.[3] But interested readers can find a number of collections of essays as well, such as *Religion and Popular Culture in America*[4] (edited by Bruce David Forbes and Jeffrey H. Mahan, now in its third edition) and *Understanding Religion and Popular Culture* (edited by Terry Ray Clark and Dan W. Clanton, Jr., and soon to be in its second edition).[5] There also are co-authored works such as *The Altars Where We Worship: The Religious Significance of Popular Culture* by Juan M. Floyd-Thomas, Stacey M. Floyd-Thomas, and Mark G. Toulouse.[6] In addition, there are a number of more targeted examinations on the religion of film, sport, hip hop, the economy, and so much more.

Theorizing Culture

Given the burgeoning scholarship on the religion of culture, it should not be surprising that there is no shortage of compelling theoretical accounts for studying culture as religious. A full account of the rich diversity of theoretical accounts would be both too long and unnecessary for my purposes, but it seems imperative to provide some general contours of that theoretical world.

David Chidester's work is often cited in this regard. Published in 2005 (one central chapter having appeared in part in *JAAR*), *Authentic Fakes* was a major step forward in theorizing culture as religious—particularly popular culture. Chidester begins by defining religion "as discourses and practices that negotiate what it is to be a human person both in relation to the superhuman and in relation to whatever might be treated as subhuman."[7] This "negotiating" is why Chidester can talk about the idea of "religious work." Obviously, religions do religious work. But, in a functionalist argument that should be overly familiar to the reader at this point, many other cultural phenomena can do religious work—because many other cultural phenomena can be effective in "forging a community, focusing desire, and facilitating exchange in ways that look just like religion."[8] In short, they are doing religious work because they are "engaged in negotiating what it is to be human."[9] These phenomena are described as "authentic fakes." They are not *really* religions, but they are authentic to the degree that they do religious work—the kind of religious work we saw, in part, in the first four chapters of this book. He summarizes:

> Although the productions of popular culture might in many ways look, sound, smell, taste, and feel like religion, there is a distinct possibility that they are not actually religious. Baseball is not a religion; Coca-Cola is not a religion; and rock 'n' roll is not a religion. But then all kinds of religious activity have been denied the status of religion, including indigenous religions labeled as superstition and alternative religious movements labeled as cults. What counts as religion, therefore, is the focus of the problem of authenticity in religion and American popular culture. Making the problem worse, some religious activity appears transparently fake, including the proliferation of invented religions on the Internet, but even fake religions can be doing a kind of symbolic, cultural, and religious work that is real.[10]

This question of what is or is not religion is avoided or at least approached from a different angle by focusing more on the functionalist questions of what is or is not religious work. In this regard, Chidester draws a compelling analogy between the study of religion in popular culture and the study of the religion of indigenous (non-Western) populations. He writes:

> The study of religion and religious diversity can be seen to have originated during the eras of exploration and colonization, with Europeans' surprising discovery of people who were presumed to lack any trace of religion. Gradually, however, European observers found ways to recognize—by comparison, by analogy, and by metaphoric transference from the familiar to the strange—the religious character of beliefs and practices among people all over the world. This discovery did not depend on intellectual innovations in defining the essence of religion; it depended on localized European initiatives that extended familiar metaphors—those that were already associated with religion, such as the belief in God, rites of worship, and the maintenance of moral order—to the strange beliefs and practices of other human populations. In the study of religion in American popular culture, I suggest, we are confronted with the same dilemma of mediating between the familiar and the strange.[11]

Just as it took a leap of imagination for early explorers and scholars to "see" the religion in "exotic" indigenous peoples (of course, sometimes referred to as savages, primitives, etc.), so do scholars today need to take a leap of imagination to see how stereotypically non-religious cultural phenomena are performing religious work.

Chidester does offer an important cautionary note. "Because the notion of 'religion' can be stretched so far as to lose any analytical usefulness, especially if we think we can use it to refer to anything and everything," he writes, "our understanding of religion requires critical and creative reworking in response to new challenges posed by globalization."[12] To claim that "anything and everything" is religious is to reduce the analytical utility of the term to nil. If everything is religious, then nothing is (since the category works only if there are things that fall outside of it). But despite this caution, Chidester's concept of religious work—drawing from sociological and anthropological sources, among others—can be seen as a crystallization of the kind of functionalist approach to the study of religion whose history has been traced in earlier chapters.

While Chidester undoubtedly holds a prominent place in the theorizing of the study of religion and (popular) culture, he is by no means alone. In 1996, *JAAR* published an issue with the theme "Religion and American Popular Culture." It includes Chidester's "The Church of Baseball, the Fetish of Coca-Cola, and the Potlatch of Rock 'n' Roll: Theoretical Models for the Study of Religion in American Popular Culture," which would later form a central chapter in his book *Authentic Fakes*. But the issue includes other theoretical approaches to the study of the religion of culture. Catherine Albanese, another prominent figure in this area of study, writes of "vernacular religion" to get at the specific phenomena we are describing. "As a linguistic form, the vernacular is, we might say, in a broad sense always creole," she writes. "That is, it always pieces and patches together its universe of meaning, appropriating terms, inflections, and structurations from numerous overlapping contexts and using them as so many ad hoc tools to order and express, to connect inner with outer, and to return to inner again."[13] Popular culture, according to Albanese, functions exactly in this way—taking bits and pieces from the "universe of meaning" (echoing the existentialist concerns of Eliade and Tillich) and putting it together in ways that lead to religious effects (such as connecting our inner life with the world around us).

In the same issue of *JAAR*, Brenda E. Brasher interrogates the concept of the cyborg as represented in modern/contemporary culture and draws important conclusions about the nature of both religion and culture. "For a substantial portion of human history overt, substantive religious groups have functioned as the cultural institutions where the boundaries of the human customarily have been addressed," she writes. "Among the many cultural tasks religious institutions historically have performed each invariably has provided potential and actual adherents with a communal response to the question of what it means to be human. ... world religions possess the common characteristic of a well-developed religious anthropology that situates the human being in relationship to the world and to the wider universe."[14] In a clever twist, Brasher moves from the concept of the mechanical cyborg that becomes human-like to the idea of human beings becoming more cyborg-like as a consequence of being increasingly intertwined with technology (computers, television, etc.). Her conclusion is helpful in thinking about human beings today and how we use culture (particular popular culture) for religious purposes. She writes of the communal and moral functions of popular culture (and, keep in mind, the cyborgs here are humans):

> Today's borged humans may or may not attend an overt religious group; but they probably do view "Seinfeld" or "Star Trek: The Next Generation" or "Oprah" "religiously" and discuss them with others, treating their fictional or quasi-fictional scenarios as a base for determining behavioral norms and creating new visions of community. I suggest that these cultural transactions constitute a form of religion; that for a select group of cyborgs' human-technical interactions constitute the social origins of much of their morality; and that, as a result, America's diverse religious market-place now incorporates a plethora of distinct popular culture faiths alongside its more traditional religions.

> ... cyborgs razor through the technologically-mediated offerings of popular culture to select what they find religiously useful. Developing their social ethics on television talk shows, their theology in science fiction television shows, movies, and books, and their sacred songs in the explosively growing rock music industry, cyborg religionists refashion the pleasure offerings of modernity into an anchor composed of the world to ground themselves within it.[15]

In short, culture (in ways we found in Kant and Hegel) provides us with a rich variety of means to make sense of who we are, to define and express our moral codes, and to construct meaning in our relationships with one another and the world around us.

While the 1996 themed issue of *JAAR* provided a collection of important essays that advanced theories about religion and popular culture, the many essays in *JAAR* in the last few decades that have focused on the religion of culture have done much to sharpen our theoretical understanding of this emerging area of scholarship. For example, in a wide-ranging review essay in 2002, Peter W. Williams examines a number of recent books about religion and space—in particular books that investigated the ways in which otherwise secular spaces fulfilled religious functions (much in the way Eliade did decades before). He realizes that calling these secular spaces "sacred" is potentially problematic. "If to designate a space as sacred is to make a political statement, let us relegate the term to nonacademic usage," he concludes. "Rather, we might instead talk about 'ritual space' as a broader category that would include sites utilized not only for Catholic masses or Aztec sacrifices but also for civic parades, football games, living rooms, or any place in which ritual performance can be identified, and devise finer categories to sort out significantly different forms of ritual from one another."[16] All spaces may not produce the same experiences (we may need "finer categories" to make those distinctions), but clearly there is significant overlap in the experiences of some secular spaces with stereotypically religious spaces.

Williams' conclusion points us in the direction of an ongoing debate among religious studies scholars about the very terminology of their trade. The use of terminology like "religion" or "religious" or even "sacred" has been critical to the study of the religion of culture. But what if the terms themselves are irretrievably problematic?

In 2010, in an article on the conceptual utility of the term "religion," Kevin Schilbrack notes that "if one argues that a culture lacking the term religion nevertheless has practices that are aptly interpreted as a religion, she need not be claiming that they are 'unconsciously' religious nor that they are 'latently' religious, but only that one can legitimately redescribe what they are doing as religious, for one's own purposes, when the label fits."[17] While Schilbrack may have been thinking more about contemporary debates about the imposing of the term "religion" on indigenous or ancient cultures that literally did not have that word (along with all its baggage), his point works just as well for scholars looking to use the term as a way of gaining insights into secular or popular phenomena. Much of the utility of studying the religion of culture is that such a "redescription" leads to new insights about the phenomenon being studied.

In a 2012 essay on *Star Wars* and the fans of the film franchise, John C. Lyden argues for a more flexible understanding of some of our key terminology. "If one is to avoid essentialist understandings of religion," he notes, "it would seem legitimate to allow the possibility that aspects of popular culture can function religiously, and adopt a sufficiently flexible understanding of the term that permits that function."[18] In reflecting on the canonicity of the films and the active and "religious" participation of fans, Lyden concludes that "[r]eligion is not dead, but the media through which it is expressed have changed."[19] As a consequence, we must have a more flexible definition of religion—and we will see below that such a flexible definition has been integral to the study of the religion of culture.

In a 2015 essay examining the 1939 World's Fair in New York City, Kati Curts interrogates the essentializing of both "religious" and "secular." In particular, she focuses on three exhibits at the Fair. "In each of these exhibits," she argues, "religious visions trafficked with secular futures, and I find in the public record of this event that, in bandying between imagery and rhetoric typically understood as either religious or secular, those invested in that World of Tomorrow reassembled these categories in their historic moment."[20] Her conclusion is one that should be well known by now by the reader of this manuscript: "there is no neat line between them [the religious and the secular], either in public life or in private experience. We know these categories are messy."[21]

The rich and diverse theoretical efforts we see in the volumes of *JAAR* (and other journals, of course) are matched in the numerous books that have appeared in the last few decades. While Chidester's book *Authentic Fakes* certainly had and continues to have a significant impact, many other books have made important theoretical contributions.

From a more theological perspective, William Dean's *The American Spiritual Culture: And the Invention of Jazz, Football and the Movies* investigates how a distinctly American cultural ethos has given rise to phenomena as varied as jazz, football, and motion pictures. In describing "spiritual culture," he compares it to an individual's faith:

> A spiritual culture provides that vision for a country, just as a spiritual faith provides that vision for a person. Further, just as a personal faith need not be *explicitly* religious to orient the person, a spiritual culture need not be *explicitly* religious to orient a country. And just as a person's spiritual faith can be unconscious, noncognitive, and emotional, so also a country's spiritual culture can be unconscious, noncognitive, and emotional.[22]

The key to this description is the idea that American spiritual culture need not be *explicitly* religious. Certainly, it includes religious institutions and practices and these played an instrumental role in its formation, but American spiritual culture is not exhausted by religion itself. There is more to it. Indeed, Dean insists that the "American spiritual culture is sometimes more vividly expressed through secular activities such as jazz, football, and the movies than through the overtly sacred activities of organized religion."[23] Dean's work is consistent in many ways with that of Mark C. Taylor, whose contributions have been detailed in the "Interlude" and will appear occasionally through the remainder of this text. Theoretically, Taylor reminds us in a number of books that religion "is often most effective when it is least obvious. Sociocultural processes that appear to be thoroughly secular harbor tacit traces of religion, which continue to influence cultural productions and reproduction in ways that usually go undetected."[24]

While Dean and Taylor come more from (though certainly not limited to) a theological perspective, recent works like *The Altars Where We Worship* (Juan M. Floyd-Thomas, Stacey M. Floyd-Thomas, and Mark G. Toulouse) and *Consuming Religion* (Kathryn Lofton) reflect a generally more religious studies approach to the study of culture. Floyd-Thomas, Floyd-Thomas, and Toulouse begin by noting that "[t]hough we claim to serve things that are sacred [gods, temples, etc.], in actuality we deem sacred those things that serve us."[25] One would be hard pressed to find a more functionalist orientation. Like Taylor, they insist that in contemporary culture "the power of religion rests in the way culture operates religiously in people's lives to sustain values and beliefs that have little to do with traditional faith expressions."[26] They proceed to investigate a wide range of "altars" (entertainment, sport, politics, etc.) where people today (primarily Americans in this case) behave religiously and have religious needs met. They conclude, "In worshiping at these altars, Americans share experiences with other human beings across countless generations who have attempted to fulfill the very human desire to create meaning in their lives."[27] In this conclusion, they share the concerns of theorists like Eliade, Tillich, and others.

Lofton argues that popular culture "supplies a terrain where individuals come together to participate in, support, or criticize an object, principle, or subject."[28] While these functions or activities may sound fairly general, she claims they are constitutive of religion itself. They also are constitutive of consumption and markets. In her book, then, she seeks "to describe how much of consumer life is itself a religious enterprise, religious in the sense of enshrining certain commitments stronger than almost any other acts of social participation."[29] Indeed, she identifies "the marketplace as the primary archive of religion" today.[30]

So, there are a wealth of theoretical options available for those who want to study the religion of culture. But all of them are ultimately functionalist and a consequence of a long history of scholarship in the study of religion—a history greatly shaped by Kant and Hegel, Durkheim and Weber, Freud and Jung, Eliade and Tillich. Once we accept this functionalist approach, then it becomes easy to see how a plethora of cultural phenomena perform these functions—perhaps even more so in our current, more secularized historical contexts. "If ... we adopt a functionalist view and understand religion as what grounds us by teaching us what the world *is*, and what our *role* in the world is," David R. Loy argues, "then it becomes obvious that traditional religions are fulfilling this role less and less, because that function is being supplanted—or overwhelmed—by other belief-systems and value-systems."[31] These other belief-systems and value-systems are not abstractions; they are the institutions, products, and practices of culture. To see how all of this theory looks in practice, let us turn to some specific areas (by no means an exhaustive sampling) or phenomena of culture.

The Religion of Culture

The Visual and Performing Arts

There has been an aesthetic dimension to religion for millennia—literature (oral or written), music, theatre, visual arts, and dance. Over that time, however, it was pretty clear that the arts were being used explicitly *for* religious purposes. For example, paintings in European history that depicted major stories or figures from the biblical tradition were meant to convey those stories to the viewer—to give some insights or power to the stories or to glorify or demonize the figure. But the arts also have existed in a much more secular context (particularly in more recent centuries) as well as for secular purposes. And, of course, the arts can exist in the very wide space between the religious and the secular—having a place on both sides of the spectrum without being easily categorized in either.

The visual arts (painting and sculpture, in particular) are ubiquitous in the history of religion. More recently, however, they have appropriated religious themes or symbols as a way of critiquing religion itself or making otherwise secular statements. Jerry D. Meyer, for example, argues that contemporary "[p]ostmodern artists intent on engaging contemporary culture in issues of political portent have referenced religious images and formats in order to invest the aesthetic artifact with a power and authority still resonating with the shadow of its former religious context."[32] For example, artists might use the imagery of the Christian crucifix in ways that critique the church's positions on women, homosexuality, sexual abuse of children in its care, and more. In this way, "the traditional figure of Christ is made to assume new roles or to foster reassessment of conventional mores."[33]

But visual arts need not engage explicitly religious themes or symbols to function religiously. We already saw with Tillich that even what seems to be explicitly secular art can express "ultimate concern" and thus function religiously. And Mark C. Taylor powerfully has advanced a Hegelian approach in which art is humanity's first revelation of truth, followed by religion, and then philosophy.[34] But the successive stages do not eliminate the previous ones. The development of religion did not bring an end to art any more than the development of philosophy brought an end to religion. And so art perseveres in giving us insights into the human condition and creating meaning—functions that are very much religious in nature.

Music also has been intertwined with religion for millennia. Floyd-Thomas, Floyd-Thomas, and Toulouse utilize Rudolf Otto's concept of the numinous to express the power of music for human beings. They note how music "connects with the depths of human emotion within a listener, allowing for a measure of vulnerability while creating an almost irresistible mood of introspection."[35] Music is pervasive throughout culture, but clearly it can impact some people more than others. "Music fills in the gaps of our lives; it encourages and consoles and heals us," they conclude. "Where music is the experience, it enables us to be introspective, to analyze our inmost yearnings and our social successes and mistakes.... For some, music powerfully shapes the actual experiences of human life."[36] In these experiences, music functions in ways that religious experiences can function.

One of the most significant musical developments of the twentieth century was the rise of "rock 'n' roll." Chidester argues that rock 'n' roll "is a religion because it enacts an intense, ritualized performance—the 'collective effervescence,' as Durkheim put it—which is generated by the interaction between ritual specialists and congregants or, in this case, between artists and audiences."[37] Chidester turns to Victor Turner's famous distinction between structure (the structure of society, from roles and tasks to hierarchies and all the rules and norms that those entail) and anti-structure or *communitas* (those structure-less experiences of unity that humans can experience with one another, that Durkheim describes as "collective effervescence") to make his point. He writes that "rock 'n' roll, as antistructure to the dominant American social structure, achieves the human solidarity, mutuality, and spontaneity that Turner captures in the term *communitas*. It happens in religious ritual; it happens in rock 'n' roll."[38] Anyone who has been to a rock concert understands Chidester's argument. The fans all are brought into a single, unified experience in which they no longer are self-conscious. They sway or sing without worrying about what others might think, because everyone else is doing the same thing. They are one with each other, and transcend the everyday world of jobs, rules, structures, and so on. For thousands of years, human beings have sought such experiences in religious settings and through religious practices. For many people today, the rock concert (or, really, any popular music concert) functions in those ancient ways.

Chidester argues that the rock concert can be understood as a kind of ritualized gift that is given by the performer(s) to the audience. Such a reading certainly is consistent with what we learn in the documentary *Long Strange Trip* (2017) about the legendary band The Grateful Dead. The followers of the band (known as "Dead Heads") often are talked about as if they are a religious community. And the band members (particularly its leader, Jerry Garcia) make clear that the music was never meant to be a commodity, but a gift to the audience.

Perhaps the most prominent individual in the development of rock 'n' roll was Elvis Presley—a performer who has drawn the attention of many scholars in religious studies. Chidester notes that Elvis "has emerged as the preeminent superhuman person in American popular culture, celebrated as an extraordinary being throughout the country, from the official sanctuary of Graceland [his home in Memphis, Tennessee] to the unofficial Web site of the First Presleyterian Church of Elvis the Divine."[39] In a *JAAR* review of a book on Elvis, Norman J. Girardot reflects more generally on Elvis Studies. He argues that "there are various Elvis 'religions' in evidence today [late 1990s] composed of different kinds of fans/disciples/believers, degrees of literalistic and symbolic 'faith,' and forms of iconic and ritual devotion."[40] For Girardot, the study of the religion of Elvis and the culture surrounding his life and music is not only important to understand the person and the culture better, but may lead to broader lessons for the study of religion. He asks: "Could it be that some careful attention to the multifarious Elvis iconolatry and cultic practices (as well as its comedic manifestations) might actually result in some interesting insight into the cultural dynamics and emotional meaning of any emergent religion in relation to the memory of a 'charismatic' foundational celebrity and the communal practices of 'fan-atic' disciples?"[41] The question, of course, is very much rhetorical and Girardot answers it in the affirmative. But the lessons from studying Elvis might go beyond even the study of "emergent religion." "Though often a risky and thankless undertaking," he concludes, "the study of Elvis culture (along with a host of other often neglected and sometimes less than serious subjects, of course) might actually be a helpful vehicle for overcoming some of the academic study of religions' disguised biases, endemic timidity, and misplaced seriousness."[42] Girardot is one of many scholars who view the study of the religion of culture to be a fruitful way of expanding our understanding of religion.

Another prominent musical genre in the United States is country music. Maxine L. Grossman explores the salvific nature of country music in a 2002 *JAAR* article. She writes:

> Salvation is the living core of religion, but salvation can stem from any sort of transformative love experience as long as it offers connection and requires sacrifice. Mamas, Daddies, and grandparents all offer a love that proves salvific but whose efficacy is only fully realized (in both senses of the word) when the children become parents themselves. Partners and spouses may offer such love, although again it is by loving back—and not merely being loved—that characters achieve their religious transformations. God and Jesus, too, in their roles as parent, lover, or friend, provide a locus for religious transformation through the divine promise of loving and being loved in return. Salvific love thus serves as a motif for religious expressions in country music that are both diverse and highly conventional.[43]

Though country music undoubtedly has a strong Christian influence and often includes lyrics that are explicitly religious and Christian in particular, its frequent focus on the salvific powers of love provides listeners from any religious or non-religious background with a compelling ethical message—a message that transcends any particular religion. "The world of country music is a Christian world, and the religion of country music is equally Christian,"

Grossman concludes. "But the country music message is one with universalist pretensions, and so, even with a Christian subtext, the religion of country music necessarily presents its truths as universal truths."[44] In this regard, we might see a parallel to Kant's treatment of Christianity. Christianity is a means by which the universal moral law is expressed—but other genuine religions may do so as well. Similarly, country music may be heavily Christian, but its moral message is universal and available to everyone.

One of the most significant musical developments in recent decades has been the emergence of rap music and the broader hip hop cultural movement. While music certainly is at the core of hip hop, it is much richer than just music— drawing upon African-American cultural history and resistance to oppression. As Monica R. Miller notes, many scholars "gesture that hip hop culture was or is simply the logical outcome, the next step in the long and enduring lineage of black cultural production as a means by which to manage struggle in American life (i.e., from spirituals to blues to hip hop)."[45]

Scholars interested in the relationship of religion to hip hop often focus on lyrics and their meaning. In this regard, they roughly fall into that camp of scholars (like Eliade and Tillich) who take a phenomenological or existential approach to religion—who understand the primary function of religion to be meaning making. Michael Eric Dyson, for example, claims that hip hop is "teeming with religious meaning, holy signifying and transcendent truths that come most alive when artists embrace their abilities to be most human and make the needs of their fellow human beings divine."[46] In his chapter in *Religion in Hip Hop: Mapping the New Terrain in the US*, Dyson focuses on the artist Jay-Z. He interprets Jay-Z as part of a much longer history of African-American religion—particularly in regard to the religious use of language. He claims that "the sermon, the performance of the oratory, links a figure like Jay-Z to critical black preaching traditions within the history itself."[47] What especially connects him to that history is that he is "making the suffering of the poor sacred, focusing on the geopolitics of urban culture, and stressing a powerful urban theodicy." But Jay-Z is not alone. Dyson sees him as just one representative of a hip hop movement that "is fueled by a deep compassion to make arguments about the vulnerable in an intelligible and publically [sic] compelling way."[48]

Indeed, hip hop, like religion, seeks to give voice to the downtrodden and oppressed—insisting both on their humanity and the need to redress the injustices in the society. This religious work is what Anthony B. Pinn describes as "nitty-gritty hermeneutics." This kind of hermeneutics is not afraid to describe and interpret the rough and often uncomfortable reality in which African

Americans live. In this regard, Pinn sees rap as being continuous with other African-American musical genres such as the blues.[49]

For Pinn, rap falls into three primary forms: "status" rap, "gangsta" rap, and "progressive" rap.[50] As musician Zachary Bain-Selbo notes, these distinctions may be a bit reductionist for such a rich cultural phenomenon as hip hop. Hip hop producer and unofficial historian Kenny Beats, for example, highlights the amazing regional diversity of hip hop (New York, Miami, West Coast, Detroit, etc.) that belies an easy division into Pinn's forms.[51] Still, those forms may be a helpful heuristic device for understanding the religious dimensions of hip hop.

"Status" rap, as the name suggests, primarily focuses on attaining the American Dream—money, fame, women (most rap artists are men), cars, houses, and more. While Pinn notes that there is an implicit critique here of American society, he is far more interested in "gangsta" and "progressive" rap.[52] He notes that "gangsta" rap "provides a brief glimpse of the interpretative honesty, roughness, and concern for personal identity inherent in nitty-gritty hermeneutics."[53] But it is "progressive" rap that puts forward the most powerful critique of American society and thus functions as a moral condemnation of the injustices at America's core. A prime example of this kind of rap is the group Public Enemy.

> Through its Islam-influenced lyrics and rebellious beats, Public Enemy provided a "jeremiad" calling attention to the hypocrisy of white America. Chuck D [the leader of the group] also reprimanded African Americans for involvement in their own oppression, while pointing out their potential for liberative action. Such a thick and layered message is the hallmark of progressive rap.[54]

The "jeremiad" is a prophetic identification of society's woes and a call for justice, such as expressed by the biblical prophet Jeremiah. Public Enemy, then, functions prophetically in its relationship to the broader society.

The prophetic function of rap is advanced even further, according to Pinn, by the group Arrested Development.

> Through raps such as "People Everyday" and "Ache'n for Acres," Arrested Development illustrates the self-destructive and community-eroding effects of consumerism and sociopolitical alienation. Seeing through the ideological platforms aimed at the extirpation of black life, Arrested Development offers a regenerative program based upon pan-African cultural nationalism, social cohesion, economic cooperation, and proactive politics.[55]

Central to the group's message is a critique of Black churches, which "enslave them [their congregations] within a web of opiatic eschatology and debilitating consternation. In this way, the essence or genuine meaning of religion is transmuted into a plea for religiously coded banality and 'turn-the-other-cheek' benignancy."[56] Pinn connects this critique of Black churches directly with the Marxist critique ("opiatic eschatology") introduced earlier in this text, concluding that the Black churches (from this perspective) "are the opium of the people" and that the "Individualistic and indolent religiosity promoted by churches is a major factor in the underdevelopment of black America."[57]

It is important to note, however, that Arrested Development's condemnation of the Black churches is not a rejection of religion *per se*. From Pinn's perspective, the group is offering another form of religiosity rather than a mere rejection of it. "Arrested Development musically outlines a religiosity committed to the hands-on deliverance of black people from a profusion of existential dilemmas, without respect to traditional theology and doctrine," Pinn concludes, adding that the group "extols the earth and calls union with the earth a 'divine' source of power and a chief objective of any vibrant religious system."[58]

Thinking about hip hop as an alternative form of religiosity leads us to seeing it as more than just rap lyrics. As artist Bernard "Bun B" Freeman states, hip hop culture "is not just a fad, but for many, a way of life and a means to contribute meaningfully to society, in general, and to communities in particular."[59] This "way of life" definitely has a strong ethical component to it. According to Freeman, hip hop "has used its platform to raise awareness and to push the culture and the world toward new levels of social consciousness and understanding. Hip hop has used its voice to call attention to global and regional humanitarian issues, as well as the individuals normally ignored by the powers that be."[60] Hip hop has defended the defenseless and sought justice for those who are victims of the system (the oppressed, the marginalized, etc.) and victims of specific agents of that system (e.g., those subject to police harassment, brutality, and even lethal force).[61] In this way, hip hop certainly can be seen as a continuation of the social justice message of Abrahamic prophetic religion—from the biblical prophets to the Christian Jesus and on to the Islamic Muhammad—but in an apparently secular cultural form.

Freeman notes that hip hop grapples with important existential and religious questions like "Who are we?" and "Why are we here?"[62] But most importantly, hip hop is about how to be a better person—another key attribute shared with institutional religion. He writes:

> I truly believe that religion should make you a better person. The virtues of the religion you follow should only make you a better person, and draw you closer to people. Religion was designed to bring people together in faith; it was not

designed to be used as a weapon to separate people. Same thing for hip hop: hip hop was created to bring people together. Not to separate. So, if hip hop makes you a better person than the religion that you practice—or the way that you've been practicing that religion—then I would rather you be a part of hip hop than a part of an organization. ... religion is hip hop, and hip hop is religion.[63]

Bringing people together and making them better people are stereotypical functions of religion.

Like Freeman, Miller also is interested in the *effects* of hip hop. In her book *Religion and Hip Hop*, she indicates her interest in "how complex configurations of human actions/activities/practices in Hip-Hop culture at times accomplish certain *effects* through religious rhetorics."[64] A good example is the work of KRS One. In a move that she describes as Tillichian, Miller claims that KRS "epistemologically relies upon and buys into a phenomenological framing of spirituality and religion to raise Hip-Hop culture to the throne of power—*as* religion."[65] In true phenomenological (and existential) fashion, "KRS relies upon the grounding of 'experience,' 'feeling,' and 'motivation' to argue that *this* Gospel [the one created by KRS] is a 'confirmation' not a re-education to those who *intuitively* acknowledge what is already present within them." As is the case with Arrested Development, KRS is not so much rejecting religion but re-framing it in the cultural phenomenon of hip hop. As Miller observes, the result is "the brilliant effect of collapsing religion as culture and culture as religion."[66] Thus, what we have is not an alternative to religion but just another cultural container for it. Miller concludes:

> By using theological language, he [KRS] is attempting to establish that like "God," Hip Hop has a "saving" ability that (divinely) inspired the development of the other ritualized elements of Hip-Hop culture such as graffiti, breakin, and fashion. Therefore, Hip Hop (as a saving force) is constructed as an invisible hand that inspires the aspirations and motivations of people to produce its cultural elements, at times divorcing Hip Hop from the people as an all-embracing divine entity.[67]

While much of Miller's work is a consideration of religious rhetoric and how it functions in hip hop, she does not want to be limited to words and the quest for meaning.[68] She rightfully sees hip hop as even more (just as one should see religion as more). The prime example is her treatment of "clowning" or "krumping"—two dance forms that emerged in Los Angeles in the hip hop movement—as chronicled in the powerful documentary *Rize* (2005). Miller cites one of the dancers in the documentary who refers to krumping as "ghetto ballet" and a form of "storytelling." "The cathartic release provided by this dance modality not only performs life's hurts and pains," Miller observes, "it offers a cultural channeling of hurt in a rather productive way."[69] Throughout the documentary we meet one young person after another who is "saved" by joining a dance group (which in some cases serves as a surrogate family), because the group becomes a safe haven from the violent and lethal gang life that is a powerful force in their environment. In describing their experiences of dance, these young people (some of them seemingly stereotypically religious and others not) often use the word "spirit" to articulate its power. As Miller notes, with one exception "no distinction was made in the film when referring to the signifier 'spirit.' Made clear however is that something 'happens'—an event of sorts—in the midst of Krumping."[70] "Belief" and "beliefs" are also used frequently, and along with "spirit" these "religious" terms "establish Krumping as something that's more than *just* dancing."[71] In sum, these terms point to krumping as a religious experience through a secular form (but, then, is it a religious form?).

Miller identifies the dancing (including its communities and attendant beliefs) as a kind of "'faith in the flesh'—not faith in a theological sense, but faith understood as emphasis and importance in and on the corporeal body."[72] But they are not just any bodies, but Black bodies—bodies that, as Ta-Nehisi Coates so powerfully describes in *Between the World and Me*, are constantly under threat of mutilation and annihilation.[73] The "event" that Miller describes then is "the cathartic release of social anxiety in a shared space of community. In Krumping, the physical body in a theoretical sense represents both the question and the answer: it is that which holds the inscription of inequality—and yet, the body becomes that which provides an artistic release of stress."[74] As a way of physically embodying the messages and meanings of hip hop (ethical, political, spiritual, and more), dance becomes a critical ritual in the religious functioning of the movement.

While hip hop culture may exemplify the connection of music and dance, the two have always gone together. "Music begs to be embodied. It compels us to move," Floyd-Thomas, Floyd-Thomas, and Toulouse write. "Dancing becomes the embodiment of our religious experience of music and provides proof that this mode of entertainment has meaning and validity. Feelings and music and body become one."[75]

Dance, of course, has been part of many religious traditions and rituals for millennia. "Scan through classics of the field and you find copious evidence that people do and have performed rhythmic bodily movement," Kimerer L. LaMothe writes, "individually or in groups, in forms carefully choreographed or spontaneously exuded, as an integral part of their religious lives."[76] But LaMothe is not simply interested in dance as an instrument of traditional religions. In examining the work of contemporary dancers and choreographers, she argues that "these artists made dances in which *dancing* itself appears as a medium for cultivating the kinds of sensory experiences that enable us to think and feel and act religiously at all."[77]

The argument here is powerful and important for the case being made in this book. Take the example of belief. Most people would assume that human beings come to hold certain beliefs and then they engage in practices that follow from and/or express those beliefs. But LaMothe reverses this thinking:

> The ritual exists as a place to practice patterns of thinking and feeling and acting that unfold a human capacity for doing so that has been discovered and practiced over time and even generations by members of their [religious] community. The ritual succeeds, in this sense, if the movements it involves quicken in participants the pleasure of their own bodily becoming. When this occurs, the ritual then becomes real or true for participants *as* the action that enabled their development into persons who *can* experience it as a blast of life-affirming, life confirming reality. They believe in what it represents.[78]

In a religious context, action (dance, in this case) leads to belief; belief does not lead to action. But what is true for a stereotypical religious context can be true in what may seem like a secular context (modern or contemporary dance, in this case). So too with meaning. LaMothe notes that "the *meaning of a phenomenon lies in the patterns of sensation and response that moving with it opens and makes possible in those who do.* The meaning is a function of the bodily becoming it enables—the world it makes possible to conceive."[79] Dance may not lead to exactly the same beliefs and meanings in all contexts (religious or secular), but it can have surprisingly similar results on the individuals involved. LaMothe's emphasis on bodily experience as opposed to or at least preceding belief (doctrine, propositions, etc.) reminds us of the fruitful lines of inquiry recently advanced by affect theory scholars.

For LaMothe, understanding how particular actions or rituals function in a religious context also can have profound consequences for the scholar's life and for how we understand the secular world around us. Her conclusion is a fitting end then to this section on the visual and performing arts:

> Finally, this analysis also suggests that the scope of the field itself is destined to evolve as we create patterns of sensation and response that embrace the bodily dimensions of religious life. For the bodily movements people make in the

study and/or practice of religion stay with them, become them, and shape their experiences in areas of their lives that may not appear as overtly religious. For example, we may begin to notice a mutually reinforcing interplay between the patterns of sensation and response we find in contemporary religious life and the day to day operations of seemingly secular culture. Tracing such patterns will further our understanding of the impact and implications of developments in religion on culture, and vice versa.[80]

Entertainment

Entertainment clearly overlaps with the performing arts. Music, dance, and theatre are performing arts, but they are integral to the entertainment industry as well. For example, contemporary television contestant shows feature individuals or groups competing in dance (*So You Think You Can Dance*) or singing (*American Idol*). And, of course, television shows and movies have their roots in theatre—a human activity that often has served religious purposes (think here of ancient Greece, Rome, and China).

Throughout the entertainment industry (our focus will be on the United States, but the lessons we learn can apply to entertainment across the globe), important cultural values are communicated to the population. Historically, such communication occurred through religious myths and rituals, but now they occur through "secular" myths in television, movies, songs, and more. Floyd-Thomas, Floyd-Thomas, and Toulouse observe:

> Myths in entertainment generally reinforce existing cultural norms. Regardless of their abilities, attitudes, and motivations, all the heroic figures discussed here represent qualities that society finds admirable and inspiring. Ultimately, their accomplishments inspire the rest of us by implying that every one of us is capable of pushing ourselves to be better than we otherwise might be. These characters are popular because they represent values connected to self-reliant and rugged individualism. They continue to reinforce specific cultural and mythical notions of the ideal person, the ideal life, and a better world, a world where evil is always defeated by good.[81]

These myths include the kind of exemplary models (Eliade) and archetypes (Jung) that institutional religion typically has provided its adherents. In short, entertainment reminds us of what we value and how we should behave. Entertainment dates back probably as far as religion itself (think here of ancient oral traditions that come down to us now as texts of myths, stories, legends, etc.), and certainly they have been intertwined in many cultures and for many centuries. At the same time, entertainment and religion can function independently—even if they are functioning in very similar ways. In this section on entertainment, we will focus on very contemporary examples—the movie industry with a foray into the relatively new phenomenon of gaming.

One of the most successful movie franchises in the history of film is *Star Wars*. The first film was released in 1977 and the final film in 2019. The nine films are three separate trilogies—a trilogy of trilogies. Over more than forty years, generations of moviegoers have been part of an elaborate mythology in which warriors of the good attempt to defeat warriors of evil—at times with the aid of "the force," a sort of spiritual power of the universe that certain exceptional human beings (they are called Jedis) can use either for good or evil.

"If there is any popular culture phenomenon that can be referred to as 'religion,' it would be the fandom associated with the *Star Wars* films," John C. Lyden insists. "In the 2001 census in many English-speaking countries, a number of people identified their religion as 'Jediism.'"[82] In his 2012 *JAAR* article, Lyden explores issues of canonicity and authority in the *Star Wars* franchise—topics associated most often with religious traditions. He argues that the films serve as sacred texts—a canon—around which community is formed and values shared. While many people may be skeptical about comparing the values and adherents of a series of films with those of an established and often ancient religious tradition, Lyden finds much more in common than we might think. He writes (this time about the television series and movies *Star Trek*):

> As I have noted elsewhere, however, there is really no reason to assume that those who utilize the stories of popular cultural texts are any less or more likely to be "responsible" to the values within them than are "traditional" religious believers. ... Not all Christians live by the Sermon on the Mount or the Ten Commandments, just as not all fans of *Star Trek* follow the Prime Directives in their daily lives. What can be said about both cases is that the narratives in question have potentially contributed in some significant way to the formation of communal identity, a set of shared ideas about ultimate meaning and values, and a set of practices that reinforce or express these.[83]

The formation of community (with its attendant meaning, values, and practices), of course, is the primary function of religion according to Durkheim.

Lyden also thinks that an exploration into the religion of culture will lead us to re-think the very idea of religion and the idea of "secular" culture. He concludes, "Religion is not dead, but the media through which it is expressed have changed, and this has changed both the 'texts' of religion which comprise its authority as well as the nature of the authorities who decide the value or interpretation of texts [in the case of *Star Wars*, those authorities are the fans themselves rather than priests or other spiritual authorities]."[84] In other words, thinking about films as texts and who is or is not empowered to create and/or interpret such texts will help us in thinking through these issues in the case of stereotypical or institutional religion. Similarly, I have argued that violence in sport (particularly American football, but also other contact sports like rugby and ice hockey) and in Quentin Tarantino films (from *Reservoir Dogs* to *Kill Bill*, *Pulp Fiction* to *Inglourious Basterds*, *Django Unchained*, *The Hateful Eight*, etc.) functions religiously—which then leads us to re-think the relationship of stereotypical or institutional religion to violence.[85]

Perhaps the most powerful and influential entertainment business ever is the Disney company. Whether through films, television, or theme parks, few Americans can escape the influence of Disney (in fact, fewer and fewer people around the globe can escape its influence). Both as an entertainment business and a pervasive cultural phenomenon, Disney has been studied by hundreds if not thousands of scholars. Religious studies scholars are no exception.

"Taken as a whole, the mythic worlds animated and brought to life in [Walt] Disney's work provide Americans with both an escape from reality and effective interpretive tools to make sense of reality," Gary Laderman writes, "in other words, his cultural legacy has as much to do with religion as it does with mass entertainment."[86] He argues that the Disney films express a number of messages that are religious in character. "These messages can be characterized as 'religious' because they teach about order, meaning, transcendence, and orientation," he observes. "In addition, like many religious expressions, they acquire social weight because they are so intimately tied to a desire to triumph over death."[87]

Though we tend to associate myths about death with religious traditions, Laderman finds similar mythological treatments of death in Disney films. In these films, death often is part of a larger battle between good and evil (e.g., the good Mufasa vs. the evil Scar in *The Lion King*). Laderman writes that the films "depict a millennial vision of the universe, where absolute good battles with absolute evil, with death usually imagined as the result of evil intentions, or as a justified fate for the unredeemable."[88] And though evil and death may have their momentary victories, good almost always reigns in the end. Such "happy endings," Laderman notes, are again stereotypically religious.

> The joyful moments following the kiss that brings Snow White out of her "sleeping death" signal another element in the Disney way of death, an element that appears in all the films and contributes to their mythic power in American

culture. That element, found in most religious systems as well, is, of course, the happy ending where death is not really the end but is defeated by the commendable main characters who live on in a safer, purified world. By the end of many Disney films, the threat of death is vanquished and, most importantly, the integrity of the family is reconstituted and made secure.[89]

The focus on family is another key element of the Disney treatment of death. While many Disney films feature the death or absence of the mother (e.g., Bambi), a more recent film revolves around the death (but not really absence) of the father. In *The Lion King*, Simba (the son) is visited by the image and voice of his "dead" father (Mufasa) and advised by him to become the king that he is meant to be. "In the Disney imaginative universe, death can be overcome and serve as a source of regeneration because there are wondrous, supernatural forces in the universe that help us face our darkest fears: abandonment, disintegration, chaos," Laderman observes. "The vibrancy of American cultural religion depends in part on the potency of family relations and the desire to perpetuate the ties that bind individuals to a family unit, realities that are stronger and more powerful than the evil forces in the cosmos that conspire to destroy families."[90] Perhaps no film demonstrates this better than *The Lion King*, where Simba's bond with his (albeit dead) father becomes the source of his strength—allowing him to defeat the evil Scar, regenerate the family, and perpetuate his lineage. As Laderman notes, in "most of his films Disney ends the story with the promise of domestic bliss, a ray of hope in an uncertain, malevolent world."[91]

For Laderman, Disney films are critical resources for understanding American popular culture and the religious elements and dimensions in it. "The centrality of death in these films mark them not only as significant cultural artifacts in the history of attitudes toward death in America," he concludes, "but as revealing cultural texts that communicate popular fears about social disorder, common fantasies about family life as a source of transcendence, and idealistic dreams about American values and virtues."[92] In all of these ways, Disney films are fulfilling stereotypically religious functions.

While Laderman focuses his analysis on Disney films and their religious dimensions, Chidester examines the role of Disney parks in the United States and around the world as a kind of religious escapism. Echoing Eliade's notions of sacred places and sacred time, he argues that "alternative worlds" of the theme parks "have become sacred places of pilgrimage in American and global popular culture. In addition to operating as sacred sites within global tourism, the Disney parks also represent a sacred time, a transcendence of the ordinary time of the present. Passing through the gates, visitors are informed, 'Here you leave today, and enter the world of yesterday, tomorrow, and fantasy."[93] Another powerful critique of Disney more generally—connecting with this idea of escapism—is made by William Arnal. Echoing the kind of Marxist critique we reviewed in Chapter 2, he argues that Disney is like religion to the extent that religion tends to be a prop or support for the dominant ideological beliefs of a culture. "Disney, in all of its manifestations—theme parks, movie productions, and so forth—appears to be simultaneously a manifestation of and a propagandistic ode to American capitalism," he writes. "Its ideological naturalizing and legitimating effects on the given social status quo can be seen necessarily to have essentially the same effects as religious discourse, which has historically served the nearly identical ideological naturalizing function in whatever cultures it has pertained to."[94] In other words, Disney naturalizes the status quo—makes it seem simply "the way things are" and unalterable—by continually affirming its basic principles and ethos through Disney films and theme parks. While Disney may provide some kind of escape, it really grounds us all in a reality that can be incredibly unjust and oppressive. Here we see again how cultural phenomena can serve functions often associated with religion—in this case a function that often can be socially problematic.

Perhaps the most impactful entertainment development in the Western world in recent years has been the rise of electronic gaming. The incredible advances in game design and equipment now allow players to enter elaborate and detailed worlds where they escape from everyday reality, meet friends, form alliances, join teams, and in many cases fight on behalf of the good to vanquish evil. "Humans seek order, meaning, and purpose," Rachel Wagner notes, "and religion and gaming are two of the places we most often turn for these comforts."[95] The key to the religion of gaming, for Wagner, is that game worlds are places where meaning exists and where the player's actions make a difference (contrast this with the modern world, Turner's world of structure, where many people might find a lack of meaning and have a general feeling of impotence in regard to their role in it). According to Wagner, the "intersection between religion and gaming, in all its forms, reveals the human fascination with orderly spaces that evoke some kind of cosmic mapping for us, assuring us that the world is a meaningful place and what we do matters."[96] In this regard, we are reminded of the importance of creation in Eliade's work—and how all creation (even virtual, perhaps) is, in some way, a re-creation of the world or the universe.

It could be that "play" is the key to the connection between religion and gaming. "Scholars who study people have rarely noticed how often the people they study engage in play and games," Shanny Luft observes. "This seems particularly to be the case in religious studies ... because religion and games can appear to be disparate aspects of human experience. But it is the interactive play element of video games that distinguishes them from other electronic media and provides the most important connection to Religious Studies."[97] In short, Luft argues that play is a much more prominent aspect of religion than we tend to think—particularly when we consider ritual activity. Such activity involves a kind of play that produces meaning—exactly what gaming also does.

This consideration of play leads us to a consideration of one of the most wildly popular aspects of contemporary culture—sport.

Sport

In the concluding chapter, I will say more about play, and sport will be used as a primary example of how cultural phenomena can effectively substitute for stereotypically religious practices and institutions. Here, however, I simply will introduce some of the myriad ways in which scholars have investigated the religion of sport.

Sport, like entertainment, dates back millennia and has been intertwined with explicitly religious activities. For example, sports in ancient Greece often were conducted in the context of larger, explicitly religious events—in fact, they were an integral part of the religious events. Today, of course, sport generally is viewed as a much more secular activity. But recent work in the study of religion and sport challenges that view.

Joseph L. Price, whose many works on religion and sport have made him a leading scholar in this area, argues that sport includes many of the basic elements and dimensions of religion and thus can function religiously. He writes of sport in the United States:

> In short, although difficulties exist in trying to specify exactly the nature and extent of sports as religion, sports do exhibit many of the characteristics of established religious traditions. Most important, they exercise a power for shaping and engaging the world for millions of devoted fans throughout America; they enable participants to explore levels of selfhood that otherwise remain inaccessible; they establish means for bonding in communal relations with other devotees; they model ways to deal with contingencies and fate while playing by the rules; and they provide the prospect for experiencing victory and thus sampling, at least in an anticipatory way, "abundant life." In America, quite simply, sports constitute a form of popular religion.[98]

This functionalist approach to thinking about sport as religion is common throughout the literature, and goes beyond even religious studies scholars. For example, philosopher Steven Connor notes, "There is no doubt that, just as sport has a claim to be called 'the religion of the twentieth century,' sporting events do have striking similarities with religious festivals, and may supply many of the same kinds of excitement and satisfaction."[99]

In *Understanding Sport as a Religious Phenomenon: An Introduction*, D. Gregory Sapp and I offer an extensive functionalist argument for sport as religion.[100] We draw on numerous disciplines—such as psychology, theology, philosophy, anthropology, and sociology—to make an argument for how sport resembles religion in some of its basic elements (myths, rituals, etc.) and provides similar goods to people (ecstasy, community, purpose, meaning, etc.) that in the past have been supplied by stereotypically religious institutions. And we demonstrate our argument across a wide range of sports—from golf to rugby, gymnastics to soccer, and many more.

Of course, many people think that comparing sport to religion is ridiculous if not blasphemous. Such people though are increasingly in the minority—especially in academic circles, but even in non-academic circles. "Whether sport is truly a religion or not will continue to be debated by scholars of religion, sports, sociology, and anthropology for decades to come," Floyd-Thomas, Floyd-Thomas, and Toulouse write. "However, few of those analyzing the question will deny that many people, fans and athletes alike, are affected, even formed, by sports, resulting in passion, practice, commitment, and community that mightily resemble or surpass the effectiveness of traditional religions."[101]

One sport particularly rich in religious elements (myths, rituals, traditions, etc.) is baseball—and that sport has been the subject of extensive analysis. In Durkheimian fashion, Chidester focuses on the sociological dimensions of the sport to identify its religious character. "Baseball is a religion because it defines a community of allegiance, the 'church of baseball,'" he writes. "In both the past and the present, this sport has operated like a religious tradition in preserving the symbols, myths, and rituals of a sacred collectivity."[102] The community he imagines is not simply local, for baseball has the ability to draw people into communal relationships in ever-expanding concentric circles. It does so through common histories, rituals, and spaces that bring people together. Chicago Cubs fans identify with one another across the country or even across the world, not simply in Chicago. The community that is formed also spans across generations—living and dead. In 2016, the Chicago Cubs broke a 108-year championship drought. During their playoff run, fans used chalk to write notes to their deceased loved ones on the exterior walls of iconic Wrigley Field (home of the team)—messages from living Cubs fans to dead ones.

Beyond any allegiance to a specific team, baseball fans in the United States generally understand themselves as a national community. As Chidester observes, "baseball supports a sense of uniformity, a sense of belonging to a vast, extended American family that attends the same church."[103] Thus, he concludes that "with its orthodoxy and heresies, its canonical myths and professions of faith, its rites of communion and excommunication, baseball appears in these terms as the functional religion of America."[104]

While Chidester's argument is about baseball more generally, other scholars have honed in on very specific aspects. For example, Paul Christopher Johnson offers a study of the fetishism surrounding Mark McGwire's record-breaking home-run baseballs. These are the balls that McGwire hit for home runs in 1998 when he set the record for most home runs in a season. In the same way that religious relics are treated like fetishes, so were/are these baseballs. "The Ball is approached, whether in Cooperstown [location of the Baseball Hall of Fame] or through the television," Johnson writes, "in order to approach a larger-than-life, super-human presence that transfixes the gaze, mediates between and structurally locates social groups by generating a shared symbolic grammar, and allows contemplation of the self-in-time. We touch the Ball to evoke memories of the past, to 'return' and thereby recharge our sense of the real in the present (Eliade)."[105] Of course, what Johnson claims about these baseballs can be true for all kinds of sports related relics—tickets from games, jerseys, programs, and much more.

Arguments for thinking about sport as religion can be extended naturally to activities that cross the divide between sport and recreation. For example, a 2007 issue of *JAAR* features a number of essays on aquatic nature religion. Among them is A. Whitney Sanford's look at the religious experience of whitewater kayaking. She argues that "whitewater paddling constitutes religious experience, that non-western terms often best describe such religious experience, and that these two facts are related and have much to tell us about religious experience, the body, the material world, and the sacred."[106] Key to her analysis is the way in which whitewater kayaking alters our understanding of the world around us. It allows us to feel more connected to it (literally, in this case, through moments of immersion in the rapids) and leads to a recognition of its sacred character. In her conclusion, she expands the lessons of her analysis beyond just kayaking. She writes, "Accounts of sacred experience through the practices of fly fishing, surfing, and whitewater kayaking reveal that for many these aquatic sports inculcate the emotion and perspective that render the material world sacred and as such should be considered religious experience."[107] Fly fishing, in fact, is taken up in an essay by Samuel Snyder. He argues that "fly fishers around the world frequently describe their experiences of fishing through the use of terms such as religious, spiritual, sacred, divine, ritual, meditation, and conversion. Further, drawing upon religious terminology, fly fishers will refer to rivers as their church and to nature as sacred."[108] As religious practices have done for millennia (recall arguments by Durkheim, Eliade, and others), these recreational activities sacralize the world for us (at least part of it).

In the concluding essay on the theme of aquatic nature religion, Bron Taylor focuses on surfing—"soul surfers" in particular. Again, he shows how this seemingly secular activity leads to experiences that adherents describe as religion, spiritual, and/or mystical, but he expands his analysis to think through how these experiences may have ethical or even political consequences. "I argue that a significant part of the evolving global, surfing world can be understood as a new religious movement in which sensual experiences constitute its sacred center," Taylor states. "These experiences, and the subcultures in which people reflect upon them, foster understandings of nature as powerful, transformative, healing, and even sacred. Such perceptions, in turn, often lead to environmental ethics and action in which Mother Nature, and especially its manifestation as Mother Ocean, is considered to be worthy of reverent care. This produces a holistic axiology that environmental ethicists label biocentrism or ecocentrism."[109] In the seemingly secular activity of surfing, Taylor finds not only powerful psychological experiences that are akin to religious experiences, but a bridge to ethical reflection and commitment (another function of religion). He concludes that "the spirituality or religion of soul surfers involves a sense of connection and belonging to nature in general and the sea in particular and produces concomitant reverence toward nature and a corresponding environmentalist ethics. Its practitioners also report that it brings a wide range of benefits: physical, psychological, and spiritual."[110]

Thus, from traditional major sports like baseball to sports or recreational activities like kayaking, fly fishing, or surfing, many scholars in religious studies are using academic tools of analysis to identify and explain the religion of sport.

Nationalism and Civil Religion

In 1967, sociologist Robert Bellah published the widely cited and critically important essay "Civil Religion in America."[111] Bellah was not the first to refer to the idea of civil religion. Indeed, it has a long history. Jean-Jacques Rousseau, for example, writes about it in *The Social Contract*—first published in 1762. But Bellah's essay is significant in that it unleashed an avalanche of research about civil religion that continues to this day.

There are varied definitions of civil religion, but for our purposes I will use it to refer to the ways in which the nation, as a cultural phenomenon, becomes the object of "worship" for its citizens; and around this nation are a set of cultural beliefs and practices that both affirm the fact that the citizens view the nation as sacred and that lead citizens to experience the nation as sacred.

Let us think just of the United States through the lens of civil religion. A beginning assumption is that citizens of the United States share enough culture in common that they can be said to be worshipping the same thing (America), that they can be said to be practicing the same civil religion. Years after the publication of his famous essay, Bellah raises this issue in "Is There a Common American Culture?" in 1998. He answers in the affirmative, insisting that "there is an enormously powerful common culture in America, and it is carried predominantly by the market and the state and by their agencies of socialization: television and education."[112] Civil religion, then, is a way of describing the religion of culture in a specific national context. But what does this civil religion look like in more detail?

A relatively recent work on this topic is Peter Gardella's *American Civil Religion: What Americans Hold Sacred*.[113] On the one hand, the title of Gardella's book tells you everything you need to know about it. It suggests that the reader will encounter descriptions of those things that Americans hold sacred. And that is exactly what the reader will find. There is no sustained argument about the existence of American civil religion. It is assumed that it exists. There also is very little in regard to arguing for or even clarifying the concept of the sacred—a term that we have learned can be ambiguous and contentious. On the other hand, the title hardly is sufficient in describing the amazing, almost encyclopedic resource that Gardella provides.

While not a sustained argument, the opening chapter of the book does include a number of key theses and definitions. Gardella notes that the "monuments, texts, and images [of American civil religion], along with the behaviors and values associated with them, amount to a real religion."[114] Furthermore, these monuments, texts, and images tell a story that is "unified by four values—personal freedom (often called liberty), political democracy, world peace, and cultural (including religious, racial, ethnic, and gender) tolerance."[115] It is a story that spans across the many phases of American history—from colonial times (the origins of the religion) to the current multicultural era.[116]

Gardella defines religion as "a system of nonrational commitments that holds life together."[117] His point in regard to American civil religion is that as citizens encounter the monuments, texts, and images that he identifies, "the emotions they feel do not arise from a rational conclusion."[118] The emotions both generate and express the "nonrational commitments" that hold together the lives of Americans. We might say that these monuments, texts, and images function to activate affects that are similar to or identical with affects found in more stereotypical religious contexts.

Much of the focus of the book is on objects and spaces. For example, the many monuments and memorials (objects) on the National Mall in Washington, D.C. (space) figure prominently in American civil religion. Indeed, Gardella argues that the nation's capital is a "sacred landscape,"[119] and that the National Mall "is the most sacred space."[120] But American civil religion is much more than just objects and spaces. Just as with any religion, it includes beliefs and rituals.

In regard to beliefs, Gardella points us to key sentences in the Declaration of Independence ("We hold these truths to be self-evident, that all men are created equal, that they are endowed by their Creator with certain unalienable Rights, that among these are Life, Liberty and the pursuit of Happiness."). He also describes sections of the Constitution and the "holiness" in which that document is held.[121] He concludes that the Constitution is "the primary document defining the values of personal freedom and political democracy that American civil religion holds sacred."[122]

Gardella identifies several rituals that are central to American Civil Religion—from the prescribed and proscribed actions that involve the flag[123] (how it is to be handled or disposed of) to the behavior of those who visit the Vietnam Veterans Memorial (the placing of wreaths, candles, pictures, gifts, and other objects at the foot of the wall).[124] These rituals both express the awe of the participants when confronted with the sacred object or space while at the same time the rituals are part of what imputes sacrality to those objects and spaces. Experiencing the nation as sacred is what compels citizens to make sacrifices for it—including the sacrifice of their lives. Sacrifice, of course, is a common action in religious traditions. Carolyn Marvin and David W. Ingle note, "both sectarian and national religions organize killing energy by committing devotees to sacrifice themselves for the group."[125]

While Gardella's book can be read as a celebration of American civil religion, he nevertheless confronts many of the issues or problems intrinsic to that tradition. For example, for whom is the American civil religion designed? Whom does it serve? While we can understand the celebration of all things good about the United States, there clearly are many populations within the country that have had mixed experiences (to say the least). Where do African Americans fit in American civil religion? Where do indigenous peoples fit? Gardella is sensitive and astute in grappling with such questions. For example, he describes the various controversies with American Indians surrounding the carving of the mountain that became Mount Rushmore.[126] He also never neglects the tragic history of slavery and Jim Crow, and recognizes the important contributions that African Americans have made in the history of the country. Indeed, he even identifies Martin Luther King, Jr. as *the* saint of American civil religion. Gardella writes that King may have done "more than anyone to turn the values of freedom and democracy into realities."[127] In a compelling chapter on King's speeches, Gardella argues that "King was using the most basic sacred text of American civil religion [Declaration of Independence] to challenge the actual practices of the United States. In this, he was following the tradition of the Hebrew prophets, who constantly used the terms of the original covenant with God to challenge the practices of Israel and Judah in their days."[128]

While many of the difficult issues Gardella examines are internal (e.g., how disparate groups can come together under a single civil religion), he also looks outward. In particular, he writes about the propensity of American civil religion to advocate for its core values, even sometimes imposing those values on other cultures and nations. He notes that for many decades the United States has been spreading the "gospel of liberty,"[129] and that doing so has led to both glorious and tragic consequences. He also notes that to the extent that the values of American civil religion overlap closely with the values of the United Nations (including the Universal Declaration of Human Rights), the American civil religion merges "with a civil religion of the world."[130]

The thoroughness of Gardella's work certainly is impressive, but it is not without its gaps when thinking about American civil religion. For example, sport is only mentioned tangentially in the text, even though it clearly plays a significant role in American civil religion. Gardella notes that 2 million people each year visit the Civil War battlefields at Gettysburg and 3 million people visit the Liberty Bell. But nearly 4 million people attend baseball games at Dodger Stadium in Los Angeles, and it is only open for eighty-one days out of the year. And while Gardella does focus on music in certain chapters, those chapters are limited to traditional patriotic and folk songs. What about Elvis, Aretha Franklin, Dolly Parton, and Miles Davis? In short, Gardella's work neglects many aspects of American popular culture (portions of which were detailed earlier in this chapter) that are critical to American civil religion.

Chidester, of course, focuses specifically on American popular culture, and like Gardella he argues that it has a missionary character—spreading its power and influence around the globe. He describes the phenomenon as "Planet America." He concludes *Authentic Fakes* in this way:

> On Planet America, popular culture has been carrying the religious dream and bearing the religious pain through vast global exchanges, with their profound local effects, all over the world. Although conventional religious institutions remain vital, defying the predictions of their demise by prophets of modernization, religious impulses have been diffused in uncontrollable, unpredictable ways through the media of popular culture. Traces of religion, as transcendence, as the sacred, as the ultimate, can be discerned in the play of popular culture. As a result, we can conclude that popular culture is doing a kind of religious work, even if we cannot predict how that ongoing religious work of American popular culture, now diffused all over the globe, will actually work for the United States of America.[131]

In thinking about how American culture as religion (or, at least, as religious) impacts the rest of the world, Brasher embraces the basic idea of civil religion but expands upon it. "In 'Civil Religion in America' Bellah predicted that the chief change ahead for civil religion would be its metamorphosis from a national to a global scale," she notes. "Almost three decades later, it is true that a global religious movement has developed as Bellah inferred; however, it is not the expanded American civil religion he anticipated but the mining of popular culture by technologically-socialized people for religious meaning that crosses the political boundaries of nation-states nearly to encompass the globe."[132] While Gardella claims that the American civil religion being exported revolves around values of liberty and democracy, Chidester and Brasher suggest that the values are more diverse and complex and are being promulgated by popular culture.

One of the primary ways in which any culture can impact those around it is through economic activity. And, of course, as the wealthiest nation on the planet, the United States can have quite an impact. Of course, that economic power and influence are part of what allows American popular culture to have a proselytizing role around the world (in other words, that power and influence open up foreign markets to American popular culture). But how Americans think about markets and the economy as well as how they proselytize capitalism around the globe also includes religious elements and dimensions. In short, the economy and economic behavior also are part of the religion of culture.

Consuming Faith and the Market as God

Much has been and can be written about the relationship of religion to economic activity. But as with other cultural phenomena investigated so far, the focus here is not on the relationship of economic activity to stereotypical institutional religion. The focus here is on how economic activity itself is religious—perhaps, especially, in our current historical moment. To make this case, let us look at the religion of economic consumption and then at the religion of markets or economies.

Kathryn Lofton provides us with a compelling analysis of the religion of consumption in *Consuming Religion*. She notes how consumerism has become central to national identity and goals—particularly in the Western world and especially in a country like the United States. Part of what it means to be an American (and to participate in American social life) is to be a consumer. "Consumerism, the theory that a progressively greater consumption of goods is economically beneficial," she writes, "has become the organizing value of social life."[133] For Lofton, it is through consumption that consumers orient themselves in the world, identify themselves, and form and express values. These functions, of course, have typically been performed by institutional religion. Sarah McFarland Taylor comes to a similar conclusion. "Thus, whether possessing the power and resources to purchase or not ..., " she argues, "we are drawn into the cosmological defining 'master logic' of consumption, its social markers of identity, and into the mystical aura of the buyosphere and its ultimate promises."[134]

Within the "buyosphere," of course, scholars have a lot of options on which to cast their analytical gaze. We already examined a phenomenon like Disney above. For Chidester, the fast-food restaurant and franchise McDonald's is of particular importance. "Anchored in a sacred institution, a 'cathedral of consumption,'" he writes, "McDonaldization might be regarded as a powerful sectarian movement within a broader 'consumer religion.'"[135] The restaurant chain is not simply a culturally meaningful institution for the consumption of food, but a symbol of a larger consumer phenomenon. Chidester concludes:

> In that consumer religion, with its places of pilgrimage, times of ritualized gift giving, and sacrosanct objects of desire, McDonald's fast-food restaurant could be regarded as a sect in the political economy of the sacred, competing for a religious market share with other sacred institutions that celebrate the spiritual ecstasy of consumerism, such as the shopping mall [which, of course, often contains a McDonald's in its food court] .... Embedded in the sacred institution of McDonald's, but extending through all social institutions, McDonaldization is the religious rationality of modern institutionalized life.[136]

In a 2017 article in *JAAR*, Dana W. Logan looks at a recent permutation of the consumer—one that nevertheless maintains religious roots. The focus of Logan's work is on actress Gwyneth Paltrow's brand *goop*—a website that sells (among other things) beauty products, clothing, and food, but really sells an upper-class lifestyle. Part of the lifestyle includes various health and wellness practices and products that require both discipline and money.

Logan observes that "*goop* is premised on the idea that its lifestyle is available not to the masses, but to the few. It presumes limited atonement, a Christian, and specifically Calvinist category."[137] But *goop* is not a religious site. While it may toy with notions of spirituality, it is really a secular website and its messaging is not stereotypically religious by any means. "*goop* is 'Calvinist' not because it is institutionally affiliated with Calvinism," Logan argues, "but because it is a cultural carrier of Calvinism's sociological tendency to enact a discipline of everyday life as evidence of election. *goop* performs rigor in an already bifurcated world, divided into the elect and the nonelect."[138] The key to separating the elect from the nonelect is a form of asceticism, and here Logan appropriates Weber in her analysis. Just as Weber examines how Calvinist asceticism could play a role in the development of capitalism (thus, the creation of wealth becomes a sign of election), so Logan sees *goop* as advocating a form of asceticism not for those who wish to increase their wealth, but for those who already are fairly wealthy. Logan writes:

> Protestant asceticism, Weber argues, is not a fight against capital accumulation as such, but rather a fight against consumer goods' degradation of character. *goop* also rejects certain constrictive effects of consumerism through rejecting the feeling of ill-chosen waste (even if it does not reject the luxury that Weber associates with Protestant asceticism). We do not have to choose between ascetic practice as affirming or rejecting the world. These ascetic practices develop disciplinary strength to resist the *effects* of accumulation (rather than the accumulation of capital itself).[139]

This asceticism does not choose poverty to avoid the spiritual dangers of wealth, it chooses the *goop* lifestyle (with its attendant luxuries) to avoid the spiritual dangers of meaningless consumerism.

What Logan finds in *goop*, however, goes beyond just the website and brand. It reflects something more significant happening in the culture. "The promotion of exclusive rigor over authenticity once again points to the strange persistence of a puritan ethic echoing in postindustrial capitalism despite evangelicalism's dominant role in American culture," Logan concludes. "As a boutique lifestyle brand (a particular outgrowth of postindustrial capitalism), *goop* demonstrates the high bar of contemporary asceticism. Like the commitment of a member of the Calvinist elect, *goop*'s spiritual path requires heavy investment [the products are expensive!]. Grace isn't cheap."[140] What we have here then is a new kind of consumerism that embraces elements of religious asceticism (without, of course, being *really* religious; or is it?). As Logan notes, "Having less is the new having more."[141]

James B. Twitchell provides us with critical insights for understanding the power of consumerism and consumer products in our lives—in particular the power of brands in our lives, whether those be as predominant as Disney or as boutique as *goop*. For Twitchell, the key to any brand's influence is storytelling, because storytelling "is the core of culture."[142] Brands tell stories—not just about themselves, but about those of us who identify with them. Disney is a brand that many people identify with—whether the theme parks are integral to the story of their families or the films form part of the narrative of their lives or both. Sports teams are brands too. People identify with certain teams. For example, fans of the Chicago Cubs baseball team not only follow the team on television and attend games, they wear clothing that identifies them as fans of the team and frequently form friendship circles around the team. In short, the sports brands form communities and consequently affect how we behave with others. Such too is the case with videogames, musicians or bands, and so many other brands. "[B]rands are the passwords in the new tribalism, the basis not just of interactions but of interior actions," Twitchell writes. "They are becoming the new Esperanto, the currency of exchange, the meaning of *habitus*, the intersection of self and other. We cluster around them as we used to cluster around sacred relics; we are loyal to them the way we are loyal to symbols such as the flag; we live through, around, and against them."[143] In other words, brands function like religions generally function. Just as religion used to provide the predominant language through which we understood our world ("currency of exchange"), so now brands do that. Just as religion used to provide the predominant meaning for our lives, so now brands do that. Just as religion used to provide the axis (think here of the totem in Durkheim's account) around which our community formed, so now brands do that. Just as religion used to provide us with a locus for our loyalty, so now brands do that. Brands, we might say, are critical mechanisms by which the religion of culture perpetuates itself—by which American civil religion, in this case, is sustained.

Much of Twitchell's focus is on cultural literacy in the Western world and the role that it plays in the community dimension of brands.

> Cultural literacy is the basis of community. Branding is one way to generate this literacy because the brand story depends not just on communal adoption (consumption) but shared individual understanding (recognition). Hard to believe, but knowing what's in a Big Mac (two all-beef patties, a special sauce ...) has much of the same kind of unifying force as knowing who played third base for the Yankees, which, in a way, has the same force as knowing what's in Deuteronomy 2:18.[144]

As the consumer world, the buyosphere, continues to provide us with an ever greater array of products and experiences, Twitchell insists that it is not the quantity that is most important. What is most important is the meaning(s) that consumers get from the products—the stories they can be a part of, the communities that they join, and the sense of identity they receive. Harley Davidson owners do not just ride the same kind of motorcycle; they share a common experience, community, and identity. "Our world is being driven primarily by the desire of the mass class of consumers, most of them young, for deep meaning *inside* the material world," Twitchell concludes. "Plenitude is no longer the goal of the developed world; finding and sharing the wealth of meaning is."[145]

It is little wonder then that consumerism may be displacing institutional religion as the preferred site for expressing our religious natures and fulfilling our religious needs. "What we increasingly share as individuals is not ancestry, religion, literature, language, or ideology but an ephemeral knowledge of the difference between Coke and Pepsi, which Prada purse is hot, or what's in a Big Mac," Twitchell argues. "What we increasingly share as nations is not a unique past [often a religious one] but the same flyby culture of what we are consuming right now."[146] In the American context, whereas once the Bible and church may have been our religious common ground, now it increasingly is the religion of culture. Lofton reaches a similar conclusion.

> Where our social and ritual interests are placed now is not in denominational tradition but workplace culture; not in inherited objects but recently purchased

goods, not archaic icons but in an endlessly rotating cast of minor and major celebrities. At the heart of each of these realignments of religious interest is the explicit monetization of value. The economy isn't understood just as an operational good but actually as an entity capable of the highest spiritual accomplishments, hence the increased diagnoses of the neoliberal economy as a *spiritual economy*. We give spiritual meaning to goods in order to express how much commodities mean to us, and also to reiterate that these goods distinguish us from others. They are *ours*, nor yours. Neoliberalism might therefore be understood as a form of religious occupation of the economy: a way of seeing the self in the world as a calculatingly sovereign person enfolded in systems of power, class, and experience through the selection of particular goods and services. The product is a material way to access something ineffable.[147]

Lofton's conclusions are an appropriate segue to the second area of analysis for us—the ways in which the economy carries with it and expresses religious elements and dimensions.

Several prominent scholars have identified the economic market as God. But what does that mean? Theologian Harvey Cox addresses the question in *The Market as God*. He describes the economy as an *ersatz religion*. "Both words are important," he writes. "It is a religion because … it exhibits all the characteristics of a classical faith. But it is ersatz because the market, like the graven idols of old, was constructed by human hands."[148] While traditional religions have God at their pinnacle, in "the new [economic] theology this celestial peak is occupied by The Market."[149] And just as traditional religions in the past permeated the everyday lives of societies, so the economy and market do today—especially in the Western world and perhaps particularly in the United States. "Today it is no longer helpful to think of markets as just particular zones or as constituting one societal institution among many," Cox observes. "We live in a new Marketist era. The Market now pervades our social imaginary."[150] For example, Cox has a chapter on the liturgical year of the market, with a special focus on Black Friday (the massive shopping day on the Friday after Thanksgiving), Christmas and the consumerism around it, and Mother's Day.[151]

David R. Loy, a Zen Buddhist scholar and teacher, also details the powerful role that the economy plays in contemporary life. In a *JAAR* article in 1997, he argues that "our present economic system should also be understood as our religion, because it has come to fulfill a religious function for us. The discipline of economics is less a science than the theology of that religion, and its god, the Market, has become a vicious circle of ever-increasing production and consumption by pretending to offer secular salvation."[152] Traditional religions generally provide promises of salvation, and usually that salvation entails the cessation of suffering and achieving of happiness (if not in this world, then at least the next). The modern economy, according to Loy, similarly promises salvation—though one limited only to this world. This salvation comes through the accumulation of wealth and the consumer goods and services that such wealth can buy. Economic growth, then, becomes the key to our secular salvation. "So our collective reaction has become the need for growth," Loy states, "the never-satisfied desire for an ever-higher 'standard of living' (because once we define ourselves as consumers we can never have too much) and the gospel of sustained economic expansion (because corporations and the GNP are never big enough)."[153] But Loy is critical of this salvation. As he notes, the happiness provided by the economy or the market is never enough. We ultimately are never satisfied, and traditional religions need to remind us of this fact. "Insofar as this strikes at the heart of the truly religious perspective—which offers an alternative explanation for our inability to be happy and a very different path to become happy—religions are not fulfilling their responsibility if they ignore this religious dimension of capitalism," Loy argues, "if they do not emphasize that this seduction is deceptive, because this solution to our unhappiness leads only to greater dissatisfaction."[154]

Also, just as is the case with stereotypical religions, the economy or the market defines who we are as human beings and what we value or should value. Loy observes, "Our humanity is reduced to a source of labor and a collection of insatiable desires; our communities disintegrate into aggregates of individuals competing to attain private ends; the earth and all its creatures are commodified into a pool of resources to be exploited to satisfy those desires."[155] As a way of understanding ourselves and the world, as a source of values, and as a means to salvation (however inadequate), it is little wonder that Loy concludes that "the market is not just an economic system but a religion—yet not a very good one, for it can thrive only by promising a secular salvation that it never quite supplies. Its academic discipline, the 'social science' of economics, is better understood as a theology pretending to be a science."[156]

While Loy and Cox may be described as scholars who have made detours in their careers to focus on economic issues, the study of the religion of the economy has become central to the scholarship of Mark C. Taylor. Through multiple works he has analyzed the entanglements of the economy with philosophy, theology, and so much more. In a Hegelian manner, Taylor claims in *Confidence Games: Money and Markets in a World without Redemption* that he is developing "a dialectic without synthesis in which religion, art, and economics progressively displace but do not replace each other. Religion first gives way to art, which then is displaced by economics."[157]

As with Cox and Loy, Taylor argues that the dominant economic system in the Western world (consumer capitalism) is more than just a mechanism for exchange of goods and services. It is an ideology and a way of life that shape how we view the world and one another. "Just as religion reconciles people to the inevitability of suffering by promising them a better life in the future," Taylor writes, "so consumer capitalism regulates behavior by holding out the prospect of a material utopia that remains an unrealizable dream for the masses."[158] Also, like Cox and Loy, Taylor sees how the market itself takes on characteristics that historically have been associated with God.

> At the turn of the new millennium, God is not dead; rather, the market has become God in more than a trivial sense: human beings freely err but the market is never wrong. Just as Calvin's providential God weaves good out of evil, so the providential market redeems losses by creating ever-greater profits. The revolution that began with the processes of privatization, deregulation, and decentralization initiated in the Protestant Reformation and extended by the network revolution unexpectedly issues in the emergence of the entrepreneurial market-state.[159]

The belief in the God-like qualities of the market goes a long way to explaining why the dominant political approach to the economy is non-interventionist. "Like the transcendent God, the market is believed to be omniscient, omnipotent, and omnipresent, and inasmuch as human beings have limited knowledge, their interventions are inevitably counterproductive," Taylor notes. "If the market knows what is best, the most prudent policy is to let it run by itself."[160]

The connection between religious concepts/attitudes and the economy extends beyond just the market as God. Think about money. Money always has had a kind of mysterious quality or even religious quality to it. For example, Taylor draws an analogy between how money functions in the economy and how Christ functions in Christianity. "As the mediator between God and man, Christ not only reconciles the divine and the human but also overcomes the oppositions dividing sinful individuals," he writes. "In a similar way, money, as the incarnation of exchange value, mediates the conflicts of individuals who are [pursuing] their own self-interests."[161]

According to Taylor, a major change that happened to money in the Western world was when it was decoupled from the gold standard. In short, it used to be that money was "backed" by gold reserves—money literally was connected to a physical object. Gold is what gave money its reality and its stability. But the gold standard was abandoned in the early 1970s.

> It is no exaggeration to insist that going off the gold standard was the economic equivalent of the death of God. God functions in religious systems like gold functions in economic systems: God and gold are believed to be the firm foundations that provide a secure anchor for religious, moral, and economic values. When this foundation disappears, meaning and value become unmoored and once trustworthy symbols and signs float freely in turbulent currents that are constantly shifting.[162]

In this analogy, truth is a consequence of the connection with gold or God. Religion, including all its moral claims, practices, doctrines, and so much more, is true because it is founded on or grounded by God. Money is true (or, in this case, we might say it has value) because it is backed by gold. Once God and gold are out of the equation, religion and money become nothing but freely floating signifiers whose truth or value is based purely on their relation to other signifiers. Taylor concludes, "Meaning and value no longer are determined by reference to a transcendental signified but now emerge through the diacritical interplay of freely floating signifiers."[163] In such a situation, faith is the only option to calm our nerves—faith that the truths of religion are still true and faith that money still has value. "In matters of economics as well as religion," Taylor argues, "*In the beginning is faith.*"[164] But it is not faith in anything transcendent, for everything now is immanent (though potentially with traces or ghosts of transcendence lingering in it).

In the same way that our religious ancestors wanted to believe in a rational and/or moral order that existed beyond or parallel to the frequently random, chaotic, and unjust reality in which they lived, modern (now, postmodern) human beings have sought to believe in an economic order that is more stable, rational, and fair than the reality in which they live. "Rationality, order, and predictability become all the more desirable in a world that appears to be increasingly irrational, chaotic, and unpredictable," Taylor observes. "The greater the uncertainty and irrationality of the real world, the greater the desire to believe in an ideal world where investors are rational and markets are efficient. But in the complexities of emerging network culture, such illusions have no future."[165] This last line gets to the key critique that Taylor makes about the current expert views of economists.

> According to the models financial economists devised, investors are rational and markets operate efficiently in a world where there is no event that is unexplainable and no risk that is unmanageable. While claiming to be realists,

these true believers imagine an ideal world at odds with the new realities emerging in network culture. Their dreams of a rationally ordered world where every risk can be hedged is as old as time itself. All such schemes are designed to escape time and history and thereby overcome the inescapable insecurity of life. In the final analysis, this dream is a religious vision in which the market is a reasonable God providentially guiding the world to the Promised Land where redemption finally becomes possible.[166]

The redemption may be a this-worldly (immanent) redemption rather than an other-worldly (transcendent) redemption, but it is a redemption nonetheless—and believing in it requires the same kind of religious faith as believing in Heaven. It is little wonder then that Taylor concludes that both "religion and financial markets are, after all, confidence games."[167]

But in an age of the death of God/gold, what happens to that confidence needed to maintain the system—either religion or the economy? What results is a crisis in confidence, one that Taylor sees as permeating Western culture.

Rather than the exception, recurrent crises of confidence in long-held beliefs and long-established institutions ranging from government, the press, and media to the church, markets, and financial institutions have become the rule. This loss of confidence is symptomatic of an often inconspicuous crisis of representation, which occurs when the referents [God, gold, etc.] that once provided secure foundations for thought and action are "liquefied" and begin to circulate freely in worldwide webs whose dynamics we do not yet understand.[168]

The crisis of confidence ties back into the abandonment of the gold standard, which seemed to provide money with a reality that it never had, but that gave people the confidence in that reality nevertheless. "When the coin of the realm is a sign, money becomes little more than a mask signifying naught," Taylor notes. "If currency is an empty cipher, the economy must be a confidence game."[169]

Through our actions (consumption) and beliefs (the market, money, economic growth, etc.), citizen-consumers believe and behave in religious ways. Few of them understand the religious elements or dimensions of what they do or what they believe, but they are acting and believing religiously nevertheless. In this way, consumerism and the economy can be seen as religious in a similar way to how many aspects of culture (some of which are examined above) are religious. And to the extent that consumerism and the economy are inextricably linked to almost all aspects of culture, they can be seen to play a critical role in our broader category of the religion of culture. Whether this critical role is benign or destructive is a question taken up in the Postscript.

Conclusion

So, what do all these investigations into the religion of culture demonstrate for us? They certainly demonstrate that religious elements and dimensions are ubiquitous in culture. In addition, we see that the predominant understanding of religion advanced by these scholars is a functionalist understanding. Religion is not a thing separate from what it does. Religion *is what it does*. It is not a cause with particular effects; it *is the effects*. We can determine that a cultural phenomenon is religious by showing that it does something that we typically see done in or by stereotypical or institutional religion. For example, the cultural phenomena that are not stereotypically religious still fulfill numerous religious functions such as:

- Distinguish the sacred from the profane in terms of spaces, times, objects, and people. In this way, the phenomena structure order out of chaos.
- Provide meaning in our lives.
- Provide ethical norms or guidelines and motivate ethical and political action.
- Help people to organize or structure their time, space, etc.
- Define reality and values (e.g., the market as god).
- Give rise to experiences of transcendence—sometimes ecstatic experiences.
- Build and/or provide access to community.
- Provide a sense of oneness either to community or to some greater "reality" (nature, the universe, etc.).

But what do we gain from looking at cultural phenomena in this way? Indeed, sociologist Steve Bruce thinks we gain very little (if anything). Bruce's concern in this regard specifically has to do with his defense of the "secularization paradigm" that we will examine more closely in the concluding chapter. But his concern is still worth considering here.

> It is unfortunately common for people to work backwards from the consequences or characteristics of religion to a redescription of secular activities as religious. People take religion seriously, so anything that people take seriously is religious. Hence the fanaticism of some football supporters is taken as warrant for treating football support as religious. Religious people often engage in collective acts of worship that temporarily take them 'out of themselves'. So, working backwards, we could say that, because it involves temporary release from the mundane, taking part in rave culture—that world of loud music, drug-taking, and collective

dancing—is religious. There seems little point in renaming as religious secular activities that have some but not many features in common with religion.[170]

I hope, by this point, the reader sees this book to be a more nuanced and compelling argument than the kind of "working backwards" that Bruce describes. But his challenge still merits a response. I would identify two reasons why the study of cultural phenomena through the multidisciplinary lenses of religious studies is beneficial.

First, concepts and theories of religious studies help to shed light on the cultural phenomena studied. In other words, we gain insights about those phenomena that we might not have gained by using other concepts or theories. The idea of religion and our theories about it are social constructs that we have devised as a way of studying particular human beliefs, practices, institutions, and communities. The history of the study of religion has led us to apply religious concepts and theories to cultural phenomena that we call secular because those phenomena do not seem to be explicitly religious. In a sense, we are engaged in the same kind of comparative enterprise that has been at the heart of the history of the study of religion. But instead of comparing Buddhist beliefs, experiences, and practices to those of Judaism, for example, we are comparing stereotypically religious beliefs, experiences, and practices to those of seemingly unreligious or secular phenomena. There are good reasons for applying religious concepts and theories and engaging in this kind of comparative work, since we continue to gain insights and knowledge about those phenomena. The results seem like a good thing to me.

Second, as a consequence of such investigations, we also may be led to see stereotypical, institutional religion differently. It is more like a sport, entertainment, and the market than we imagine. It is a brand. Like a sport, stereotypical, institutional religion divides us into teams with specific loyalties, forming communities of distinct beliefs, and providing opportunities for ecstatic experiences. Like entertainment, stereotypical, institutional religion provides powerful narratives that reveal to us the human condition, move us emotionally, and shape how we view each other and the world. Like the market, stereotypical, institutional religion provides the norms of human interaction, gives us goals or goods to achieve, and convinces us that there is a stable reality or foundation underlying the world in which we live. And like a brand, it is a locus around which our lives and communities often revolve. In other words, the comparative work advocated here demystifies stereotypical, institutional religion—allowing us to see it in a new light.

In sum, the idea of religion gives us a common and powerful language to understand the most important aspects or elements of some of what human beings do individually and collectively. Religion is less a thing out there in the world, than a language for effectively talking about humanly important things. In that sense, religion cannot be restricted to a church, mosque, temple, or other stereotypically religious institution.

Bruce seems concerned about the kind of work detailed and described in this chapter because he has an interest in defending and advancing an argument (one, by the way, to which I am sympathetic) about secularization. So, what about the future of religion—stereotypical or not? And what does the future hold for the study of religion? We take up these questions in the concluding chapter.

6

What Happens Next? Some Concluding Remarks

In the previous chapter I detailed an inevitable consequence of the history of the study of religion (at least that history as shaped by some of its most prominent figures). My claim is that that history leads us to understand culture more deeply—in all of its glorious and amazing diversity. This greater understanding is what I call the religion of culture. But the history of the study of religion also leads to taking institutional religion down a peg or two—down from what many people may think is its rightful place at the top of culture (or, at least, as a unique part of culture). I have argued that institutional religion is not at the top of culture or a unique part of culture. It is merely one of many cultural phenomena that express what we can call our religious nature. So, to some extent, the subtitle of this work is misleading. Institutional religion is not so much "irrelevant," but simply only as relevant as other cultural phenomena.

This final chapter goes one step further. The question now is "What happens next?" And here the subtitle becomes more appropriate. For once institutional religion becomes just one of many cultural phenomena, it really does become irrelevant to many people. It is not the only means to salvation (worldly salvation, in this case), to insights about the human condition, to questions and answers about who we are and how we should be, and so much more that we typically identify with institutional religion. So, what *does* happen next? What does the future hold for institutional religion? These are questions, of course, that are central to thinking about secularization. So, in this chapter we will do some of that thinking. We will look at several accounts of secularism and secularization, consider humanism as an alternative to institutional religion (using sport as an example), make a few predictions about the future of religion (including the study of religion), and end with hope—hope that the very dramatic cultural changes that I think we are going through will nonetheless continue us on a path to a greater understanding of the human condition and lead to even more effective ways for us to be together.

The Truth and Folly of Secularization

We already have encountered several theorists who thought about secularization and secularism, even if they did not always use the terminology. For example, Sigmund Freud argues that humanity is growing out of its adolescence (characterized by religious belief and behavior) and into adulthood (characterized by reason and science). Karl Marx claims that as human beings (led by workers) liberate themselves (a kind of worldly salvation) from the tyranny of capitalism, they will put religion behind them and work toward creating the communist ideal (a sort of heaven on earth). My focus here, however, will be on more contemporary theorists.

There are many different questions and approaches for thinking about secularization and secularism. I will focus on three key sets of questions.

1. Is secularization occurring? In other words, are we becoming a secular society?
2. What are the causes of secularization? And did/do those causes necessarily lead to secular societies?
3. What does the future hold? Are human beings inevitably going to be more secular? Is religion (as we typically understand it) really going away? And how do these cultural changes impact individuals and societies?

These are incredibly weighty questions, and answers are by no means easy or clear. But they are the kinds of questions that I argue follow directly out of the history of the study of religion that I have shared in this work. We will begin with the first set of questions, but all of these questions are intertwined and so cannot be easily delineated.

Prominent theologian John Milbank claims, "In the early twenty-first century, the global presence of religion is growing—in terms of active numbers in the Third World, and more sporadically in terms of public influence in the West."[1] This "return of religion" argument certainly is not limited to Milbank. Many theologians and scholars of religion make it. They point to the rise of fundamentalisms, for example, as evidence of the endurance of religion—especially in places like Africa and the Middle East (Islam) and the United States (conservative or evangelical Christianity). Milbank and others make interesting arguments, but they often fail to account for or even attend to the wealth of data that undermines their positions.

One of the most renowned sociologists studying secularism and secularization is Steve Bruce. In *Secularization: In Defence of an Unfashionable Theory*, Bruce presents the kind of data that makes a powerful argument that secularization is indeed occurring—and has been for quite some time. The "unfashionable theory" that he seeks to defend is what he calls the "secularization paradigm."

Bruce explains that the secularization paradigm "aims to explain one of the greatest changes in social structure and culture: the displacement of religion from the centre of human life."[2] This cultural change perhaps is most prominent in the Western world, and that is the focus of Bruce's work and will be for us as well. Bruce relies extensively on polling and survey data to advance his argument. For example, he notes the dramatic decline in European countries in those who claim religious affiliation or attend church on a regular basis. Though the numbers alone are striking (e.g., between 1970 and 1999, the number of Belgians who said they attend church once a week or more declined from 52 percent to 10 percent; in religiously fervent Ireland, 1,375 men joined the priesthood in 1965, but only 201 did so in 1994, and only 61 in 2000), what Bruce finds most compelling is "the pattern. In no cases has there been a reversal of decline."[3] Even in the United States, which is considered to be much more religious than its Western counterparts, church attendance has declined significantly in the last century.[4] In addition, the number of people who claim to have no religion has increased from 2 percent in 1948 to as much as 16 percent in the first decade of the twenty-first century.[5] Indeed, a 2019 Pew Research Center survey indicates that a quarter of the American population claim to be atheist, agnostic, or "nothing in particular"[6]—hardly the "return of religion" championed by Milbank and others. The headline to the Pew report states it starkly: "In U.S., Decline of Christianity Continues at Rapid Pace"—and, just to be clear, Christianity is *not* being replaced by some other institutional religion in the United States.

According to Bruce, even those who continue to claim some religious identification have been changed by secularization—particularly in regard to the Western turn toward reason and science. For Bruce, we see this change in the increasingly liberal character of Western churches and their members. He writes:

> Few Protestants now believe that the Bible is the revealed Word of God, that Christ really was the Son of God, that God created the world in six days, that the Bible miracles really happened, that there is an actual heaven and hell, and so on.

Rather, the basic Christian ideas have been internalized and psychologized. Evil and sin have been turned into alienation and unhappiness. The vengeful God has been replaced by Christ the inspiring Big-brother or Christ the therapist. The purpose of religion is no longer to glorify God: it is to help find peace of mind and personal satisfaction.[7]

These changes in the beliefs of the adherents are reflected in the power of the churches as well. "The once-hegemonic churches have lost significant power, prestige, and popularity, and the new entrants to the market have made little headway in filling the gaps," Bruce concludes. "Across almost all strands of Christianity there has been a significant decline in doctrinal orthodoxy, a shift in focus from the next world to this one, and a weakening of the ties of obedience."[8]

Bruce uses the idea of a garden as a metaphor for what is happening across Western culture. "The best way I can convey the change from the religious to the secular is to use the metaphor of an abandoned garden in the countryside," he writes. "Without constant pruning, selective breeding, and weeding, the garden loses its distinctive character, as it is overtaken by the greater variety of plant species in the surrounding wilderness."[9] In this case, the change to a more secular society was not the consequence of some radical digging up of the garden (religion), but simply thoughtlessness and neglect. People (most, at least) did not so much actively attack religion; they simply stopped caring about it.

There are a number of causes that Bruce provides for this cultural change. For example, the privatization of religion that works hand-in-hand with Western individualism robs religion of much of its power. In other words, when institutional religion becomes more of an individual preference rather than a societal norm, it is well on its way to decline. Bruce insists that he is "making an empirical causal claim: because privatized, compartmentalized, and individualized religion attracts less commitment, is harder to maintain, and is more difficult to pass on intact to the next generation, it fails to make up the ground lost by, and declines faster than, traditional religion."[10] For Bruce, the modern world is characterized by individual freedom or autonomy. As such, individuals are choosing other cultural institutions or activities for meaning, significance, social bonds, and more. "At its most general," he writes, "modernization increases the autonomy of the individual, increases the degree of variation in the religious culture, and weakens the plausibility of religious belief systems."[11]

The cultural shift to greater and greater individualism and freedom is not something that Bruce sees changing in the future. In fact, recent history (the last fifty years or so) would indicate that we are trending toward greater individualism and freedom. Consequently, traditional religion will find itself in an ever more challenging environment in competing for people's attention, commitment, and devotion. "Given the almost universal preference for greater personal autonomy and the strong international pressures that promote it," he predicts, "it is difficult to see how any religious tradition, no matter how popular, can remain immune."[12]

If I were to extend the garden metaphor, I would say that the other "plant species" that are coming to overtake the garden are all those cultural phenomena discussed in the last chapter that fulfill many of the functions that stereotypical or institutional religion fulfills. I noted in the last chapter that Bruce is reticent to call such cultural phenomena "religious," but he nevertheless recognizes their role in displacing traditional religion. For him, such displacement is further confirmation of secularization. He concludes, "That people once found relief from their mundane lives through prayer, worship, and meditation and now find it through rave music and pretending to be someone else on the Internet seems like secularization."[13]

Years before Bruce, another prominent sociologist was making similar claims about secularization and its inevitability. In *The Sacred Canopy: Elements of a Sociological Theory of Religion*, Peter L. Berger defines secularization as "the process by which sectors of society and culture are removed from the domination of religious institutions and symbols."[14] He also identifies several potential causes.

- Protestantism eliminated the church as the intermediary between God and the individual. Thus, there was a diminishment of the role of the church in the Western world—accelerating secularization.[15]
- Individualism (which Berger connects historically to Protestantism in the Western world) has led to institutional religion being a private affair rather than a public one. Private religiosity "cannot any longer fulfill the classical task of religion, that of constructing a common world within which all of social life receives ultimate meaning binding on everybody."[16] When institutional religion no longer serves that (Durkheimian?) function, it loses its power and influence—thus accelerating secularization.
- Religious pluralism has challenged the objective truth and credibility of all religions. "The pluralistic situation multiplies the number of plausibility structures competing with each other. *Ipso facto*, it relativizes their religious contents," Berger argues. "More specifically, the religious contents are 'de-objectivated,' that is, deprived of their status as taken-for-granted, objective reality in consciousness."[17] In a situation of religious monopoly, the single

religion seems obviously true to people. In a situation of religious pluralism, all religions may lose their obviousness or givenness.
- Religious pluralism creates a sort of consumer market for religion—a market where choices are not about the "truth" but merely one's taste or preference. As Berger claims, "the dynamics of consumer preference is introduced into the religious sphere. Religious contents become subjects of 'fashion.'"[18] Again, in the pluralistic religious marketplace, any particular religion loses its power and influence over adherents—thus accelerating secularization.

As a consequence of these and other reasons, Berger concludes that "Probably for the first time in history, the religious legitimations of the world have lost their plausibility not only for a few intellectuals and other marginal individuals but for broad masses of entire societies."[19]

Berger is no Freud or Marx. He does not champion secularization. He is concerned about the process of secularization and worries about the impact on people. He believes that it leads to "severe anomy and existential anxiety."[20] As we already have seen, these are concerns shared by Durkheim, Weber, Jung, Eliade, and Tillich. In *The Sacred Canopy*, Berger does seem resigned not only to the process of secularization but to its continued gains in the Western world. More recently, however, he has argued that his previous position was wrong. He now claims that "the assumption that we live in a secularized world is false. The world today ... is as furiously religious as it ever was, and in some places more so than ever."[21] As evidence, Berger notes the rise in the last half century of "conservative or orthodox or traditionalist movements that are on the rise almost everywhere."[22] Berger grants that Europe may be an exception to his argument, but without the kind of data that we saw with Bruce it is hard to believe his claim that there "is no reason to think the world of the twenty-first century will be any less religious than the world is today."[23] As we saw with Bruce, there is in fact good reason to think that the twenty-first century will be less religious (in that stereotypical sense) than the twentieth century.

"The religious impulse, the quest for meaning that transcends the restricted space of empirical existence in this world, has been a perennial feature of humanity," Berger notes. "It would require something close to a mutation of the species to extinguish the impulse for good."[24] In some ways, I agree with Berger. The problem is that he views this impulse as leading to the continuation of stereotypical, institutionalized religion. My claim, of course, is that we can both affirm this impulse (we can call it religious or something else; the terminology ultimately is not important) while recognizing that stereotypical, institutionalized religion is fading. The impulse simply is finding other cultural phenomena to serve and express itself. Part of the problem with Berger is an uncritical acceptance of a strict, impermeable dichotomy of the religious and the secular.

Anthropologist Talal Asad argues that we need to contest the boundary between the religious and the secular. He sees the divide between the religious and the secular going back centuries. In the Western world, he agrees with others in identifying the Reformation as a critical moment in that divide—the beginning of the withdrawal of religion from the public sphere and into the private sphere alone (a withdrawal typically in the Western world). But this withdrawal not only changed Western society, it shaped how we defined religion. Asad writes:

> By the time we get to Kant, one can see how a private religion of sentimental sociability was beginning to take the place of a public religion of passionate conviction. It has become a commonplace among historians of modern Europe to say that religion was gradually compelled to concede the domain of public power to the constitutional state, and of public truth to natural science. But perhaps it is also possible to suggest that in this movement we have the construction of religion as a new historical object: anchored in personal experience, expressible as belief-statements, dependent on private institutions, and practiced in one's spare time.[25]

In other words, it is not simply that there were religion and the secular world in some distant past, and then the process of secularization changed the balance of power. The very idea of religion and the idea of the secular grew out of the historical dynamics that occurred over several centuries (some of it, especially in regard to the study of religion, covered in previous chapters). Religion and the secular, as categories, were created together by philosophers, scholars of religion, and many other thinkers across academic disciplines.

Asad's approach is to avoid essentialism of any kind. There is not some essential religion and some essential secular. Rather, these are contested and contentious terms that have changed throughout history.[26] Thus, in *Formations of the Secular* he writes:

> The analyses that I offer here are intended as a counter to the triumphalist history of the secular. I take the view, as others have done, that the "religious" and the "secular" are not essentially fixed categories. However, I do not claim that if one stripped appearances one would see that some apparently secular institutions were *really* religious. I assume, on the contrary, that there is nothing *essentially* religious, nor any universal essence that defines "sacred language" or "sacred experience."[27]

Of course it is true that the religious and the secular are social constructs that are inherently unstable and dynamic. That said, this fact then gives scholars like myself and all those highlighted in the previous chapter the freedom to play with the language of religion vis-a-vis a wide variety of cultural phenomena. Some of that play may seem pointless or even silly in the end, but some of it will help reveal important insights about those phenomena—insights that other language might not reveal.

Perhaps the most prominent recent scholar on the secular is philosopher Charles Taylor. His monumental work *A Secular Age* has become the kind of work that must be grappled with (and for good reason) by anyone writing on the subject. So, here we go.

Though Taylor mentions Tillich and Eliade really only in passing, his approach nevertheless echoes the kind of phenomenological and existential orientation we found in those scholars. Early in his work he declares that his focus is "on the different kinds of lived experiences involved in understanding your life in one way or the other, on what it's like to live as a believer or an unbeliever."[28] Thinking historically, his question is: "Why was it virtually impossible not to believe in God in, say, 1500 in our Western society, while in 2000 many of us find this not only easy, but even inescapable?"[29]

For Taylor, there are a number of ways in which we can distinguish the lived experience of the believer from that of the unbeliever. It is not simply about whether or not one believes in certain propositions. It has to do with how one understands oneself in the world, in relation to other people, in relation to possible unseen forces, powers, or spirits, and in relation to the idea of God. Here are just a few examples.

- **Fullness**: For Taylor, "fullness" is a lived condition. It is when "life is fuller, richer, deeper, more worthwhile, more admirable, more what it should be."[30] How that is achieved will differ depending on whether one is a believer or unbeliever. Taylor notes that "for believers, the account of the place of fullness requires reference to God, that is, to something beyond human life and/or nature; where for unbelievers this is not the case; they rather will leave any account open, or understand fullness in terms of a potentiality of human beings understood naturalistically."[31] Historically, then, "we have moved from a world in which the place of fullness was understood as unproblematically outside of or 'beyond' human life, to a conflicted age in which this construal is challenged by others which place it (in a wide range of different ways) 'within' human life."[32] To return to a distinction that has been central to this work and that Taylor famously embraces, we have here the difference between a transcendent orientation as opposed to an immanent orientation.

- **Enchanted (religious) versus disenchanted (secular) worlds**: The idea of enchantment or disenchantment has been prevalent in the discussion of secularism. For Taylor, "disenchantment is the dissolution of the 'enchanted' world, the world of spirits and meaningful causal forces, of wood sprites and relics."[33] Most importantly, for someone who lives in an enchanted world, meaning comes from outside the "natural" world (transcendent); while for someone who lives in a disenchanted world, meaning may be generated and shared among individuals but it is still restricted to the human psyche and the here and now (immanent).
- **Porous (religious) versus buffered (secular) self**: The difference between the porous self and the buffered self is connected with the enchanted/disenchanted distinction. The porous self is one that lives in an enchanted world where the various spirits and forces can permeate their being and have effects. The buffered self lives in the disenchanted world—immune to those same spirits and forces mainly as a consequence of a rational and/or scientific rejection of them.

The major historical shift that Taylor brilliantly details in philosophy, religion, social sciences, and more is the move from a world that includes a strong sense of transcendence (that there are spirits, forces, gods or God, etc., that influence or impact us and that are sources of meaning) to one of immanence where everything is of this world (there is no transcendent). Taylor describes the latter as the immanent frame. He writes that "this frame constitutes a 'natural' order, to be contrasted to a 'supernatural' one, an 'immanent' world, over against a possible 'transcendent' one."[34] Key characteristics of the immanent frame include modern science, individualism, the buffered self, instrumental reason, and "action in secular time."[35] "This immanent frame is neither atheistic nor theistic," Benjamin Schewel claims. "It simply brackets metaphysical and theological concerns in a way that premodern cultures did not and leaves the decision about whether or in which way to believe up to individuals."[36] Here we see the consequences of individualism and the privatization of religion.

In *Sources of the Self*, published nearly twenty years before *A Secular Age*, Taylor elaborates on how important frameworks or frames are for individuals. He states that he wants "to defend the strong thesis that doing without frameworks is utterly impossible for us."[37] Frameworks are critical to our very ability to have an identity. Our identities then guide us in figuring out what is good or bad, who we are or who we ought to be, and what is meaningful or not.[38] Our identities also connect us with specific communities.[39]

Religious or transcendent frames have their problems, but they generally are effective in helping people construct the kind of full identities described above. The immanent frame, then, comes with certain dangers. Taylor identifies a number of aspects of what he calls the "malaise of immanence":

> I have distinguished three forms which the malaise of immanence may take: (1) the sense of the fragility of meaning, the search for an over-arching significance; (2) the felt flatness of our attempts to solemnize the crucial moments of passage in our lives; and (3) the utter flatness, emptiness of the ordinary.[40]

All three forms are central to Eliade's critique of modern Western society and remind us of Durkheim's concern about anomie. For Taylor, the problem of meaning is particularly important, and really is the umbrella under which the latter two forms fall (the "flatness" of "crucial moments of passage" and the "utter flatness, emptiness of the ordinary" are both a result of a lack of meaning). "This malaise is specific to a buffered identity," Taylor notes, "whose very invulnerability opens it to the danger that not just evil spirits, cosmic forces or gods won't 'get to' it, but that nothing significant will stand out for it."[41]

Certainly, Taylor believes that the problem of meaning is particularly acute for modern humanity, but he is careful to note that this does not mean that the problem of meaning has been at the forefront of all of history. In other words, it is too simplistic to argue that human beings always have sought meaning to their lives—and that the lack of meaning in the secular age necessarily means that religious ages were all about providing meaning. "Just because this [problem of meaning] looms as [a] big issue for *us* in a secular age," Taylor observes, "it is all too easy to project it on all times and places. But there is in the end something incoherent in this move."[42] The problem of meaning for those in the secular age may not be the same kind of problem of meaning for those in religious ages. As Taylor notes, just "because everyone recognizes that they [the 'malaise of immanence' in all its forms] come onto our horizon, or onto our agenda, with the eclipse of transcendence," it "doesn't follow that the only cure for them is a return to transcendence."[43]

Whether or not a simple "return to transcendence" is helpful or even possible, Taylor clearly believes that modern humanity needs something to address the "malaise of immanence." The challenge of the problem of meaning is not just for the individual, it is a social problem because it undermines our belief and trust in institutions and one another. "As our public traditions of family, ecology, even polis are undermined or swept away," Taylor notes, "we need new languages of personal resonance to make crucial human goods alive for us again."[44]

These new languages are necessarily accompanied by new practices and new social forms that help human beings address their most pressing needs. But they are not created *ex nihilo*. They develop out of a long religious history and thus bear the imprint of that history. In this regard, Taylor acknowledges the prevalence of what we might call remnants of the past—sometimes diminished versions of earlier beliefs or practices, sometimes radically transformed versions of earlier beliefs or practices. Midway through *A Secular Age*, Taylor draws an important analogy between religious "ghettos" (particularly those of the Catholic Church) and secular clubs or political/social organizations.

> [The ghetto] was meant to ensure that people would be schooled, play football, take their recreation, etc., exclusively among co-religionists. The Catholic Church was the major architect of such ghettos, building them even in the Anglo-Saxon world; but in the Netherlands, for instance, Protestants did likewise. As a matter of fact, one might even claim that the "Confessional Age" extends beyond the boundaries of Christian Churches. One can see certain analogies with Social Democratic and later Communist parties, with their women and youth groups, sports clubs, cultural organizations, and the like. The aims here were not dissimilar to those underlying Catholic "ghettos": to penetrate more deeply the lives of the followers, to bond them more closely together, and to minimize contact with outsiders.[45]

The more modern clubs and organizations came to function much like churches, helping to create identity and solidarity among the people. Where once our identities were tied to the church and then later to the nation, Western culture provides its citizens with so many other ways in which to identify oneself. "One could argue that for many young people today, certain styles, which they enjoy and display in their more immediate circle, but which are defined through the media, in relation to admired stars—or even products—occupy a bigger place in their sense of self," Taylor speculates, "and that this has tended to displace in importance the sense of belonging to large scale collective agencies, like nations, not to speak of churches, political parties, agencies of advocacy, and the like."[46] Here, Taylor is pointing to what I have called the religion of culture, which, among other functions, provides a variety of opportunities for community building and identity formation.

Of course, identity formation and community building are intrinsically intertwined. Identity formation always is achieved with others, and community building necessarily leads to identity. For identity formation or community building to occur, people must first be brought together. Bringing people together has been a crucial function fulfilled by religious institutions. Today, being with others is achieved in other ways. As Taylor notes, for example, "city life has developed other ways of being-with, for instance, as we each take our Sunday walk in the park; or as we mingle at the summer street-festival, or in the stadium before the play-off game."[47]

For Taylor, certain forms of "being-with" give rise to powerful emotional and communal experiences. In this regard, he borrows Victor Turner's distinction between structure and *communitas* (anti-structure)—a distinction we highlighted in Chapter 2. He writes:

> We have a sense of it [*communitas*] in our daily lives. We still feel the need to "get away from it all", to cut out and "recharge our batteries", away, on holiday, outside our usual roles. There are certainly carnival-type moments: public holidays, football matches—here, like their predecessors, hovering on the brink, sometimes over the brink of violence. Communitas breaks out in moments of exceptional danger or bereavement, as with the crowds mourning Princess Di.[48]

The reason why we need these experiences of *communitas*, of course, is that living only in and through structure is unbearable. As Taylor notes, "the pains of structure, its rigidities, injustices, insensitivity to human aspiration and suffering, having lost their earliest social outlet, drive us back to this dream [of *communitas*]. We have probably not seen the last of it."[49]

Not only is the dream not dead, but we in fact find ways to bring it to reality on a regular basis. We already have indicated where Taylor sees it throughout contemporary society—in the festival or carnival experiences that periodically break through our everyday plodding through structure. These are powerful communal experiences. "People still seek those moments of fusion, which wrench us out of the everyday, and put us in contact with something beyond ourselves," he writes. "We see this in pilgrimages, mass assemblies like World Youth Days, in one-off gatherings of people moved by some highly resonating event, like the funeral of Princess Diana, as well as in rock concerts, raves, and the like."[50] Each such occasion "connects us again to the 'communitas' dimension of our society, where beyond the hierarchical divisions of the established order, we are together as equal human beings."[51]

Besides Turner, Taylor also turns to Durkheim to explicate the point he is making—particularly Durkheim's notion of "collective effervescence." Using rock concerts and Princess Di's funeral as examples, Taylor insists that these communal events give rise to "an emotion, a powerful common feeling [collective effervescence]. What is happening is that we are all being touched together, moved as one, sensing ourselves as fused in our contact with something greater, deeply moving, or admirable; whose power to move us has been immensely magnified by the fusion."[52]

These occasions—carnivalesque as well as funerary—are "an important continuing form of religious and quasi-religious life in our own day. It has to be part of any description of the place of the spiritual in our society."[53] For Taylor, modern humanity, however secular we may be, still has the ability and the need to experience "moments of fusion in a common action/feeling, which both wrench us out of the everyday, and seem to put us in touch with something exceptional, beyond ourselves. Which is why some have seen these moments as among the new forms of religion in our world. I think there is something to this idea."[54] In other words, despite the rejection of the transcendent in the secular (immanent) world, human beings still engage in activities that provide experiences of transcendence—though in this case it is not God or the gods that are the objects of the experiences, but (as Durkheim teaches us) ourselves *writ large*, ourselves as society. Taylor writes that the "festive remains a niche in our world, where the (putatively) transcendent can erupt into our lives, however well we have organized them around immanent understandings of order."[55] Here Taylor returns to the notion of *the* transcendent as a thing (even if "putatively"). My point is that we can have the experience of transcendence *without* any transcendent reality—for the "transcendent" in this case is a fully immanent reality.

Clearly, Taylor sees remnants of religious expression and behavior in seemingly secular activities and institutions. It seems odd to me that more scholars have not paid more attention to this remnant aspect of Taylor's work. Most of their focus tends to be on the historical narrative (to what extent it is accurate) or to his treatment of humanism (often referred to as "exclusive humanism" or "modern humanism") and its inadequacies. Simply put, this humanism "recognizes no more constitutive goods external to us."[56] Early in *A Secular Age*, Taylor presents his thesis that "the coming of modern secularity ... has been coterminous with the rise of a society in which for the first time in history a purely self-sufficient humanism came to be a widely available option." This humanism entails "accepting no final goals beyond human flourishing, nor any allegiance to anything else beyond this flourishing."[57] This flourishing returns us to the idea of "fullness." And it is here that Taylor identifies a critical shortcoming of humanism. "Exclusive humanism must find the ground and contours of fullness in the immanent sphere, in some condition of human life, or feeling, or achievement," Taylor writes. "The door is barred against further discovery [e.g., something transcendent]."⁵⁸ Taylor is concerned particularly with the impacts on moral life. Can we form moral communities in the absence of the transcendent? "That I am left with only human concerns doesn't tell me to take universal human welfare as my goal; nor does it tell me that freedom is important, or fulfillment, or equality," Taylor observes. "Just being confined to human goods could just as well find expression in my concerning myself exclusively with my own material welfare, or that of my family or immediate milieu."⁵⁹

The perceptive reader will see in Taylor's critique an implicit nostalgia. The lack of clear moral guidance in the immanent frame suggests that somehow it was present and/or effective in more religious time periods. Of course, history would tell us differently as we run through the millennia of human atrocities. It also is unclear to me at least that the remnants of religious life described above are so inadequate in the modern context—inadequate in helping overcome what Taylor perceives as the shortcomings of humanism.

Regardless of how we assess Taylor's more normative judgments, however, it is clear that he provides us with a subtle, complex, and compelling narrative. It certainly is not a narrative like Freud or Marx with the complete destruction of stereotypical or institutional religion—or even the more nuanced narrative of Bruce with the steady decline of such religion. At the same time, he is not predicting some kind of return or revival of religion as with Berger. Laurens ten Kate insists that "Taylor strongly opposes this diagnosis of our time that religion would be 'returning,' and that we would now enter a post-secular era. Religion is not returning in our time, because it was never gone in the first place."⁶⁰ But religion might not look a lot like it has in the past. As German McKenzie notes, Taylor's view is that "secularization in the West is in reality one of religious transformation: old religious forms decline but give place to new ones"⁶¹—some of which, I would add, look distinctly secular to the untrained eye. In this sense, McKenzie is right in concluding that Taylor's narrative helps us recognize that "there has been a relocation of religion within society and individual life."⁶²

By obfuscating, in a fruitful way, the divide between the secular and the religious, I think Taylor is firmly in a camp (I am not sure what to call this camp) with Asad and Mark C. Taylor. And to the extent that he recognizes the remnants of religious belief and practices in what is otherwise secular, I think Taylor's argument has some affinities with mine—though my narrative is more narrowly focused on the history of the study of religion rather than the broader and grander (and more amazing) narrative that he provides of the Western intellectual tradition. Mark C. Taylor summarizes well this shared position:

> For theologians as well as psychologists, sociologists, and anthropologists, secularization appeared to be an inescapable by-product of modernization. Furthermore, these analysts argued that the interrelated processes of modernization and secularization are irreversible. Religion appeared to be a primitive vestige that modern people and societies inevitably would leave behind. It is now obvious that this line of analysis is completely wrong: religion *never* disappears. When seemingly absent, religion actually takes different forms, which often are unrecognizable to traditionalists. Since proponents of the secularization theory had a limited understanding of religion, they were not able to understand emerging alternative forms of spirituality and could not appreciate the complicated ways in which religion indirectly informs all culture and society.[63]

So where does this leave us? "Both those who hope that unbelief will encounter its own limitations and aridity, and will peter out in a general return to orthodoxy; and those who think that all this represents an historic march towards reason and science, seem doomed to disappointment," Charles Taylor writes. "Over time, there seems no stable resolution."[64] It is not that the traditional secularization thesis is completely false. And certainly those defenders of traditional religion make good points about the persistence and importance of their institutions. But neither side has a convincing account of the twists and turns of how we got to this moment (Taylor believes he does), and certainly none of them has a good idea of where we are heading. Taylor is humble about predicting the future, but he does share some hints about where we may be headed:

> Thus my own view of "secularization"... is that there has certainly been a "decline" of religion. Religious belief now exists in a field of choices which include various forms of demurral and rejection; Christian faith exists in a field where there is also a wide range of other spiritual options. But the interesting story is not simply one of decline, but also of a new placement of the sacred or spiritual in relation to individual and social life. This new placement is now the occasion for recompositions of spiritual life in new forms, and for new ways of existing both in and out of relation to God.[65]

In the previous chapter I shared a plethora of examples of what we might call "secular spiritual options"—what I describe as the religion of culture. My claim is that these phenomena are "recompositions of spiritual life in new forms"— recompositions that may or may not be experienced by people in terms of divine relations, but nevertheless are firmly akin to stereotypical religious beliefs, experiences, and practices.

Humanism and Culture and the Example of Sport[66]

To more deeply understand the import of the cultural transformations described above, I want to think through humanism as a helpful conceptual tool and sport as an illustrative cultural model. I will begin, however, with play. After briefly introducing the concepts of play and sport, I then will defend one understanding of humanism, one informed significantly by the work of philosopher Richard Rorty. Finally, I will analyze sport through this humanist lens and argue that it can serve as an exemplary cultural phenomenon for a humanist vision of the future—a more hopeful vision than the negative or at least ambiguous one we get from Charles Taylor.

Play and Sport

While play often is reduced to a characteristic of childhood, it really permeates the developmental spectrum. Broadly speaking, play is associated predominantly with recreation (e.g., hiking and dancing) and sport (e.g., competitive activities like baseball and rugby). Johan Huizinga, whose *Homo Ludens: A Study of the Play Element in Culture* is a classic in the field, asserts that play "is a voluntary activity or occupation executed within certain fixed limits of time and place, according to rules freely accepted but absolutely binding, having its aim in itself and accompanied by a feeling of tension, joy and the consciousness that it is 'different' from 'ordinary life.'"[67] In terms of the emotional experience of play, he adds that the "play-mood is one of rapture and enthusiasm, and is sacred or festive in accordance with the occasion. A feeling of exaltation and tension accompanies the action, mirth and relaxation follow."[68] We might see play as a key element (*the* key element?) that distinguishes the sacred from the profane—a distinction that has been central to so many of the theoretical developments in this book (e.g., Durkheim, Eliade, and more).

For Huizinga, play is "primordial."[69] It precedes all civilization or culture. In fact, it is the very basis of civilization or culture. In this sense, play is the fundamental human practice or disposition from which civilization or culture (including art, religion, recreation, sport, and much more) develops. Huizinga insists that "play is older and more original than civilization" and that "culture arises in the form of play … it is played from the very beginning."[70] Even more strongly, Huizinga argues that the "spirit of playful competition is, as a social impulse, older than culture itself and pervades all life like a veritable ferment. … We have to conclude, therefore, that civilization is, in its earliest phases, played.

It does not come *from* play like a babe detaching itself from the womb: it arises *in* and *as* play, and never leaves it."[71] Without the impulse to play—with each other in what become games and dance, with sounds that become music, with words that become poetry and literature—there would be no human culture.

Philosopher Hans-Georg Gadamer argues for a different kind of primordiality of play. He gives ontological priority to play over any subjects of play. It is play—the to-and-fro of the activity—that gives rise to the player consciousness. It is little wonder then that players can be absorbed into the play itself, since the play precedes their existence as players. We might say that the players do not play; instead, the players are played by play.[72] Gadamer adds that such absorption also occurs to the spectator (e.g., in an athletic contest or at a theatre).[73] Like the players, the spectators "lose" themselves in the play itself. In both cases, the boundary between the subjects and play is dissolved—and only play remains. This dissolving of boundaries occurs wherever play is—from rudimentary children's games to symphony concerts, from theatrical productions to top-level sporting events, from religious rituals to dance clubs. Play might be understood as the conceptual umbrella under which all kinds of cultural phenomena fall. It then is a critical link that ties religion to all those other cultural phenomena.

These arguments about play may strike many people as counter-intuitive. Play seems so frivolous and trivial (after all, it is *just* play) while culture and civilization (the arts, law, religion, etc.) seem so important and serious. Play seems meaningless, while culture and civilization seem to be the very basis of meaning. But play *does* have meaning. As philosopher Randolph Feezell notes, "play is a free activity, intrinsically valued and therefore meaningful, joyous, or happy, ending in a consummation or fulfillment [not just accomplishing a task or winning a game, but even simply playing well]."[74] In his insightful treatment of play, Gadamer concludes:

> Play has a special relation to what is serious. …[P]lay itself contains its own, even sacred, seriousness. Yet, in playing, all those purposive relations that determine active and caring existence have not simply disappeared, but are curiously suspended. The player himself knows that play is only play and that it exists in a world determined by the seriousness of purposes. But he does not know this in such a way that, as a player, he actually *intends* this relation to seriousness. Play fulfills its purpose only if the player loses himself in play. Seriousness is not merely something that calls us away from play; rather, seriousness in playing is necessary to make the play wholly play. Someone who doesn't take the game seriously is a spoilsport. … The player knows very well what play is, and that what he is doing is "only a game"; but he does not know what exactly he "knows" in knowing that.[75]

Theologian Robert Ellis similarly notes that "a strangely paradoxical thing about sport *for the vast majority* of those who play and those who watch, is that *sport is terribly important but also utterly unimportant.* ... Like play, sport is a kind of serious irrelevance. Worship is often described in similar ways."[76] Here again, play is that element that links religious behavior to a secular phenomenon like sport.

This "strangely paradoxical thing," as Ellis describes play, may strike many people as absurd. And, indeed, play is absurd. But the absurdity of play is not because it is meaningless. Its absurdity arises from the intensity of our play and the feeling that it is the most important activity we could be doing and, on reflection, that we are engaged in *merely* play or that "it's only a game." For Feezell, this gives rise to the dominant attitude of the player: irony.[77] It is ironic that we can be engaged in something so fully, immersed in it to the point that we truly transcend the sense of self, and yet upon reflection realize that the game is still just a game. (I will return to this irony below with Rorty and a humanist interpretation of play and sport.)

Play occurs in an incredible array of cultural phenomena. From art to politics, courtship to music, there may not be any cultural phenomena devoid of the element of play. Perhaps no where do we see it so prominently, however, than in our games—from the most developmentally early games of peek-a-boo with a baby to the most highly skilled and competitive sports. In his amazingly creative and insightful *The Grasshopper: Games, Life and Utopia*, philosopher Bernard Suits provides us with a compelling account of our games and sports—an account that, not surprisingly, relies heavily on the concept of play.

Suits defines play as "all of those activities which are intrinsically valuable to those who engage in them."[78] Games and sports are specific examples of such activities. Suits wonderfully and succinctly states that "playing a game is the voluntary attempt to overcome unnecessary obstacles."[79] This definition is short but rich. Obviously, the definition is about "play." We know that play is "voluntary." If one is forced to engage in an activity, then it would be hard to believe that they are playing at anything. And games always include rules that make the activity more difficult—that become "unnecessary obstacles." The game of basketball would be easier without having to dribble the ball. Golf would be immensely easier if one could just walk over and place the ball in the cup with one's hand rather than having to use a stick to strike the ball into the hole. We willingly accept these rules or obstacles in our games and sports because they pose for us a challenge and our achievement and even excellence in these games and sports are "intrinsically valuable."

Because they are so intrinsically valuable, Suits concludes that games and sports must be central to any utopian vision. He writes (via his philosophical character "Grasshopper"):

> I believe that Utopia is intelligible, and I believe that game playing is what makes Utopia intelligible. What we have shown thus far is that there does not appear to be any thing to *do* in Utopia, precisely because in Utopia all instrumental activities have been eliminated. There is nothing to strive for precisely because everything has already been achieved. What we need, therefore, is some activity in which what is instrumental is inseparably combined with what is intrinsically valuable, and where the activity is not itself an instrument for some further end. Games meet this requirement perfectly. For in games we must have obstacles which we can strive to overcome *just so that* we can possess the activity as a whole, namely, playing the game.[80]

In a utopian world where all our most basic needs (food, shelter, health, comfort, etc.) are met, we would spend our time playing. Such play can manifest in a wide variety of activities, including music, art, theatre, and much more. But the paradigmatic forms of play are games and sports.

Humanism and Pragmatism

Humanism is hardly about utopian visions. But key principles or tendencies in the humanist tradition overlap or intersect with much of what has been said above about play. In this section, I will focus on certain characteristics of humanism that will set the stage for thinking about sport through a humanist lens.[81]

For our purposes, it is important to think of humanism as a philosophy or outlook that focuses on the human ability to live moral and meaningful lives in the absence of religious beings or realities that stereotypically provide us with a moral code or capacity and are the basis or foundation of meaning in our lives.[82] As theologian and humanist Anthony B. Pinn writes, humanism is "that stance toward life that rejects the demands of gods and smirks at metaphysics meant to push humans beyond their flesh in the world."[83]

For the humanist, we are all alone in the world, but that does not mean that we should or will live immorally. Nor does it entail that our lives cannot be meaningful. Stephen Law notes that there are many factors to a meaningful life—factors that do not depend on religion or religious ideas. These factors include "a project freely chosen, a project that is not deeply immoral, a project pursued with some dedication and skill, engagement in activities that help or enrich the lives of others, and so on."[84]

Humanism is the idea that living a flourishing or meaningful life is the only reasonable goal for human beings, and that such a goal is both worthy and attainable in spite of the absence of a god or similar entity. Indeed, for some, a flourishing or meaningful life is really only attainable once religion in jettisoned—once we realize that meaning is a wholly human construct.

The modern philosophical tradition of American pragmatism overlaps significantly with the humanist outlook. Two of the founding figures were William James and fellow philosopher John Dewey. James claims that pragmatism "is primarily a method of settling metaphysical disputes that otherwise might be interminable."[85] It does so by determining what the practical consequences are of the two sides (or three sides, etc.) in the dispute. "Whenever a dispute is serious," James insists, "we ought to be able to show some practical difference that must follow from one side or the other's being right."[86] So what practical differences matter? Here is where pragmatism provides a very humanistic response: the differences that matter are those that promote human well-being and flourishing—those that allow us to achieve our aims. "The whole function of philosophy ought to be to find out what definite difference it will make to you and me," James concludes, "at definite instants of our life, if this world-formula or that world-formula be the true one."[87] When we cannot find such a practical difference (such as in interminable, metaphysical disputes typically associated with religion), then the dispute is meaningless. In other words, there is no point in even trying to resolve such disputes (besides, they are interminable and thus not ultimately resolvable).

This focus on practical effects is central to the pragmatic definition of truth. As James argues, "truths should *have* practical consequences."[88] Indeed, James connects pragmatism to humanism when he writes that the latter is "conceiving the more 'true' as the more 'satisfactory'" (referencing Dewey).[89] This understanding of truth relies on human effort alone. It is not provided through divine revelation or by any other way outside of our control. "There is but one sure road of access to truth," Dewey insists, "the road of patient, cooperative inquiry operating by means of observation, experiment, record and controlled reflection."[90]

A more contemporary pragmatist, whose work is central to the argument to be made here, is Richard Rorty. Rorty embraces the pragmatist rejection of correspondence theories of truth, insisting that our aim should be achieving descriptions of the world (and ourselves) that are more useful than less useful—the more useful tending to lead to flourishing and meaningful lives, the less useful tending to lead to diminished lives and suffering.[91] This conception of truth is dependent on a community that acknowledges the usefulness of certain descriptions of the world. "The core of Dewey's thought was an insistence that nothing—not the Will of God, not the Intrinsic Nature of Reality, not the Moral Law—can take precedence over the result of agreement freely reached by members of a democratic community," Rorty observes. "The pragmatist claim that truth is not correspondence to the intrinsic nature of something that exists independently of our choice of linguistic descriptions is another expression of this insistence."[92] Indeed, Rorty acknowledges that language—which is necessarily communal—is central to the pragmatist position. Rorty argues that "since truth is a property of sentences, since sentences are dependent for their existence upon vocabularies, and since vocabularies are made by human beings, so are truths."[93] Truth is not something "out there" in the world or even beyond in some transcendent realm or mind of God; it is fully immanent—a function of our linguistic practices that are, necessarily, wholly social practices.

This pragmatist position has three important implications for my argument—represented by Rorty's focus on contingency, irony, and solidarity. First, the pragmatist position entails a radical contingency. Truth is historically and culturally contingent. What "works" or is most "useful" is likely to vary across time and peoples. This variance may not be radically so. For example, cultures across the planet and through the ages have claimed that the taking of innocent life (murder) is wrong. It works or is useful for cultures to make this determination and to prohibit such actions. So too with lying, cheating, physical or mental abuse, and other immoral actions. There is no reason to ground the prohibition against these immoral actions in the laws of the universe or the mind of God. But what works or is useful at one time may not be so at another time. New vocabularies may prove to be better. For most people in the Western world, we no longer find it useful (let alone just or appropriate) to describe homosexual acts as abominations or sins against God. This change from the past (many people believe) is progress. Progress can be understood as the result of a "contest between an entrenched vocabulary which has become a nuisance and a half-formed new vocabulary which vaguely promises great things."[94] As those "great things" come to fruition, the old vocabulary becomes an historical artifact and the new vocabulary becomes our common sense.[95]

For Rorty, the historical process of recognizing the radical contingency of our claims about the world and ourselves is the process of "de-divination." This process is not simply one by which we realize that our most trusted truths are not grounded in the divine will and handed down to us through revelation—a realization endorsed by humanists. It also is a process by which we also realize that our most trusted truths are not grounded in some infallible reason. Here we see the humanist's philosophical suspicion of religious truths turned back upon the philosophical enterprise itself.[96]

According to Rorty, the Enlightenment faith in reason (think of Kant and Hegel, for example) is just another version of the blind or naïve religious faith that it sought to upend. Rorty concludes that the "process of de-divination … would, ideally, culminate in our no longer being able to see any use for the notion that finite, moral, contingently existing human beings might derive the meanings of their lives from anything except other finite, mortal, contingently existing human beings."[97] In other words, the process of de-divination supports humanism—a humanism that acknowledges our radical contingency and is willing continually to question our deepest held beliefs.[98]

The second important implication of the pragmatist position is the attitude that Rorty thinks we *ought* to take to the radical contingency that he describes. This attitude is irony. Rorty identifies the ironist as "the sort of person who faces up to the contingency of his or her own most central beliefs and desires—someone sufficiently historicist and nominalistic to have abandoned the idea that those central beliefs and desires refer back to something beyond the reach of time and chance."[99] But the ironist is the hero of Rorty's story not just because she faces up to contingency, but because she can commit herself to her "central beliefs and desires" in spite of their contingency. That ability to commit in spite of contingency is what makes her ironic. At its most extreme, Rorty's position entails that in a community of ironists there can be a belief that "can still regulate action, can still be thought worth dying for, among people who are quite aware that this belief is caused by nothing deeper than contingent historical circumstance."[100] Because the belief is contingent, however, even if one is willing to die for it, we can hope that one might not be willing to kill for it.

It is hard to imagine the ironist as a deeply religious person. Generally, those who espouse religious beliefs reject the contingency of those beliefs. Religious beliefs are thought to be eternal or at least express eternal truths. But, for Rorty, it also is hard for the ironist to be a typical philosopher—since the ironist does not believe that philosophizing will lead to foundational or eternal truths that are any more necessary (not contingent) than many of those religious truths that they are meant to replace.[101] While the ironist probably cannot be deeply religious or typically philosophical, she can be a humanist. In fact, the (pragmatist) ironist and the humanist can be seen as two sides of the same coin.

If discovering foundational principles or truths cannot be a legitimate goal for the philosopher or theologian, what can we achieve? For Rorty, solidarity is one achievable aim—and this is the third important implication of his pragmatic position. In typical fashion, Rorty insists that we cannot think our way to solidarity. There is no fundamentally convincing argument that can lead to strong human connection and community. "Solidarity is not discovered by reflection but created," he argues. "It is created by increasing our sensitivity to the particular details of the pain and humiliation of other, unfamiliar sorts of people."[102] Moral progress, then, is "the ability to see more and more traditional differences (of tribe, religion, race, customs, and the like) as unimportant when compared with similarities with respect to pain and humiliation—the ability to think of people wildly different from ourselves as included in the range of 'us.'"[103] When we learn about the "pain and humiliation" of others, an experience we share with them, we expand our empathetic circle and eventually will try to alleviate their suffering (or, at a minimum, try to avoid contributing to their suffering).

So where do we learn about the pain and humiliation, the suffering, of others? It certainly will not be in dry though rationally sound philosophical treatises. This does not mean that Rorty finds no place for the philosopher. But given his position, the way we think about the role of the philosopher changes dramatically. No longer is the philosopher charged with discovering the foundational principles of the mind or the universe. The philosopher no longer serves the role of a theologian in disguise. Instead, the philosopher is a cultural critic. And the element of culture that Rorty champions in particular is literature.

Given the inadequacy of philosophy or theology to provide us with a foundation for human solidarity, Rorty claims that "novels and ethnographies which sensitize one to the pain of those who do not speak our language must do the job which demonstrations of a common human nature were supposed to do."[104] For Rorty, in a conclusion that reminds us of Hegelian historical stages, the turn to literature is simply the next stage in a historical trajectory. He argues that "the intellectuals of the West have, since the Renaissance, progressed through three stages: they have hoped for redemption first from God, then from philosophy, and now from literature."[105]

What Rorty means by literature or a literary culture, however, is more expansive than just stereotypical texts like novels or even ethnographies. As he explains:

> As I am using the terms "literature" and "literary culture," a culture which has substituted literature for both religion and philosophy finds redemption neither in a non-cognitive relation to a non-human person [theology] nor in a

cognitive relation to propositions [philosophy], but in non-cognitive relations to other human beings, relations mediated by human artifacts such as books and buildings, paintings and songs.[106]

These human artifacts, elements of what I call the religion of culture, expand our imagination.[107] "The advantage that well-read, reflective, leisured people have when it comes to deciding about the right thing to do is that they are more imaginative," Rorty concludes, "not that they are more rational. Their advantage lies in being aware of many possible practical identities, and not just one or two. Such people are able to put themselves in the shoes of many different sorts of people."[108] It is not reason that leads to empathy and solidarity, but imagination—an imagination sparked by our human artifacts. It is an imagination, I would argue, that is cultivated and enriched by the religion of culture.

If various human artifacts can mediate our relationships with one another, expanding our empathy and leading to human solidarity, what about the human artifact that is the focus of this section? What about sport?

Sport and Humanism: Present and Future

In *Humanism: Essays on Race, Religion and Popular Culture*, Pinn draws on Albert Camus' reading of the myth of Sisyphus—the Greek hero condemned for all of eternity to push a boulder up a hill. Upon reaching the top, he must watch it roll back down the hill. He then begins the process of rolling it back up the hill—doing this over and over again forever. Pinn summarizes the conclusion that Camus draws from the myth, a conclusion that represents well the humanist perspective. He writes, "Happiness and absurdity are linked. Struggle serves as that linkage."[109] The human condition is absurd. In a universe that is inhospitable and meaningless, humans nevertheless struggle to make themselves at home and to lead meaningful lives. We cannot finally be successful in this struggle. We never can feel completely at home in the universe. There are finally no foundations for a meaningful life. But this does not entail that we cannot make a home, that we cannot have meaning. However, the struggle simply cannot be won by appeal to some divine revelation. Nor can it be won by some appeal to a principle or rule of reason. We are condemned, like Sisyphus, to a constant struggle. But in the struggle, we *can* find happiness. Indeed, Camus concludes and Pinn affirms, we must imagine Sisyphus happy in the end. In short, happiness is not found in the winning of the struggle, but in the very struggle itself.

There are few cultural phenomena that manifest the Sisyphean lesson better than play and sport. While winning a game certainly is the aim of many if not most sports, the winning is never final. Even at the end of a season, the champion remains as such only for a year—at which point a new champion is crowned. Sisyphus was a Greek hero, but today he could be a Major League Baseball player, a college soccer player, or a professional golfer. While they rejoice in their victories, they know those victories are fleeting. Their struggles are unending, but they nevertheless find happiness and meaning in what they do. But can we view what they do in light of the deeper pragmatist philosophy that illuminates the humanist perspective? Let us look at Rorty's three key concepts of contingency, irony, and solidarity to answer this question.

Contingency: While play may be a universal characteristic of the human condition, it is hard to imagine anyone denying the historical and cultural contingency of our games and sports. Baseball, for example, has an historical origin—beginning in the United States in the nineteenth century. Though there are debates about activities that might have influenced its development and particular details about its origin, there is no doubt that it is a historical and cultural phenomenon. Even the most committed athlete or devout fan recognizes that it was not given to humanity through some divine revelation or dispensation. Nor is the game a necessary consequence of some transcendent rationality. In other words, it is fully humanly created, fully immanent, and different circumstances and variables might have led to a very different game.

Think about the dimensions of a baseball diamond. While many aficionados will sing the praises of those dimensions, there is no necessity to the fact that the distance between the bases is 90 feet. It seems perfectly natural to us now, but the distance could have been different. And for the player and the fan, the game looks and feels like it does because of that distance. Certain plays only occur the way they do because of that distance. But it could have been otherwise. Early developers of the game could have made the distance 100 feet. This would have changed the game (most likely providing an advantage to the defense, since the runner would need to travel farther to reach a base safely). But, of course, if the distance had been set at 100 feet, then the subsequent game would have seemed perfectly natural to both players and fans. Or think about the distance from the pitcher's mound to home plate—60 feet, 6 inches. This distance strikes us as even more contingent, even arbitrary. Why the 6 inches? And why 60 feet? Why not 70 feet, 7 inches? The distance could have been 70 feet, 7 inches, and undoubtedly this distance would have changed the nature of the game (in this case, probably providing an advantage for the batter, who would have just slightly more time to watch the ball and decide whether or not to swing). And, again, if the distance had been different then players and fans would have found the game played with different dimensions to be just as "natural" as the game played today.

But not only could our sports have been radically different than they are, we could be different too. I will use myself as an example of how contingencies affect the loyalties and passions of all of us. I was raised in the American South in the United States. As a fairly typical American boy, I grew up playing the major sports of baseball, basketball, and football (hockey was not very prominent in the American South in the 1970s). I rooted for the Boston Celtics in basketball because the first basketball team I played on at the Boys Club in Nashville, Tennessee, wore green and claimed the name "Celtics." I identified myself as a Minnesota Vikings fan in football because my father's side of the family came from North Dakota and Minnesota and they were all Vikings' fans. I became a Boston Red Sox fan in baseball because my little league team for many years was the Red Sox, and the first World Series I remember watching was the 1975 classic between the Red Sox and the Cincinnati Reds. Though the Red Sox lost that series, I became enamored with the long-suffering team that played under the "Curse of the Bambino."[110] Years later I would become a much more devoted fan of baseball's most lovable losers—the Chicago Cubs. This devotion started in 1984 when my mother finally relented and subscribed to cable television—leading me to discover WGN television out of Chicago, which at that time broadcasted most Cubs games. Again, I bought into more mythology, this time the "Curse of the Billy Goat,"[111] that apparently kept the Cubs out of the World Series from 1945 onward. Of course, you cannot win a World Series without participating in one. The Cubs finally broke the curse in 2016 and won the World Series for the first time since 1908.

As many people know, the sport that dominates the American South is college football. Though I grew up in Nashville rooting for the Vanderbilt University Commodores, my allegiance changed quickly and powerfully when I went to the University of Tennessee as an undergraduate. From that time to this day, I have been a loyal Tennessee Volunteers fan for football and really all college sports.

As is abundantly clear, the fact that I ever identified with the Celtics, Vikings, Red Sox, or Cubs is a matter of historical and cultural contingency— as is the fact that I have such a deep love and commitment for the University of Tennessee and the athletic teams that represent it. There is no necessity (rational, metaphysical, or otherwise) for the sporting identifications I have. There is no necessity to the fact that I identify as a golfer. If my father had not played golf and taught me the game as a young teenager, I might not even be a golfer (which might have been better for my mental health; thanks

Dad). And, to return to where we started, there is no necessity that the sports that dominate the lives of so many of us even have to be the way they are. They could all be very different. In short, radical contingency runs through it all—from the very nature of the games we play to the sporting identities we embrace.

Identity, of course, is a central function of religion. Many people find it of "ultimate concern" (Tillich) that they are Christian or Buddhist or Muslim. But all of these identifications are just as contingent as my sports identities. What is true with sport and religion is true with all of our loyalties and passions. They are all contingent. As the humanist would insist, they are all immanent and humanly constructed—no gods or greater forces made them so. The identities of the politically liberal, Catholic, and Red Sox fan in Boston are all just as contingent as those of the politically conservative, Southern Baptist, and Braves fan in Atlanta.

Irony: Given such ubiquitous contingency, what is the kind of attitude that an athlete or spectator should take toward the sports that they love? For Rorty, of course, it would be an ironic attitude. I argue that not only is this the attitude that we *should* have toward our sports, but it is the attitude that most athletes or spectators *do* have.

The ironic attitude that I am arguing for here has two distinct characteristics. First, there is the recognition by the athlete or spectator of the contingency just described. And, second, there is a passion or commitment toward the game or sport that suggests that it is of ultimate importance and even, for some, a matter of life or death (figuratively speaking).

There is ample evidence of the second characteristic of the ironic attitude—a characteristic similar to one that we found intrinsic to play, where the athlete or fan "loses" herself or transcends herself in play itself. Athletes regularly devote their lives to their sport. Such devotion may require years of (sometimes grueling and painful) training, extended absences from friends and family, and time away from the pursuit of other goods in life (marriage, children, etc.). Certain sports can be extremely destructive to the body. American football, for example, regularly leads to players with broken bones, damaged joints, and concussions. American football also is one of a handful of sports (we might include automobile racing, boxing, and a few others) where deaths may be rare (as with all sports) but possible. In short, athletes often have a passion and commitment to their sport that suggests that they consider it to be of ultimate importance and worthy of significant sacrifices—that the sport is a matter of life and death (generally figuratively speaking, but sometimes literally).

What about the spectators? They do not put their bodies (let alone their lives) on the line as do the athletes, but they nevertheless commit enormous amounts of time and emotional energy to their sports, teams, and individual players. They also, of course, spend enormous amounts of money watching and following their sports, teams, and individual players. Every sport has a wealth of stories about the devotion of its fans. For example, one can read novelist Nick Hornby's *Fever Pitch*, his memoir of what it means to be a fan of the Arsenal soccer team.[112] Or think about the fanaticism we see for college football in the American South.[113] Many books recount the extreme behavior of fans to follow their teams and express their devotion. For example, one can read journalist Warren St. John's *Rammer Jammer Yellow Hammer: A Road Trip into the Heart of Fan Mania* about devotees of the University of Alabama football team—about fans who arrange weddings around football Saturdays, who check themselves out of the hospital just before surgery in order to attend a game, and much more.

Culturally speaking, sport dominates many cultures—perhaps none more so than the United States. Newspapers more often than not have entire sections devoted only to sport. There are dozens of cable channels that provide nothing else but sports programming. Millions of Americans participate in one or more sports—everything from biking to golf, from ultimate frisbee to pick-up games of basketball. And tens of millions of Americans regularly attend or follow sporting events. The Super Bowl, the championship game of the National Football League, has a television audience of well over 100 million people each year—equating to approximately a third of the US population. Of course, such numbers are dwarfed by the viewership of international sporting events like the Olympics or the soccer World Cup. By one estimate, over 3 billion people watched the 2018 World Cup, approaching nearly half of the world's population.[114] It would be fair to say that few cultural phenomena approach the level of popularity that sport does.

For both athletes and spectators, sport is a matter (again, to use Tillich's term) of "ultimate concern"—providing a sense of belonging in the world, identity, community, life lessons, and more. At the same time that both athletes and spectators will tell you how important their sports are, and despite the fact that their behavior often suggests that their sports are *the* most important things in their lives, almost all of them will admit that their sports are *not* the most important things in the world. Most of them will admit, in fact, that their sports are *not* a matter of life and death. Here, we have the first characteristic of the ironic attitude—a recognition of the ultimate contingency of sport.

While athletes and spectators talk and act as if their sports are the most important things in the world, that they are a matter of "ultimate concern," of life and death, when challenged on the issue they almost always will admit that there are much more important things in life. They will admit that the love of family and friends is more important; that being a "good" person is more important; that easing the suffering of others (let alone stopping oneself from causing suffering) is more important. They recognize the contingency of something about which they usually have "ultimate concern." Generally speaking, this is what separates the religious devotion and fervor that many athletes and spectators have toward their sports[115] from what we have seen through millennia in regard to stereotypical or institutional religion. The latter often has led to terrible atrocities because groups take their "truths" to be so important and beyond question that the suffering and death of other human beings can be justified by the defense or advancement of those "truths." While the sporting world has had its share of terrible human beings (i.e., "assholes" might be the appropriate term), very few athletes or spectators seek to inflict pain or suffering on other athletes and spectators—certainly not in any permanent sense or outside of the confines of the sporting event. And very few athletes or spectators have ever murdered anyone to defend the honor of their team or to advance the cause of their fan community—unlike so many religious people throughout human history.

The ironic attitude allows the player and spectator to experience sport in powerfully meaningful ways—as they "lose" or transcend themselves in the play that is manifested in sports and that lies at the center of the human condition. Sports provide meaning for both athletes and fans, but the athletes and fans recognize them to be immanent, contingent, human creations. As such, they may be worth our time, energy, and resources, but they are not worth dying for (not intentionally) nor worth killing for.

Solidarity: The ironic attitude that athletes and spectators tend to have about their sports allows them to feel empathy toward one another and thus to achieve or at least advance some sense of solidarity.

Let me paint a picture that illustrates well both the ironic attitude and the openness to solidarity—a picture that fits well with the moral outlook expressed in Rorty's work. Imagine the end of a hard-fought American football game or a rugby match (men's or women's) or a World Cup soccer game (men's or women's). The athletes have competed with great passion and even, at times, significant violence. The fans have "booed" or "cheered" the players, and often screamed insults and obscenities at the referees. The game or match is itself a narrative, a dramatic story that plays out over a number of hours (here we see a close connection with Rorty's prioritization of literature). The tension can be intense, the pressure building on the players and the spectators nervously watching the action. At certain moments, it seems there is nothing in the world more important, more significant, more meaningful than the action on the field and the outcome of the game or match. What is happening on the field is of "ultimate concern." What then happens when it is all over? What happens when the intensity dissipates, and the outcome is known? What typically happens is the players meet in the middle of the field and congratulate or console one another. They renew old friendships and wish one another well. Fans of the losing team may begrudgingly rub shoulders with fans of the winning team, but they too (with rare exceptions) exhibit the kind of sportsmanship shown by the athletes. For the winning fans know how fickle (contingent) sports are. They know that the next time they easily could be on the losing side of the narrative. We can say that they empathize with the losing fans, just as the winning players empathize with the losing players. We legitimately can say that sports build a kind of solidarity among the athletes and spectators.

This solidarity even exists among players and fans in the most heated of rivalries. In the American South, no football rivalry is stronger than that between the University of Alabama and Auburn University. The two teams play every year in their last game of the regular season, a game famously referred to as the Iron Bowl. In describing the rivalry that consumes all of the state of Alabama, journalist Clay Travis writes:

> In Alabama, every house is divided. Somehow, someway, if you live in the state your blood seeps across the Auburn-Alabama partition, which means that whatever happens in this game can't be forgotten for an entire year. The sting of defeat is unavoidable, inescapable, since you are surrounded by your gridiron enemies, and cannot help but run into neighbors and family members who will bask in the glory of their win. In Alabama, the Iron Bowl loss stings like a paper cut that is reopened anew each morning for a year. Even worse, on the day after the big game, Alabama and Auburn fans have to come together at church and accidentally touch hands when the offering plate is passed. Even religious life does not allow any measure of avoidance.[116]

Note, however, that the fans *do* go to church with one another. Indeed, it is remarkable how peaceful the rivalry can be. As Travis writes after witnessing the 2006 Iron Bowl:

> By the end of the night, Alabama and Auburn fans have come together in the bars of Tuscaloosa [Alabama]. I don't see any fights or near fights. ... The anger, aggression, and distaste have been washed away and, at least for one night, the

two warring armies of Alabama fandom have lain down their weapons. By the end of the night, the state of Alabama is once more one nation, under God ... [117]

Even with alcohol perhaps serving as a peace-making lubricant (though, sometimes, it can have the opposite effect), we see the kind of solidarity that comes from fans understanding the pain and suffering that can result from a loss. Victory, it is understood, is always temporary (next year may be different). It is always contingent. In addition, fans know that despite the incredible importance they put on the game, there are other things that are so much more important. For example, two events in 2010 and 2011 wonderfully exemplify how the ironic attitude can open us to solidarity and moral concern for one another. In 2010, a crazed Alabama fan poisoned the oak trees on Toomer's Corner in the city of Auburn, Alabama (the site is popular with Auburn fans, who strew the trees with toilet paper after football victories). There was an outpouring of concern and support (both moral and financial) from the Alabama team and its fans as everyone condemned the action and helped rectify the situation. Just a year later, a major tornado tore through Tuscaloosa (home of the University of Alabama), killing dozens of citizens (including several University of Alabama students). Auburn coaches, players, and fans joined with Alabamians from across the state and rushed to Tuscaloosa to help clean up and care for the survivors.

The members of the Auburn and Alabama communities may not know it (in fact, I am almost certain they do not), but they exemplify Rorty's ironic attitude. Even though their rivalry is incredibly important and deeply meaningful to them, they recognize the contingency of it. Such recognition opens them to an empathy for and a solidarity with one another. And, I argue, such irony and solidarity are hardly unique among them. Such irony and solidarity are typical of the overwhelming majority of athletes and fans. Human history would have been much less bloody if more people could have had such irony about their religious beliefs, experiences, and practices—perhaps leading to a sense of solidarity that would have prevented so much suffering and death.

Conclusion

Of course, it might be worthwhile to have a quick "reality check" about the power and importance of sport. At their most significant level, Rorty's positions about contingency, irony, and solidarity are focusing on some pretty weighty issues. His primary interest is not in whether or not sports fans are nice to each other or even come to one another's aid on occasion. His primary interest revolves around how to avoid having religious and/or political ideologues perpetrate atrocities against other people (or even their own people). He wants to help us figure out how to commit ourselves to fight against the pain and suffering caused by such ideologues even when we realize the utter contingency of that commitment. In other words, how can we commit to the principle of "do no harm" or even the principle of "ease the pain and suffering of others" when there are no foundations or fundamental grounding for those principles? The principles are merely cultural and historical contingencies, artifacts that I have inherited. Why should I follow them? Even more, why should I sacrifice my time, resources, or even life to follow them?

For Rorty, the ironic attitude allows us to recognize the contingency of such principles while still passionately defending their power and meaning in our lives. These principles may even be worth dying for. Sport, frankly, is not operating at such a significant level. But what I hope to have shown is that sport at least can serve as a kind of training ground for the type of ironist that Rorty believes is critical to a more peaceful future. In that regard, I argue that sport is a kind of training ground for a humanist future—one that recognizes the human origin (contingency) of our greatest ideals (human rights, justice, democracy, etc.), but one that also recognizes that those ideals are valuable and worth defending, preserving, and advancing.

By training us in the ironic attitude, sport prepares us to avoid the pitfalls of the religious and/or political ideologies that tarnish our history and continue to threaten us today. While certainly simple human greed and cruelty have been enough to cause harm for thousands of years, the belief that one's ideology is absolutely true and of the highest value (higher, for example, than avoiding suffering, preventing death, respecting others, or even promoting happiness) undoubtedly has led to some of the world's worst atrocities. The evidence litters our history—from the Crusades to the terrorist attacks of 9/11, from the Reign of Terror of the French Revolution to the Cultural Revolution in Maoist China.

Why should sport matter to the humanist? Because sport draws upon our fundamental nature as beings who play. It teaches us that we can passionately and meaningfully engage in play while also recognizing the fundamental contingency of the very activities that manifest play. In other words, sport (at its best) can help us to have the kind of attitudes and character that make for a good ironist (in Rorty's sense) and a good humanist.

My claim, in fact, is that the good ironist and the good humanist, while not identical, are two sides of the same coin. Both reject metaphysical claims about institutions, practices, and values that really are humanly created; insist that morality and meaning can be affirmed by human beings even in the absence of religious or philosophical foundationalism; and recognize that human flourishing in solidarity with one another is the good or goal that we legitimately can pursue within the parameters of the human condition.

As our societies become more secular, we desperately need institutions like sport that can serve as training grounds for good ironists and good humanists. Consequently, the advocate for humanism has good reason not only to promote institutions like sport, but to protect them against capitalism, nationalism, and other forces that threaten their intrinsic nature (play) and leave them ineffective in achieving their more noble ends. As a cultural phenomenon, however, the value of sport in this regard is not unique. Other cultural phenomena can have similar value—theatre, art, film, dance, literature, music, and so much more. Indeed, the argument made here for sport is true more generally for all phenomena that are constitutive of the religion of culture.

Highly Speculative Conclusions, Part One: The Future of Institutional Religion and the Study of It

In bringing this work to a close, I want to share some speculative conclusions. This first part focuses on the future of institutional religion and the study of religion. The second part focuses on the future of humanity more generally. These are speculative musings, but they are not random or arbitrary. In fact, I think they follow from so much of what has been detailed in this book. But the future is always a dangerous thing to predict, and I certainly am humbled by the task. My view is so limited, regardless of how informed I think it is.

So, what is going to happen to institutional religion? Juan M. Floyd-Thomas, Stacey M. Floyd-Thomas, and Mark G. Toulouse note the kind of contemporary individualism that has come to shape religious expression today. In *The Altars Where We Worship*, they observe that many people seek a "more inward and insular religion" that threatens our ability to form genuine community and work with one another for the common good.[118] In short, they recognize the potential dangers of our historical transformations and the particular moment in which we live—dangers that I elaborate upon in the Postscript. At the same time, they challenge the very divide between the sacred and profane, the divide that I have traced in part through these chapters and likewise find problematic. "The notion of a radical separation between the sacred and the secular is an assumption more than an actuality," they write. "In many instances, a shared realm of human experience runs through them both. Human beings seek an escape from the mundane or a notion of transcendence in the sacred and a feeling of the presence (or immanence) of the divine in the everydayness of their lives."[119] Consequently, while they do not use the same terminology that I do, the "religion of culture," they nevertheless recognize the same phenomenon occurring. Their conclusion is worth quoting at length:

> Finding no salvation in religion, Americans have laid our fair share, if not our all, at the altars of body and sex, big business, entertainment, politics, sports, and science and technology. Organized religion has you shuffling between who you are and what you are expected to become, appearing to make religion an out-of-body experience more than an embodied one. For many Americans, religion attempts to make you "so heavenly minded that you are no earthly good." A good percentage of "nones," as well as a growing number of the American population, are looking for new places and spaces where they can find inspiration without being judged, where they can have both their humanity affirmed and their natural sensations nurtured.[120]

In other words, many Americans (and increasingly people around the world) are disenchanted with institutional religion. But they need functional equivalents to meet their basic human needs—needs that I would argue are both individual and communal. My claim, of course, is that they have been seeking to have those needs met in the religion of culture.

So, if I have to make a prediction, I will say that I think institutional religion will continue to decline in popularity and relevance. I think Bruce and others are right in highlighting the pattern of decline, and I do not see anything in the near future that indicates any change in that pattern. If this prediction is true, then what happens to the study of religion?

Unlike some scholars and administrators who might suggest or call for the faculty in religious studies departments to be absorbed into other departments (sociology, psychology, etc.), I believe there still is a benefit to having distinct religious studies departments. The kind of work described in the previous chapter will continue to make the study of religion (particularly the religion of culture) important and relevant. It is wonderfully interdisciplinary work that is cultivated in religious studies departments but might be limited or diminished in single discipline departments. This interdisciplinary work will continue to complicate the very idea of religion for us. But such complication is not a bad thing. Complicating matters is one of the ways in which the academic world advances its work. Nor is it a new thing. While we might like to imagine a simpler time ("back in the day") when religion was religion and scholars knew what they were studying, such a simpler time may be more of an illusion than a reality.

In part, we must recognize that the very idea of religion is contested. As Asad notes, "there cannot be a universal definition of religion, not only because its constituent elements and relationships are historically specific, but because that definition is itself the historical product of discursive processes."[121] Brent Nongbri's work is instructive in this regard. He traces the history of the use of "religion" in the Western world and particularly in academic circles. He concludes that "religion is not a universally applicable first-order concept that matches a native discursive field in every culture across time and throughout history."[122] But that does not mean we should give up on the study of religion or the use of the concept. Indeed, Nongbri argues that we should think of the concept as a "second-order, redescriptive concept" that can be useful in gaining insights into all sorts of cultural phenomena. He even makes a suggestion at the end of his historical work that parallels the claims in this book:

> If we shift away from the essentialist standpoint [about religion], we might ask different questions, such as "How might we understand human behavior differently if we, as a thought exercise, regard capitalism as a religion?" Such an inquiry could provoke a series of strategic comparisons involving gods and invisible market forces, catechumens reciting creeds and advertisers' sloganeering. This kind of exercise helps us see phenomena in new ways and should be encouraged. I think, then, there is still a place for "the study of religion" in the modern world, provided that those doing the study adopt a self-conscious and critical attitude that has often been lacking.[123]

Nongbri rejects an essentialist understanding of religion, recognizing the historical contingency of the concept. But that does not mean that it cannot be useful to us, and I hope that the preceding chapters have illustrated that fact. In a wonderful essay on the work of Jonathan Z. Smith, Sam Gill brings together in his conclusion several threads that have been woven throughout this book:

> Our academic play, like any, is bound by the rules that distinguish the activity. Our subjects may support many profiles and show many faces through the acts of our interpretations—they are puppets of our choices of theory. Still, underlying our understanding of what is academic is the philosophical assumption that our subjects exist independent of what we write of them. Thus, academic writing is distinguished from the novel by our acknowledgment that we cannot say simply

anything we want about our subjects. As academics, we are bound by the rules of our play to have our stories constrained by our real subjects.[124]

There is no "essence" or "essential nature" to religion. As academics, we are engaged in a kind of play. Our theories are our basic equipment, and when we use them to interpret religious beliefs, experiences, and practices (however broadly construed), we do so in a playful manner. In the process, knowledge and insights about those beliefs, experiences, and practices emerge—knowledge and insights that are, from a pragmatist perspective, useful to us. At the same time, our use of the equipment of religious studies (such as those detailed in Chapters 1 through 4, with examples shared in Chapter 5) does not allow us to say anything we want about cultural phenomena and the people engaged with them. Here the analogy to literary interpretation might be useful. Just because a great (or even a terrible) novel is subject to various interpretations, that does not mean that any interpretation is valid. Some will be better than others to the extent that they are tethered to the actual text and/or the historical context of the author and its audience. The study of the religion of culture does not mean "anything goes," and some scholarship in the area is better than others.

The study of the religion of culture necessarily puts into question what we think we know about religion (not just culture). Take, for example, Monica R. Miller's *Religion and Hip Hop*. As we learned in the previous chapter, she has challenged scholars who have reduced the religion of hip hop to lyrics and meaning. But that reduction is a consequence of what those scholars think of religion. As she observes, "after much excavation, endlessly searching for the construction of meaning, I realized that what we as scholars call religion—isn't so religious after all. We must begin again. We must begin by rethinking the religious."[125] She adds that "we must get beyond our modernist lenses of religion *as* feeling, and get up to speed with religion *as* effect, strategy, and manufacturing of social, cultural, and political interests. Chasing meaning is like chasing waterfalls—it is an impossible and endless task."[126] In this regard, she is rejecting the kind of phenomenological or existential approach we detailed in Chapter 4.[127] Such an approach privatizes religion and fails to understand its greater (for example) political and economic contexts and effects. Such an approach would miss so much of what hip hop is all about (giving voice to the voiceless, embodying historical and current oppression, resisting the powers that be, etc.). Thus, a "way forward would focus less on proving the meaningful merit of cultural activity, and more on exploring the *contexts* that house the production of meaning."[128]

This destabilizing approach to religious studies—putting in question definitions of religion, being self-conscious about the contingencies of our theories, exploring the religious elements and dimensions of seemingly non-religious phenomena, and so much more—also complements more recent efforts to query the Western (white) colonial and hegemonic origins and continuing legacy of those origins in the study of religion. I am thinking here of the work of Charles Long, someone who was a real forerunner in the critical investigation of race and colonialism in the study of religion.[129] More recently, anthropologist Johannes Fabian[130] and religious studies scholar David Chidester[131] have made important contributions on these questions. Even more recently, Christopher M. Driscoll and Monica R. Miller have pushed our questioning even further in their powerful collection of essays, *Method as Identity: Manufacturing Distance in the Academic Study of Religion*.[132] All of these authors recognize that the study of religion is bound up with Western (white) notions of rationality and progress, and it is shaped as well by the European colonizing project. As Driscoll and Miller observe, the Western study of religion "is from its inception organized around the propagation of a white myth of progress positing white men the most advanced at studying and classifying earlier forms."[133]

In tracing some of the history of the study of religion and the impact of central figures in that history, I necessarily have focused on Western, white men and on topics that they found important. That white men dominate the history of the study of religion is a consequence of white (male) supremacy—unjustly limiting educational opportunities for women and people of color as well as publishing and teaching opportunities even for those able to be educated. But Chapter 5 has a much richer diversity of scholars—a consequence of both a focus on more contemporary scholarship and a broadening of what are considered to be appropriate research topics. I believe the study of the religion of culture, to the extent that it questions the received wisdom of the past (again, overwhelmingly from white men) and pushes us into new areas of inquiry, promises a more diverse religious studies academic community and more diversity in its areas of study.

Of course, it remains important and relevant to study the beliefs, experiences, and practices of institutional religion both past and present, and certainly insightful work will continue to be done in these areas. And, undoubtedly, there will be people who continue to argue that there is something distinct about stereotypical religion that makes it unlike any other cultural phenomenon. They are the "essentialists" of whom Nongbri speaks. In this book, Eliade represents this argument best. There also are contemporary efforts along these lines too, but these efforts are less and less convincing. For example, let us take a brief look at Christian Smith's book *Religion: What It Is, How It Works, and Why It Matters*.

"*Religion is a complex of culturally prescribed practices, based on premises about the existence and nature of superhuman powers, whether personal or impersonal,*" Smith asserts, "*which seek to help practitioners gain access to and communicate or align themselves with these powers, in hopes of realizing human goods and avoiding things bad.*"[134] As a sociologist, it is not a surprise that Smith places greater emphasis on practices rather than beliefs—though the former do not exist without the latter.[135] The key to religion for Smith is what he identifies as "causal attribution," the idea that superhuman powers can be identified as the cause of something that happens to the believer/practitioner. "The most essential dynamic that makes religion work is *the human making of causal attributions to superhuman powers*," Smith concludes. "Apart from the central process of making attributions, religion would collapse."[136]

Of course, religion is not simply causal attribution. Smith identifies a host of "secondary products, features, and powers"—including identity and community formation, forms of expression, social control, and more.[137] But these are secondary in part because they are not exclusive or unique to religion.[138] Other cultural institutions (social, political, etc.) also have such products, features, and powers. What is unique or exclusive to religion are superhuman powers that we can tap into in order to advance our self-interest. In other words, religion does things for us—it functions as an aid in achieving our aims. "Human beings practice religion (when they do) ultimately because they believe that it will help them in their larger life quests to better realize their natural human ends," Smith claims. "Practicing religion, in short, appears to many people to be in their basic interest."[139]

Again, religion does a lot for people, but what religion essentially is, for Smith, has to do with these superhuman powers and how they can be causes for good on our behalf. Everything else is important, but secondary. Take Smith's treatment of identity formation.

> When religion provides meaningful identities to people, that is one more motive for them—in the absence of more powerful counteracting influences—to practice religion. Religion, by my account, did not arise in order to provide such identities; that is not its primary source. But after developing for other, more basic reasons, religion's provision of personal, social, and collective identities became another, reinforcing cause of people's ongoing religious practice.[140]

There is a lot to unpack in this passage. First, how can Smith write with such confidence about how religion (all religions) arose? As the first four chapters of this book indicate and even as Smith acknowledges, religions function in multiple ways for people. How can we pick out just one that was *the* cause of all of them? Second, even today, people seem to join institutional religions for a lot of reasons (their "motives," as Smith says, may be mixed). They may even join for reasons that are, in Smith's terms, "secondary." In fact, they may not even believe in superhuman powers, but really want to be part of a community or simply enjoy certain friendships or even like the weekly potluck meal. Years ago I attended a Zen Buddhist temple in Chicago. While I found Buddhism's metaphysical claims interesting, I did not believe in them. I attended because I enjoyed the meditative practice and the weekly messages, not because I believed in any superhuman powers (Buddhist or otherwise). And I certainly did not believe that some supernatural being was going to bring me good fortune. Was I really engaged in religious practice for "secondary" reasons? By Smith's definition, was I engaged in religious practice at all? Third, what about people like the sports fan who engages in ritual practices to help their team win (e.g., wearing a "lucky" jersey on game day), but does so in an ironic way? They seem to believe in some sort of impersonal superhuman power, but in an ironic sense described above. If questioned, they probably would admit that their ritual practice does not *really* help their team win, but they continue to engage in those practices. Even more stereotypically religious people may engage in traditional rituals in a similarly ironic manner. Does Smith's approach exclude such people from the category of religion? If so, why would we want to do that?

While Smith's work serves as an excellent introduction to the study of religion, it nevertheless has essentialist tendencies that limit its utility. His work limits the use of the term "religion" to particular kinds of phenomena—in particular phenomena that involve people who explicitly acknowledge superhuman powers. Indeed, Smith uses superhuman powers as the definitional dividing line between what is religion and what is not religion—with the latter including Confucianism, Reform Judaism, Unitarian Universalism, Scientology, Alcoholics Anonymous, astrology, Star Trek fandom, and many more "arguably ambiguous case[s]."[141] I can say with some confidence (I once was a member of a Unitarian Universalist church) that some people who identify as Unitarian Universalist would be surprised to learn that they were not part of a religion. Certainly, many people at the church did not believe in superhuman powers, but many others did believe. Most of them, however, most likely believed that they were part (in an unambiguous way) of a religion and were engaged in religious practices.[142]

Smith's approach explicitly or implicitly discourages our application of our scholarly tools to other phenomena that might be revealed in ever-increasingly insightful ways. Monica R. Miller might describe it as a "top-down approach"—one that "begins with traditional categorical religious assumptions" and that thus "offers at best a thin analysis of the changing cartography of what we identify *as* religious in culture."[143] She insists that "as scholars of religious studies we can approach cultural practices with the understanding that there is nothing in and of itself unique about religion. Of greater interest is the exploration of *why* certain social processes come to be understood and classified *as* religious, and furthermore what these classifications accomplish among particular groups across time and space."[144] In regard to Smith's approach, is it simply another example of a "protective strategy" that we see in Eliade and Tillich (Chapter 4) and critiqued by the likes of Proudfoot (Chapter 3) and others? What are the cultural or political advantages sought (even if merely within the academy) by drawing a bright line—as Smith does—between what is religion and what is not? What value judgments (implicit or explicit) are being made about various cultural phenomena? Is hip hop a lesser cultural phenomenon than the Baptist Church simply because the latter is a "religion" and the former is not?

Smith's work represents the kind of approach that I move away from in this book. Because in this book, in my story, religious studies recognizes that the sacred is not just transcendent but is immanent. That recognition then may be a cause (one of many) of our increasing turn to the immanent in order to experience the sacred, thus making institutional religion (focused on the transcendent) increasingly irrelevant. But there nevertheless is a lot of continuity between the study of religion as handed down through recent centuries and what I advocate for in the study of the religion of culture. In writing about himself and other comparative religion scholars in the latter half of the twentieth century, Charles H. Long states that "we are attempting to find those existential structures of the life of human communities across space and time which concretely gave and give expression to who and what we are in the scheme of things."[145] I think many if not most of the scholars featured in Chapter 5, those engaged in the study of the religion of culture, are attempting to achieve much of what Long describes.

The study of the religion of culture, however, is not simply about how religious expression has changed and is changing. It also is about where we think religion is going or if it is going anywhere. As Jonathan Sheehan writes, "'What was religion?' is not the question on the table. Rather, it is 'What will religion become?'"[146] Smith insists that "until human nature fundamentally changes, many humans will almost certainly want to continue to practice religion."[147] In part, much of this book affirms something like his claim about human nature, but it diverges greatly in regard to what it means to "practice religion." While Smith understands religion as closely circumscribed, I understand it as a term to describe beliefs, experiences, and practices that have a sort of "family resemblance" (to use Ludwig Wittgenstein's idea). Thus, whereas Smith's claim must commit him to the idea that stereotypical or institutional religion is likely to continue for some time (contrary to the kind of data that Bruce, for example, presents), my approach does not really need stereotypical or institutional religion (it is, as I have argued, irrelevant). Thus, I agree with Smith when he states that religion "will be a significant part of human life and societies as long as the human condition is like what it is now."[148] I strongly disagree, however, with the highly constrictive definition of religion that Smith uses. I also think that we might want to question whether the future "human condition" will be as "it is now," just as we legitimately might wonder if the "human condition" now is the same as what it used to be. As Charles Taylor's work suggests, human beings and what they are capable of believing and doing today may not be quite the same as human beings 500 years ago. Maybe the secular age changes us. I think there might be something to this claim, but I think it necessarily leads to the abandonment of stereotypical or institutional religion rather than the end of religious experience or even religious life all together. But now we are drifting into areas best covered in the next section.

Highly Speculative Conclusions, Part Two: The Future of Humanity

While Taylor's *A Secular Age* (2007) is kind of a crowning achievement to a truly spectacular career, his theorizing about contemporary culture certainly dates back several decades. To begin this section, I want to return to his book *Hegel and Modern Society*, which was published in 1979. Here we again see the impact of Hegel on the thought of a major contemporary figure.

Taylor writes that "Modern civilization has ... seen the proliferation of Romantic views of private life and fulfillment, along with a growing rationalization and bureaucratization of collective structures, and a frankly exploitative stance towards nature."[149] In short, modern civilization is characterized by individualism (and some degree of self-absorption) at the personal level and utilitarianism at the social level. Taylor is concerned in particular with individualism. "Individualism comes ... when men cease to identify with the community's life, when they 'reflect', that is, turn back on themselves, and see themselves most importantly as individuals with individual goals," he claims, drawing upon Hegel. "This is the moment of dissolution of a *Volk* and its life."[150] In this situation, people feel alienated from their society, its institutions, and its goals or norms—all of which are not individual, but collective.[151] Taylor notes that alienation "arises where the important ideas of man and society and their relation to nature embodied in the institutions of a given society cease to be those by which its members identify themselves."[152] Stereotypical or institutional religion, as just one institution in society, suffers as a consequence, and certainly individualism has accelerated our arrival into a secular age and the alienation that accompanies it.

Hegel can be credited for playing a significant role in the development of the modern conception of the self—particularly given the central role he plays in the Western world in championing the idea of freedom. At the same time, we see his awareness of the dangers of that freedom—especially to our institutions and the possibility of social cohesion. Taylor notes that Hegel "has paradoxically helped both to bring this modern doctrine [freedom and its accompanying self-dependence] to its most extreme expression and to show the dilemma in which it involves us." Hegel not only recognizes the merits of the rise of individualism in the Western world (freedom, human and civil rights, democracy, etc.), but also recognizes the costs (alienation, decline or even collapse of certain institutions, etc.). Taylor describes the conflict of goods here as "Hegel's dilemma."

> Thus Hegel's dilemma for modern democracy, put at its simplest, is this: the modern ideology of equality and of total participation leads to a homogenization of society. This shakes men loose from their traditional communities, but cannot replace them as a focus of identity. Or rather, it can only replace them as such a focus under the impetus of militant nationalism or some totalitarian ideology which would depreciate or even crush diversity and individuality. It would be a focus for some and would reduce the others to mute alienation. Hegel constantly stresses that the tight unity of the Greek city state cannot be recaptured in the modern world that has known the principle of individual freedom.[153]

Hegel and Taylor, of course, are both right. We cannot return to some earlier age. The secular age is here to stay. So, what is Hegel's response to this dilemma? "Hegel's answer ... is to give social and political differentiation a meaning by seeing them as expressive of cosmic order, but he conceives this order as the final and complete fulfilment of the modern aspiration to autonomy," Taylor concludes. "It is an order founded on reason alone, and hence is the ultimate object of the free will."[154] This triumph of reason, of course, is that final unfolding of history and full revelation of Spirit. But reason has done little to truly unite people into communities and combat alienation (outside of scientific communities, perhaps, or the academy). And while nationalism and other such radical ideologies may help to curb the detrimental effects of individualism and alienation, we know how dangerous those can be (e.g., look no further than twentieth-century fascism in Europe or Stalin's lethal rule of communist Russia).

So, are we simply stuck with Hegel's dilemma? Taylor leans more toward a standard religious response to this dilemma, though this response likely looks very different from any other religious responses in history.[155] In this regard, he is consistent with the work of Josef Pieper, the mid-twentieth century Catholic philosopher (Taylor, by the way, is also a philosopher with a Catholic background) whose more popular books focus on the modern world, leisure, and festival.

Pieper is a champion of leisure, especially given what he sees as the increasing domination of materialism and work in the contemporary world. "If the essence of 'proletarian' is the fact of being fettered to the process of work," he writes, "then the central problem of liberating men from this condition lies in making a whole field of significant activity available and open to the working man—of activity which is *not* 'work'; in other words: in making the sphere of real leisure available to him."[156] While we may think of leisure mainly as engaging in recreation, hobbies, entertainment, or even just as inactivity (the opposite of work), Pieper thinks of it as a "mental and spiritual attitude" and even a "condition of the soul."[157] The sphere of leisure is culture—"everything that lies beyond the utilitarian world" of work or labor.[158] Certainly the many phenomena that I have included under the umbrella of the religion of culture would fit here with Pieper's definition of leisure and culture. But there are many places where my work diverges from Pieper's work. He is skeptical about the centrality of play in culture,[159] something that I argued for earlier in this chapter. He also insists that more stereotypical religious institutions, attitudes, and practices must be at the core of leisure and culture—an insistence that I resist.

It is in his account of festival that we can best understand Pieper's view. "To celebrate a festival means to do something which is in no way tied to other goals, which has been removed from all 'so that' and 'in order to,'" he states. "True festivity cannot be imagined as residing anywhere but in the realm of activity that is meaningful in itself."[160] While the festival certainly may include "jesting, gaiety, and laughter," it "becomes true festivity only when man affirms the goodness of his existence by offering the response of joy."[161] This affirmation of our existence is central to what Pieper identifies as divine worship, and it is here that he insists on the religious dimension of the festival and consequently of true leisure. The festival and leisure are gifts, and the only appropriate response is to praise God for them.[162]

But it is not the case that particular phenomena are either really festivals or they are not. It appears that Pieper imagines a sort of spectrum, across which many different phenomena may fall. He observes that "real festivity cannot be restricted to any one particular sphere of life, neither to the religious nor to any other; it seizes and permeates all dimensions of existence—so that from a mere description of the proceedings we cannot easily tell whether a festival is 'really' a social, economic, athletic, or church event, a fair, a dance, or a feast."[163] Thus, Pieper concludes that the "core and source of festivity itself remains inviolably present in the midst of society."[164] In a passage that should remind the reader of Tillich and the "ultimate concern" that permeates the human condition, Pieper insists that there "are worldly, but there are no purely profane, festivals. And we may presume that not only can we not find them, but that they cannot exist. A festival without gods is a non-concept, is inconceivable."[165] Then, in a passage that also should remind the reader of Durkheim's "collective effervescence" and Turner's *communitas*, Pieper argues that "ideally speaking, festivals should be public affairs of concern to the political community; during festivals social differences should be abolished; social and political peace, real 'fraternization,' should be considered the fruits, or even the preconditions, of festivals."[166]

At this point, Pieper might seem like a welcome "fellow traveler" for advocates of the religion of culture. Certainly, the religion of culture includes the kind of festivals and festivity that Pieper seems to be celebrating. But Pieper does not go as far as I do here. For example, he claims that "festivals are doomed unless they are preceded by the pattern of ritual religious praise. That is the fire that kindles them. But it is that very thing—praise of God—which constitutes almost the entire content of Christian ritual—virtually the only ritual, incidentally, which continues to have meaning within those civilizations that stem from Europe."[167] So, on that spectrum of festivals, there are those that are more genuine and efficacious (these are explicitly Christian) and then there are those that have elements of "real" festivals but in the end are poor substitutes (these might be various phenomena that fall into the category of the religion of culture). Pieper refers to the latter as "artificial festivals." He even admits that "for a time at least, [they] can thrive and even exert a more or less convincing spell—especially if the combined powers of the pseudo-arts, entertainment, sensationalism, and manipulated illusion are brought to bear, and if in addition the political rulers command and control such 'spontaneous festive gladness.'"[168]

This brief foray into Pieper's work is useful in that it illustrates in another way the crux of the issue when thinking about the future of humanity. Can "artificial festivals" (concerts, sporting events, etc.) come to function as robustly as Pieper believes stereotypical religious festivals function—especially in regard to their communal effects? More generally, as we drift away from the explicitly religious institutions and practices that for millennia were the basis of our culture, can secular institutions and practices effectively replace them? Can secular institutions and practices function just as well as the explicitly religious institutions and practices in meeting so many of the basic individual and social needs that we identified in the earlier chapters of this work? Charles Taylor has doubts, and Pieper thinks not.[169] But the answer to both these questions, from my perspective, is "yes." I am tentative, however, about that answer. I am more confident in the religion of culture's ability to meet individual needs. But I am concerned about the role that economic concerns (the market) may play here. So, I am tentative because I am not sure that the religion of culture is sufficient to produce the kind of communities and social capital needed today. We are right to be concerned about contemporary individualism and its effects on community (see the Postscript for more along these lines). And I think the "jury is still out" on whether or not the religion of culture has the resources to obviate the worst effects of individualism—particularly in its consumer form.

Still, I stand by the basic claim that human beings have some fairly stable needs and desires (some of which roughly can be considered religious), and that those needs and desires can be met in stereotypically religious ways (institutional religion) but also through a variety of cultural phenomena. If religion, like money, is a "confidence game" as Mark Taylor argues, then indeed the "dilemma is no longer how to recover confidence but to learn how to live without it."[170] My basic claim is that we indeed can learn to live without that confidence—that we can come to live an ironic life in Rorty's sense—and that the religion of culture can help us do just that. I believe, to borrow a phrase from Akeel Bilgrami, that we can and are experiencing "*secular* forms of reenchanting the world,"[171] and that reenchantment will help us persevere.

But what if those "religious" needs and desires are not as stable as I claim? What if human beings simply are becoming radically different than they have been in the past? I suppose I have to grant that possibility. But we have thousands of years of evidence against such a shift, and for now the best we can do is think about the future of human beings as we know human beings to be.

So, in the end, I have hope that humanity can move beyond stereotypical or institutional religion and still be okay. In other words, I have hope (faith?) in that ironic life for which Rorty advocates. Thus, it may be appropriate to finish with Rorty. In describing the kind of faith that he associates with pragmatism, he writes that it is:

> ... a faith in the future possibilities of mortal humans, a faith which is hard to distinguish from love for, and hope for, the human community. I shall call this fuzzy overlap of faith, hope, and love "romance." Romance, in this sense, may crystallize around a labor union as easily as around a congregation, around a novel as easily as around a sacrament, around a God as easily as around a child.[172]

As for me, I cannot think of a better way of concluding than by declaring myself a romantic in this sense.

Postscript: A Cautionary Tale

The argument that various cultural phenomena can fill the void left by the absence of institutional religion, that they actually can replace or substitute for stereotypical or institutional religion, often is met with skepticism. While I hope the last chapter addressed some concerns, I still have some as well. In particular, I am concerned about the rise of consumerism in the Western world (and increasingly around the globe). I am concerned that cultural phenomena (particularly popular culture) may not be able in the end to fulfill our "religious" needs—especially if they are corrupted (the phenomena as well as the needs) by mere economic ends and rampant consumerism.

Human beings have engaged in economic behavior for millennia. But only in more recent times has the economy come to dominate our lives and our relationships with one another. As Jean-Pierre Dupuy claims, we have become *homo economicus*. "Little by little, Economy emancipated itself from the shackles of the sacred. Once held in check by religion, and then by politics, it has today become both our religion *and* our politics," Dupuy writes. "No longer subject to any higher authority, it cannot decide our future, or make us a world in which to live: it has become our future *and* our world."[1] As with Mark C. Taylor's critique of economy detailed in Chapter 5, Dupuy is pointing us to the often hidden, and thus more pernicious, power of economy over our lives.

The particular form of economic life that dominates today is consumer capitalism—and it is consumerism that poses itself as the dark side of the religion of culture. The danger is when consumerism runs wild through cultural phenomena and institutions—including stereotypical or institutional religion, of course, but also all those phenomena and institutions that function religiously. This dark side should make us skeptical about the possibility that some elements of culture simply can replace stereotypical or institutional religion.

Some sections of this Postscript appeared in my article "Popular Culture and the Naked Self" in *Divinatio*, no. 30 (2009), pp. 85–100. I received great assistance from Dimitri Ginev in preparing and publishing that article, and I thank the journal for permission to use parts of it here.

Popular Culture and Fetishism

Philosophy "rock star" Slavoj Zizek takes exception to those who smugly proclaim that Western culture has entered successfully a post-ideological age—one free of both political ideology and religious dogma. In such an age, people no longer hold to deep beliefs about religion or history or politics. They do not need Hegel or Jesus Christ, Moses or Marx. They have become more pragmatic creatures who make rational choices based on their self-interest—whether that be economic or psychological, political or sexual. They are freed from ultimately foundationless doctrines such as Christianity or Marxism and they are all the better as a consequence. This post-ideological age is one vision of the culmination of the process of secularization.

Zizek tells the story of a man whose wife died of cancer rather suddenly. The man dealt remarkably well with her passing. But his friends noticed that whenever he talked about his wife he held a hamster in his hands—his wife's beloved pet. Months later the hamster died, the man had an emotional breakdown, and he had to be hospitalized for severe depression. In this philosophical parable, the death of the wife is the death of ideologies and the hamster is the fetish that allows people to persevere in the absence of ideologies. So, Zizek asks the post-ideologist, "*where is your hamster—the fetish which enables you to (pretend to) accept reality 'the way it is'?*"[2]

One could argue that it is in popular culture that we find an array of fetishistic objects that serve our post-ideological and secular Western culture. From television shows to Barbies, from movies to sports teams, people find a fetish that serves to fill the void left by the absence of religious and political ideologies. These ideologies, with their attendant practices and institutions, fulfilled many of our "religious" needs. Those needs remain, by and large, so the fetish (like the hamster) serves as a psychological substitute. Despite the therapeutic benefits, however, one could argue that in a viciously circular manner popular culture fetishes depend upon and promote a kind of self that is feeble and diminished—a kind of self that we would be wise to avoid. And a collection of such selves raises serious social and political concerns. To understand the objects of fetishism in contemporary culture, we have to understand how commodities work in social relations.

Marx describes a commodity as "an object outside us, a thing that by its properties satisfies human wants of some sort or another."[3] Commodities have a mystical or mysterious character to them. Produced by human beings, they take on a life of their own—detached from the hands that make them. They become the locus of social relations, to the extent that the consumers and the producers are only in a relationship through the commodity itself. Marx compares commodities to the gods of the religious world.

> In that [religious] world the productions of the human brain appear as independent beings endowed with life, and entering into relation both with one another and the human race. So it is in the world of commodities with the products of men's hands. This I call the Fetishism which attaches itself to the products of labour, so soon as they are produced as commodities, and which is therefore inseparable from the production of commodities.[4]

Thus, the attachment to or even craving of commodities is fetishism. The commodities that we desire fulfill our needs "of some sort or another." While some of these needs may be necessary for our survival (basic sustenance, shelter, etc.), commodity fetishism speaks more to deeper psychological or existential needs such as human relations and meaning—needs we often might describe as religious. Commodity fetishism speaks in particular to those needs that arise in response to traumatic change, such as, today, the fall of ideological structures (religious or political) as a consequence of the process of secularization. These needs often are even more powerful than those associated with our survival, and they explain the powerful draw that commodities have on us. This power of commodities is of particular interest to someone like Zizek, drawing on the psychoanalytic work of Jacques Lacan as well as Marxist theory.

Zizek makes an important distinction between a symptom and a fetish. Take again the case of the death of a loved one:

> In the case of a symptom, I "repress" this death, I try not to think about it, but the repressed trauma returns in the symptom; in the case of a fetish, on the contrary, I "rationally" fully accept this death, and yet I cling to the fetish, to some feature that embodies for me the disavowal of this death. In this sense, a fetish can play a very constructive role in allowing us to cope with the harsh reality: fetishists are not dreamers lost in their private worlds, they are thoroughly "realists," able to accept the way things effectively are—since they have their fetish to which they can cling in order to cancel the full impact of reality.[5]

The man whose wife died could repress his sadness and try not to think about her. He could throw himself, for example, into his work—perhaps even in an obsessive manner. Here his repressed mourning shows itself in his symptom, in his obsessive dedication to his job. On the other hand, he might rationally accept the death and talk about it freely—but only with the aid of the fetish. In this case, the hamster helps him to deal with the burden of the reality that he does not repress but that he also cannot accept completely. As Zizek concludes, "a fetish is the embodiment of the lie which enables us to sustain the unbearable truth. … In this sense, a fetish can play a very constructive role of allowing us to cope with harsh reality."[6]

Zizek's work abounds with examples of fetishes in Western, capitalist culture. Money is a good one. He writes that "a bourgeois subject knows very well that there is nothing magic about money, that money is just an object which stands for a set of social relations, but he nevertheless *acts* in real life as if he believed that money is a magical thing."[7] Western Buddhism is often a target for Zizek—and, in a sense, is a fetish. While practitioners go about their daily business immersed in the manipulations and exploitations of capitalism, they can act (through Buddhist practices) as if they are detached from it.[8] Thus, they can believe themselves to be free of that system's injustices and cruelties while knowing they are not.

The commodities of popular culture are fetishistic as well. While we know that they are merely social constructions, often mindless distractions, and ultimately meaningless, we act as if they are important and increasingly structure our lives around them—be it the ritualistic viewing of our favorite weekly television show or the obsessive fascination with our celebrities or our potentially unhealthy identification with our chosen sports team.

Max Horkheimer and Theodor Adorno were powerful critics of popular culture—in particular what they called the "culture industry," which was emerging in the middle of the twentieth century. Adorno writes, "Before the theological caprices of commodities, the consumers become temple slaves. Those who sacrifice themselves nowhere else can do so here, and here they are fully betrayed."[9] They are betrayed because the commodities never satisfy their needs, at least not enough or for long enough. Adorno, in his typically bleak manner, concludes: "Without admitting it they [the consumers of commodities] sense that their lives would be completely intolerable as soon as they no longer clung to satisfactions which are none at all."[10] For Zizek, the satisfactions are "none at all" because, like Coca-Cola, they never really satisfy us. He claims that Coke's "strange taste does not seem to provide any particular satisfaction; it is not directly pleasing and endearing; however, it is precisely as such, as transcending any immediate use-value (unlike water, beer or wine, which definitely do quench our thirst or produce the desired effect of satisfied calm), that Coke functions as the direct embodiment of '*it*': of the pure surplus of enjoyment over standard satisfactions, of the mysterious and elusive X we are all after in our compulsive consumption of merchandise."[11] Whether or not we agree with this negative assessment of Coke (he might have a better case with Diet Coke), Zizek's point is clear: consumption never ultimately satisfies us. As he concludes, "every satisfaction opens up a gap of 'I want more!'"[12] But the problem is not simply that we can never consume enough, it is that there is a fundamental *lack* in all consumption. It is not that I cannot drink enough Cokes. Whether I drink 10 or 10,000, my consumption of each one is an experience of lack—of the failure of the commodity to satisfy my real need. Thus, it is not surprising, as Juliet Schor reports, that roughly half the population in the United States (the wealthiest country on the planet) claims that "they cannot afford everything they really need."[13]

So, what can we take from Marx and Zizek? First, from Marx we must recognize that fetishes (in this case in regard to commodities) represent or embody social relations, but in an alienated way. We are not directly in relationships with others, for these relationships only are mediated through commodities. And from Zizek we see that fetishes help us to deal with a reality that we do not repress, but with which we only can cope by virtue of the fetish. So if fetishes are a sign of alienation from others, from social relations; and they are a sign of alienation from reality, because we fundamentally cannot cope with reality (the post-ideological reality) directly but only through fetishistic mediation; and if popular culture can be seen as an array of fetishistic objects and phenomena; then popular culture in the end is dependent on a socially isolated and psychologically impaired self for its success *and* in its standard mode of operation popular culture promotes such a self. Stated another and shorter way, popular culture depends upon and promotes the "naked" self.

"What Do You Mean I'm Naked?"

One description and critique of the naked self can be found in the work of Alasdair MacIntyre. Throughout much of his career, but particularly in his work *After Virtue*, MacIntyre makes a compelling argument that moral life is not a matter of rational assent to a set of transcendental philosophical or logical rules of conduct (contra Kant, for example). Instead, moral life is grounded in communities that have a certain history and that are bound to a certain tradition or traditions that provide the justification for the moral life lived in those communities (more Hegelian in this sense). This does not mean that there is no place for ethical reflection, but that community, history, and tradition precede that reflection and only on the foundation of that community, history, and tradition will the judgments and actions from that reflection be justified. The broader criticism here is of the stereotypical, liberal rational being or modern self. This self is defined by its rational capabilities rather than by the intricate web of relationships that form a substantive understanding of the self—a web that includes other selves in the community, the history of that community, and the traditions that provide myths, legends, rituals, and so much more that explain what it means to be in this intricate web. This web provides meaning to those within it, so a self outside a web is threatened by meaninglessness (think here of Durkheim's anomie). MacIntyre calls such a self the "modern" self and links it to the idea of an "emotivist" self—a self with no moral orientation but simply expressing its emotions or preferences through its language and actions. Such a self "lost its traditional boundaries provided by a social identity [formed through communities and their traditions] and a view of human life as ordered to a given end [as defined by communities and their traditions]."[14] MacIntyre describes well what I mean by naked self.

MacIntyre's project is both descriptive and prescriptive. He is describing the nature of the self. He also is describing what he takes to be changes in our understanding of the self, changes that can be traced philosophically back to Kant in the eighteenth century but that have had a broader and more pervasive impact among twentieth-century liberal democracies in the West. These democracies, increasingly secularized, fundamentally presuppose the naked self because the laws and norms of modern states draw more from reason and rational deliberation than community, history, and tradition. But MacIntyre is also prescribing a remedy to what he takes to be a contemporary social disease, and his remedy is to reinvigorate our traditions (his tradition of choice is Catholicism, though other traditions might be equally worthwhile) as sites where people can once again be whole selves (one might say "clothed selves" or what Charles Taylor might call a "full" self). In short, MacIntyre views secularization as harmful to individuals and communities, and only a return to our (overwhelmingly religious) traditions might allow us to avoid secularism's most insidious effects (meaninglessness, anomie, etc.).

Of course, there are some advantages to the naked self—especially in a pluralistic society. If we are all clothed selves, divided into separate communities, histories, and traditions, how can we form one society or one nation? Will these divisions simply lead to conflict? Have they not done so throughout human history? Do we really want a bunch of conflicting moral codes instead of one morality to which we can all rationally assent? MacIntyre is aware of these problems. But, for MacIntyre, the costs of the naked self (moral ambiguity, anxiety concerning life's purposes, loss of meaning, etc.) far outweigh the advantages (independence, possibility of an intercultural, rational moral code, etc.). In other words, MacIntyre's solution to "Hegel's dilemma" (as Taylor describes it) is (in some sense) a return to the past.

The Pop Self

MacIntyre's analysis can be applied to the self of popular culture. Popular culture treats the self not as grounded in a rich tradition that provides meaning and purpose, but as groundless—capable of being swayed and manipulated to consume this product or that form of entertainment. The popular culture self is conceived as one that has certain desires or cravings that are not bound to a community, history, or tradition. We come into the world as naked (literally and figuratively) individual consumers and we die that way.

The naked selves of American culture are easy pickings for businesses and corporations that provide consumer services and goods. The efforts of businesses and corporations have been made easier by what Schor calls the "new consumerism."[15] The new consumerism entails that citizens (consumers) not only compare their wealth and possessions to others in their income groups, but to others who tend to make much more money than they do. The result is "upscale spending," when you (the middle-class American in this example) try to keep up with the well-to-do folks you see on television as well as the Joneses (your neighbors) who live next door. Here again, the products I consume are fetishistic commodities—serving the psychological needs arising from my failure to have genuine social relationships with rich people *or* my neighbors. What relationships I have are viewed through the prism of consumer culture and mediated through commodities.

In *Born to Buy*, Schor reveals the way American children are acculturated into consumer society. At an extremely early age, an American child recognizes popular brands and already begins demanding them. Such a child obviously is not experiencing some kind of postmodern or post-ideological abyss that consumer items abate in a fetishistic manner. But such a child is being trained to overvalue or even mystify consumer items, preparing him or her for adulthood when these items—along with other popular culture creations—can ease his or her post-ideological angst. Even as children, however, the deleterious effects of consumerism are apparent:

> American children are deeply enmeshed in the culture of getting and spending, and they are getting more so. We find that the more enmeshed they are, the more they suffer for it. The more they buy into the commercial and materialist messages, the worse they feel about themselves, the more depressed they are, and the more they are beset by anxiety, headaches, stomachaches, and boredom. The bottom line on the culture they're being raised in is that it's a lot more pernicious than most adults have been willing to admit.[16]

While keeping up with the Joneses (the neighbors) next door may prod us to immerse ourselves in consumer culture, we increasingly do not even know our neighbors—let alone have strong relationships with them. Robert D. Putnam, in his acclaimed *Bowling Alone: The Collapse and Revival of American Community*, pores over an incredible array of data to show that Americans increasingly have been disconnected from their communities and less involved in civic and political life.[17] Increasingly, we do not go to church together, volunteer in community organizations, or (famously) participate in bowling leagues—the kind of activities that build social capital and strong communities (communities that can address effectively their pressing problems and improve lives). More and more of our time and attention are directed toward individual consumption. The consequence is a general lack of interest in knowing who our neighbors are— let alone socializing with them. Such indifference is compounded by the strategy of "market segmentation" that draws upon individual preference and further isolates individuals from what we might call their "natural" communities— those based on neighborhood geography, school districts, etc. On the one hand, companies utilizing market segmentation draw upon similarities within a particular group and offer products to its specific needs or wants. On the other hand, such a strategy accentuates dividing lines among the population, whether along the lines of race, age, class, ethnicity, or more. It also cuts across "natural" communities, appealing to consumers from one end of the country to the other. As Lizabeth Cohen concludes in her book *A Consumers' Republic: The Politics of Mass Consumption in Postwar America*, market segmentation strengthened "the boundaries between social groups, it contributed to a more fragmented America."[18]

Not only do American wealth and a plethora of consumer goods divide us, they also do not appear to be making us happier. This is the "lack" Zizek finds in Coca-Cola. While Americans have lots of "stuff," we have it all as isolated individuals—increasingly isolated from one another and any tradition that would provide meaning or purpose to our work and lives. Putnam details the decline in social participation rates of American citizens. They simply are not "joiners" like they used to be, and consequently they are not "doers" in regard to organizations or associations that serve the common good. Rampant consumerism and the individualism of much of popular culture may not be solely to blame, but certainly they are contributing factors.

The "Community" of Naked Selves

Many scholars argue that popular culture is a creator of community rather than a hindrance to it. In fact, I make that argument in this book. And we might conclude that some community is better than none at all. Certainly there are those in the Harley-Davidson community or the Star Trek (Trekkers) community, but these are more exceptions than the rule. Such communities entail a kind of lifestyle that accompanies the consumer product in a way that most consumer products do not (though certainly advertisers, whether for The Gap or Coca-Cola, try to convince us that their products are lifestyle choices). And I could go further. By appealing to individual needs or wants and emphasizing consumer choice, market segmentation contributes to the prevalence of naked selves and generally a very weak form of community. You join your consumer community and remain with it as long as it brings you enjoyment and makes you feel good. When it no longer does that, you move on to another consumer product and join a new community. As we saw in Chapter 6, Steve Bruce and Peter Berger (among many others) note how religious pluralism can lead to a form of religious consumerism and then weak commitment among adherents. What is true in the religious context (marketplace?) would seem to be even more so in communities that revolve around secular consumer products.

Consumer preference and its attendant weak commitment translate poorly to our natural communities of neighborhoods, school districts, and towns—places where we need to be able to work with one another to resolve conflicts and figure out solutions to local problems, where conflicts and problems can appear intractable and our continued efforts depend on our acting as citizens and not consumers. No wonder we increasingly find ourselves shut up in our homes with curtains drawn. Zizek describes us as monads. He asks, "Are we not more and more monads with no direct windows onto reality, interacting alone with the PC screen, encountering only the virtual simulacra, and yet immersed more than ever in the global network, synchronously communicating with the entire globe?"[19] (Zizek, *On Belief*, 26). Communities of monads or naked selves do not tackle local problems or generate long-lasting commitments to the community. Remember, the commodities of popular culture—the real locus of consumer communities—are only mediators of social relationships. The commodities of popular culture ultimately obfuscate these relationships. Thus, the genuine community that can arise from social relationships is missing in popular culture.

In Guy Debord's analysis, the commodities of popular culture are "spectacles." Spectacles are cultural productions that act upon the masses like an opiate (reminiscent here of Marx's critique of religion)—leading people through a life detached from the real processes of existence and from real relationships. Spectacles also function to the benefit of the "haves" rather than the "have nots." Spectacles implicitly or explicitly support or justify the existing socio-economic order. They rarely put the existing order in question. The spectacle thus functions in much the same way that religion does. In the society of the spectacle, the "illusory paradise that represented a total denial of earthly life is no longer projected into the heavens, it is embedded in earthly life itself."[20] The spectacle gives the illusion of "heaven on earth"—leaving people unconscious to the real world, particularly the world of capitalist exploitation, alienation, and general social injustice. The spectacle certainly functions religiously, but to our detriment. As a result, genuine community is impossible. He concludes:

> The spectacle keeps people in a state of unconsciousness as they pass through practical changes in their conditions of existence. Like a fictitious god, it engenders itself and makes its own rules. It reveals itself for what it is: an autonomously developing separate power, based on the increasing productivity resulting from an increasingly refined division of labour into parcelised gestures dictated by the independent movement of machines, and working for an ever-expanding market.[21]

The consequence of the society of the spectacle for the workers or the "have nots" is that the fundamental structure of the socio-economic world remains outside of one's control. He or she is simply a cog in the structure, with little dignity or respect—except, Debord notes, as a consumer. "Once his workday is over, the worker is suddenly redeemed from the total contempt toward him that is so clearly implied by every aspect of the organization and surveillance of production," he writes, "and finds himself seemingly treated like a grownup, with a great show of politeness, in his new role as a consumer."[22] He is the consumer of spectacles, ranging from the hottest concert experience to the newest technological gadget. These are all designed to usher the worker through life without ever confronting reality (e.g., the socio-economic structure itself or genuine human relations not distorted by that very structure) or even questioning it. Thus, the spectacles are not real. "The real consumer has become a consumer of illusions," Debord argues. "The commodity is this materialized illusion, and the spectacle is its general expression."[23] The commodity is not real just like the fetish is not real—for they both really only stand in for something else.

Our desires for these commodities also are produced and sold to us. In other words, the manufacturing of commodities, of spectacles, goes hand-in-hand with the manufacturing of the desires for those commodities. We see here the "replacing [of] the satisfaction of primary human needs (now scarcely met) with an incessant fabrication of pseudoneeds."[24] Debord adds, "Consumers are filled with religious fervour for the sovereign freedom of commodities whose use has become an end in itself. Waves of enthusiasm for particular products are propagated by all the communications media."[25] This propagation is ubiquitous today, given the wide range of media vehicles for advertisers and marketers. Human desires or needs are actually being generated on a daily if not hourly basis. The *real* need that is met, of course, is the need of the system or structure itself. The "pseudoneeds" all "ultimately come down to the single pseudoneed of maintaining the reign of the autonomous economy."[26] This need is met quite well, while the needs of the workers/consumers are met sporadically and unsatisfactorily. Debord concludes: "The image of blissful social unification through consumption merely *postpones* the consumer's awareness of the actual divisions until his next disillusionment with some particular commodity. Each new product is ceremoniously acclaimed as a unique creation offering a dramatic shortcut to the promised land of total consummation."[27] In other words, we falsely believe that our consumption helps us to create community, but it really only obfuscates the divisions (mainly economic, but not exclusively so) that ultimately prevent any genuine unity. As DeBord concludes, "Spectators [or we can say, consumers] are linked solely by their one-way relationship to the very centre that keeps them isolated from each other. The spectacle thus reunites the separated, but it reunites them only *in their separateness.*"[28]

Defining community or distinguishing between kinds of communities, however, is difficult. I think this is reflected in one of cultural theorist Henry Jenkins' most influential essays, "*Star Trek* Rerun, Reread, Rewritten: Fan Writing as Textual Poaching."[29] In the essay he slips from using scare quotes around the word community to not using scare quotes. Does this suggest his own ambivalence about these consumer communities and the naked selves of which they are constituted? Putnam expresses such ambivalence in looking at internet communities, many of which center on shared interests about particular commodities (e.g., BMW automobile owners). He argues that these communities fail to generate the kind of social capital of more traditional communities—the kind of social capital that forms the glue of communities and helps to get community projects and initiatives done. He also fears the spectre of "cyberbalkanization." "Local heterogeneity [found in traditional or natural communities] may give way to more focused virtual homogeneity as communities coalesce across space," Putnam writes. "Internet technology allows and encourages infrared astronomers, oenophiles, Trekkies, and white supremacists to narrow their circle to like-minded intimates."[30] In other words, we end up with geographical locations where citizens are members of a variety of virtual communities but do not even know their neighbors. Consequently, they are incapable of generating the kind of social capital necessary to accomplish anything for the neighborhood.

The proliferation of naked selves and the weak communities that follow pose some negative consequences for social and political life. The consumer of popular culture is an isolated individual. There is nothing that binds the consumer with his or her fellow citizens other than the act of consumption. There are no common traditions or codes of conduct like we find in stereotypical or institutional religion.

Schor cites research that indicates the more concerned people are with financial gain and material possessions, the less likely they are to have community affiliations.[31] Of course, many consumers share a particular product of popular culture in common. Harley Davidson motorcycle owners form a community of sorts, as do (we might suppose) Starbucks coffee drinkers or fans of the television series *Lost*. But even here we fail to reach any level of political critical mass. We do not have political community. We have groupings as a consequence of market segmentation. As naked selves we are incapable of genuine community and thus incapable of real political action. This makes us vulnerable to the machinations of the state and, of course, the culture industry.

Cohen notes that market segmentation of consumer culture has long since made its way into the political arena. In other words, not only are consumers divided through market segmentation, but citizens are divided as well—into liberals and conservatives, the religious and non-religious, gay rights advocates and their opponents, and, of course, (in the United States) Pro-Choicers and Pro-Lifers. In such a public square, politicians rarely focus on the common good. They focus on the *goods* of constituencies instead. Cohen concludes that "just as segmented buyers of goods seek the best match for their distinctive tastes and desires with what is available in the commercial marketplace, so segmented citizens have similarly come to expect the political marketplace—consisting of candidates, government agencies, and PACs—to respond to their needs and interests narrowly construed."[32] In short, citizens—full citizens, clothed in the familiarity of community, history, and tradition—have been turned into naked consumers.

We certainly must avoid the nostalgic trap of imagining some utopian past of fully engaged citizens and robust communities. Genuine communities always have been hard to come by, and even when they have come about they often have engaged in atrocious behavior (think of racist cities in the American South, the plight of homosexuals in homophobic communities, etc.). Nor should we always glorify religious traditions. They frequently have divided people as much as bringing them together in community. And religion often has functioned like a commodity as well. But the absence of a utopian past need not prevent us from recognizing the inadequacies or perniciousness of our current situation.

Liquid modernity

The cautionary tale of this Postscript may be hard to understand or at least hard to stomach. It may not be dystopic, but it still paints a fairly negative picture of contemporary humanity in Western consumer societies. Perhaps nobody has revealed the nature of this contemporary predicament better than Zygmunt Bauman. In particular, his notion of liquid modernity and all that it entails offers a significant challenge to those (like me) who may sing the praises of the religion of culture.

"What makes modernity 'liquid,'" Bauman writes, "and thus justifies the choice of name, is its self-propelling, self-intensifying, compulsive and obsessive 'modernization', as a result of which, like liquid, none of the consecutive forms of social life is able to maintain its shape for long."[33] Modernity is understood here as a period in which nothing is stable. There are no foundations (neither ideological belief structures nor rich and self-evident traditions). Everything is free-floating (thus, the imagery of liquid). In such an environment, we will see, consumerism has free rein.

Bauman accepts the standard postmodern assumption that grand religious or political narratives have gone by the wayside. Humanity is not on some inevitable march to eternal salvation after the coming apocalypse (as least salvation for some) or to an idyllic communist utopia or really to anything fundamentally different than what we have now. Certainly there is progress, but the progress is limited to ever new and improved products, increased leisure time, or even the creation of new pleasures of which we cannot even dream at the moment. In place of the grand narratives of the past we simply have consumerism—the overarching means by which we organize our society and increasingly our lives. Bauman defines consumerism as

> a type of social arrangement that results from recycling mundane, permanent and so to speak 'regime-neutral' human wants, desires and longings into the *principal propelling and operating force* of society, a force that coordinates systemic reproduction, social integration, social stratification and the formation of human individuals, as well as playing a major role in the processes of individual and group self-identification and in the selection and pursuit of individual life policies.[34]

In consumerism, material goods and life experiences must be produced. But they are not the most important products. The most important products are desires themselves. That is what makes consumerism today so unique. As Bauman concludes, "consumerism, in sharp opposition to the preceding forms of life, associates happiness not so much with the *gratification* of needs ... as with an *ever rising volume and intensity* of desires, which imply in turn prompt use and speedy replacement of the objects intended and hoped to gratify them."[35] While this may sound sad, what else do we have? We do not *really* believe in religious or political narratives anymore. They do not ground us—helping us to form communities, guiding our decisions and actions, and providing our lives with a grander and transcendent context of meaning. In such a situation, all we have is consumption. We are fully victims (even more so, since we see ourselves as incredibly free rather than victimized) to what Adorno and Horkheimer call the culture industry or Debord calls the society of the spectacle.

The new regime of consumerism changes everything. Take happiness for example. "Our society of consumers is perhaps the only society in human history that promises happiness in *earthly life*, and happiness *here* and *now*, in every successive 'now'—an undelayed and continuous happiness," Bauman writes, "and the only society that refrains from justifying any variety of *un*happiness, refuses to tolerate it, and presents it as an abomination that calls for punishment of the culprits and compensation for the victims."[36] Happiness is not simply a goal in life, but an obligation—an obligation that left unfulfilled must be punished by social ostracism.

But the fixation on happiness also is misleading, because the whole consumer economy only works when we are *not* completely happy. As Bauman notes (similar to Zizek), "the promise of satisfaction remains seductive only as long as the desire stays *ungratified*."[37] In other words, "Consumer society thrives as long as it manages to render the *non-satisfaction* of its members (and so, in its own terms, their unhappiness) *perpetual*. The explicit method of achieving such an effect is to denigrate and devalue consumer products shortly after they have been hyped into the universe of the consumers' desires."[38] Think here of the succession of new iPhones. The newest version certainly has some improvements and new features, but the most important effect of the new iPhone (from the perspective of the consumer society, which is the only perspective that matters) is to "denigrate and devalue" the older version I have in my pocket. Thus, I am no longer happy with my old iPhone and desire the new one. And so the cycle begins, one iPhone after another for as far into the future as we can see. It only ends in the grave (undoubtedly with my phone buzzing or ringing because I could not figure out how to change the notification setting). "The function of culture is not to satisfy existing needs, but to create new ones—while simultaneously maintaining needs already entrenched or permanently unfulfilled," Bauman concludes. "Its chief concern is to prevent a feeling of satisfaction in its former subjects and charges, now turned into clients, and in particular to counteract their perfect, complete and definitive gratification, which would leave no room for further, new and as yet unfulfilled needs and whims."[39]

This description of our predicament sounds fairly dour. And, of course, defenders of the current consumerist regime would insist that there are good reasons for another assessment. For example, they might point to the incredible freedom that accompanies consumer society. We have an amazing array of consumer choices and we have the freedom to choose which ones might make us happy. But in a way analogous to Weber's "iron cage," Bauman argues that choice is exactly the problem. We may have choice, but we do not have the choice to choose or not. We have to play the consumer game whether we want to or not (indeed, the overwhelming majority of people could no more imagine *not* playing the game than they could imagine not being human). And the objects or experiences from which we choose are not limitless and are not a matter of our choosing. "Choice is yours," Bauman insists, "but making choices is obligatory [just as being happy is obligatory], and the limits on what you are allowed to choose are non-negotiable."[40] The fact that we have choice gives us a false sense of freedom,[41] which (of course) makes our victimization by the culture industry all the easier. This freedom that is not really freedom is one of the dominant characteristics of the "society of consumers."

> The 'society of consumers', in other words, stands for the kind of society that promotes, encourages or enforces the choice of a consumerist lifestyle and life strategy and dislikes all alternative cultural options; a society in which adapting to the precepts of consumer culture and following them strictly is, to all practical intents and purposes, the sole unquestionably approved choice; a feasible, and so also a plausible choice—and a condition of membership.[42]

A final characteristic of the consumer condition is worth noting—the ways in which consumers themselves become products.

> In most descriptions, the world formed and sustained by the society of consumers stays neatly divided into things *to be chosen* and their *choosers*; commodities and their consumers: things to be consumed and the humans to consume them. In fact, however, the society of consumers is what it is precisely because of being nothing of the sort; what sets it apart from other types of society is exactly the *blurring*, and ultimately the *effacing* of the divisions listed above.[43]

In other words, the "most prominent feature of the society of consumers—however carefully concealed and most thoroughly covered up—is the *transformation of consumers into commodities*."[44] One sees this commodification of consumers starkly in the way in which consumer data are bought and sold on the internet—data specifically intended to be used to create new desires among consumers to perpetuate the consumer economy. But more profoundly we see this commodification in the way that the very project of being a human being is now a kind of product. When there are no grand narratives and no religious or political foundations for my identity, then my identity becomes a product—something I produce through the consumption that comes to define me. "In the liquid modern society of consumers no identities are gifts at birth, none is 'given', let alone given once and for all and in a secure fashion," Bauman observes. "Identities are projects: tasks yet to be undertaken, diligently performed and seen through to infinitely remote completion."[45] This fluidity of identity ultimately does not serve the consumer, but rather the culture industry.

> Rather than a gift ... identity is a sentence to lifelong hard labour. For the producers of avid and indefatigable consumers and for the sellers of consumer goods it is also an inexhaustible source of capital—a source that tends to grow bigger with each scoop. Once set in motion in early childhood, the composing and dismantling of identity becomes a self-propelling and self-invigorating activity.[46]

Who am I? At one point in the life cycle I am part of the counter culture with a leather jacket and a motorcycle; then a young professional with a casual business suit and minivan; then an old hipster with a beret and classic sports car; then ... In short, I constantly am changing because there is no solid ground to my identity. And the consumer products that I purchase (clothes, vehicles, entertainment, etc.) are not just expressions of those changing identities but *constitutive of them*. In other words, I am not intrinsically a hipster who then buys a beret; I buy the beret and become a hipster. And here then we have the sum of my life—the continual obligation (yes, another one) to create my identity, to create myself.

A primary concern for Bauman is how the society of consumers functions (or does not function) ethically. Our communities often are the sources of our norms and values and shape us as moral beings. But what kind of communities do we even have in a society of consumers? Like the rest of liquid modern realities, communities in the society of consumers hold only a weak resemblance to genuine communities. Part of the problem is simply the sheer number of potential groups to which we can belong. "In its contemporary liquid-modern rendition, belonging to one entity may be shared and practiced simultaneously with belonging to other entities in almost any combination, without necessarily provoking condemnation or repressive measures of any kind," Bauman observes. "Accordingly, attachments have lost much of their past intensity."[47]

There are moments of togetherness, of course, but they are fleeting and generate few bonds and even less loyalty. Bauman identifies contemporary carnivals (we might think here of Debord's spectacles) as prime examples. "The function (and seductive power) of liquid modern carnivals," he claims, "lies in the momentary resuscitation of the togetherness that has sunk into a coma."[48] Here we have Durkheim's "collective effervescence" or Turner's *communitas*— states of consciousness and togetherness that are stereotypical goals of religious practice. Going to the sporting event or the music festival does give rise to some sort of togetherness and altered consciousness, but it hardly forms a lasting community. It certainly does not generate the kind of emotional attachment or social capital needed for people to solve difficult social or political problems or to make sacrifices for the group.

Bauman conceptualizes the individual's capitulation to the group or the society as a surrender to the "totality."[49] Such individual surrender certainly can have its downside (e.g., blind nationalism, fascism), but it also is the foundation of our duty not only to the group, society, or nation, but to one another. In the society of consumers, Bauman insists, "No lasting bonds emerge in the activity of consumption."⁵⁰ Without those bonds and awash in the consumerist ethos, everything about morality changes.

> The concepts of responsibility and responsible choice, which used to reside in the semantic field of ethical duty and moral concern for the Other, have moved or have been shifted to the realm of self-fulfillment and calculation of risks. In the process, the Other as the trigger, the target, and the yardstick for a responsibility accepted, assumed, and fulfilled has all but disappeared from view, having been elbowed out or overshadowed by the actor's own self. "Responsibility" means now, first and last, *responsibility to oneself* ("You owe this to yourself," as the outspoken traders in relief from responsibility indefatigably repeat), while "responsible choices" are, first and last, such moves as serve well the interests and satisfy the desires of the actor and stave off the need to compromise.⁵¹

Morality in liquid modernity entails a strange kind of duty to constantly form our identity through our consumption. "Changing identity, discarding the past and seeking new beginnings, struggling to be born again," Bauman writes, "these are promoted by that culture as a *duty* disguised as a privilege."⁵² Another way of putting it is that "the ethical guideline of the consuming life … has to be to avoid *staying satisfied*,"⁵³ because only continual dissatisfaction can keep the consumer society going. Even some of our most basic moral orientations, such as sympathy and care for the poor, become twisted. Rather than sympathy, the poor in the society of consumers become suspect and denigrated because of their inability to participate in the consumer society. "While the poor are banished from the streets, they can also be banished from the recognizably *human* community: from the world of *ethical* duties," Bauman argues. "This is done by rewriting their stories away from the language of deprivation to that of depravity. The poor are portrayed as lax, sinful and devoid of moral standards."⁵⁴ In a world of consumer "choice" and "freedom," only those who have some sort of failing or defect would not participate in that world or choose its happiness.

In the end, Bauman, like others mentioned earlier, presents us with a disturbing view of our current society of consumers and the culture industry that shapes and perpetuates it. It is a view that serves as a powerful challenge to the idea, advanced in previous chapters, that the products of that culture industry effectively can take up the functions (from individual identity to community formation) of stereotypical religious institutions—at least as we might imagine those institutions to function in an ideal world.

Peek-a-boo

Neil Postman, in his seminal work *Amusing Ourselves to Death: Public Discourse in the Age of Show Business*, describes us as entering a "peek-a-boo" world. The "peek-a-boo" world is one "where now this event, now that, pops into view for a moment, then vanishes again. It is a world without much coherence or sense; a world that does not ask us, indeed, does not permit us to do anything; a world that is, like the child's game of peek-a-boo, entirely self-contained. But like peek-a-boo, it is also endlessly entertaining."[55]

While Postman is concerned here mainly with television and in particular television news, his analogy can be applied to all of popular culture. Popular culture commodities or spectacles come at us faster than we can consume them—more demanding our attention as we finally focus on one. There is no coherent or unified purpose or meaning to it all. An even better analogy than peek-a-boo may be our dog Zoe. On walks she constantly is moving her nose along the ground, rapidly shifting from one direction to another—briefly stopping to sniff something (goose poop, a sewer manhole cover, etc.) before moving on to another smell. Are we not just like her in regard to our commodities—moving rapidly from one consumer product, one spectacle, to another? Of course, for Zoe, her behavior is instinct. We, however, are trained animals—trained by the culture industry.

The ways that popular culture exploits and encourages naked selves are depressing and do not bode well for us as individuals. This sense of foreboding gets worse when we begin to consider the social and political consequences. We increasingly are a mere collection of individuals rather than a community. One might wonder if there is any hope for our future. Adorno perhaps foresaw this predicament when he wrote:

> The neon signs which hang over our cities and outshine the natural light of the night with their own are comets presaging the natural disaster of society, its frozen death. Yet they do not come from the sky. They are controlled from earth. It depends upon human beings themselves whether they will extinguish these lights and awake from a nightmare which only threatens to become actual as long as men believe in it.[56]

If this "nightmare" can be avoided or, in a more dire sense, if we can wake up from the "nightmare" we already have begun dreaming, it is going to take a re-orientation of our perspective to our popular culture. It is going to take a renewed affirmation of the "fully clothed" self—the self intricately bound in a web of community, history, and tradition. And such an affirmation itself will require the realization that the fetishes of popular culture, no matter how good they might seem, are poor substitutes for the human relationships that nourish our lives and upon which our political fate depends. Stereotypical or institutional religion often has been the ground upon which community has been built, history remembered, and traditions perpetuated. Its absence cannot easily be compensated for by the religion of culture. I say "cannot easily" because I do not think it is impossible. But it will require us to draw upon what is best, most powerful, and most efficacious in the religion of culture—and defend it against the dangers of consumerism and mere economic interests.

Conclusion

I am convinced that we have natural "religious" needs that can be met outside of stereotypical religious traditions. At the same time, there may be limits to the effectiveness of the religion of culture to meet those needs. And, what happens when these needs are manipulated and exploited by the culture industry? As theologian Harvey Cox writes about "The Market," uncontrolled economic logic can "intrude and distort other vital institutions such as the family, the arts, education, and religion."[57] If economic logic wins out, we likely will end up with rather pathetic selves and weak communities.

In Chapter 5, I turned to Mark C. Taylor and others to describe how there are religious elements and dimension to the economy and economic behavior—especially in more recent times. I think this is a bad development, and Taylor certainly has detailed well the dangers of the economic "confidence game."[58] Even worse, perhaps, is when economic aims and logic corrupt other cultural phenomena. We know what it can do to religion (we can trace a sad history in this regard from the selling of indulgences in the medieval Catholic church all the way to corrupt and disgraced televangelists today). But given that I used sport as an exemplary model in the last chapter, let me return to that seemingly secular cultural phenomenon. Indeed, sport may even be a prime example of a cultural phenomenon where nefarious economic aims and logic come to counter or even destroy its positive values.

Cultural critic Dave Zirin describes sport as "suffocated" by "corporate greed" and "commercialism."[59] He even describes the world of sport, at least from the perspective of the fan, as a *Terrordome*—harkening back to the image of the Superdome in New Orleans and the suffering of those trapped there in the aftermath of Hurricane Katrina.

While the profiteers of sport can include universities, college coaches, and the National Collegiate Athletic Association, all of whom profit from the "free" labor of student athletes, Zirin's main targets are professional leagues and owners. And though he details well their power, he does not think that athletes and fans are helpless. He instead thinks we (I am including myself here) have a chance. He writes: "By speaking out for the political [and, I would add, spiritual] soul of the games we love, we begin to impose our ideas on the world of sports—a counter morality to compete with the yawning hypocrisy of the pro leagues."[60] It is in this way that Zirin sees sport as a "site of resistance" and a source of hope in a social ethos dominated by economic self-interest. He believes sport "can become an arena where the ideas of our society are not only presented but also challenged. Just as sports can reflect the dominant ideas of our society, they can also reflect struggle."[61] Just like any religion when it is functioning at its social best, sport has the ability to question our social norms and values and change the world for the better.[62]

At the end of our book *Understanding Sport as a Religious Phenomenon: An Introduction*, Greg Sapp and I write:

> Like the ancient Greeks, whose games also came to be corrupted by politics and money, we need to recognize the critical importance of our games as well. Our games are *not* "just" play. Play is an intrinsic and critical human quality that is manifested through sport. It should not be taken lightly. And while sport may be "secular" in some sense, it nevertheless is "sacred secular." We should treat it as carefully as we should treat all that is "holy."[63]

What is true for sport is true of other cultural phenomena that feed our minds and souls and help us to bond with one another. The religion of culture—which includes much of popular culture, but not necessarily all of it—always is threatened by our baser instincts and motivations. What this Postscript has shown is that we must be ever vigilant against the inroads of economic aims and logic and the consumer ethos that it engenders. Only in this way can we protect our cultural phenomena, allowing them to meet our "religious" needs to whatever extent they can.

Notes

Introduction

1. Eric J. Sharpe, *Comparative Religion: A History*, second edition (LaSalle, IL: Open Court, 1986).
2. Walter H. Capps, *Religious Studies: The Making of a Discipline* (Minneapolis, MN: Augsburg Fortress, 1995).
3. Daniel L. Pals, *Eight Theories of Religion*, second edition (New York: Oxford University Press, 2006).
4. Christopher M. Driscoll and Monica R. Miller, *Method as Identity: Manufacturing Distance in the Academic Study of Religion* (New York: Lexington Books, 2019).
5. Additional materials from a number of these scholars can be found in the endnotes.

Chapter 1

1. Immanuel Kant, *Toward Perpetual Peace and Other Writings on Politics, Peace, and History*, translated by David L. Colclasure (New Haven, CT: Yale University Press, 2006), 17.
2. The combination of rationalism, cultural maturity, and the civilizational mission of the Western world was used in particularly destructive ways in the history of Western colonialism and genocide.
3. Immanuel Kant, *Groundwork of the Metaphysic of Morals*, translated by H.J. Paton (New York: Harper & Row, Publishers, 1964), 61.
4. Kant, *Groundwork*, 62.
5. Kant, *Groundwork*, 64.
6. Kant, *Groundwork*, 100.
7. Kant, *Groundwork*, 108.
8. "Hypothetical imperatives declare a possible action to be practically necessary as a means to the attainment of something else that one wills (or that one may will). A categorical imperative would be one which represented an action as objectively necessary in itself apart from its relation to a further end" (Kant, *Groundwork*, 82).
9. Kant describes duty as *"the necessity to act out of reverence for the law"* (*Groundwork*, 68)—the moral law that is a product of my rationality.
10. Kant, *Groundwork*, 88.
11. Kant, *Groundwork*, 96.

12 The third formulation builds off of the second, but (to my mind) does little to advance the argument. It simply states that we should act as if all human beings were part of a "Kingdom of Ends." By doing so, we would avoid treating other human beings simply as means (returned us to the second formulation).
13 See Immanuel Kant, *Critique of Practical Reason*, translated by Lewis White Beck (New York: Macmillan Publishing Company, 1956), 126–36.
14 Kant, *Critique*, 134.
15 Immanuel Kant, *Religion within the Limits of Reason Alone*, translated by Theodore M. Greene and Hoyt H. Hudson (New York: Harper & Row, Publishers, 1960), 3.
16 Kant, *Religion*, 3.
17 Kant, *Religion*, 56.
18 Kant, *Religion*, 47.
19 Kant, *Religion*, 158.
20 Kant, *Religion*, 161.
21 Kant, *Religion*, 91. Burkhard Tuschling states that the ethical commonwealth "represents the final end (*summum bonum*), the higher possible good *in the world* and the telos of history—of humanity's coming to the final point of its perfectibility and rationality" (Burkhard Tuschling, "*Rationis societas*: Remarks on Kant and Hegel," in *Kant's Philosophy of Religion Reconsidered*, edited by Philip J. Rossi and Michael Wreen (Bloomington, IN: Indiana University Press, 1991), 186).
22 Kant, *Religion*, 139.
23 Kant, *Religion*, 155.
24 Kant, *Religion*, 102.
25 Kant, *Religion*, 95.
26 Kant warns, "To deem this statutory faith … as essential to the service of God generally, and to make it the highest condition of the divine approval of man, is *religious illusion* whose consequence is a *pseudo-service*, that is, pretended honoring of God through which we work directly counter to the service demanded by God Himself" (*Religion*, 156).
27 Kant, *Religion*, 79.
28 Kant, *Religion*, 167–8.
29 Kant, *Religion*, 181.
30 Kant, *Religion*, 163.
31 Kant, *Religion*, 105.
32 Kant, *Religion*, 129.
33 Kant, *Religion*, 9.
34 Tuschling, "*Rationis*," 187.
35 Kant, *Religion*, 107.
36 Kant, *Religion*, 112.
37 Charles Taylor, *A Secular Age* (Cambridge, MA: Harvard University Press, 2007), 312.

38 Georg Wilhelm Friedrich Hegel, *Phenomenology of Spirit*, translated by A.V. Miller (New York: Oxford University Press, 1977), 6.
39 Georg Wilhelm Friedrich Hegel, *Lectures on the Philosophy of Religion*, translated by E.B. Speirs and J. Burdon Sanderson (New York: The Humanities Press, 1974), 53.
40 This account necessarily abbreviates Hegel's much more elaborate account of the relationship of Spirit to the world. That more elaborate account is summarized when Hegel writes: "Spirit is the content of its consciousness at first in the form of *pure substance*, or is the content of its pure consciousness. This element of Thought is the movement of descending into existence or into individuality. The middle term between these two is their synthetic connection, the consciousness of passing into otherness, or picture-thinking as such. The third moment is the return from picture-thinking and otherness, or the element of self-consciousness itself. These three moments constitute Spirit" (Hegel, *Phenomenology*, 464). Here we see the way in which Hegel's understanding of Spirit mirrors a kind of evolutionary development of the human species and human rationality. The intricate link among human beings, Spirit, and reason is highlighted in this passage from Hegel:

> [T]here cannot be a Divine reason and a human, there cannot be a Divine Spirit and a human, which are *absolutely different*. Human reason—the consciousness of one's being—is indeed reason; it is the divine in man, and Spirit, in so far as it is the Spirit of God, is not a spirit beyond the stars, beyond the world. On the contrary, God is present, omnipresent, and exists as Spirit in all spirits. God is a living God, who is acting and working. (Hegel, *Lectures*, 33)

41 Hegel, *Lectures*, 33. Charles Taylor provides the following summary: "Hegel's Spirit, or *Geist*, although he is often called 'God' and although Hegel claimed to be clarifying Christian theology, is not the God of traditional theism; he is not a God who could exist quite independently of men, even if men did not exist, as the God of Abraham, Isaac and Jacob before the creation. On the contrary, he is a spirit who lives as spirit only through men [sic]. They are the vehicles, and the indispensable vehicles, of his spiritual existence, as consciousness, rationality, will" (Charles Taylor, *Hegel and Modern Society* (Cambridge, UK: Cambridge University Press, 1979), 11).
42 Hegel, *Phenomenology*, 414.
43 Hegel insists that "no man is so utterly ruined, so lost, and so bad, nor can we regard any one as being so wretched that he has no religion whatever in him, even if it were only that he has the fear of it, or some yearning after it, or a feeling of hatred towards it" (*Lectures*, 5).
44 Hegel, *Lectures*, 206.
45 Hegel, *Lectures*, 246.
46 "It is thus *One Individuality* which, presented in its essence as God, is honored and enjoyed in *Religion*," Hegel writes, "which is exhibited as an object of sensuous

contemplation in *Art*; and is apprehended as an intellectual conception, in *Philosophy*" (Georg Wilhelm Friedrich Hegel, *The Philosophy of History*, translated by J. Sibree (New York: Willey Book Co., 1944), 49).

47 Hegel, *Lectures*, 138.
48 Hegel, *Lectures*, 20. He elaborates:

> The object of religion as well as of philosophy is eternal truth in its objectivity, God and nothing but God, and the explication of God. Philosophy is not a wisdom of the world, but is knowledge of what is not of the world; it is not knowledge which concerns external mass, or empirical existence and life, but is knowledge of that which is eternal, of what God is, and what flows out of His nature. For this His nature must reveal and develop itself. Philosophy, therefore, only unfolds itself when it unfolds religion, and in unfolding itself it unfolds religion. (Hegel, *Lectures*, 19)

49 Hegel, *History*, 53.
50 Mark C. Taylor writes: "His monumental philosophical system is best understood as a comprehensive philosophy of culture in which representations, ideas, and concepts influence and are influenced by history. Neither arbitrary nor directionless, the course of history, according to Hegel, follows a strict dialectical progression in which later stages bring to fruition and replace preceding stages. Within this trajectory, religion gives way to art, which, in turn, culminates in philosophy. Having become free from images and representations, philosophy brings nature, history, and self-consciousness to conceptual clarity and perfect transparency" (*Confidence Games: Money and Markets in a World Without Redemption* (Chicago: The University of Chicago Press, 2004), 25).
51 Hegel, *Phenomenology*, 298.
52 Hegel, *Lectures*, 2.
53 Hegel, *Phenomenology*, 265.
54 Hegel, *Phenomenology*, 213.
55 Taylor, *Hegel*, 81.
56 Taylor, *Hegel*, 87.
57 Hegel, *History*, 38.
58 Hegel, *History*, 39.
59 Hegel, *Lectures*, 246.
60 Hegel, *History*, 74.
61 Language plays a particularly critical role for Hegel: "Language is self-consciousness existing *for others*, self-consciousness which *as such* is immediately *present*, and as *this* self-consciousness is universal. It is the self that separates itself from itself, which as pure 'I'='I' becomes objective to itself, which in this objectivity equally preserves itself as *this* self, just as it coalesces directly with other selves and is *their* self-consciousness" (Hegel, *Phenomenology*, 395).

62 Hegel, *Lectures*, 246.
63 Hegel, *Phenomenology*, 492.
64 Hegel, *History*, 9. He adds that "Reason governs the world, and has consequently governed its history" (Hegel, *History*, 25).
65 Hegel, *Phenomenology*, 488.
66 Hegel, *Phenomenology*, 493.
67 Hegel, *History*, 17.
68 Tuschling, "Rationis," 190.
69 Friedrich Schleiermacher, *On Religion: Speeches to Its Cultured Despisers*, translated by Richard Crouter (New York: Cambridge University Press, 1988), 31.
70 Schleiermacher, *On Religion*, 19.
71 Compare Schleiermacher here to this statement from Hegel:

> Feeling is a form, or mould, for every possible kind of content, and this content receives no determination therefrom which could affect its own independent existence, its being in-and-for self. Feeling is the form in which the content appears as perfectly accidental, for it may just as well be posited by my caprice, or good pleasure, as by Nature. The content as it exists in feeling thus appears as not absolutely determined on its own account, as not posited through the Universal, through the Notion. (Hegel, *Lectures*, 131)

72 Schleiermacher, *On Religion*, 54.
73 Schleiermacher, *On Religion*, 112.
74 Schleiermacher, *On Religion*, 59.
75 Schleiermacher, *On Religion*, 111.
76 Ludwig Feuerbach, *Essence of Christianity*, translated by George Eliot (New York: Prometheus Books, 1989), xv.
77 Feuerbach, *Essence*, xix.
78 Feuerbach, *Essence*, xviii.
79 Feuerbach, *Essence*, 2.
80 Feuerbach, *Essence*, 3.
81 "In the object [God] which he contemplates," Feuerbach writes, "man becomes acquainted with himself; consciousness of the objective is the self-consciousness of man. We know the many by the object, by his conception of what is external to himself; in it his nature becomes evident; this object is his manifested nature, his true objective *ego*" (Feuerbach, *Essence*, 5).
82 Feuerbach, *Essence*, 13. Feuerbach uses an anatomical analogy to emphasize this point: "As the action of the arteries drives the blood into the extremities, and the action of the veins brings it back again, as life in general consists in a perpetual systole and diastole; so is it in religion. In the religious systole man propels his own nature from himself, he throws himself outward; in the religious diastole he receives the rejected nature into his heart again" (Feuerbach, *Essence*, 31).

83 Feuerbach, *Essence*, 12–13.
84 Feuerbach, *Essence*, 40–1.
85 Feuerbach, *Essence*, 36.
86 Feuerbach, *Essence*, 289.
87 Feuerbach writes about the relationship of morality to religion: "Only in its morality does the essence of a religion realise, reveal itself: morality alone is the criterion, whether a religious dogma is felt as a truth or is a mere chimera" (Feuerbach, *Essence*, 336).
88 Feuerbach, *Essence*, 46.
89 Feuerbach, *Essence*, 47.
90 Feuerbach, *Essence*, 47.
91 Feuerbach, *Essence*, 49.
92 Feuerbach, *Essence*, xvi.
93 Feuerbach, *Essence*, 282.
94 Karl Marx, *Karl Marx: The Essential Writings*, second edition, edited by Frederic L. Bender (Boulder, CO: Westview Press, 1972), 45.
95 Marx, *Writings*, 46.
96 Marx, *Writings*, 46.
97 Daniel L. Pals writes: "Religion, he says, is pure illusion. Worse, it is an illusion with most definitely evil consequences. It is the most extreme example of ideology, of a belief system whose chief purpose is simply to provide reasons—excuses, really—for keeping things in society just the way the oppressors like them" (*Seven Theories of Religion* (New York: Oxford University Press, 1996), 138).
98 Marx, *Writings*, 46. Pals concludes: "For him, belief in God and in some heavenly salvation is not just an illusion; it is an illusion that paralyzes and imprisons. It paralyzes workers by drawing off into fantasy the very motives of anger and frustration they need to organize a revolt. Desire for heaven makes them content with earth. At the same time, religion also imprisons; it promotes oppression by presenting a system of belief which declares that poverty and misery are facts of life which ordinary people must simply accept and embrace" (Pals, 143).

Chapter 2

1 James Spickard, *Alternative Sociologies of Religion: Through Non-Western Eyes* (New York: New York University Press, 2017), 27.
2 Spickard, *Alternative Sociologies of Religion*, 78.
3 Spickard, *Alternative Sociologies of Religion*, 2.
4 Portions of this section on Durkheim are revised from *Understanding Sport as a Religious Phenomenon: An Introduction* (New York: Bloomsbury, 2016), which I co-authored with D. Gregory Sapp.

5   Emile Durkheim, *The Elementary Forms of Religious Life*, translated by Karen E. Fields (New York: The Free Press, 1995), 34.
6   Robert N. Bellah, "Durkheim and Ritual," in *The Cambridge Companion to Durkheim*, edited by Jeffrey C. Alexander and Philip Smith (Cambridge, UK: Cambridge University Press, 2005), 184.
7   Spickard, *Alternative Sociologies of Religion*, 68.
8   Durkheim, *Elementary Forms*, 41.
9   Durkheim, *Elementary Forms*, 44.
10 Chris Shilling, "Embodiment, Emotions, and the Foundations of Social Order: Durkheim's Enduring Contribution," in *The Cambridge Companion to Durkheim*, edited by Jeffrey C. Alexander and Philip Smith (Cambridge, UK: Cambridge University Press, 2005), 213–14.
11 Durkheim, *Elementary Forms*, 267.
12 Durkheim, *Elementary Forms*, 16.
13 Durkheim, *Elementary Forms*, 271.
14 Victor Turner, *Dramas, Fields, and Metaphors: Symbolic Action in Human Society* (Ithaca, NY: Cornell University Press, 1974), 55.
15 Durkheim, *Elementary Forms*, 330.
16 Durkheim, *Elementary Forms*, 347.
17 Durkheim, *Elementary Forms*, 350.
18 Robert Alun Jones, "Practices and Presuppositions: Some Questions about Durkheim and *Les Formes elementaires de la vie religieuse*," in *The Cambridge Companion to Durkheim*, edited by Jeffrey C. Alexander and Philip Smith (Cambridge, UK: Cambridge University Press, 2005), 81.
19 Durkheim, *Elementary Forms*, 385.
20 The experience of "collective effervescence" may be similar to what Mihaly Csikszentmihalyi describes as the experience of "flow." I will leave that discussion, however, for Chapter 5.
21 As Roger Friedland concludes: "Effervescent aggregation performs, expresses, mimes, indeed, is, the enabling powers of collective life, upon which not only does the finest within us depend, but from which we derive our meaning and our material existence, indeed which enables us to be" ("Drag kings at the totem Ball: the erotics of collective representation in Emile Durkheim and Sigmund Freud," in *The Cambridge Companion to Durkheim*, edited by Jeffrey C. Alexander and Philip Smith (Cambridge, UK: Cambridge University Press, 2005), 243).
22 Spickard, *Alternative Sociologies of Religion*, 69.
23 Shilling, "Embodiment," 221.
24 Elisa Heinamaki, "Durkheim, Bataille, and Girard on the Ambiguity of the Sacred: Reconsidering Saints and Demoniacs," *Journal of the American Academy of Religion*, vol. 83, no. 2 (2015), 518.

25 Victor Turner, *The Ritual Process: Structure and Anti-Structure* (New York: Aldine de Gruyter, 1995), 131–2.
26 Turner, *Dramas*, 272.
27 Turner, *Ritual Process*, 132.
28 Turner, *Dramas*, 56.
29 Turner, *Ritual Process*, 139.
30 Durkheim, *Elementary Forms*, 386.
31 Durkheim, *Elementary Forms*, 429.
32 Edward A. Tiryakian, "Durkheim, Solidarity, and September 11," in *The Cambridge Companion to Durkheim*, edited by Jeffrey C. Alexander and Philip Smith (Cambridge, UK: Cambridge University Press, 2005), 309.
33 Lawrence A. Scaff, "Weber on the Cultural Situation of the Modern Age," in *The Cambridge Companion to Weber*, edited by Stephen Turner (Cambridge, UK: Cambridge University Press, 2000), 104–6.
34 Scaff, "Weber," 104.
35 Scaff, "Weber," 104.
36 Scaff, "Weber," 105.
37 Max Weber, *Economy and Society*, Volume 1, edited by Guenther Roth and Claus Wittich (Berkeley, CA: University of California Press), 426.
38 Weber, *Economy*, 426.
39 Weber, *Economy*, 400.
40 Weber, *Economy*, 480.
41 Max Weber, *The Protestant Ethic and the "Spirit" of Capitalism and Other Writings*, edited by Peter Baehr and Gordon C. Wells (New York: Penguin Books, 2002), 35.
42 Weber, *Protestant*, 36.
43 Weber, *Protestant*, 122. On this point, intellectual biographer Fritz Ringer writes: "Max Weber took Karl Marx very seriously, not only because he considered him the creator of an extremely fruitful ideal type, but also because he respected his practice as an economic and social historian. On the other hand, he flatly rejected the notion that all causal connections in history can ultimately be traced back to economic conditions, however defined, or that all historical processes are essentially unidirectional" (*Max Weber: An Intellectual Biography* (Chicago: The University of Chicago Press, 2004), 113).
44 Weber, *Protestant*, 12.
45 Weber, *Protestant*, 23.
46 Weber, *Protestant*, 28.
47 Weber, *Protestant*, 19.
48 Weber, *Protestant*, 1.
49 Weber, *Protestant*, 4.
50 Weber, *Protestant*, 16. I have altered the particulars of the example for the ease of the reader.

51 Weber, *Protestant*, 4–5.
52 Weber, *Protestant*, 29.
53 Luther, Martin, *Martin Luther: Selections from His Writings*, edited by John Dillenberger (New York: Anchor Books, 1961), 493.
54 Weber, *Protestant*, 69.
55 Weber, *Protestant*, 73.
56 Weber, *Protestant*, 73.
57 Weber, *Protestant*, 76.
58 Weber, *Protestant*, 77–8.
59 Weber, *Protestant*, 107.
60 Weber, *Protestant*, 81–2.
61 Weber, *Protestant*, 83.
62 Weber, *Protestant*, 104.
63 Weber, *Economy*, 544.
64 Weber, *Protestant*, 68.
65 Weber concludes: "Christian asceticism, which was originally a flight from the world into solitude, had already once dominated the world on behalf of the Church from the monastery, by renouncing the world. In doing this, however, it had, on the whole, left the natural, spontaneous character of secular everyday life unaffected. Now it would enter the market place of life, slamming the doors of the monastery behind it, and set about permeating precisely this secular everyday life with its methodical approach, turning it toward a rational life *in* the world, but neither *of* this world nor *for* it" (Weber, *Protestant*, 104–5).
66 Weber, *Economy*, 588.
67 The successful business person "was given the comforting assurance that the unequal distribution of this world's goods was the special work of the providence of God, who by means of these distinctions, and his 'particular' grace, was working out his secret purposes, of which we know nothing" (Weber, *Protestant*, 119).
68 Weber, *Protestant*, 110.
69 Weber writes: "And if that restraint on consumption is *combined with* the freedom to strive for profit, the result produced will inevitably be the *creation of capital* through the *ascetic compulsion to save*" (Weber, *Protestant*, 116–17).
70 Weber, *Protestant*, 115.
71 Weber, *Protestant*, 120–1.
72 Weber, *Protestant*, 121.
73 Guy Debord, *Society of the Spectacle*, translated by Ken Knabb (London: Rebel Press, n.d.).
74 Alan Sica summarizes well this viewpoint in his analysis of Weber, and is worth quoting at length: "Western, modernized, rationalized humans have become childish in their demands upon each other and upon their environments, social and ecological, as have peoples in other parts of the world who have begun imitating

this general model of behavior and social organization. When it suits their private short-term desires, they exhibit 'rationality' in the purest economic meaning of the term. Yet after their materials and status needs are more or less satisfied, at least temporarily, they turn for relief from regimentation and predictable tedium to those very realms of social life, those zones of solace, wherein rationality has the least play and the least likely future influence. That is, they rush to those few remaining human or animal intimates still available to them, to aesthetic realms of abandon which seem ever more important (perhaps the hallmark of 'post-modern culture'), and to a revived yet only half-believed supernatural realm of doctrine and chant that requires, in order to work properly, a suspension of modern scientific principles that educated people find very difficult to manage—except those in dire psychological straits" ("Rationalization and Culture," in *The Cambridge Companion to Weber*, edited by Stephen Turner (New York: Cambridge University Press, 2000), 57).
75 Ringer, 158.

Chapter 3

1   Sigmund Freud, *New Introductory Lectures on Psycho-Analysis*, translated and edited by James Strachey (New York: W. W. Norton & Company, 1965), 222.
2   Robert A. Paul, "Freud's Anthropology: A Reading of the 'Cultural Books,'" in *The Cambridge Companion to Freud*, edited by Jerome Neu (New York: Cambridge University Press, 1991), 276.
3   "It is our suspicion that during the human family's primaeval period castration used actually to be carried out by a jealous and cruel father upon growing boys, and that circumcision, which so frequently plays a part in puberty rites among primitive peoples, is a clearly recognizable relic of it" (Freud, *Introductory*, 108).
4   "One day the brothers who had been driven out came together, killed and devoured their father and so made an end of the patriarchal horde" (Sigmund Freud, *Totem and Taboo: Some Points of Agreement between the Mental Lives of Savages and Neurotics*, translated by James Strachey (New York: W. W. Norton & Company, 1950), 141).
5   Freud, *Totem*, 142. See also Sigmund Freud, *Moses and Monotheism*, translated by Katherine Jones (New York: Vintage Books, 1939), 103.
6   We also have here the Oedipus complex, since at least some of the women the young men desired were their mothers (Freud, *Totem*, 156).
7   Freud, *Totem*, 143.
8   Freud, *Totem*, 145.
9   Freud, *Totem*, 148.
10 Freud, *Totem*, 150.

11 Freud, *Totem*, 145.
12 Freud, *Totem*, 150. Thus, he adds: "The problem of the relation between animal and human sacrifice thus admits of a simple solution. The original animal sacrifice was already a substitute for a human sacrifice—for the ceremonial killing of the father; so that, when the father-surrogate once more resumed its human shape, the animal sacrifice too could be changed back into a human sacrifice" (Freud, *Totem*, 151).
13 Freud, *Totem*, 153.
14 Freud, *Totem*, 146.
15 Daniel L. Pals notes: "For Freud, then, the murder in the prehistoric herd is an event of momentous importance in the history of human social life. In the powerful emotions is produced, we find the origin of religion. In the incest taboo—the agreement to protect the clan in its aftermath—we can see the origin of morality and the social contract. Taken together, totem and taboo thus form the very foundation of all that later comes to be called civilization" (*Seven Theories of Religion* (New York: Oxford University Press, 1996), 70).
16 Freud, *Introductory Lectures*, 93.
17 Freud, *Introductory Lectures*, 91.
18 Freud, *Introductory Lectures*, 138.
19 Sigmund Freud, *Civilization and Its Discontents*, translated by James Strachey (New York: W. W. Norton & Company, 1961), 69.
20 An important benefit of this mutual cooperation is the protection of individuals against nature. See Sigmund Freud, *The Future of an Illusion*, translated by James Strachey (New York: W. W. Norton & Company, 1961), 15, 16.
21 Freud, *Civilization*, 46–7.
22 To be clear on some basic terminology, Freud writes that "we will describe the fact that an instinct cannot be satisfied as a 'frustration', the regulation by which this frustration is established as a 'prohibition' and the condition which is produced by the prohibition as a 'privation'" (Freud, *Future*, 10).
23 Freud, *Future*, 7.
24 Freud, *Future*, 6.
25 Freud, *Civilization*, 49.
26 Freud, *Civilization*, 49.
27 Freud, *Civilization*, 58.
28 Carl E. Schorske, "Freud: The Psychoarcheology of Civilizations," in *The Cambridge Companion to Freud*, edited by Jerome New (New York: Cambridge University Press, 1991), 8.
29 Freud, *Civilization*, 66.
30 Freud, *Future*, 11.
31 For Freud, conscience "is the internal perception of the rejection of a particular wish operating within us" (Freud, *Totem*, 68). Conscience then leads to the development of a sense of guilt in the individual (Freud, *Civilization*, 79, 89, 97).

32 Freud, *Future*, 11.
33 Freud, *Future*, 18.
34 Freud, *Future*, 21.
35 Freud, *Future*, 31.
36 Freud, *Future*, 31.
37 Freud, *Civilization*, 20.
38 Freud, *Future*, 42–3.
39 As Paul summarizes the argument, religion "is the neurosis of civilization, the price civilized people pay for the instinctual renunciations demanded of them. Nor is it just any neurosis; it is specifically a neurosis of the obsessive-compulsive type" (Paul, "Freud's anthropology," 270).
40 Freud, *Totem*, 88.
41 Freud, *Totem*, 90.
42 Freud, *Future*, 28.
43 Freud, *Future*, 38.
44 Freud, *Future*, 49.
45 Freud, *Future*, 50.
46 In regard to commandments and laws that previously were seen as the merely arbitrary declarations of a divine being or beings, Freud writes: "People could understand that they are made, not so much to rule them as, on the contrary, to serve their interests; and they would adopt a more friendly attitude to them, and instead of aiming at their abolition, would aim only at their improvement. This would be an important advance along the road which leads to becoming reconciled to the burden of civilization" (Freud, *Future*, 41).
47 John Deigh, "Freud's Later Theory of Civilization: Changes and Implications," in *The Cambridge Companion to Freud*, edited by Jerome Neu (New York: Cambridge University Press, 1991), 287.
48 Deigh, "Freud's Later Theory of Civilization," 287.
49 Freud, *Future*, 56.
50 Carl Jung, *Modern Man in Search of a Soul*, translated by W.S. Dell and Cary F. Baynes (New York: Houghton Mifflin Harcourt, 1933), 240.
51 Philip Rieff, *The Triumph of the Therapeutic: Uses of Faith after Freud* (Chicago: The University of Chicago Press, 1966), 88.
52 Carl Jung, *The Archetypes and the Collective Unconscious*, translated by R.F.C. Hull (Princeton, NJ: Princeton University Press, 1969), 3.
53 Jung, *Archetypes*, 42.
54 Carl Jung, *Two Essays on Analytical Psychology*, translated by R.F.C. Hull (Princeton, NJ: Princeton University Press, 1966), 145.
55 Jung, *Modern*, 186.
56 Jung, *Archetypes*, 22.
57 Jung, *Archetypes*, 22.

58   Jung, *Essays*, 147.
59   Jung, *Archetypes*, 282.
60   Jung, *Essays*, 154.
61   Jung, *Essays*, 162.
62   Jung, *Archetypes*, 278.
63   Jung, *Archetypes*, 42.
64   Jung, *Archetypes*, 82.
65   Jung, *Archetypes*, 82.
66   Jung, *Essays*, 65.
67   Jung, *Archetypes*, 48.
68   Jung, *Archetypes*, 160. He makes an even clearer connection with instincts when he writes: "there is good reason for supposing that the archetypes are the unconscious images of the instincts themselves, in other words, that they are *patterns of instinctual behaviour*" (Jung, *Archetypes*, 44).
69   Jung, *Archetypes*, 286–7. He also writes: "They are images spring from the life, the joys and sorrows, of our ancestors; and to life they seek to return, not in experience only, but in deed. Because of their opposition to the conscious mind they cannot be translated straight into our world; hence a way must be found that can mediate between conscious and unconscious reality" (Jung, *Essays*, 79).
70   Jung, *Archetypes*, 48.
71   Jung, *Archetypes*, 5.
72   Jung, *Archetypes*, 154.
73   Carl Jung, "Approaching the Unconscious," in *Man and His Symbols*, edited by Carl Jung (New York: Dell Publishing, 1968), 68.
74   Jung, *Modern*, 166.
75   Jung, *Modern*, 169, 170.
76   Jung, *Essays*, 234.
77   Jung, *Essays*, 173.
78   Jung, *Essays*, 174.
79   Jung, *Archetypes*, 40.
80   Ann Belford Ulanov, "Jung and Religion: The Opposing Self," in *The Cambridge Companion to Jung*, edited by Polly Young-Eisendrath and Terence Dawson (New York: Cambridge University Press, 2008), 324.
81   Ulanov, "Jung and Religion," 326.
82   Jung, *Modern*, 197.
83   Jung, *Archetypes*, 62.
84   Jung, *Archetypes*, 16.
85   Jung, "Approaching," 84.
86   Jung, "Approaching," 85.
87   Jung, *Modern*, 126.

88 Jung, *Modern*, 244.
89 Rieff, *The Triumph of the Therapeutic*, 133.
90 See Jung, *Archetypes*, 94, 253, and *Essays*, 72.
91 Pals, *Seven Theories*, 77.
92 Rieff summarizes well Jung's view: "To end the spiritual impoverishment of Western culture, Jung recommends the following: that the rationalist suppression of myth and of other manifestations of the unconscious need mitigation, but not by a new theology or by new dogmas; rather, by a therapeutic release of the myth components from the collective unconscious. The neurosis of modernity is defined by Jung as the suppression of precisely those irrational components. Therefore, Jung is recommending an essentially private religiosity without institutional reference or communal membership for the individual in need of an integrated symbolism. In this sense, Jung is anti-institutional; he suspects that institutions rapidly rationalize a symbol system, rendering it rigid for the individual, thus to become a negative factor in the process of 'individuation'" (Rieff, 134).
93 This section is revised from my article, "Affect Theory, Spirituality, and Sport," that appeared in a special issue of the online journal *Religions* (Summer 2019). Many thanks to Tracy Trothen, who organized and edited the special issue, and to the peer reviewers who provided helpful feedback.
94 Donovan O. Schaefer, *Religious Affect: Animality, Evolution, and Power* (Durham, NC: Duke University Press, 2015), 4.
95 Schaefer, *Religious*, 23.
96 John Corrigan, "Introduction: How Do We Study Religion and Emotion?," in *Feeling Religion*, edited by John Corrigan (Durham, NC: Duke University Press, 2017), 9.
97 Schaefer, *Religious*, 15.
98 Schaefer, *Religious*, 94.
99 Schaefer, *Religious*, 24. He adds: "Affects invert the metaphysical emphasis on the human's rational sovereignty over its body, retracing us as nests of animal becoming, finding pleasure in spinning out of control. Affective economies are directed by compulsions—by autotelic forces that derail the abacus of rational self-interest" (Schaefer, *Religious*, 166).
100 Donovan O. Schaefer, "Beautiful Facts: Science, Secularism, and Affect," in *Feeling Religion*, edited by John Corrigan (Durham, NC: Duke University Press, 2017), 70.
101 David Morgan, "Emotion and Imagination in the Ritual Entanglement of Religion, Sport, and Nationalism," in *Feeling Religion*, edited by John Corrigan (Durham, NC: Duke University Press, 2017), 225.
102 Schaefer, "Beautiful," 79.

103 Schaefer also is interested in how affects are related to power. For him, "Affects fuse together to shape the planes of interface between bodies and power" (Schaefer, "Beautiful," 77). He also states, "Affect theory in all its forms is designed to profile the operations of power outside of language and the autonomous, reasoning human subject" (Schaefer, *Religious*, 23). Schaefer's work in this direction is interesting and worth engaging, but not critical for our purposes.
104 Schaefer, *Religious*, 39.
105 Schaefer, *Religious*, 9–10.
106 Schaefer, *Religious*, 24.
107 Schaefer, *Religious*, 134. He adds: "Religion is an extraordinarily powerful distribution network through the global nervous system of affect" (Schaefer, *Religious*, 175).
108 Religion also is an area where Schaefer analyzes power. He notes, "Religion, like other forms of power, moves bodies by creating affective ligatures between bodies and their worlds" (Schaefer, *Religious*, 179). In other words, religions "like other formations of power, are reservoirs of compulsory links to the world" (Schaefer, *Religious*, 207). In the end, he concludes: "Affects wordlessly crawl through our bodies on the way to the world, producing systems of power as they do—some of which get called religious" (Schaefer, *Religious*, 218).
109 Schaefer, *Religious*, 8. Also see Schaefer, *Religious*, 54, 59.
110 Wayne Proudfoot, *Religious Experience* (Berkeley, CA: University of California Press, 1985), 75–8.
111 William James, *The Varieties of Religious Experience* (New York: Collier Books, 1961), 42.
112 Proudfoot, *Religious*, 11.
113 Proudfoot, *Religious*, 11.
114 Proudfoot, *Religious*, 18.
115 Proudfoot, *Religious*, 40.
116 Proudfoot, *Religious*, 36.
117 Proudfoot, *Religious*, 92–3.
118 Proudfoot, *Religious*, 93.
119 Proudfoot, *Religious*, 102.
120 Proudfoot, *Religious*, 196.
121 Proudfoot, *Religious*, 197.
122 Proudfoot, *Religious*, 195.
123 Proudfoot, *Religious*, 200.
124 Proudfoot, *Religious*, 231.
125 Mihaly Csikszentmihalyi, *Flow: The Psychology of Optimal Experience* (New York: HarperCollins, 1990), 4.
126 Csikszentmihalyi, *Flow*, 72.

127 Howard Slusher, "Sport and the Religious," in Charles S. Prebish, *Religion and Sport: The Meeting of Sacred and Profane* (Westport, CT: Greenwood Press, 1993), 191.
128 Slusher, "Sport and the Religious," 191.
129 For a critique of Proudfoot, see G. William Barnard, "Explaining the Unexplainable: Wayne Proudfoot's *Religious Experience*," *Journal of the American Academy of Religion*, vol. 60, no. 2 (1992), 231–56. Interested readers might then want to consult Proudfoot's response and Barnard's rejoinder in the *Journal of the American Academy of Religion*, vol. 61, no. 4 (1993), 793–812.
130 Schaefer, *Religious*, 117.
131 Schaefer, *Religious*, 209.
132 Abby Kluchin, "At the Limits of Feeling: Religion, Psychoanalysis, and the Affective Subject," in *Feeling Religion*, edited by John Corrigan (Durham, NC: Duke University Press, 2017), 257.
133 Morgan, "Emotion," 223.
134 Morgan, "Emotion," 228.
135 Morgan, "Emotion," 230.
136 Morgan, "Emotion," 238.
137 Ann Taves, *Religious Experience Reconsidered: A Building-Block Approach to the Study of Religion and Other Special Things* (Princeton, NJ: Princeton University Press, 2009), 21. It should be noted that Taves recognizes a fair amount of agreement between her position and Proudfoot's work (Taves, 93).
138 Taves, *Religious Experience Reconsidered*, 162.

Chapter 4

1 Mircea Eliade, *The Sacred & Profane: The Nature of Religion*, translated by Willard R. Trask (New York: Harcourt Brace Jovanovich, 1959), 162.
2 Mircea Eliade, *Myths, Dreams, and Mysteries: The Encounter between Contemporary Faiths and Archaic Realities*, translated by Philip Mairet (New York: Harper & Row Publishers, 1960), 9.
3 Eliade, *Sacred*, 165.
4 Mircea Eliade, *The Quest: History and Meaning in Religion* (Chicago: The University of Chicago Press, 1969), 4.
5 Jason N. Blum, "Retrieving Phenomenology of Religion as a Method for Religious Studies," *Journal of the American Academy of Religion*, vol. 80, no. 4 (2012), 1032. He adds that "phenomenology of religion does not posit the existence of transcendent, religious, or sacred realities, nor does it endorse the perspective of the religious subject or assume the truth of religion. Rather, it employs epoche and

suspends judgment concerning these matters, and instead focuses on interpreting the consciousness and experience of the imminent religious subject" (1043).

6   Eliade, *Quest*, 10.
7   Mircea Eliade, *Ordeal by Labryinth: Conversations with Claude-Henri Rocquet*, translated by Derek Coltman (Chicago: The University of Chicago Press, 1982), 121.
8   Eliade, *Quest*, 2.
9   Eliade, *Quest*, 19.
10 Mircea Eliade, *No Souvenirs: Journal, 1957–1969*, translated by Fred H. Johnson, Jr. (New York: Harper & Row Publishers, 1977), 55.
11 See Eliade, *Quest*, 21–2.
12 Eliade, *Myths, Dreams*, 14.
13 Mircea Eliade, *Shamanism: Archaic Techniques of Ecstasy*, translated by Willard R. Trask (Princeton, NJ: Princeton University Press, 1964), xvii.
14 Russell T. McCutcheon, *Manufacturing Religion: The Discourse on Sui Generis Religion and the Politics of Nostalgia* (New York: Oxford University Press, 1997), 35.
15 Eliade, *Myths, Dreams*, 17.
16 Eliade, *Myths, Dreams*, 18.
17 Eliade, *Sacred*, 28.
18 Eliade, *Sacred*, 11.
19 Eliade, *Sacred*, 14.
20 Eliade, *Sacred*, 64.
21 Eliade, *Sacred*, 100.
22 Mircea Eliade, *The Myth of the Eternal Return, or, Cosmos and History*, translated by Willard R. Trask (Princeton, NJ: Princeton University Press, 1954), 4.
23 Eliade, *Myth*, 42, 43.
24 Eliade, *Patterns in Comparative Religion*, translated by Rosemary Sheed (New York: Sheed & Ward, 1958), xiv, 13.
25 Eliade, *Patterns in Comparative Religion*, 447.
26 Eliade, *Patterns in Comparative Religion*, 11.
27 Eliade, *Patterns in Comparative Religion*, 367.
28 Eliade, *The Sacred & Profane*, 21, 26.
29 Eliade, *The Sacred & Profane*, 88–9.
30 Eliade, *Patterns in Comparative Religion*, 407.
31 For Eliade, "any human act whatever acquires effectiveness to the extent to which it exactly *repeats* an act performed at the beginning of time by a god, a hero, or an ancestor" (*Myth*, 22).
32 Eliade, *Myth*, 52.
33 Eliade, *Sacred*, 23.

34 Eliade, *Sacred*, 50.
35 Eliade, *Sacred*, 204.
36 Eliade, *Sacred*, 204.
37 Mircea Eliade, *Autobiography, Volume II: 1937–1960: Exile's Odyssey*, translated by Mac Linscott Ricketts (Chicago: The University of Chicago Press, 1988), 84–5.
38 Eliade, *Sacred*, 209.
39 Eliade, *Sacred*, 210.
40 Eliade, *Myths, Dreams*, 24.
41 Eliade, *Patterns*, 398.
42 Eliade, *Myths, Dreams*, 28.
43 Eliade, *Patterns*, 400.
44 Eliade, *Myths, Dreams*, 33.
45 Eliade, *Sacred*, 24.
46 Eliade, *Sacred*, 45.
47 Eliade, *Patterns*, 379.
48 Mircea Eliade, *Journal III: 1970–1978*, translated by Teresa Lavender Fagan (Chicago: The University of Chicago Press, 1989), 284.
49 Eliade, *Sacred*, 206–7.
50 David Chidester, *Authentic Fakes: Religion and American Popular Culture* (Berkeley, CA: University of California Press, 2005), 1.
51 Chidester, *Authentic Fakes*, 18.
52 Chidester, *Authentic Fakes*, 231.
53 Eliade, *Myths, Dreams*, 237.
54 Eliade, *Ordeal*, 148.
55 Eliade, *Sacred*, 168.
56 Eliade, *Patterns*, 455–6.
57 Eliade, *Sacred*, 185–6.
58 Eliade, *Sacred*, 203.
59 Eliade, *Myth*, 151.
60 Eliade, *Myth*, 161.
61 Eliade suggests that Christianity can play a particularly helpful role in this regard. See Eliade, *Myth*, 162.
62 Eliade, *Autobiography II*, 102.
63 Eliade, *Sacred*, 201–2.
64 Eliade, *Quest*, 58.
65 Eliade, *Quest*, 62. Eliade also writes: "The hermeneutic necessary for the revelation of the meanings and the messages hidden in myths, rites, symbols, will also help us to understand both depth psychology and the historical age into which we are entering and in which we will be not only surrounded but also dominated by the 'foreigners,' the non-Occidentals. It will be possible to decipher the 'Unconscious,'

as well as the 'Non-Western World,' through the hermeneutic of the history of religions" (Eliade, *Souvenirs*, 70).

66 Eliade, *Quest*, 3.
67 Eliade, *Quest*, 67.
68 Eliade, *Quest*, 69.
69 Eliade, *Souvenirs*, 17.
70 Many scholars have been critical of Eliade's humanist project, believing it is an obstacle to the proper study of religion—particularly in terms of understanding religion in its full cultural, political, economic, and historical context. One compelling critique is Russell McCutcheon. He writes: "The new humanism is therefore idealist insofar as it proposes that social change occurs from the inside out; that is, beliefs are altered first through the interpreter's contact with a text or ritual, and only then can social values change and lead to the creation of a new social arrangement … It is also elitist and romantic insofar as it proposes that social change occurs from the top down and that the peasants and cultural elites share essential similarities that transcend their class and economic disparities" (McCutcheon, *Manufacturing*, 71).
71 Charles H. Long, *Significations: Signs, Symbols, and Images in the Interpretation of Religion* (Philadelphia: Fortress Press, 1986), 51. Christopher M. Driscoll and Monica R Miller add: "Eliade was convinced that the history of religions—what he ultimately came to call a humanist endeavor—would serve a vital role in translating across the many cultural and ethnic worlds continuously colliding across the shrinking globe in the wake of World War II" (*Method as Identity: Manufacturing Distance in the Academic Study of Religion* (New York: Lexington Books, 2019), 79).
72 See Steven Pinker's *The Better Angels of Our Nature: Why Violence Has Declined* (New York: Penguin Books, 2012).
73 Jonathan Z. Smith, "Tillich['s] Remains … ", *Journal of the American Academy of Religion*, vol. 78, no. 4 (2010), 1147.
74 Paul Tillich, *Systematic Theology: Volume Three: Life and the Spirit: History and the Kingdom of God* (Chicago: The University of Chicago Press, 1963), 118.
75 Paul Tillich, "Art and Ultimate Reality," *Dimensions* (1959), 2.
76 Paul Tillich, *Theology of Culture*, edited by Robert C. Kimball (New York: Oxford University Press, 1959), 5–6.
77 Tillich, *Theology*, 7.
78 Tillich, *Theology*, 7.
79 Tillich, *Theology*, 7–8.
80 Tillich, *Theology*, 8.
81 Tillich, *Theology*, 8. He adds: "Reductive profanization may succeed in abolishing religion as a special function, but it is not able to remove religion as a quality that is found in all functions of the spirit—the quality of ultimate concern" (Tillich, *Systematic*, 102).

82	Tillich, *Theology*, 40.
83	Tillich, *Theology*, 42.
84	Tillich, *Systematic*, 130.
85	Tillich, *Systematic*, 130. He adds: "Faith is actual in all life processes—in religion, in the other functions of the spirit, and in the preceding realms of life—in so far as they condition the actualization of the spirit" (Tillich, *Systematic*, 134).
86	Tillich, *Systematic*, 131.
87	Tillich, *Theology*, 41.
88	Tillich, *Theology*, 49.
89	Tillich, *Theology*, 51.
90	Tillich, *Systematic*, 155. He adds: "It is most important for the practice of the Christian ministry, especially in its missionary activities toward those both within and without the Christian culture, to consider pagans, humanists, and Jews as members of the latent Spiritual Community and not as complete strangers who are invited into the Spiritual Community from outside" (Tillich, *Systematic*, 155).
91	Tillich, *Systematic*, 213.
92	Tillich, *Theology*, 51.
93	Tillich, *Theology*, 58–9.
94	Tillich, *Theology*, v.
95	Tillich, *Theology*, 27. For Tillich, the root or basis of this relationship is found in language. He writes, "Intended or not, it [ultimate concern] expresses itself in the most basic of all cultural creations, in human language, and thence it permeates the whole life of a society" (Tillich, *Theology*, 178).
96	Tillich, *Systematic*, 111.
97	Tillich, *Systematic*, 247.
98	Tillich, *Theology*, 42.
99	Tillich, *Theology*, 42.
100	Tillich, *Theology*, 46–7.
101	Tillich, "Art," 3.
102	Tillich, *Systematic*, 64.
103	As Tillich insists, "the manifestation of the ultimate in the visual arts is not dependent on use of works which traditionally are called religious art" (Tillich, "Art," 11).
104	Tillich, *Systematic*, 201.
105	Tillich, *Theology*, 70.
106	Tillich, *Systematic*, 254.
107	Tillich, *Systematic*, 254.
108	Tillich, *Systematic*, 38.
109	Tillich, *Systematic*, 44. He adds: "The commandments of the moral law are valid because they express man's essential nature and put his essential being against him in his state of existential estrangement" (Tillich, *Systematic*, 46).

110 Tillich, *Systematic*, 95.
111 Tillich, *Systematic*, 95.
112 Tillich, *Systematic*, 274–5.
113 Tillich, *Systematic*, 97.
114 Tillich, *Systematic*, 97.
115 Tillich, *Systematic*, 248.
116 Tillich, *Systematic*, 248.
117 Kelton Cobb, "Reconsidering the Status of Popular Culture in Tillich's Theology of Culture," *Journal of the American Academy of Religion*, vol. 63, no. 1 (1995), 80.

Interlude

1 Mark C. Taylor, *After God* (Chicago: The University of Chicago Press, 2007), xiii.
2 Taylor, *After*, 3.
3 Taylor, *After*, 64.
4 Taylor, *After*, 73.
5 Taylor, *After*, 101.
6 Mark C. Taylor, *About Religion: Economies of Faith in Virtual Culture* (Chicago: The University of Chicago Press, 1999), 34.
7 "When the True is finally grasped as subject, God becomes fully embodied in nature as well as history and both self and world are completely transformed," Taylor writes. "This transformation reverses the interrelated processes of desacralization and disenchantment by revealing the sacred in the midst of what had seemed profane. With this twist, secularity appears to be the fulfillment rather than the simple negation of religion" (Taylor, *After*, 153).
8 Taylor, *After*, 157.
9 Taylor, *After*, 158.
10 "While intending to reduce the divine to the human, these hermeneuticists of suspicion actually remain haunted by the ghost of religion they struggle to dispel," Taylor concludes. "When read against the grain, their socioeconomic, psychological, and aesthetic theories of religion imply an irreducible altarity in the midst of immanence and the presence it is supposed to realize" (Taylor, *After*, 184).
11 Taylor, *After*, 201.
12 Taylor, *About*, 178.
13 Taylor, *After*, 2–3.
14 Taylor, *After*, 10.
15 Taylor, *After*, 132.
16 Taylor, *About*, 148.

Chapter 5

1. To make the text less cumbersome, I will use the phrase "religion of culture" to denote the study of the religious elements or dimensions of cultural phenomena that otherwise are not considered religious.
2. The exact number is debatable. Some articles may have been left out since they focused more on the intersection of religion with culture rather than the religious elements or dimensions of culture. An example of the former might be an article about Baptists engaging with or critiquing popular music and dancing. On the other hand, an example of the latter would be a study on the religious aspects of dance itself.
3. David Chidester, *Authentic Fakes: Religion and American Popular Culture* (Berkeley, CA: University of California Press, 2005).
4. Bruce David Forbes and Jeffrey H. Mahan, eds, *Religion and Popular Culture in America*, third edition (Berkeley, CA: University of California Press, 2017).
5. Terry Ray Clark and Dan W. Clanton, Jr., eds, *Understanding Religion and Popular Culture* (New York: Routledge, 2012).
6. Juan M. Floyd-Thomas, Stacey M. Floyd-Thomas, and Mark G. Toulouse, *The Altars Where We Worship: The Religious Significance of Popular Culture* (Louisville, KY: Westminster John Knox Press, 2016).
7. Chidester, *Authentic*, vii–viii.
8. Chidester, *Authentic*, viii.
9. Chidester, *Authentic*, 18.
10. Chidester, *Authentic*, 9.
11. Chidester, *Authentic*, 49–50.
12. Chidester, *Authentic*, 29.
13. Catherine Albanese, "Religion and American Popular Culture: An Introductory Essay," *Journal of the American Academy of Religion*, vol. 64, no. 4 (1996), 740.
14. Brenda E. Brasher, "Thoughts on the Status of the Cyborg: On Technological Socialization and Its Link to the Religious Function of Popular Culture," *Journal of the American Academy of Religion*, vol. 64, no. 4 (1996), 814.
15. Brasher, "Thoughts on the Status," 821–2.
16. Peter W. Williams, "Sacred Space in North America," *Journal of the American Academy of Religion*, vol. 70, no. 3 (2002), 607.
17. Kevin Schilbrack, "Religions: Are There Any?", *Journal of the American Academy of Religion*, vol. 78, no. 4 (2010), 1125.
18. John C. Lyden, "Whose Film Is It, Anyway? Canonicity and Authority in *Star Wars* Fandom," *Journal of the American Academy of Religion*, vol. 80, no. 3 (2012), 783.
19. Lyden, "Whose Film Is It," 783.

20 Kati Curts, "Temples and Turnpikes in 'The World of Tomorrow': Religious Assemblage and Automobility at the 1939 New York World's Fair," *Journal of the American Academy of Religion*, vol. 83, no. 3 (2015), 725.
21 Curts, "Temples and Turnpikes," 725.
22 William Dean, *The American Spiritual Culture: And the Invention of Jazz, Football and the Movies* (New York: Continuum, 2003), 20.
23 Dean, *American Spiritual Culture*, 114.
24 Mark C. Taylor, *About Religion: Economies of Faith in Virtual Culture* (Chicago: The University of Chicago Press, 1999), 148.
25 Floyd-Thomas, Floyd-Thomas, and Toulouse, *The Altars Where We Worship*, 2.
26 Floyd-Thomas, Floyd-Thomas, and Toulouse, *The Altars Where We Worship*, 6.
27 Floyd-Thomas, Floyd-Thomas, and Toulouse, *The Altars Where We Worship*, 11.
28 Kathryn Lofton, *Consuming Religion* (Chicago: The University of Chicago Press, 2017), 4.
29 Lofton, *Consuming*, 6.
30 Lofton, *Consuming*, 6.
31 David R. Loy, "The Religion of the Market," *Journal of the American Academy of Religion*, vol. 65, no. 2 (1997), 275.
32 Jerry D. Meyer, "Profane and Sacred: Religious Imagery and Prophetic Expression in Postmodern Art," *Journal of the American Academy of Religion*, vol. 65, no. 1 (1997), 19.
33 Meyer, "Profane and Sacred," 42.
34 M.C. Taylor, *About*, 177.
35 Floyd-Thomas, Floyd-Thomas, and Toulouse, *The Altars Where We Worship*, 86.
36 Floyd-Thomas, Floyd-Thomas, and Toulouse, *The Altars Where We Worship*, 88.
37 Chidester, *Authentic*, 34.
38 Chidester, *Authentic*, 47.
39 Chidester, *Authentic*, 33.
40 Norman J. Girardot, "*Ecce* Elvis: 'Elvis Studies' as a Postmodernist Paradigm for the Academic Study of Religion," *Journal of the American Academy of Religion*, vol. 68, no. 3 (2000), 604.
41 Girardot, "*Ecce* Elvis," 604.
42 Girardot, "*Ecce* Elvis," 612.
43 Maxine L. Grossman, "Jesus, Mama, and the Constraints on Salvific Love in Contemporary Country Music," *Journal of the American Academy of Religion*, vol. 70, no. 1 (2002), 92.
44 Grossman, "Jesus, Mama, and the Constraints," 110.
45 Monica R. Miller, "Real Recognize Real: Aporetic Flows and the Presence of New Black Godz in Hip Hop," in *Religion in Hip Hop: Mapping the New Terrain in the US*, edited by Monica R. Miller, Anthony B. Pinn, and Bernard "Bun B" Freeman (New York: Bloomsbury, 2015), 201.

46 Michael Eric Dyson, "Preface," in *Religion in Hip Hop: Mapping the New Terrain in the US*, edited by Monica R. Miller, Anthony B. Pinn, and Bernard "Bun B" Freeman (New York: Bloomsbury, 2015), xix.
47 Michael Eric Dyson, "God Complex, Complex Gods, or God's Complex: Jay-Z, Poor Black Youth, and Making 'The Struggle' Divine," in *Religion in Hip Hop: Mapping the New Terrain in the US*, edited by Monica R. Miller, Anthony B. Pinn, and Bernard "Bun B" Freeman (New York: Bloomsbury, 2015), 55. He adds, "Jay-Z is fundamentally linked whether consciously or unconsciously, to this tradition of black preaching and rhetorical performativity" (56).
48 Dyson, "God complex," 68.
49 The blues subsequently are connected to Black spirituals, but very much in a critical way. In the blues, "the promises of the spirituals were weighed and tested in light of life's controlling hardships, and utopian ideals were found wanting" (Anthony B. Pinn, "Rap Music and Its Message: On Interpreting the Contact between Religion and Popular Culture," in *Religion and Popular Culture in America*, third edition, edited by Bruce David Forbes and Jeffrey H. Mahan (Oakland, CA: University of California Press, 2017), 393).
50 Pinn, "Rap Music," 398.
51 For an excellent discussion by Kenny Beats, listen to this Broken Record podcast: https://brokenrecordpodcast.com/all#/episode-90-kenny-beats-1/.
52 For a very creative treatment of the politically progressive aspect of rap music, also see Pinn's "Zombies in the Hood: Rap Music, Camusian Absurdity, and the Structuring of Death," in *Religion in Hip Hop: Mapping the New Terrain in the US*, edited by Monica R. Miller, Anthony B. Pinn, and Bernard "Bun B" Freeman (New York: Bloomsbury, 2015).
53 Pinn, "Rap Music," 402.
54 Pinn, "Rap Music," 404.
55 Pinn, "Rap Music," 404.
56 Pinn, "Rap Music," 405.
57 Pinn, "Rap Music," 406.
58 Pinn, "Rap Music," 406.
59 Bernard "Bun B" Freeman, "Afterword: An Insider Perspective," in *Religion in Hip Hop: Mapping the New Terrain in the US*, edited by Monica R. Miller, Anthony B. Pinn, and Bernard "Bun B" Freeman (New York: Bloomsbury, 2015), 218.
60 Freeman, "Afterword," 219.
61 Freeman writes: "Where there are perceived instances of abuse, brutality, and civil rights violations by police, the hip hop community has helped make the issues at hand not only visualized, but vocalized" (Freeman, "Afterword," 219).
62 Freeman, "Afterword," 220.
63 Bernard "Bun B" Freeman, "Bun B on Religion and Hip Hop: An Interview (by Biko Gray) with Bun B," in *Religion in Hip Hop: Mapping the New Terrain in the US*,

edited by Monica R. Miller, Anthony B. Pinn, and Bernard "Bun B" Freeman (New York: Bloomsbury, 2015), 134.
64 Monica R. Miller, *Religion and Hip Hop* (New York: Routledge, 2013), 10.
65 Miller, *Religion*, 58.
66 Miller, *Religion*, 62.
67 Miller, *Religion*, 61.
68 Miller insists: "In analyzing what the use of religion accomplishes, beyond perpetual quests for meaning figured as religious, we can achieve a more robust examination of religion in the interests of and for various human efforts, rather than stopping at explicating such efforts as existential pursuits and questioning" (Miller, *Religion*, 91).
69 Miller, *Religion*, 158.
70 Miller, *Religion*, 161.
71 Miller, *Religion*, 162.
72 Miller, *Religion*, 151.
73 Ta-Nehisi Coates, *Between the World and Me* (New York: Spiegel & Grau, 2015).
74 Miller, *Religion*, 165.
75 Floyd-Thomas, Floyd-Thomas, and Toulouse, *The Altars Where We Worship*, 87.
76 Kimerer L. LaMothe, "What Bodies Know about Religion and the Study of It," *Journal of the American Academy of Religion*, vol. 76, no. 3 (2008), 580–1.
77 LaMothe, "What Bodies Know," 585.
78 LaMothe, "What Bodies Know," 587.
79 LaMothe, "What Bodies Know," 588.
80 LaMothe, "What Bodies Know," 595.
81 Floyd-Thomas, Floyd-Thomas, and Toulouse, *The Altars Where We Worship*, 75.
82 John C. Lyden, "Whose Film," 775.
83 Lyden, "Whose Film Is It," 781–2.
84 Lyden, "Whose Film Is It," 783.
85 See my chapter "On the Sacred Power of Violence in Popular Culture," in *Understanding Religion and Popular Culture*, edited by Terry Ray Clark and Dan W. Clanton, Jr. (New York: Routledge, 2012).
86 Gary Laderman, "The Disney Way of Death," *Journal of the American Academy of Religion*, vol. 68, no. 1 (2000), 27.
87 Laderman, "Disney," 37.
88 Laderman, "Disney," 40.
89 Laderman, "Disney," 43.
90 Laderman, "Disney," 43–4.
91 Laderman, "Disney," 44.
92 Laderman, "Disney," 44.
93 Chidester, *Authentic*, 145–6.

94 William Arnal, "The Segregation of Social Desire: 'Religion' and Disney World," *Journal of the American Academy of Religion*, vol. 69, no. 1 (2001), 17.
95 Rachel Wagner (with Heidi A. Campbell, Shanny Luft, Rabia Gregory, Gregory Price Grieve, and Xenia Zeiler), "Gaming Religionworlds: Why Religious Studies Should Pay Attention to Religion in Gaming," *Journal of the American Academy of Religion*, vol. 84, no. 3 (2016), 645.
96 Wagner, "Gaming Religionworlds," 646.
97 Shanny Luft (with Heidi A. Campbell, Rachel Wagner, Rabia Gregory, Gregory Price Grieve, and Xenia Zeiler), "Gaming Religionworlds: Why Religious Studies Should Pay Attention to Religion in Gaming," *Journal of the American Academy of Religion*, vol. 84, no. 3 (2016), 647–8.
98 Joseph L. Price, "The 'Godding Up' of American Sports," in *Religion and Popular Culture in America*, third edition, edited by Bruce David Forbes and Jeffrey H. Mahan (Oakland, California: University of California Press, 2017), 306.
99 Steven Connor, *A Philosophy of Sport* (London: Reaktion Books, 2011), 82.
100 Eric Bain-Selbo and D. Gregory Sapp, *Understanding Sport as a Religious Phenomenon: An Introduction* (New York: Bloomsbury, 2016). Bain-Selbo also has published a similar work that focuses specifically on college football in the America South: *Game Day and God: Football, Faith, and Politics in the American South* (Macon, GA: Mercer University Press, 2012).
101 Floyd-Thomas, Floyd-Thomas, and Toulouse, *The Altars Where We Worship*, 162.
102 Chidester, *Authentic*, 33.
103 Chidester, *Authentic*, 36.
104 Chidester, *Authentic*, 39.
105 Paul Christopher Johnson, "The Fetish and McGwire's Balls," *Journal of the American Academy of Religion*, vol. 68, no. 2 (2000), 260.
106 A. Whitney Sanford, "Pinned on Karma Rock: Whitewater Kayaking as Religious Experience," *Journal of the American Academy of Religion*, vol. 75, no. 4 (2007), 876.
107 Sanford, "Pinned on Karma Rock," 893.
108 Samuel Snyder, "New Streams of Religion: Fly Fishing as a Lived, Religion of Nature," *Journal of the American Academy of Religion*, vol. 75, no. 4 (2007), 897.
109 Bron Taylor, "Surfing into Spirituality and a New, Aquatic Nature Religion," *Journal of the American Academy of Religion*, vol. 75, no. 4 (2007), 925.
110 B. Taylor, "New Streams of Religion," 945.
111 Robert Bellah, "Civil Religion in America," *Daedalus*, vol. 96, no. 1 (1967).
112 Robert N. Bellah, "Is There a Common American Culture?" *Journal of the American Academy of Religion*, vol. 66, no. 3 (1998), 616.

113 Peter Gardella, *American Civil Religion: What Americans Hold Sacred* (New York: Oxford University Press, 2014). See my full review of this book in the *Journal of American Studies*, vol. 49 (2015).
114 Gardella, *American Civil Religion*, 2.
115 Gardella, *American Civil Religion*, 3.
116 Gardella, *American Civil Religion*, 4.
117 Gardella, *American Civil Religion*, 5.
118 Gardella, *American Civil Religion*, 6.
119 Gardella, *American Civil Religion*, 149.
120 Gardella, *American Civil Religion*, 323.
121 Gardella, *American Civil Religion*, 117.
122 Gardella, *American Civil Religion*, 131.
123 Gardella, *American Civil Religion*, 81.
124 Gardella, *American Civil Religion*, 321.
125 Carolyn Marvin and David W. Ingle, "Blood Sacrifice and the Nation: Revisiting Civil Religion," *Journal of the American Academy of Religion*, vol. 64, no. 4 (1996), 767.
126 Gardella, *American Civil Religion*, 232–45.
127 Gardella, *American Civil Religion*, 302.
128 Gardella, *American Civil Religion*, 306.
129 Gardella, *American Civil Religion*, 293.
130 Gardella, *American Civil Religion*, 268.
131 Chidester, *Authentic*, 231.
132 Brasher, "Thoughts on the Status of the Cyborg," 824.
133 Lofton, *Consuming*, 8.
134 Sarah McFarland Taylor, "Shopping, Religion, and the Sacred 'Buyosphere,'" in *Religion and Popular Culture in America*, third edition, edited by Bruce David Forbes and Jeffrey H. Mahan (Oakland, CA: University of California Press, 2017), 256.
135 Chidester, *Authentic*, 139.
136 Chidester, *Authentic*, 139.
137 Dana W. Logan, "The Lean Closet: Asceticism in Postindustrial Consumer Culture," *Journal of the American Academy of Religion*, vol. 85, no. 3 (2017), 604.
138 Logan, "The Lean Closet," 604–5.
139 Logan, "The Lean Closet," 618.
140 Logan, "The Lean Closet," 621–2.
141 Logan, "The Lean Closet," 622.
142 James B. Twitchell, *Branded Nation: The Marketing of Megachurch, College Inc., and Museumworld* (New York: Simon & Schuster, 2004), 5.
143 Twitchell, *Branded Nation*, 24–5.

144 Twitchell, *Branded Nation*, 275.
145 Twitchell, *Branded Nation*, 299.
146 Twitchell, *Branded Nation*, 294.
147 Lofton, *Consuming*, 9.
148 Harvey Cox, *The Market as God* (Cambridge, MA: Harvard University Press, 2016), 8.
149 Cox, *Market*, 8.
150 Cox, *Market*, 43.
151 Cox, *Market*, 210–31.
152 David R. Loy, "The Religion of the Market," *Journal of the American Academy of Religion*, vol. 65, no. 2 (1997), 275.
153 Loy, "*Religion*," 281.
154 Loy, "*Religion*," 278.
155 Loy, "*Religion*," 285.
156 Loy, "*Religion*," 289.
157 Mark C. Taylor, *Confidence Games: Money and Markets in a World without Redemption* (Chicago: The University of Chicago Press, 2004), 3.
158 Mark C. Taylor, *After God* (Chicago: The University of Chicago Press, 2007), 216.
159 Taylor, *After*, 239.
160 Taylor, *After*, 359. Elsewhere he writes: "When understood in this way, the mind of the market appears to be the functional equivalent of the mind of God, whose all-knowing invisible hand creates and maintains order in what otherwise would be a chaotic universe" (Taylor, *Confidence*, 246).
161 Taylor, *Confidence*, 106.
162 Taylor, *Confidence*, 6.
163 Taylor, *About*, 165.
164 Taylor, *Confidence*, 124.
165 Taylor, *Confidence*, 276.
166 Taylor, *Confidence*, 301.
167 Taylor, *Confidence*, 122. Jean-Pierre Dupuy makes a similar argument about capitalism: "What makes capitalism possible is the belief that it is immortal. What may be called the original sin of capitalism lies concealed in the fact that the future must endlessly stretch out before it if, at any given moment, it is to be able to deliver on its promises. This is the source of the cult of growth" (Jean-Pierre Dupuy, *Economy and the Future: A Crisis of Faith*, translated by M.B. DeBevoise (East Lansing, MI: Michigan State University Press, 2014), 84).
168 Taylor, *Confidence*, 25.
169 Taylor, *Confidence*, 50.
170 Steve Bruce, *Secularization: In Defence of an Unfashionable Theory* (New York: Oxford University Press, 2011), 80–1.

Chapter 6

1. John Milbank, "The Legitimacy and Genealogy of Secularization in Question," in *Radical Secularization: An Inquiry into the Religious Roots of Secular Culture*, edited by Stijn Latre, Walter Van Herck, and Guido Vanheeswijck (New York: Bloomsbury, 2015), 83.
2. Steve Bruce, *Secularization: In Defence of an Unfashionable Theory* (New York: Oxford University Press, 2011), 1.
3. Bruce, *Secularization*, 10.
4. Bruce, *Secularization*, 159.
5. Bruce, *Secularization*, 158.
6. Pew Research Center, "In U.S., Decline of Christianity Continues at Rapid Pace: An Update on America's Changing Religious Landscape" (Washington, DC: Pew Research Center, 2019), https://www.pewforum.org/2019/10/17/in-u-s-decline-of-christianity-continues-at-rapid-pace/ Accessed September 20, 2020.
7. Bruce, *Secularization*, 13.
8. Bruce, *Secularization*, 14.
9. Bruce, *Secularization*, 19.
10. Bruce, *Secularization*, 48.
11. Bruce, *Secularization*, 199.
12. Bruce, *Secularization*, 201.
13. Bruce, *Secularization*, 112.
14. Peter L. Berger, *The Sacred Canopy: Elements of a Sociological Theory of Religion* (New York: Doubleday, 1967), 107.
15. Berger, *Sacred*, 112.
16. Berger, *Sacred*, 133–4.
17. Berger, *Sacred*, 151.
18. Berger, *Sacred*, 145–6.
19. Berger, *Sacred*, 124.
20. Berger, *Sacred*, 125.
21. Peter L. Berger, "The Desecularization of the World: A Global Overview," in *The Desecularization of the World: Resurgent Religion and World Politics*, edited by Peter L. Berger (Grand Rapids, MI: William B. Eerdmans Publishing Company, 1999), 2.
22. Berger, "Desecularization," 6.
23. Berger, "Desecularization," 12.
24. Berger, "Desecularization," 13.
25. Talal Asad, *Genealogies of Religion: Discipline and Reasons of Power in Christianity and Islam* (Baltimore, MD: The Johns Hopkins University Press, 1993), 207.
26. Even fairly recently, scholars continue to treat the two categories in a somewhat essentialist way. For example, take Nancy T. Ammerman's introduction to the

edited volume *Everyday Religion: Observing Modern Religious Lives* (New York: Oxford University Press, 2007). She writes, "We do not, however, assume that 'religious' and 'secular' are zero-sum realities tightly bounded against each other. We leave open the possibility that the boundaries between them are permeable" (9). But not only is there a "possibility" here, it is an actuality. And it is such because the two categories are not, in fact, "realities" out in the world. They merely are conceptual tools (contested and fluid ones at that) that here and there provide useful insights into human behavior and beliefs.

27 Talal Asad, *Formations of the Secular: Christianity, Islam, Modernity* (Stanford, CA: Stanford University Press, 2003), 25.
28 Charles Taylor, *A Secular Age* (Cambridge, MA: Harvard University Press, 2007), 4–5.
29 C. Taylor, *Secular*, 25.
30 C. Taylor, *Secular*, 5.
31 C. Taylor, *Secular*, 8.
32 C. Taylor, *Secular*, 15. Michael Warner, Jonathan VanAntwerpen, and Craig Calhoun describe it this way: "This sense of heightened meaning and connection is always possible within humanist and naturalist frames of reference: this is the way life should be. But to most moderns, this strong sense of the fullness of the world, of the wonder of it that goes beyond everyday concerns about health, material prosperity, politics, even justice, is available only occasionally. Some people may seem to have more consistent access to it, and this may be a source of their inspirational leadership, extraordinary commitments, or saintliness. But it is typically episodic, available only for moments, perhaps aided by ritual but sometimes just surprising us. And fullness is less available now than it used to be, when it seemed routinely the case that the material world was not all that there was" ("Editor's Introduction," in *Varieties of Secularism in a Secular Age* (Cambridge, MA: Harvard University Press, 2010), 12).
33 C. Taylor, *Secular*, 553.
34 C. Taylor, *Secular*, 542.
35 C. Taylor, *Secular*, 566.
36 Schewel adds that the immanent frame "allows diverse social spheres to develop according to their own internal logics and, thus, to proceed unconstrained by overarching religious-metaphysical systems" (Benjamin Schewel, "Transformational Post-Secularism: An Overlooked Strand of Thought," *Journal of the American Academy of Religion*, vol. 87, no. 4 (2019), 1098).
37 Charles Taylor, *Sources of the Self: The Making of the Modern Identity* (Cambridge, MA: Harvard University Press, 1989), 27.
38 Taylor writes: "My identity is defined by the commitments and identifications which provide the frame or horizon within which I can try to determine from case

to case what is good, or valuable, or what ought to be done, or what I endorse or oppose" (C. Taylor, *Sources*, 27).

39 Taylor notes, "The full definition of someone's identity thus usually involves not only his stand on moral and spiritual matters but also some reference to a defining community" (C. Taylor, *Sources*, 36).

40 C. Taylor, *Secular*, 309.
41 C. Taylor, *Secular*, 303.
42 C. Taylor, *Secular*, 680.
43 C. Taylor, *Secular*, 309.
44 C. Taylor, *Sources*, 513.
45 C. Taylor, *Secular*, 472.
46 C. Taylor, *Secular*, 484.
47 C. Taylor, *Secular*, 481.
48 C. Taylor, *Secular*, 50.
49 C. Taylor, *Secular*, 54.
50 C. Taylor, *Secular*, 516–17.
51 C. Taylor, *Secular*, 469.
52 C. Taylor, *Secular*, 482.
53 C. Taylor, *Secular*, 469.
54 C. Taylor, *Secular*, 482–3.
55 C. Taylor, *Secular*, 518. It is important to note at least one qualification that Taylor makes in this regard—though I do not think it is a critical one. Taylor writes in regard to festive occasions: "Some moments of this kind are, indeed, the closest analogues to the Carnival of previous centuries. They can be powerful and moving, because they witness the birth of a new collective agent out of its formerly dispersed potential. They can be heady, exciting. But unlike Carnival, they are not enframed by any deeply entrenched if implicit common understanding of structure and counter-structure" (C. Taylor, *Secular*, 715).
56 C. Taylor, *Sources*, 94.
57 C. Taylor, *Secular*, 18.
58 C. Taylor, *Secular*, 769.
59 C. Taylor, *Secular*, 572.
60 Lauren ten Kate, "To World or Not to World: An Axial Genealogy of Secular Life," in *Radical Secularization?: An Inquiry into the Religious Roots of Secular Culture*, edited by Stijn Latre, Walter Van Herck, and Guido Vanheeswijck (New York: Bloomsbury, 2015), 208.
61 McKenzie, *Interpreting Charles Taylor's Social Theory on Religion and Secularization: A Comparative Study* (Cham, Switzerland: Springer, 2017), 144–5.
62 McKenzie, *Interpreting*, 175. This reading of Taylor seems pretty straightforward to me, and is consistent with that of others. For example, Charles Lockwood

writes: "Taylor is not denying that something called secularization has occurred in Western modernity. Rather, his intention is to offer a more accurate account of the process. Instead of treating secularization merely as a story of religion's decline, as in mainstream theory, Taylor characterizes it in terms of religion's transformation" ("Apologetics and Anti-Apologetics in Taylor's *A Secular Age*," in *Radical Secularization?: An Inquiry into the Religious Roots of Secular Culture*, edited by Stijn Latre, Walter Van Herck, and Guido Vanheeswijck (New York: Bloomsbury, 2015), 154).

63 Mark C. Taylor, *Confidence Games: Money and Markets in a World without Redemption* (Chicago: The University of Chicago Press, 2004), 29–30.
64 C. Taylor, *Secular*, 303.
65 C. Taylor, *Secular*, 437.
66 This section is a revision of my entry in the *Oxford Handbook on Humanism* (New York: Oxford University Press, 2019). I thank Oxford University Press for permission to reuse some of that material. I also thank the editor, Anthony Pinn, for his ample assistance in helping me craft that original article.
67 Johan Huizinga, *Homo Ludens: A Study of the Play Element in Culture* (Boston: The Beacon Press, 1955), 28.
68 Huizinga, *Homo Ludens*, 132.
69 Huizinga, *Homo Ludens*, 3. As theologian Michael Novak writes: "The basic reality of all human life is play, games, sport; these are the realities from which the basic metaphors for all that is important in the rest of life are drawn. ... *Being, beauty, truth, excellence, transcendence*—these words [are] grown in the soil of play ... Art, prayer, worship, love, civlization: these thrive in the field of play" (Michael Novak, *The Joy of Sports: Endzones, Bases, Baskets, Balls, and the Consecration of the American Spirit*, revised edition (Lanham, MD: Madison Books, 1994), xvii). He adds, "Play is the most human activity. It is the first act of freedom" (Novak, *The Joy of Sports*, 32).
70 Huizinga, *Homo Ludens*, 75, 46. Novak reverses the typical argument that play represents some kind of human diversion when he writes, "Cease play, cease civilization. Work is the diversion necessary for play to survive" (Novak, 43).
71 Huizinga, *Homo Ludens*, 173. Roger Caillois makes a similar argument about the central role of play in the development of culture (Roger Callois, *Man, Play and Games*, translated by Meyer Barash (Chicago, IL: University of Illinois Press, 2001)).
72 Hans-Georg Gadamer, *Truth and Method*, second revised edition, translation revised by Joel Weinsheimer and Donald G. Marshall (New York: Continuum, 1994), 103–5.
73 Gadamer, *Truth*, 126–8.
74 Randolph Feezell, *Sport, Play & Ethical Reflection* (Chicago, IL: University of Illinois Press, 2004), 50.
75 Gadamer, *Truth*, 102.

76 Robert Ellis, *The Games People Play: Theology, Religion, and Sport* (Eugene, OR: Wipf & Stock, 2014), 215.
77 Feezell, *Sport*, 55–7, 74–6.
78 Bernard Suits, *The Grasshopper: Games, Life, and Utopia*, third edition (Tonawanda, NY: Broadview Press, 2014), 176.
79 Suits, *The Grasshopper*, 43.
80 Suits, *The Grasshopper*, 188–9.
81 In *Humanism: A Very Short Introduction*, philosopher Stephen Law identifies seven characteristics of humanism: (1) a belief in the value of science and reason; (2) atheism or at least an agnostic stance toward religion; (3) the belief that human beings have only this life on earth (i.e., no afterlife); (4) commitment to the importance of moral values; (5) belief in the importance of moral autonomy; (6) belief that humans can have meaningful lives without God or a similar entity providing that meaning; and (7) belief in the value of secularism, in which the state takes a neutral stance toward religion (Stephen Law, *Humanism: A Very Short Introduction* (New York: Oxford University Press, 2011), 1–3).
82 As philosopher and psychologist William James argues, humanism "is willing to let finite experience be self-supporting" (William James, *Pragmatism and Other Writings*, edited by Giles Gunn (New York: Penguin Books, 2000), 163). For a summary of James' account of humanism, see his essay "Humanism and Truth" (James, 167).
83 Anthony B. Pinn, *Humanism: Essays on Race, Religion and Popular Culture* (New York: Bloomsbury, 2015), 2.
84 Law, 123.
85 James, 25.
86 James, 25.
87 James, 27.
88 James, 146.
89 James, 148.
90 John Dewey, *A Common Faith*, second edition (New Haven, CT: Yale University Press, 1934), 30. Dewey contrasts this approach to religious claims to truth that are dependent on authority or individual revelation. He writes: "The method of intelligence [the pragmatic method] is open and public. The doctrinal method [religion] is limited and private" (Dewey, 37).
91 Richard Rorty, *Philosophy and Social Hope* (New York: Penguin Books, 1999), 27.
92 Rorty, *Social Hope*, 237–8.
93 Richard Rorty, *Contingency, Irony, and Solidarity* (New York: Cambridge University Press, 1989), 21.
94 Rorty, *Contingency*, 9.
95 Rorty elaborates: "the terms used by the founders of a new form of cultural life will consist largely in borrowings from the vocabulary of the culture which they are hoping to replace" (Rorty, *Contingency*, 56).

96 The process of de-divination is a difficult one. Rorty notes that iconoclastic philosopher Friedrich Nietzsche saw poets as the only ones who could really grapple with the contingency he describes. He adds: "The rest of us are doomed to remain philosophers, to insist that there really is only one true lading-list, one true description of the human situation, one universal context of our lives. We are doomed to spend our conscious lives trying to escape from contingency rather than, like the strong poet, acknowledging and appropriating contingency" (Rorty, *Contingency*, 28).

97 Rorty, *Contingency*, 45.

98 Rorty provides the following summary of the historical trajectory of Western thought: "once upon a time we felt a need to worship something which lay beyond the visible world. Beginning in the seventeenth century we tried to substitute a love of truth for a love of God, treating the world described by science as a quasi divinity. Beginning at the end of the eighteenth century we tried to substitute a love of ourselves for a love of scientific truth, a worship of our own deep spiritual or poetic nature, treated as one more quasi divinity" (Rorty, *Contingency*, 22). What he recommends, however, is that we "get to the point where we no longer worship *anything*, where we treat *nothing* as a quasi divinity, where we treat *everything*—our language, our conscience, our community—as a product of time and chance" (Rorty, *Contingency*, 22).

99 Rorty, *Contingency*, xv.

100 Rorty, *Contingency*, 189. These would be "people who combined commitment with a sense of the contingency of their own commitment" (Rorty, *Contingency*, 61).

101 Rorty summarizes this position: "Philosophers have often described religion as a primitive and insufficiently reflective attempt to philosophize. But … a fully self-conscious literary culture would think of both religion and philosophy as largely obsolete, yet glorious, literary genres. They are genres in which it is now becoming increasingly difficult to write, but their replacements might never have emerged had they not been read as swerves away from religion, and later as swerves away from philosophy. Religion and philosophy were stepping-stones, stages in a continuing process of maturation" (Rorty, *Cultural*, 95).

102 Rorty, *Contingency*, xvi.

103 Rorty, *Contingency*, 192.

104 Rorty, *Contingency*, 94.

105 Richard Rorty, *Philosophy as Cultural Politics: Philosophical Papers, Volume 4* (New York: Cambridge University Press, 2007), 91.

106 Rorty, *Cultural*, 93.

107 Rorty writes of the power of imagination: "we see both intellectual and moral progress not as a matter of getting closer to the True or the Good or the Right, but as an increase in imaginative power. We see imagination as the cutting edge

of cultural evolution, the power which—given peace and prosperity—constantly operates so as to make the human future richer than the human past. Imagination is the source both of new scientific pictures of the physical universe and of new conceptions of possible communities. It is what Newton and Christ, Freud and Marx, had in common: the ability to redescribe the familiar in unfamiliar terms" (Rorty, *Social Hope*, 87).

108 Rorty, *Cultural*, 201–2.
109 Pinn, *Humanism*, 148.
110 It is believed by many that the long World Series championship drought of the Red Sox (they won in 1918 and then not again until 2004) was a consequence of selling future legend Babe Ruth to the New York Yankees during the 1919–20 off season. The Red Sox would go eighty-six years before winning another title, while Babe Ruth would go on to become one of the greatest players in the history of the game and the Yankees the sport's most dominant and successful team.
111 The story goes that William Sianis, owner of the Billy Goat Tavern in Chicago, was a big Cubs fan. During the 1945 World Series in which the Cubs were participating, he bought a ticket for his goat and brought the goat to game four. As a result of complaints from other patrons, Sianis and his goat were asked to leave, at which point Sianis reportedly cursed the Cubs.
112 Nick Hornby, *Fever Pitch* (New York: Riverhead Books, 1998).
113 Or, perhaps, it *is* a religion. For an argument along these lines, see Eric Bain-Selbo's *Game Day and God: Football, Faith, and Politics in the American South*.
114 See https://www.cnn.com/2013/10/03/world/world-cup-fast-facts/index.html.
115 For a comprehensive argument in this regard, see Eric Bain-Selbo and D. Gregory Sapp's *Understanding Sport as a Religious Phenomenon: An Introduction*.
116 Clay Travis, *Dixieland Delight: A Football Season on the Road in the Southeastern Conference* (New York: HarperCollins, 2007), 286.
117 Travis, *Dixieland Delight*, 305.
118 Juan M. Floyd-Thomas, Stacey M. Floyd-Thomas, and Mark G. Toulouse, *The Altars Where We Worship: The Religious Significance of Popular Culture* (Louisville, KY: Westminster John Knox Press, 2016), 186.
119 Floyd-Thomas, Floyd-Thomas, and Toulouse, *The Altars Where We Worship*, 12.
120 Floyd-Thomas, Floyd-Thomas, and Toulouse, *The Altars Where We Worship*, 186.
121 Asad, *Genealogies*, 29.
122 Brent Nongbri, *Before Religion: A History of a Modern Concept* (New Haven, CT: Yale University Press, 2013), 158.
123 Nongbri, *Before Religion*, 156.
124 Sam Gill, "No Place to Stand: Jonathan Z. Smith as *Homo Ludens*, The Academic Study of Religion *Sub Specie Ludi*," *Journal of the American Academy of Religion*, vol. 66, no. 2 (1998), 310.
125 Monica R. Miller, *Religion and Hip Hop* (New York: Routledge, 2013), 2.

126 Miller, *Religion and Hip Hop*, 70.
127 Miller writes: "Although Tillich's loose positioning of religion (as questions and concerns of 'ultimacy') makes room for interpretation beyond strict Christian assumptions, this positioning situates religiosity within the problematic realm of private experience, presence, and meaning grounded in existentialist concerns. While this formulation enables exploration beyond religiously explicit rhetorical pronouncements in rap, the housing of 'ultimate concern' (Tillich) and 'orientation' ([Charles] Long) remains phenomenologically situated within a (Christian) inheritance and intellectual genealogy that's preoccupied with apprehending meaning itself" (Miller, 93).
128 Miller, *Religion and Hip Hop*, 155.
129 See Long's *Significations: Signs, Symbols, and Images in the Interpretation of Religion* (Aurora, CO: The Davies Group, 1999).
130 See Fabian's *Time and the Other: How Anthropology Makes Its Object* (New York: Columbia University Press, 2002) and *Out of Their Minds: Reason and Madness in the Exploration of Central Africa* (Berkeley, CA: University of California Press, 2000).
131 See Chidester's *Savage Systems: Colonialism and Comparative Religion in South Africa* (Charlottesville, VA: University of Virginia Press, 1996) and *Empire of Religion: Imperialism and Comparative Religion* (Chicago: University of Chicago Press, 2014).
132 Christopher M. Driscoll and Monica R. Miller, *Method as Identity: Manufacturing Distance in the Academic Study of Religion* (New York: Lexington Books, 2019).
133 Driscoll and Miller, *Method as Identity*, 15.
134 Christian Smith, *Religion: What It Is, How It Works, and Why It Matters* (Princeton, NJ: Princeton University Press, 2017), 22.
135 C. Smith, *Religion*, 41.
136 C. Smith, *Religion*, 136.
137 C. Smith, *Religion*, 78–80.
138 C. Smith, *Religion*, 81.
139 C. Smith, *Religion*, 205.
140 C. Smith, *Religion*, 220.
141 C. Smith, *Religion*, 49.
142 In his 1982 book *Imagining Religion: From Babylon to Jonestown* (Chicago: The University of Chicago Press, 1982), Jonathan Z. Smith writes of religious studies: "Scholars have engaged in the quest for the unique and definitive *sine qua non*, the 'that without which' religion would not be religion but rather an instance of something else. In the main, the results of this enterprise have not been convincing; they have failed to achieve consensus" (5). It would seem, to take Christian Smith as an example, that history is indeed doomed to repeat itself.
143 Miller, *Hip Hop*, 73.

144 Miller, *Hip Hop*, 178.
145 Long, *Significations*, 24.
146 Jonathan Sheehan, "When Was Disenchantment? History and the Secular Age," in *Varieties of Secularism in a Secular Age*, edited by Michael Warner, Jonathan VanAntwerpen, and Craig Calhoun (Cambridge, MA: Harvard University Press, 2010), 232.
147 C. Smith, 5.
148 C. Smith, 251.
149 Charles Taylor, *Hegel and Modern Society* (Cambridge, UK: Cambridge University Press, 1979), 69.
150 C. Taylor, *Hegel*, 89.
151 C. Taylor, *Hegel*, 88.
152 C. Taylor, *Hegel*, 124.
153 C. Taylor, *Hegel*, 113.
154 C. Taylor, *Hegel*, 114.
155 For two interesting takes on Taylor's views, I recommend Guido Vanheeswijck's "Beyond Radical Secularlization and Radical Orthodoxy?" and Gerbert Faure's "Religion, Modernity and the Notion of Subtler Languages" in *Radical Secularization?: An Inquiry into the Religious Roots of Secular Culture*, edited by Stijn Latre, Walter Van Herck, and Guido Vanheeswijck (New York: Bloomsbury, 2015).
156 Josef Pieper, *Leisure: The Basis of Culture*, translated by Alexander Dru (San Francisco: Ignatius Press, 1963), 63.
157 Pieper, *Leisure*, 46.
158 Pieper, *Leisure*, 71.
159 Pieper, *In Tune with the World: A Theory of Festivity*, translated by Richard and Clara Winston (South Bend, Indiana: St. Augustine's Press, 1963), 10–11.
160 Pieper, *In Tune*, 9.
161 Pieper, *In Tune*, 29.
162 Pieper, *In Tune*, 71.
163 Pieper, *In Tune*, 33.
164 Pieper, *In Tune*, 86.
165 Pieper, *In Tune*, 34.
166 Pieper, *In Tune*, 69.
167 Pieper, *In Tune*, 37.
168 Pieper, *In Tune*, 62–3.
169 I would add here too the work of William Dean, whose interests cross from theology to democracy. He writes that "discovering that religious therapies stand on no independent evidence, Americans will drop them and turn to whatever other public therapy is more powerful. American democracy may need a spiritual culture, but if that culture can supply no evidence for a God or some other reality

that can give that culture what it cannot provide for itself, then that culture will do little to preserve democracy. In short, the skepticism that is setting in forebodes a dangerous future" (William Dean, *The American Spiritual Culture: And the Invention of Jazz, Football and the Movies* (New York: Continuum, 2002), 42).
170   Mark C. Taylor, *About Religion: Economies of Faith in Virtual Culture* (Chicago: The University of Chicago Press, 1999), 28.
171   Akeel Bilgrami, "What Is Enchantment?," in *Varieties of Secularism in a Secular Age*, edited by Michael Warner, Jonathan VanAntwerpen, and Craig Calhoun (Cambridge, MA: Harvard University Press, 2010), 155.
172   Richard Rorty, "Religious Faith, Intellectual Responsibility, and Romance," in *The Cambridge Companion to William James*, edited by Ruth Anna Putnam (New York: Cambridge University Press, 1997), 96.

Postscript

1   Jean-Pierre Dupuy, *Economy and the Future: A Crisis of Faith*, translated by M.B. DeBevoise (East Lansing, MI: Michigan State University Press, 2014), xiii.
2   Slavoj Zizek, "Afterword: *With Defenders Like These, Who Needs Attackers?*" in *The Truth of Zizek*, edited by Paul Bowman and Richard Stamp (New York: Continuum, 2007), 252.
3   Karl Marx, *The Portable Karl Marx*, edited by Eugene Kamenka (New York: Viking Penguin, 1983), 437.
4   Marx, *Portable*, 447.
5   Slavoj Zizek, *On Belief* (New York: Routledge, 2001), 13–14.
6   Slavoj Zizek, *The Universal Exception*, edited by Rex Butler and Scott Stephens (New York: Continuum, 2006), 253.
7   Zizek, *Universal*, 254–5.
8   Zizek, *Universal*, 254.
9   Theodor Adorno, *The Culture Industry* (New York: Routledge, 1991), 39.
10 Adorno, *Culture*, 103.
11 Slavoj Zizek, *The Fragile Absolute—or, Why Is the Christian Legacy Worth Fighting for?* (New York: Verso, 2000), 22.
12 Zizek, *Fragile*, 22.
13 Juliet Schor, *The Overspent American: Why We Want What We Don't Need* (New York: HarperCollins, 1998), 6.
14 Alasdair MacIntyre, *After Virtue: A Study in Moral Theory*, 2nd edition (Notre Dame, IN: University of Notre Dame Press, 1984), 34.
15 Schor, *Overspent*, 5.
16 Juliet Schor, *Born to Buy* (New York: Scribner, 2005), 173.

17 Robert D. Putnam, *Bowling Alone: The Collapse and Revival of American Community* (New York: Simon & Schuster, 2001).
18 Lizabeth Cohen, *A Consumer's Republic: The Politics of Mass Consumption in Postwar America* (New York: Vintage Books, 2003), 331.
19 Zizek, *On Belief*, 26.
20 Guy Debord, *Society of the Spectacle*, translated by Ken Knabb (London: Rebel Press, 2006), 12.
21 Debord, *Society*, 14.
22 Debord, *Society*, 22.
23 Debord, *Society*, 24.
24 Debord, *Society*, 25.
25 Debord, *Society*, 33.
26 Debord, Society, 25.
27 Debord, *Society*, 34.
28 Debord, *Society*, 16.
29 Henry Jenkins, "*Star Trek* Rerun, Reread, Rewritten: Fan Writing as Textual Poaching," in *Popular Culture: A Reader*, edited by Raiford Guins and Omayra Zaragoza Cruz (Thousand Oaks, CA: Sage Publications, 2005).
30 Putnam, *Bowling Alone*, 178.
31 Schor, *Born*, 174.
32 Cohen, *A Consumer's Republic*, 343.
33 Zygmunt Bauman, *Culture in a Liquid Modern World*, translated by Lydia Bauman (Malden, MA: Polity Press, 2011), 11.
34 Zygmunt Bauman, *Consuming Life* (Malden, MA: Polity Press, 2007), 28.
35 Bauman, *Consuming*, 31.
36 Zygmunt Bauman, *Does Ethics Have a Chance in a World of Consumers?* (Cambridge, MA: Harvard University Press, 2008), 167.
37 Bauman, *Consuming*, 46.
38 Bauman, *Consuming*, 47.
39 Bauman, *Culture*, 17.
40 Bauman, *Does*, 145.
41 Bauman, *Consuming*, 74.
42 Bauman, *Consuming*, 53.
43 Bauman, *Consuming*, 12.
44 Bauman, *Consuming*, 12.
45 Bauman, *Consuming*, 110.
46 Bauman, *Consuming*, 111.
47 Bauman, *Does*, 23.
48 Bauman, *Consuming*, 76.
49 Bauman, *Consuming*, 75. Elsewhere he writes: "Hardly any belonging engages the 'whole self,' as each person is involved, not just in the course of her or his life but

at any moment of life, in multiple belongings, so to speak. Being loyal only in part, or loyal 'a la carte,' is no longer viewed as necessarily tantamount to disloyalty, let alone betrayal" (Bauman, *Does*, 24).
50 Bauman, *Consuming*, 78.
51 Bauman, *Does*, 52–3.
52 Bauman, *Consuming*, 100.
53 Bauman, *Consuming*, 98.
54 Bauman, *Consuming*, 127.
55 Neil Postman, *Amusing Ourselves to Death: Public Discourse in the Age of Show Business*, 20th Anniversary Edition (New York: Penguin, 2006), 77.
56 Adorno, *Culture*, 96.
57 Harvey Cox, *The Market as God* (Cambridge, MA: Harvard University Press, 2016), 242.
58 In this regard, I particularly commend his book *Confidence Games: Money and Markets in a World without Redemption* (Chicago: University of Chicago Press, 2008).
59 Dave Zirin, *Welcome to the Terrordome: The Pain, Politics, and Promise of Sports* (Chicago: Haymarket Books, 2007), 22.
60 Zirin, *What's*, 292.
61 Zirin, *What's*, 21.
62 I identify this function of sport as its "prophetic dimension." For more in this regard, see my essay "Sport and Social Change: The Prophetic Dimension," in *The Prophetic Dimension of Sport*, edited by Terry Shoemaker (New York: Springer, 2018). For an application of some of these ideas to the plight of African-American athletes in the United States, see Harry Edwards, *The Revolt of the Black Athlete*, 50th Anniversary Edition (Chicago: University of Illinois Press, 2017) and William C. Rhoden, *Forty Million Dollar Slaves: The Rise, Fall, and Redemption of the Black Athlete* (New York: Three Rivers Press, 2006).
63 Eric Bain-Selbo and D. Gregory Sapp, *Understanding Sport as Religious Phenomenon: An Introduction* (New York: Bloomsbury, 2016), 143.

Bibliography

Adorno, Theodor. *The Culture Industry*. New York: Routledge, 1991.
Albanese, Catherine. "Religion and American Popular Culture: An Introductory Essay," *Journal of the American Academy of Religion*, vol. 64, no. 4 (1996).
Ammerman, Nancy T. "Introduction," in *Everyday Religion: Observing Modern Religious Lives*, edited by Nancy T. Ammerman. New York: Oxford University Press, 2007.
Arnal, William. "The Segregation of Social Desire: 'Religion' and Disney World," *Journal of the American Academy of Religion*, vol. 69, no. 1 (2001).
Asad, Talal. *Genealogies of Religion: Discipline and Reasons of Power in Christianity and Islam*. Baltimore, MD: The Johns Hopkins University Press, 1993.
Asad, Talal. *Formations of the Secular: Christianity, Islam, Modernity*. Stanford, CA: Stanford University Press, 2003.
Bain-Selbo, Eric. "Popular Culture and the Naked Self," *Divinatio*, no. 30 (2009).
Bain-Selbo, Eric. *Game Day and God: Football, Faith, and Politics in the American South*. Macon, GA: Mercer University Press, 2012.
Bain-Selbo, Eric. "On the Sacred Power of Violence in Popular Culture," in *Understanding Religion and Popular Culture*, edited by Terry Ray Clark and Dan W. Clanton, Jr. New York: Routledge, 2012.
Bain-Selbo, Eric. "Sport and Social Change: The Prophetic Dimension," in *The Prophetic Dimension of Sport*, edited by Terry Shoemaker. New York: Springer, 2018.
Bain-Selbo, Eric. "Affect Theory, Spirituality, and Sport," *Religions*, vol. 10, no. 8 (Summer 2019).
Bain-Selbo, Eric and D. Gregory Sapp. *Understanding Sport as a Religious Phenomenon: An Introduction*. New York: Bloomsbury, 2016.
Barnard, G. William. "Explaining the Unexplainable: Wayne Proudfoot's *Religious Experience*," *Journal of the American Academy of Religion*, vol. 60, no. 2 (1992).
Barnard, G. William. "Rejoinder," *Journal of the American Academy of Religion*, vol. 61, no. 4 (1993).
Bauman, Zygmunt. *Consuming Life*. Malden, MA: Polity Press, 2007.
Bauman, Zygmunt. *Does Ethics Have a Chance in a World of Consumers?* Cambridge, MA: Harvard University Press, 2008.
Bauman, Zygmunt. *Culture in a Liquid Modern World*, translated by Lydia Bauman. Malden, MA: Polity Press, 2011.
Beats, Kenny. *Broken Record* podcast, episode 90. https://brokenrecordpodcast.com.
Bellah, Robert. "Civil Religion in America," *Daedalus*, vol. 96, no. 1 (1967).
Bellah, Robert N. "Is There a Common American Culture?," *Journal of the American Academy of Religion*, vol. 66, no. 3 (1998).

Bellah, Robert N. "Durkheim and ritual," in *The Cambridge Companion to Durkheim*, edited by Jeffrey C. Alexander and Philip Smith. Cambridge, UK: Cambridge University Press, 2005.

Berger, Peter L. *The Sacred Canopy: Elements of a Sociological Theory of Religion*. New York: Doubleday, 1967.

Berger, Peter L. "The Desecularization of the World: A Global Overview," in *The Desecularization of the World: Resurgent Religion and World Politics*, edited by Peter L. Berger. Grand Rapids, MI: William B. Eerdmans Publishing Company, 1999.

Bilgrami, Akeel. "What Is Enchantment?," in *Varieties of Secularism in a Secular Age*, edited by Michael Warner, Jonathan VanAntwerpen, and Craig Calhoun. Cambridge, MA: Harvard University Press, 2010.

Blum, Jason N. "Retrieving Phenomenology of Religion as a Method for Religious Studies," *Journal of the American Academy of Religion*, vol. 80, no. 4 (2012).

Brasher, Brenda E. "Thoughts on the Status of the Cyborg: On Technological Socialization and Its Link to the Religious Function of Popular Culture," *Journal of the American Academy of Religion*, vol. 64, no. 4 (1996).

Bruce, Steve. *Secularization: In Defence of an Unfashionable Theory*. New York: Oxford University Press, 2011.

Callois, Roger. *Man, Play and Games*, translated by Meyer Barash. Chicago: University of Illinois Press, 2001.

Capps, Walter H. *Religious Studies: The Making of a Discipline*. Minneapolis, MN: Augsburg Fortress, 1995.

Chidester, David. *Savage Systems: Colonialism and Comparative Religion in South Africa*. Charlottesville, VA: University of Virginia Press, 1996.

Chidester, David. *Authentic Fakes: Religion and American Popular Culture*. Berkeley, CA: University of California Press, 2005.

Chidester, David. *Empire of Religion: Imperialism and Comparative Religion*. Chicago: University of Chicago Press, 2014.

Clark, Terry Ray and Dan W. Clanton, Jr., editors. *Understanding Religion and Popular Culture*. New York: Routledge, 2012.

Coates, Ta-Nehisi. *Between the World and Me*. New York: Spiegel & Grau, 2015.

Cobb, Kelton. "Reconsidering the Status of Popular Culture in Tillich's Theology of Culture," *Journal of the American Academy of Religion*, vol. 63, no. 1 (1995).

Cohen, Lizabeth. *A Consumer's Republic: The Politics of Mass Consumption in Postwar America*. New York: Vintage Books, 2003.

Connor, Steven. *A Philosophy of Sport*. London: Reaktion Books, 2011.

Corrigan, John. "Introduction: How Do We Study Religion and Emotion?," in *Feeling Religion*, edited by John Corrigan. Durham, NC: Duke University Press, 2017.

Cox, Harvey. *The Market as God*. Cambridge, MA: Harvard University Press, 2016.

Csikszentmihalyi, Mihaly. *Flow: The Psychology of Optimal Experience*. New York: HarperCollins, 1990.

Curts, Kati. "Temples and Turnpikes in 'The World of Tomorrow': Religious Assemblage and Automobility at the 1939 New York World's Fair," *Journal of the American Academy of Religion*, vol. 83, no. 3 (2015).

Dean, William. *The American Spiritual Culture: And the Invention of Jazz, Football and the Movies*. New York: Continuum, 2003.

Debord, Guy. *Society of the Spectacle*, translated by Ken Knabb. London: Rebel Press, 2006.

Deigh, John. "Freud's Later Theory of Civilization: Changes and Implications," in *The Cambridge Companion to Freud*, edited by Jerome Neu. New York: Cambridge University Press, 1991.

Dewey, John. *A Common Faith*, second edition. New Haven, CT: Yale University Press, 1934.

Driscoll, Christopher M. and Monica R. Miller. *Method as Identity: Manufacturing Distance in the Academic Study of Religion*. New York: Lexington Books, 2019.

Dupuy, Jean-Pierre. *Economy and the Future: A Crisis of Faith*, translated by M.B. DeBevoise. East Lansing, MI: Michigan State University Press, 2014.

Durkheim, Emile. *The Elementary Forms of Religious Life*, translated by Karen E. Fields. New York: The Free Press, 1995.

Dyson, Michael Eric. "God Complex, Complex Gods, or God's Complex: Jay-Z, Poor Black Youth, and Making 'The Struggle' Divine," in *Religion in Hip Hop: Mapping the New Terrain in the US*, edited by Monica R. Miller, Anthony B. Pinn, and Bernard "Bun B" Freeman. New York: Bloomsbury, 2015.

Dyson, Michael Eric. "Preface," in *Religion in Hip Hop: Mapping the New Terrain in the US*, edited by Monica R. Miller, Anthony B. Pinn, and Bernard "Bun B" Freeman. New York: Bloomsbury, 2015.

Edwards, Harry. *The Revolt of the Black Athlete*, 50th Anniversary Edition. Chicago: University of Illinois Press, 2017.

Eliade, Mircea. *The Myth of the Eternal Return, or, Cosmos and History*, translated by Willard R. Trask. Princeton, NJ: Princeton University Press, 1954.

Eliade, Mircea. *Patterns in Comparative Religion*, translated by Rosemary Sheed. New York: Sheed & Ward, 1958.

Eliade, Mircea. *The Sacred & Profane: The Nature of Religion*, translated by Willard R. Trask. New York: Harcourt Brace Jovanovich, 1959.

Eliade, Mircea. *Myths, Dreams, and Mysteries: The Encounter between Contemporary Faiths and Archaic Realities*, translated by Philip Mairet. New York: Harper & Row Publishers, 1960.

Eliade, Mircea. *Shamanism: Archaic Techniques of Ecstasy*, translated by Willard R. Trask. Princeton, NJ: Princeton University Press, 1964.

Eliade, Mircea. *The Quest: History and Meaning in Religion*. Chicago: The University of Chicago Press, 1969.

Eliade, Mircea. *No Souvenirs: Journal, 1957–1969*, translated by Fred H. Johnson, Jr. New York: Harper & Row Publishers, 1977.

Eliade, Mircea. *Ordeal by Labryinth: Conversations with Claude-Henri Rocquet*, translated by Derek Coltman. Chicago: The University of Chicago Press, 1982.

Eliade, Mircea. *Autobiography, Volume II: 1937–1960: Exile's Odyssey*, translated by Mac Linscott Ricketts. Chicago: The University of Chicago Press, 1988.

Eliade, Mircea. *Journal III: 1970–1978*, translated by Teresa Lavender Fagan. Chicago: The University of Chicago Press, 1989.

Ellis, Robert. *The Games People Play: Theology, Religion, and Sport*. Eugene, OR: Wipf & Stock, 2014.

Fabian, Johannes. *Out of Their Minds: Reason and Madness in the Exploration of Central Africa*. Berkeley, CA: University of California Press, 2000.

Fabian, Johannes. *Time and the Other: How Anthropology Makes Its Object*. New York: Columbia University Press, 2002.

Faure, Gerbert. "Religion, Modernity and the Notion of Subtler Languages", in *Radical Secularization?: An Inquiry into the Religious Roots of Secular Culture*, edited by Stijn Latre, Walter Van Herck, and Guido Vanheeswijck. New York: Bloomsbury, 2015.

Feezell, Randolph. *Sport, Play & Ethical Reflection*. Chicago, IL: University of Illinois Press, 2004.

Feuerbach, Ludwig. *Essence of Christianity*, translated by George Eliot. New York: Prometheus Books, 1989.

Floyd-Thomas, Juan M., Stacey M. Floyd-Thomas, and Mark G. Toulouse. *The Altars Where We Worship: The Religious Significance of Popular Culture*. Louisville, KY: Westminster John Knox Press, 2016.

Forbes, Bruce David and Jeffrey H. Mahan, editors. *Religion and Popular Culture in America*, third edition. Berkeley, CA: University of California Press, 2017.

Freeman, Bernard "Bun B." "Afterword: An insider perspective," in *Religion in Hip Hop: Mapping the New Terrain in the US*, edited by Monica R. Miller, Anthony B. Pinn, and Bernard "Bun B" Freeman. New York: Bloomsbury, 2015.

Freeman, Bernard "Bun B." "Bun B on religion and hip hop: An interview (by Biko Gray) with Bun B," in *Religion in Hip Hop: Mapping the New Terrain in the US*, edited by Monica R. Miller, Anthony B. Pinn, and Bernard "Bun B" Freeman. New York: Bloomsbury, 2015.

Freud, Sigmund. *Moses and Monotheism*, translated by Katherine Jones. New York: Vintage Books, 1939.

Freud, Sigmund. *Totem and Taboo: Some Points of Agreement between the Mental Lives of Savages and Neurotics*, translated by James Strachey. New York: W. W. Norton & Company, 1950.

Freud, Sigmund. *Civilization and Its Discontents*, translated by James Strachey. New York: W. W. Norton & Company, 1961.

Freud, Sigmund. *The Future of an Illusion*, translated by James Strachey. New York: W. W. Norton & Company, 1961.

Freud, Sigmund. *New Introductory Lectures on Psycho-Analysis*, translated and edited by James Strachey. New York: W. W. Norton & Company, 1965.

Friedland, Roger. "Drag Kings at the Totem Ball: The Erotics of Collective Representation in Emile Durkheim and Sigmund Freud," in *The Cambridge Companion to Durkheim*, edited by Jeffrey C. Alexander and Philip Smith. Cambridge, UK: Cambridge University Press, 2005.

Gadamer, Hans-Georg. *Truth and Method* (second revised edition), translation revised by Joel Weinsheimer and Donald G. Marshall. New York: Continuum, 1994.

Gardella, Peter. *American Civil Religion: What Americans Hold Sacred*. New York: Oxford University Press, 2014.

Gill, Sam. "No Place to Stand: Jonathan Z. Smith as *Homo Ludens*, The Academic Study of Religion *Sub Specie Ludi*," *Journal of the American Academy of Religion*, vol. 66, no. 2 (1998).

Girardot, Norman J. "*Ecce* Elvis: 'Elvis Studies' as a Postmodernist Paradigm for the Academic Study of Religion," *Journal of the American Academy of Religion*, vol. 68, no. 3 (2000).

Grossman, Maxine L. "Jesus, Mama, and the Constraints on Salvific Love in Contemporary Country Music," *Journal of the American Academy of Religion*, vol. 70, no. 1 (2002).

Hegel, Georg Wilhelm Friedrich. *The Philosophy of History*, translated by J. Sibree. New York: Willey Book Co., 1944.

Hegel, Georg Wilhelm Friedrich. *Lectures on the Philosophy of Religion*, translated by E.B. Speirs and J. Burdon Sanderson. New York: The Humanities Press, 1974.

Hegel, Georg Wilhelm Friedrich. *Phenomenology of Spirit*, translated by A.V. Miller. New York: Oxford University Press, 1977.

Heinamaki, Elisa. "Durkheim, Bataille, and Girard on the Ambiguity of the Sacred: Reconsidering Saints and Demoniacs," *Journal of the American Academy of Religion*, vol. 83, no. 2 (2015).

Hornby, Nick. *Fever Pitch*. New York: Riverhead Books, 1998.

Huizinga, Johan. *Homo Ludens: A Study of the Play Element in Culture*. Boston: The Beacon Press, 1955.

James, William. *The Varieties of Religious Experience*. New York: Collier Books, 1961.

James, William. *Pragmatism and Other Writings*, edited by Giles Gunn. New York: Penguin Books, 2000.

Jenkins, Henry. "*Star Trek* Rerun, Reread, Rewritten: Fan Writing as Textual Poaching," in *Popular Culture: A Reader*, edited by Raiford Guins & Omayra Zaragoza Cruz. Thousand Oaks, CA: Sage Publications, 2005.

Johnson, Paul Christopher. "The Fetish and McGwire's Balls," *Journal of the American Academy of Religion*, vol. 68, no. 2 (2000).

Jones, Robert Alun. "Practices and Presuppositions: Some Questions about Durkheim and *Les Formes elementaires de la vie religieuse*," in *The Cambridge Companion to Durkheim*, edited by Jeffrey C. Alexander and Philip Smith. Cambridge, UK: Cambridge University Press, 2005.

Jung, Carl. *Modern Man in Search of a Soul*, translated by W.S. Dell and Cary F. Baynes. New York: Houghton Mifflin Harcourt, 1933.

Jung, Carl. *Two Essays on Analytical Psychology*, translated by R.F.C. Hull. Princeton, NJ: Princeton University Press, 1966.

Jung, Carl. "Approaching the Unconscious," in *Man and His Symbols*, edited by Carl Jung. New York: Dell Publishing, 1968.

Jung, Carl. *The Archetypes and the Collective Unconscious*, translated by R.F.C. Hull. Princeton, NJ: Princeton University Press, 1969.

Kant, Immanuel. *Critique of Practical Reason*, translated by Lewis White Beck. New York: Macmillan Publishing Company, 1956.

Kant, Immanuel. *Religion Within the Limits of Reason Alone*, translated by Theodore M. Greene and Hoyt H. Hudson. New York: Harper & Row, Publishers, 1960.

Kant, Immanuel. *Groundwork of the Metaphysic of Morals*, translated by H.J. Paton. New York: Harper & Row, Publishers, 1964.

Kant, Immanuel. *Toward Perpetual Peace and Other Writings on Politics, Peace, and History*, translated by David L. Colclasure. New Haven, CT: Yale University Press, 2006.

Kate, Laurens ten. "To World or Not to World: An Axial Genealogy of Secular Life," in *Radical Secularization?: An Inquiry into the Religious Roots of Secular Culture*, edited by Stijn Latre, Walter Van Herck, and Guido Vanheeswijck. New York: Bloomsbury, 2015.

Kluchin, Abby. "At the Limits of Feeling: Religion, Psychoanalysis, and the Affective Subject," in *Feeling Religion*, edited by John Corrigan. Durham, NC: Duke University Press, 2017.

Laderman, Gary. "The Disney Way of Death," *Journal of the American Academy of Religion*, vol. 68, no. 1 (2000).

LaMothe, Kimerer L. "What Bodies Know about Religion and the Study of It," *Journal of the American Academy of Religion*, vol. 76, no. 3 (2008).

Law, Stephen. *Humanism: A Very Short Introduction*. New York: Oxford University Press, 2011.

Lockwood, Charles. "Apologetics and Anti-Apologetics in Taylor's *A Secular Age*," in *Radical Secularization?: An Inquiry into the Religious Roots of Secular Culture*, edited by Stijn Latre, Walter Van Herck, and Guido Vanheeswijck. New York: Bloomsbury, 2015.

Lofton, Kathryn. *Consuming Religion*. Chicago: The University of Chicago Press, 2017.

Logan, Dana W. "The Lean Closet: Asceticism in Postindustrial Consumer Culture," *Journal of the American Academy of Religion*, vol. 85, no. 3 (2017).

Long, Charles H. *Significations: Signs, Symbols, and Images in the Interpretation of Religion*. Philadelphia: Fortress Press, 1986.

Loy, David R. "The Religion of the Market," *Journal of the American Academy of Religion*, vol. 65, no. 2 (1997).

Luft, Shanny (with Heidi A. Campbell, Rachel Wagner, Rabia Gregory, Gregory Price Grieve, and Xenia Zeiler). "Gaming Religionworlds: Why Religious Studies Should Pay Attention to Religion in Gaming," *Journal of the American Academy of Religion*, vol. 84, no. 3 (2016).

Luther, Martin. *Martin Luther: Selections from His Writings*, edited by John Dillenberger. New York: Anchor Books, 1961.

Lyden, John C. "Whose Film Is It, Anyway? Canonicity and Authority in *Star Wars* Fandom," *Journal of the American Academy of Religion*, vol. 80, no. 3 (2012).

MacIntyre, Alasdair. *After Virtue: A Study in Moral Theory*, second edition. Notre Dame, IN: University of Notre Dame Press, 1984.

Marvin, Carolyn and David W. Ingle. "Blood Sacrifice and the Nation: Revisiting Civil Religion," *Journal of the American Academy of Religion*, vol. 64, no. 4 (1996).

Marx, Karl. *Karl Marx: The Essential Writings*, second edition, edited by Frederic L. Bender. Boulder, CO: Westview Press, 1972.

Marx, Karl. *The Portable Karl Marx*, edited by Eugene Kamenka. New York: Viking Penguin, 1983.

McCutcheon, Russell T. *Manufacturing Religion: The Discourse on Sui Generis Religion and the Politics of Nostalgia*. New York: Oxford University Press, 1997.

McKenzie, German. *Interpreting Charles Taylor's Social Theory on Religion and Secularization: A Comparative Study*. Cham, Switzerland: Springer, 2017.

Meyer, Jerry D. "Profane and Sacred: Religious Imagery and Prophetic Expression in Postmodern Art," *Journal of the American Academy of Religion*, vol. 65, no. 1 (1997).

Milbank, John. "The Legitimacy and Genealogy of Secularization in Question," in *Radical Secularization: An Inquiry into the Religious Roots of Secular Culture*, edited by Stijn Latre, Walter Van Herck, and Guido Vanheeswijck. New York: Bloomsbury, 2015.

Miller, Monica R. *Religion and Hip Hop*. New York: Routledge, 2013.

Miller, Monica R. "Real Recognize Real: Aporetic Flows and the Presence of New Black Godz in Hip Hop," in *Religion in Hip Hop: Mapping the New Terrain in the US*, edited by Monica R. Miller, Anthony B. Pinn, and Bernard "Bun B" Freeman. New York: Bloomsbury, 2015.

Morgan, David. "Emotion and Imagination in the Ritual Entanglement of Religion, Sport, and Nationalism," in *Feeling Religion*, edited by John Corrigan. Durham, NC: Duke University Press, 2017.

Nongbri, Brent. *Before Religion: A History of a Modern Concept*. New Haven, CT: Yale University Press, 2013.

Novak, Michael. *The Joy of Sports: Endzones, Bases, Baskets, Balls, and the Consecration of the American Spirit*, revised edition. Lanham, MD: Madison Books, 1994.

Pals, Daniel L. *Seven Theories of Religion*. New York: Oxford University Press, 1996.

Pals, Daniel L. *Eight Theories of Religion*, second edition. New York: Oxford University Press, 2006.

Paul, Robert A. "Freud's Anthropology: A Reading of the 'Cultural Books,'" in *The Cambridge Companion to Freud*, edited by Jerome Neu. New York: Cambridge University Press, 1991.

Pew Research Center. "In U.S., Decline of Christianity Continues at Rapid Pace: An Update on America's Changing Religious Landscape." Washington, DC: Pew Research Center, 2019. https://www.pewforum.org/2019/10/17/in-u-s-decline-of-christianity-continues-at-rapid-pace/ Accessed September 20, 2020.

Pieper, Josef. *In Tune with the World: A Theory of Festivity*, translated by Richard and Clara Winston. South Bend, IN: St. Augustine's Press, 1963.

Pieper, Josef. *Leisure: The Basis of Culture*, translated by Alexander Dru. San Francisco: Ignatius Press, 1963.

Pinker, Steven. *The Better Angels of Our Nature: Why Violence Has Declined*. New York: Penguin Books, 2012.

Pinn, Anthony B. *Humanism: Essays on Race, Religion and Popular Culture*. New York: Bloomsbury, 2015.

Pinn, Anthony B. "Zombies in the Hood: Rap Music, Camusian Absurdity, and the Structuring of Death," in *Religion in Hip Hop: Mapping the New Terrain in the US*, edited by Monica R. Miller, Anthony B. Pinn, and Bernard "Bun B" Freeman. New York: Bloomsbury, 2015.

Pinn, Anthony B. "Rap Music and Its Message: On Interpreting the Contact between Religion and Popular Culture," in *Religion and Popular Culture in America*, third edition, edited by Bruce David Forbes and Jeffrey H. Mahan. Oakland, CA: University of California Press, 2017.

Postman, Neil. *Amusing Ourselves to Death: Public Discourse in the Age of Show Business*, 20th Anniversary Edition. New York: Penguin, 2006.

Price, Joseph L. "The 'Godding Up' of American Sports," in *Religion and Popular Culture in America*, third edition, edited by Bruce David Forbes and Jeffrey H. Mahan. Oakland, CA: University of California Press, 2017.

Proudfoot, Wayne. *Religious Experience*. Berkeley, CA: University of California Press, 1985.

Proudfoot, Wayne. "Response," *Journal of the American Academy of Religion*, vol. 61, no. 4 (1993).

Putnam, Robert D. *Bowling Alone: The Collapse and Revival of American Community*. New York: Simon & Schuster, 2001.

Rhoden, William C. *Forty Million Dollar Slaves: The Rise, Fall, and Redemption of the Black Athlete*. New York: Three Rivers Press, 2006.

Rieff, Philip. *The Triumph of the Therapeutic: Uses of Faith after Freud*. Chicago: The University of Chicago Press, 1966.

Ringer, Fritz. *Max Weber: An Intellectual Biography*. Chicago: The University of Chicago Press, 2004.

Rorty, Richard. *Contingency, Irony, and Solidarity*. New York: Cambridge University Press, 1989.

Rorty, Richard. "Religious Faith, Intellectual Responsibility, and Romance," in *The Cambridge Companion to William James*, edited by Ruth Anna Putnam. New York: Cambridge University Press, 1997.

Rorty, Richard. *Philosophy and Social Hope*. New York: Penguin Books, 1999.

Rorty, Richard. *Philosophy as Cultural Politics: Philosophical Papers, Volume 4*. New York: Cambridge University Press, 2007.

Sanford, A. Whitney. "Pinned on Karma Rock: Whitewater Kayaking as Religious Experience," *Journal of the American Academy of Religion*, vol. 75, no. 4 (2007).

Scaff, Lawrence A. "Weber on the Cultural Situation of the Modern Age," in *The Cambridge Companion to Weber*, edited by Stephen Turner. Cambridge, UK: Cambridge University Press, 2000.

Schaefer, Donovan O. *Religious Affect: Animality, Evolution, and Power*. Durham, NC: Duke University Press, 2015.

Schaefer, Donovan O. "Beautiful Facts: Science, Secularism, and Affect," in *Feeling Religion*, edited by John Corrigan. Durham, NC: Duke University Press, 2017.

Schewel, Benjamin. "Transformational Post-Secularism: An Overlooked Strand of Thought," *Journal of the American Academy of Religion*, vol. 87, no. 4 (2019).

Schilbrack, Kevin. "Religions: Are There Any?," *Journal of the American Academy of Religion*, vol. 78, no. 4 (2010).

Schleiermacher, Friedrich. *On Religion: Speeches to Its Cultured Despisers*, translated by Richard Crouter. New York: Cambridge University Press, 1988.

Schor, Juliet. *The Overspent American: Why We Want What We Don't Need*. New York: HarperCollins, 1998.

Schor, Juliet. *Born to Buy*. New York: Scribner, 2005.

Schorske, Carl E. "Freud: The Psychoarcheology of Civilizations," in *The Cambridge Companion to Freud*, edited by Jerome Neu. New York: Cambridge University Press, 1991.

Sharpe, Eric J. *Comparative Religion: A History*, second edition. LaSalle, IL: Open Court, 1986.

Sheehan, Jonathan. "When Was Disenchantment? History and the Secular Age," in *Varieties of Secularism in a Secular Age*, edited by Michael Warner, Jonathan VanAntwerpen, and Craig Calhoun. Cambridge, MA: Harvard University Press, 2010.

Shilling, Chris. "Embodiment, Emotions, and the Foundations of Social Order: Durkheim's Enduring Contribution," in *The Cambridge Companion to Durkheim*, edited by Jeffrey C. Alexander and Philip Smith. Cambridge, UK: Cambridge University Press, 2005.

Sica, Alan. "Rationalization and Culture," in *The Cambridge Companion to Weber*, edited by Stephen Turner. New York: Cambridge University Press, 2000.

Slusher, Howard. "Sport and the Religious" in *Religion and Sport: The Meeting of Sacred and Profane*, edited by Charles S. Prebish, Westport, CT: Greenwood Press, 1993.

Smith, Christian. *Religion: What It Is, How It Works, and Why It Matters*. Princeton, NJ: Princeton University Press, 2017.

Smith, Jonathan Z. *Imagining Religion: From Babylon to Jonestown*. Chicago: The University of Chicago Press, 1982.

Smith, Jonathan Z. "Tillich['s] Remains ...," *Journal of the American Academy of Religion*, vol. 78, no. 4 (2010).

Snyder, Samuel. "New Streams of Religion: Fly Fishing as a Lived, Religion of Nature," *Journal of the American Academy of Religion*, vol. 75, no. 4 (2007).

Spickard, James. *Alternative Sociologies of Religion: Through Non-Western Eyes*. New York: New York University Press, 2017.

St. John, Warren. *Rammer Jammer Yellow Hammer: A Road Trip into the Heart of Fan Mania*. New York: Crown Publishers, 2004.

Suits, Bernard. *The Grasshopper: Games, Life, and Utopia*, third edition. Tonawanda, NY: Broadview Press, 2014.

Taves, Ann. *Religious Experience Reconsidered: A Building-Block Approach to the Study of Religion and Other Special Things*. Princeton, NJ: Princeton University Press, 2009.

Taylor, Bron. "Surfing into Spirituality and a New, Aquatic Nature Religion," *Journal of the American Academy of Religion*, vol. 75, no. 4 (2007).

Taylor, Charles. *Hegel and Modern Society*. Cambridge, UK: Cambridge University Press, 1979.

Taylor, Charles. *Sources of the Self: The Making of the Modern Identity*. Cambridge, MA: Harvard University Press, 1989.

Taylor, Charles. *A Secular Age*. Cambridge, MA: Harvard University Press, 2007.

Taylor, Mark C. *About Religion: Economies of Faith in Virtual Culture*. Chicago: The University of Chicago Press, 1999.

Taylor, Mark C. *Confidence Games: Money and Markets in a World without Redemption*. Chicago: The University of Chicago Press, 2004.

Taylor, Mark C. *After God*. Chicago: The University of Chicago Press, 2007.

Taylor, Sarah McFarland. "Shopping, Religion, and the Sacred 'Buyosphere,'" in *Religion and Popular Culture in America*, third edition, edited by Bruce David Forbes and Jeffrey H. Mahan. Oakland, CA: University of California Press, 2017.

Tillich, Paul. "Art and Ultimate Reality." *Dimensions* (1959).

Tillich, Paul. *Theology of Culture*, edited by Robert C. Kimball. New York: Oxford University Press, 1959.

Tillich, Paul. *Systematic Theology: Volume Three: Life and the Spirit: History and the Kingdom of God*. Chicago: The University of Chicago Press, 1963.

Tiryakian, Edward A. "Durkheim, solidarity, and September 11," in *The Cambridge Companion to Durkheim*, edited by Jeffrey C. Alexander and Philip Smith. Cambridge, UK: Cambridge University Press, 2005.

Travis, Clay. *Dixieland Delight: A Football Season on the Road in the Southeastern Conference*. New York: HarperCollins, 2007.

Turner, Victor. *Dramas, Fields, and Metaphors: Symbolic Action in Human Society*. Ithaca, NY: Cornell University Press, 1974.

Turner, Victor. *The Ritual Process: Structure and Anti-Structure*. New York: Aldine de Gruyter, 1995.

Tuschling, Burkhard. "*Rationis societas*: Remarks on Kant and Hegel," in *Kant's Philosophy of Religion Reconsidered*, edited by Philip J. Rossi and Michael Wreen. Bloomington, IN: Indiana University Press, 1991.

Twitchell, James B. *Branded Nation: The Marketing of Megachurch, College Inc., and Museumworld*. New York: Simon & Schuster, 2004.

Ulanov, Ann Belford. "Jung and Religion: The Opposing Self," in *The Cambridge Companion to Jung*, edited by Polly Young-Eisendrath and Terence Dawson. New York: Cambridge University Press, 2008.

Vanheeswijck, Guido. "Beyond Radical Secularlization and Radical Orthodoxy?" in *Radical Secularization?: An Inquiry into the Religious Roots of Secular Culture*, edited by Stijn Latre, Walter Van Herck, and Guido Vanheeswijck. New York: Bloomsbury, 2015.

Wagner, Rachel (with Heidi A. Campbell, Shanny Luft, Rabia Gregory, Gregory Price Grieve, and Xenia Zeiler). "Gaming Religionworlds: Why Religious Studies Should Pay Attention to Religion in Gaming," *Journal of the American Academy of Religion*, vol. 84, no. 3 (2016).

Warner, Michael and Jonathan VanAntwerpen, and Craig Calhoun. "Editor's Introduction," in *Varieties of Secularism in a Secular Age*, edited by Michael Warner, Jonathan VanAntwerpen, and Craig Calhoun. Cambridge, MA: Harvard University Press, 2010.

Weber, Max. *Economy and Society*, Volume 1, edited by Guenther Roth and Claus Wittich. Berkeley, CA: University of California Press, 1978.

Weber, Max. *The Protestant Ethic and the "Spirit" of Capitalism and Other Writings*, edited by Peter Baehr and Gordon C. Wells. New York: Penguin Books, 2002.

Williams, Peter W. "Sacred Space in North America," *Journal of the American Academy of Religion*, vol. 70, no. 3 (2002).

Zirin, Dave. *What's My Name, Fool? Sports and Resistance in the United States*. Chicago: Haymarket Books, 2005.

Zirin, Dave. *Welcome to the Terrordome: The Pain, Politics, and Promise of Sports*. Chicago: Haymarket Books, 2007.

Zizek, Slavoj. *The Fragile Absolute—or, Why Is the Christian Legacy Worth Fighting for?* New York: Verso, 2000.

Zizek, Slavoj. *On Belief*. New York: Routledge, 2001.

Zizek, Slavoj. *The Universal Exception*, edited by Rex Butler and Scott Stephens. New York: Continuum, 2006.

Zizek, Slavoj. "Afterword: *With Defenders Like These, Who Needs Attackers?*" in *The Truth of Zizek*, edited by Paul Bowman and Richard Stamp. New York: Continuum, 2007.

Index

Adorno, Theodor 206, 221
Adorno, Theodor, and Max Horkheimer
    206
affect theory 64–79
Albanese, Catherine 117
Ammerman, Nancy T. 252–3 n. 26
Arnal, William 135
Asad, Talal 163–4, 191
atheism 23, 25

Bain-Selbo, Eric 133, 263 n. 62
Bain-Selbo, Eric, and D. Gregory Sapp
    137, 223
Bain-Selbo, Zachary 126
Bauman, Zygmunt 215–20, 262–3 n. 49
Bellah, Robert N. 28–9, 140, 143
Berger, Peter 161–3
Bilgrami, Akeel 201
Blum, Jason N. 83, 239–40 n. 5
Boston Red Sox ("Curse of the Bambino")
    182, 258 n. 110
Brasher, Brenda E. 117–18, 143
Bruce, Steve 153–5, 159–61, 197

Caillois, Roger 255 n. 71
Calvinism 41–4
Camus, Albert 180
Chicago Cubs ("Curse of the Billy Goat")
    137–8, 182, 258 n. 111
Chidester, David 91–2, 115–16, 123,
    134–5, 137–8, 143, 144–5, 193
Coates, Ta-Nehisi 129
Cobb, Kelton 104
Cohen, Lizabeth 210, 214–15
Connor, Steven 137
consumerism 144–8, 203–23
    and community 211–15
    liquid modernity 215–20
    "naked" self 207–9
    pop self 209–11
Corrigan, John 65
Cox, Harvey 148, 222

Csikszentmihalyi, Mihaly 73
Curts, Kati 119

Dean, William 119–20, 260–1 n. 169
Debord, Guy 44, 212–13
Deigh, John 56
Dewey, John 176, 256 n. 90
Driscoll, Christopher M., and Monica R.
    Miller 2, 193, 242 n. 71
Dupuy, Jean-Pierre 203, 251 n. 167
Durkheim, Emile 28–36, 45–6, 106, 168–9
    collective effervescence 33–5, 90,
        168–9, 230 n. 21
    totemism 29–30
Dyson, Michael Eric 125, 247 n. 47

Eliade, Mircea 66–8, 75–9, 81–96, 98,
    103–4, 107, 240 n. 31, 241 n. 61,
    241–2 n. 65, 242 n. 70, 242 n. 71
    homo religious 84, 89
    New Humanism 94
    sacred 84–92
    sui generis 83–4
Ellis, Robert 174
Enlightenment 5, 6, 19, 24–5
ethics 5–25
existentialist approach 81, 83, 103, 164

Fabian, Johannes 193
Feezell, Randolph 173–4
Feuerbach, Ludwig 19–23, 228 n. 81, 228
    n. 82, 229 n. 87
    atheism 23
Floyd-Thomas, Juan M., and Stacey
    M. Floyd-Thomas and Mark G.
    Toulouse 120–1, 122, 129, 131, 137,
    189–90
Freeman, Bernard "Bun B" 127–8, 247 n. 61
Freud, Sigmund 47–57, 79, 107, 158, 233
    n. 3, 233 n. 4, 234 n. 12, 234 n.
    15, 234 n. 22, 234 n. 31, 235 n. 39,
    235 n. 46

and Jung 57, 63–4
civilization 50–3
future of religion 54–7
id, ego, and superego 50–1
social contract theory 51
totemism 48–50
Friedlander, Roger 230 n. 21
functionalism 2–3, 35–6, 45–6, 57, 64, 79, 105, 113–55, 201, 203, 220

Gadamer, Hans-Georg 173
Gardella, Peter 140–3
Gill, Sam 191–2
Girardot, Norman J. 123–4
Grossman, Maxine L. 124–5

Heinamaki, Elisa 34
Hegel, Georg Wilhelm Friedrich 14–19, 77, 106, 197–9, 209, 226 n. 40, 226 n. 43, 226–7 n. 46, 227 n. 48, 227 n. 61, 228 n. 64, 228 n. 71
culture 16–17
history 17–18
and Kant 18
moral life 17
Hornby, Nick 184
Huizinga, Johan 172–3
humanism 172–89, 256 n. 81, 256 n. 82
and pragmatism 175–80, 256 n. 90

immanence and transcendence 25, 31, 44, 46, 47, 57, 85–6, 94, 100–1, 103, 109–11, 151–2, 164–73, 177, 181, 183, 196
irony (ironic life) 174, 178, 183–5, 201–2

James, William 68–9, 176, 256 n. 82
Jenkins, Henry 213–14
Johnson, Paul Christopher 138
Jones, Robert Alun 33
Journal of the American Academy of Religion 114, 245 n. 2
Jung, Carl 57–64, 79, 107
archetypes 59–64, 236 n. 68, 236 n. 69, 237 n. 92
art 61
collective unconscious 58–64
and Freud 57, 63–4
individuation 61–2
literature 60–1
spiritual crisis 62–4

Kant, Immanuel 5–14, 106, 224 n. 8, 224 n. 9, 225 n. 26
and Hegel 18
Religion within the Limits of Reason Alone 11–14
Kate, Laurens ten 170
Kluchin, Abby 75

Laderman, Gary 133–4
LaMothe, Kimerer 129–31
Law, Stephen 175, 256 n. 81
Lockwood, Charles 254–5 n. 62
Lofton, Kathryn 120–1, 144, 147–8
Logan, Dana W. 145–6
Long, Charles H. 95, 193, 196
Loy, David R. 121, 148–9
Luft, Shanny 135–6
Luther, Martin 39–41
Lyden, John C. 119, 132–3

MacIntyre, Alasdair 207–9
Marvin, Carolyn, and David W. Ingle 141–2
Marx, Karl 23–4, 158, 204–5, 229 n. 97, 229 n. 98
McCutcheon, Russell 84, 242 n. 70
McKenzie, German 170
Meyer, Jerry D. 122
Milbank, John 158–9
Miller, Monica R. 125, 128–9, 192, 196, 248 n. 68, 259 n. 127
Morgan, David 66, 75–6, 77–8

Nongbri, Brent 191, 193–4
Novak, Michael 255 n. 69, 255 n. 70

Otto, Rudolf 67, 68, 75, 79

Pals, Daniel L. 229 n. 97, 229 n. 98, 234 n. 15
Paul, Robert A. 48, 235 n. 39
phenomenological approach 67, 81–2, 103–4, 164, 239–40 n. 5
Pieper, Josef 199–201
festival 199–201
Pinn, Anthony B. 125–7, 175, 180, 247 n. 49, 247 n. 52
play 135–6, 172–5, 191–2, 199, 223, 255 n. 69, 255 n. 70, 255 n. 71
Postman, Neil 221

Presley, Elvis 123–4
Price, Joseph L. 136–7
Proudfoot, Wayne 68–78, 239 n. 137
　descriptive and explanatory reduction 71–2
　on Schleiermacher 69–70
　use of Stanley Schacter 71
Putnam, Robert D. 210–11, 214

Reformation 39–44
religion of culture 3–4, 113–55, 180, 193, 199–201, 203, 220, 222–3, 245 n. 1
　civil religion 140–4, 147
　　Martin Luther King, Jr. 142
　consumerism 144–8
　　brands 146–7
　　Gwyneth Paltrow's *goop* 145–6
　economy (markets) 148–52, 251 n. 160, 251 n. 167
　　money 150–1
　entertainment
　　Disney 133–5, 146
　　electronic gaming 135–6
　　Star Wars 132–3
　sport(s) 136–9, 142–3, 146
　　aquatic sports/recreation 138–9
　　baseball 137–8
　visual and performing arts 121–31
　　dance 129–31
　　hip hop 125–9, 247 n. 49, 247 n. 52, 247 n. 61, 248 n. 68; Arrested Development 126–7; Jay-Z 125, 247 n. 47; KRS One 128; krumping 128–9; Public Enemy 126; *Rize* 128–9
　　music 122–9; country music 124–5; Elvis Presley 123–4; rock 'n' roll 123–4; The Grateful Dead 123
　　visual arts 122
religious studies (academic study of religion) 190–7
Rieff, Philip 57, 63, 237 n. 92
Ringer, Fritz 45, 231 n. 43
Rorty, Richard 176–80, 256 n. 95, 257 n. 96, 257 n. 98, 257 n. 100, 257 n. 101, 257–8 n. 107
　contingency 177–8
　irony (ironic life) 178, 201–2

literature 179–80
on Enlightenment 178
on John Dewey 177
solidarity 178–9

Sanford, A. Whitney 138–9
Scaff, Lawrence A. 36
Schaefer, Donovan O. 65–8, 74–5, 77, 237 n. 99, 238 n. 103, 238 n. 107, 238 n. 108
Schewel, Benjamin 165, 253 n. 36
Schilbrack, Kevin 118–19
Schleiermacher, Friedrich 19–21, 68, 69–70, 228 n. 71
Schor, Juliet 207, 209–10, 214
Schorske, Carl E. 52
secularism (secularization) 45, 63, 113, 158–71, 189–202, 204–5
Sheehan, Jonathan 196–7
Shilling, Chris 29–30, 33
Sica, Alan 232–3 n. 74
Slusher, Howard 73–4
Smith, Christian 194–7
Smith, Jonathan Z. 75, 96–7, 259 n. 142
Snyder, Samuel 139
Spickard, James V. 27–8, 29, 33
sport(s) 31–2, 73–4, 172–5, 180–9, 222–3
　baseball 181
　contingency 181–3
　irony 183–5
　solidarity 185–7
St. John, Warren 184
Suits, Bernard 174–5

Taves, Ann 76–7, 239 n. 137
Taylor, Bron 139
Taylor, Charles 253–4 n. 38, 254 n. 39
　on Hegel 17, 197–9, 209, 226 n. 41
　humanism 169–71, 253 n. 32
　on Kant 14
　secularism (secularization) 164–73, 197, 201, 253 n. 36, 254 n. 55, 254–5 n. 62
Taylor, Mark C. 108–11, 149–52, 222, 244 n. 7, 244 n. 10, 251 n. 160
　on Hegel 109–10, 227 n. 50
　immanence and transcendence 109–11
　Jean-Jacques Rousseau 109

John Calvin 109
Martin Luther 108
Protestant Reformation 108–9
secularism 108, 110–11, 171
Thomas Altizer 110
Taylor, Sarah McFarland 144
The Grateful Dead 123
Tillich, Paul 96–104, 107, 242 n. 81, 243 n. 85, 243 n. 90, 243 n. 95, 243 n. 103, 243 n. 109, 253 n. 32, 253 n. 36
    art 101
    literature 101–2
    moral life 102
    secular culture 103
    Spirit 100–3
    theology of culture 97–103
    transcendence 102
    ultimate concern 97–8
Tiryakian, Edward A. 35

Turner, Victor 31–2, 168
    communitas 34–5, 90, 168
Tuschling, Burkhard 13, 225 n. 21
Twitchell, James B. 146–7

Ulanov, Ann Belford 61

Wagner, Rachel 135
Warner, Michael, and Jonathan VanAntwerpen and Craig Calhoun 253 n. 32
Weber, Max 36–46, 106, 231 n. 43
    The Protestant Ethic and the "Spirit" of Capitalism 37–45, 232 n. 65, 232 n. 67, 232 n. 69, 232–3 n. 74
Williams, Peter W. 118

Zirin, Dave 222–3
Zizek, Slavoj 204–7, 211–12